Python® & AI

Python® & AI

by John C. Shovic, PhD, and
Mary "Marz" Everett, PhD

Python® & AI For Dummies®

Published by: **John Wiley & Sons, Inc.,** 111 River Street, Hoboken, NJ 07030-5774, www.wiley.com

For general information on our other products and services, please contact our Customer Care Department within the U.S. at 877-762-2974, outside the U.S. at 317-572-3993, or fax 317-572-4002. For technical support, please visit https://hub.wiley.com/community/support/dummies.

Wiley publishes in a variety of print and electronic formats and by print-on-demand. Some material included with standard print versions of this book may not be included in e-books or in print-on-demand. If this book refers to media that is not included in the version you purchased, you may download this material at http://booksupport.wiley.com. For more information about Wiley products, visit www.wiley.com.

Library of Congress Control Number is available from the publisher.

ISBN 978-1-394-41346-1 (pbk); ISBN 978-1-394-41348-5 (ebk); ISBN 978-1-394-41347-8 (ebk)

Printed and bound by CPI Group (UK) Ltd, Croydon, CR0 4YY

C9781394413461_240626

Contents at a Glance

Table of Contents

Introduction

Welcome, AI aficionados! If you picked up this book, you're probably aware that the field of artificial intelligence (AI) is enormous and omnipresent. Its abilities are sometimes magical, sometimes bewildering, and sometimes completely incomprehensible.

Many AI tools are concentrated in one particular snake-named programming language: Python. Whether you are interested in Python and want to level up your AI skills, or are interested in AI but have no clue how to start programming for it, this book gives you the tools you need. We cover many different aspects of AI (data, models, and training) and provide hands-on Python programs for you to test them out. We draw from our experience in teaching and research at a university robotics center, where we use Python and AI every day.

We've been spending the last several years in our careers applying AI solutions to problems primarily in the manufacturing and agriculture industries, and we've learned a lot along the way. AI isn't just a large language model app on your phone that can helpfully assure you no hospital is needed when you accidentally brush your teeth with anti-itch cream (long story). AI encompasses a wide range of models, techniques, processes, and search methods that suit an array of problems. Not every technique is a solution for every scenario, though. We put our experience to work when explaining how certain models fit certain situations better.

About This Book

This book is intended to be a reference for implementing the full AI toolchain in the Python programming language. We devote chapters to every part of the process, including Python fundamentals, manipulating and formatting data, installing and using AI libraries, and evaluating the models and algorithms. John says that while he did his doctoral dissertation on the AI technique of expert systems, he is thrilled to be obsoleted by these new techniques in this book. Really.

This book isn't intended to be comprehensive — there are many more AI techniques than are dreamt of in our philosophy! — but it is intended to give you the essential skills and point you to places where you can learn more. This book provides an overview of many different kinds of AI algorithms, but users often gravitate toward one type of model or another. Your new favorite technique may only be a few chapters away. (We'll give you a hint: How about those genetic algorithms?)

If you're new to programming, it's okay to read the book in order, as we start with programming and AI basics and gradually implement more complex models. But you can just as easily get comfortable in one section and skip over to another. Absolutely zero judgment if no universe exists where you care about linear regression. Seriously.

Getting "dangerous" in programming AI techniques with Python can happen surprisingly fast — no prior experience required. That being said, as with any new skills, mastery takes persistence and a willingness to try and try again. This book gives you a solid starting point for beginning an AI journey, but don't be discouraged if you break a few things on the way to success. Marz spent her first day of graduate school blowing up a robot, which was perhaps not the best start to her career. Running into problems is part of the process — but we've included plenty of troubleshooting tips throughout the book to help you if you get stuck.

One of the best features of this book (other than presenting information in the easy-to-read *Dummies* format) is the sheer number of projects you get to try. We recommend implementing all the projects on your computer — there's nothing that quite stirs the emotions like seeing your very own AI model solve a problem. We have projects that analyze steel plates, projects that classify handwritten numbers, and projects that magically draw a box around a rubber duck you hold up to your webcam. It's spectacular to learn about AI, but way more fun to create it. We stuffed the book full of programs for you to write, play with, break, improve, and eventually use to take over the world (okay, maybe not that last one).

Curiosity is the most important skill you bring to developing AI with Python. As you'll learn, models range from simple to complex, and techniques won't always behave like you want them to. We cover plenty of tricks to help you analyze problems that can be solved with AI, but we also try to get you thinking about how our modern-day solutions can be improved.

Foolish Assumptions

We assume that, while you're curious about AI, you haven't actually implemented any AI models yet — we'll get to those! We also assume that you don't have prior Python language experience (or any programming experience, for that matter). However, we do assume:

- You are familiar with the basic workings of a computer, including how to install software and manage your file system.
- You have a computer accessible to you for projects in this book.
- You have an Internet connection that will help you access project materials.

Icons Used in This Book

Throughout this book, icons in the margins highlight certain types of valuable information that call out for your attention. Here are the icons you'll encounter and a brief description of each.

TIP

The Tip icon marks tips and shortcuts you can use on a variety of topics. They are usually informed by personal experience we have with the subject or tool.

REMEMBER

Remember icons mark the information that's especially important to know, but easy to forget!

TECHNICAL STUFF

The Technical Stuff icon marks information of a highly technical nature that you can normally skip over. It will often give more detail about a technical subject or point you to resources that will let you dive deeper into a topic.

WARNING

The Warning icon tells you to watch out! It marks important information that may save you headaches or avoid particularly catastrophic situations. We don't use this icon very often, so make sure to take note when we do!

Beyond the Book

Besides the contents you will find in the book, you can also access other cool materials:

- **Cheat Sheet:** A cheat sheet provides you with even more information and guidance related to AI and Python. You can find the Cheat Sheet for this book at `www.dummies.com`. Type **Python & AI For Dummies** in the Search box and click the Cheat Sheet option that appears.

» **Companion files:** The source code referenced in this book is available for download. You can find these files on this book's page at `www.dummies.com/go/python&aifd`. Just enter the book title in the Search box, click Books on the page that appears, click the book's title, and scroll down the page to Downloads.

Where to Go from Here

You can start anywhere in this book — but if you've never programmed in Python before, Chapter 1 is an excellent way to begin. If you have done some programming and have a little more familiarity with AI (but not implementing it), you can skip to Chapter 4, where we cover machine learning libraries. If your true love lies with neural network architectures, Chapter 8 is the place for you. If you want to learn about the latest and greatest advanced AI models, head on over to Chapter 16. If you picked up this book for the sole express purpose of fulfilling your lifelong dream to build a rubber duck detector, you're among friends! Oh, and that's found in Chapter 15.

1 Getting Started with Python and AI

IN THIS PART . . .

Discover what the Python programming language is and how it's become the leading language to work with AI.

Review fundamental programming concepts, including libraries, lists, loops, and functions.

Explore the two main subfields of AI: expert systems or rule-based approaches and machine learning.

Understand the different types of data and how to work with datasets.

IN THIS CHAPTER

» Answering the question, "Why Python for AI?"

» Reviewing the Python programming environment components

» Writing your first Python program

» Exploring useful Python functionality

Chapter 1 Starting with Python Basics

Welcome to the wonderful world of using Python with artificial intelligence (AI)! In this chapter, you get your feet wet by exploring what the Python programming language is and how it's become the leading language to work with AI tools. You get acquainted with fundamental programming concepts: text editors, the Python language interpreter, and the terminal. You write your very first Python program using Microsoft Visual Studio Code (VS Code) and Anaconda. You explore more Python concepts, including libraries, lists, loops, and functions, in your second written program. Finally, you learn some tips and tricks for debugging programs and writing great software. Ready to start exploring?

Using Python to Work with AI

The world of AI is vast, but the Python programming language has emerged as one of the most popular ways to create, test, and use AI tools. It's a good idea to understand some of the basics behind the language itself and the many ways it's used in the AI industry.

What Is Python?

Python is a programming language like C/C++, Java, and Rust. Programming languages use written commands to control underlying computer resources. Collections of written commands are called *programs* or *software*. People who write programs are called programmers, coders, software engineers, developers, computer scientists, or sleep-deprived, coffee-slurping zombies, depending on how soon a project is due.

The type of programming language you use determines how you format the commands you give the computer, what command capabilities you have at your disposal, and how the commands will actually access the computer resources you want to use. Python is a very flexible and versatile language, with a user-friendly command-writing structure (also called a *syntax*). Because the syntax is user-friendly, many people have written collections of software in Python that can be reused by other developers. These reusable pieces of code are called *libraries* or *packages*.

Libraries of reusable code are common in many programming languages, which reduces the amount of software other developers have to rewrite. Python calls its libraries *packages*, which are directories of individual Python files implementing the reusable code. Individual files within a package are called *modules*.

When your computer carries out an instruction written in a programming language, it's executing that command. Python is an *interpreted* language, which means that it uses another piece of software (the interpreter) to translate and run the written commands on your computer, usually line by line. A *compiled* language (like C/C++) first translates all the commands in the program and then runs them on your computer. Compiled languages tend to run faster since they can use the translation step to make optimizations, but interpreted languages are easy to prototype and often are simple to use on multiple types of computers.

The Python Software Foundation (`www.python.org`) maintains the language, hosts package repositories, and coordinates the development of new versions. They have excellent documentation on their website if you want to dive deeper into the world of the language! For this book, we cover a lot of the basics of Python as well as how the language relates to AI development.

Why use Python with AI?

Out of the many, many (seriously . . . so many!) programming languages in existence, it's fair to ask, How did Python become the top contender for AI developers? It turns out, Python had a lot of the right characteristics at the right time, which include:

- Simplicity
- Numerous AI-focused packages
- High community support

Simplicity

Python's syntax — the structure of writing commands in the language — is easy to read, especially compared to many other programming languages. Many of the keywords you use when creating programs have intuitive meanings, and Python enforces a spacing scheme that makes programs easy to scan at a glance. The simple syntax of Python has made it a low-barrier-to-entry language — simply put, you don't have to be a computer scientist to learn Python. You don't even have to be a computer scientist to be good at Python! Anyone can pick it up and put it to work automating digital tasks.

Numerous AI-focused packages

Python has a huge ecosystem of libraries and packages that are useful for AI tasks. AI has a lot of interconnected components, including data preparation, model development, and model evaluation. There's a wealth of libraries written in Python that handle every component, allowing you to write less software and focus more on tailoring an AI model to your application. These include data manipulation tools like Pandas (Chapter 3), machine learning model libraries like scikit-learn (Chapter 4), and deep-learning powerhouses like Keras and PyTorch (Chapter 10). Chances are, for whatever AI-integrated task you have in mind, someone has written a Python library that takes the pain out of accomplishing it.

High community support

Having software available for AI tasks is great — unless no one bothered to explain how to use it (and if that seems ridiculous, ask any embedded systems engineer — it happens). Python, fortunately, has a large and active user base that documents their projects, creates tutorials for packages, and helps users debug problems. All developers at some point hit a wall with a program they're writing. The Python community has made it much easier to find and diagnose problems, push through the wall, and keep going.

It's no secret that interest in AI has exploded. Python has made it possible for many different people to interact with, develop for, and push the boundaries of AI — no engineering or computer science background required. It's one of the reasons reading this book is so exciting — you get to program with these tools directly.

TECHNICAL STUFF

Python (an interpreted language) runs much more slowly than a compiled language. This has been noted as a major flaw when it comes to AI development, because many models rely on compute speed to increase their training performance. However, Python lends itself to implementing complex AI algorithms with much less overhead than other languages. A lot of optimizations have been tried and tested with Python to increase its speed in the training phase.

Setting Up a Python Programming Environment

The Appendix of this book walks you through the installation process for a Python programming environment. There are multiple pathways to working with Python, and they require different resources. However, most of them have the following components in common:

- Text editor
- Python interpreter
- Terminal
- Integrated development environment (IDE)

TIP

If this is your first time programming in a computer language, it can be a little confusing at first to figure out where each of these components lives on your computer and how each of them contributes to creating an output. We'll go over each of these individually. If you've programmed before, this is a good review, but you can also skip ahead to the next section if you have a good grasp on these concepts.

Text editor

A text editor is used to write Python commands that make up Python programs. That's it. You can use a simple document editor, a notepad app, or just about anything that lets you write text. There's no special software strictly needed to write down the Python commands you want your computer to run. However, it's common for developers to use special software to write these programs with features that make programming mistakes easier to catch and fix.

A file that contains your written Python commands is called a *Python program* or a *Python script*. Again, there's nothing special about this file, except that the name must end in the extension `.py`. This extension lets the computer know that this file is meant to be run by the Python interpreter, and it will contain commands written in the Python programming language. In most of this book, we'll use Anaconda as our Python virtual environment and interpreter, and VS Code as our IDE (which is a combination text editor and terminal). We give instructions for installing these and the relevant extensions in the appendix.

Python interpreter

The Python interpreter is the software installed on your computer that translates commands written in your Python file into actions that your computer executes. On most computers available today, this software doesn't come pre-installed so you have to find a version to put on your machine that works for your needs. You can install a Python interpreter directly on your system (especially in Linux and Mac operating systems), or you can install virtual environment software, which allows you to interact with a Python interpreter in a more managed way. The Anaconda virtual environment software is popular for managing different versions of Python interpreters and packages depending on your needs. Most of this book's examples are run in an Anaconda environment.

TIP

Virtual environments are often considered "best practice" for implementing a Python environment, especially if you are starting out. Virtual environments allow you to keep Python interpreter versions — and packages installed with them — inside a specific namespace. If you accidentally install the wrong version of a package or mess up the namespace, this lets you revert to a fresh, clean base environment. It's an extra safeguard when experimenting with new libraries.

Terminal

The terminal is a program available on most operating systems that allows you to give your computer commands. It's also the big black rectangle you see inside every movie hacking scene ("I'm in."). The type of commands your computer accepts depends on your operating system — which is usually Windows, Mac, or some version of Linux (like Ubuntu). The terminal lets you command your computer to use the Python interpreter to execute a Python program. In most cases, you do this using the `python` keyword. To execute a Python program, you open a terminal on your computer and type:

```
python <program_name>.py
```

There are different types of terminals, but your operating system usually restricts your options. While the above command works on most operating systems to "run" your Python program, there are definitely some "gotchas" that might prevent this from happening! We'll go through these when we start programming.

You can give lots of other commands to your operating system by using the terminal. The terminal will print the output of the programs or indicate where a mistake in the program was made that prevented it from running. Being familiar with some basic terminal commands in your operating system will go a long way in beginning your programming journey. Plus, you can impress your non-programmer friends just by opening a terminal. Once, when caught off guard by a random school tour, one of Marz's students opened several programs on his computer just to look busy and "techie" for the crowd. It turns out he was just changing his monitor settings.

Integrated development environment

The last component — an integrated development environment (IDE) — is a software program that combines multiple elements together. Most commonly, an IDE will bundle a text editor for writing programs with a terminal interface for running them. The text editor will allow you to view your files and write commands in them, and will usually highlight mistakes or provide coding help to make your programming more efficient. Another part of the program has a terminal, where you can type commands into your operating system to run the Python programs. In this book, most examples use VS Code, a free IDE from Microsoft, which works for many programming languages. Other popular Python-focused IDEs include PyCharm and Spyder.

Another common Python programming IDE is Google Colab, which is available with a Google account. This allows you to use Python entirely in your browser (without installing anything extra), and instead of using a terminal, you can run code (written in code blocks or code cells) directly. We use Colab in Chapter 15 because this gives us access to advanced computer resources useful for more complex AI models. Figure 1-1 gives an overview of how the different Python programming components fit together.

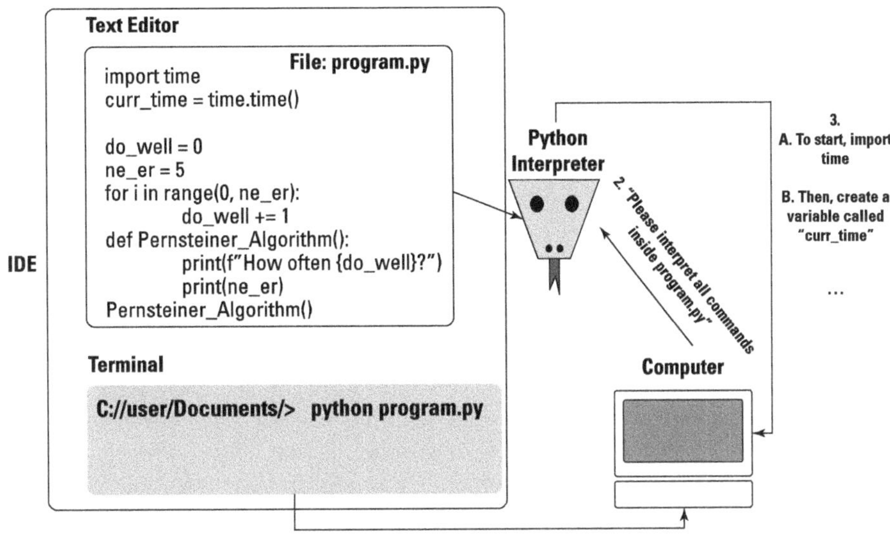

FIGURE 1-1: Python programming components and how they work together.

First-Time Python Programming Gotchas

While Python is comparatively easy to pick up, there are definitely some pitfalls to watch out for. If you run into issues, don't panic — every first-time programmer makes mistakes! The Internet is a great resource for troubleshooting, but we'll also include some resources for navigating common sources of problems.

Understanding the terminal

The terminal is a common cause of tears for new programmers. After all, you just started learning a new programming language — only to realize that in order to test your new language skills, you also have to learn how to talk to your computer in its own language! Terminals execute your commands to the operating system from a location in your computer's file system. For example, if you try to run the Python interpreter on a Python file, but your terminal is not located inside the same folder as the file, nothing will happen. Frustrating!

Figure 1-2 displays a diagram of a general terminal in most operating systems.

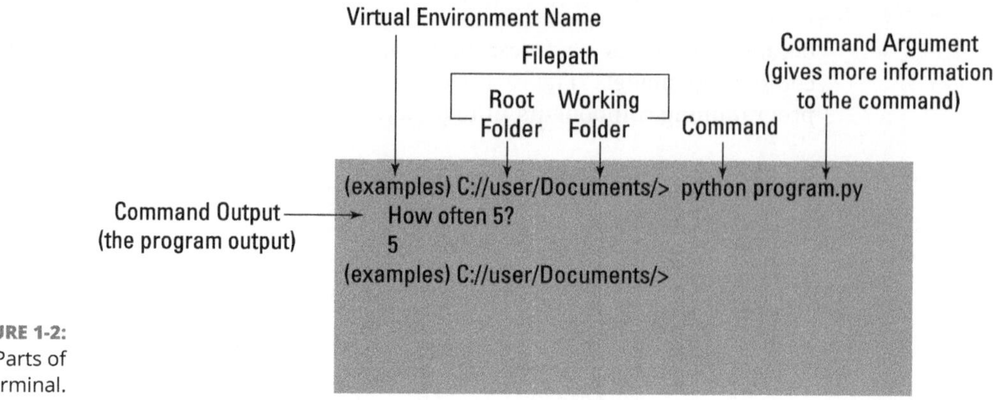

FIGURE 1-2: Parts of a terminal.

The filepath, which displays your location in the file system, is printed on the right, and you can type commands to the left of it. If you are working in a virtual environment, the name of the environment you are working in will be printed inside parentheses on the extreme right. In many IDEs (and even graphical file systems), you can open a terminal inside a given folder to start with, which helps. There are also a couple of commands that help you navigate the location inside the terminal. After you type a command in your terminal, press **Enter** on your keyboard to execute it.

To print a list of files and folders in your current terminal location, you can type:

```
ls
```

in a Linux/Mac environment, or

```
dir
```

in a Windows environment. Go ahead — open a terminal (Mac/Linux), a command prompt (Windows), or the Anaconda Prompt (Windows/Linux), and try it out!

To change the location of the terminal, you can type:

```
cd <folder_name>
```

in all three environments. If you need to go up a folder, you can type:

```
cd ..
```

So, if you have a folder structure that looks like:

top

middle

bottom

And your terminal is currently in the "middle" folder, you would type:

```
cd bottom
```

to change to the "bottom" folder and

```
cd ..
```

to go back to the "top" folder.

Sometimes, you have a lot of output printed in your terminal, which can be annoying. If you want to clear the terminal output, type:

```
cls
```

in a Windows environment, and

```
clear
```

in a Linux/Mac environment.

Generally, pressing the up arrow on your keyboard will bring up your most recently run command, which is a time saver (repeatedly pressing the up arrow will cycle through your command history). Pressing the tab key on your keyboard while writing out a filename will usually attempt to autocomplete the filename with matching files inside the folder.

Using different virtual environments

If you are working with a virtual environment, another common pitfall is not having the right environment active when you try to run a command. Speaking from experience, this encompasses something like 70 percent of the first-time "gotchas!" when working with Python. For an Anaconda environment, you also might need to initialize the terminal to be able to work with Anaconda. If Anaconda is already initialized, you'll see

```
(base)
```

in front of the filepath. If that's missing, you may need to run:

```
conda init
```

inside the terminal. To change to your particular virtual environment, run:

```
conda activate <environment_name>
```

For example, if I have a virtual environment named "examples," I would run:

```
conda activate examples
```

Python packages you install are tied to a given environment. If you are getting a "package missing" error on a package you know you already installed, you are probably in the wrong environment. You can always run:

```
conda deactivate
```

to get back into your base environment.

Installing Python packages

Installing Python packages is crucial to running many of the examples in this book. The commands to do this can vary slightly depending on how you installed the Python interpreter. If you have it installed directly on your system, you can usually run:

```
pip install <package_name>
```

Or:

```
python -m pip install <package_name>
```

for a given library (Pip is a Python package manager). For Anaconda, you would run:

```
conda install <package_name>
```

For example, if you want to install the pandas Python package, you would run one of these:

```
pip install pandas
python -m pip install pandas
conda install pandas
```

TIP

Anaconda comes with a lot of packages installed by default. Usually, the package manager will tell you during the installation process if a package is already present. It typically won't reinstall the package unless you ask it to get a specific version of the software.

Creating a Virtual Environment

With the basics out of the way, you are now ready to write your first Python program. To begin, you'll create a virtual environment that you'll use to run examples in this book. You have a few options to do this. If you installed Anaconda Navigator along with Anaconda, you can do this graphically in Windows/Linux.

Open Anaconda Navigator. On the left is a side navigation bar. Click the Environments tab and then click the + sign that appears on top of the word Create at the bottom of the window (see Figure 1-3). Type **examples** in the new window that pops up, and make sure Python is checked. Then click Create to initialize the new environment (this may take a few minutes).

If you don't have Anaconda Navigator, you can open a terminal (Terminal, Command Prompt, or Anaconda Navigator, depending on your system). If the Anaconda base environment is not yet initialized (it should be in Anaconda Navigator already if you're using that program), run:

```
conda init
```

Then, to create the virtual environment, run:

```
conda create -n examples
```

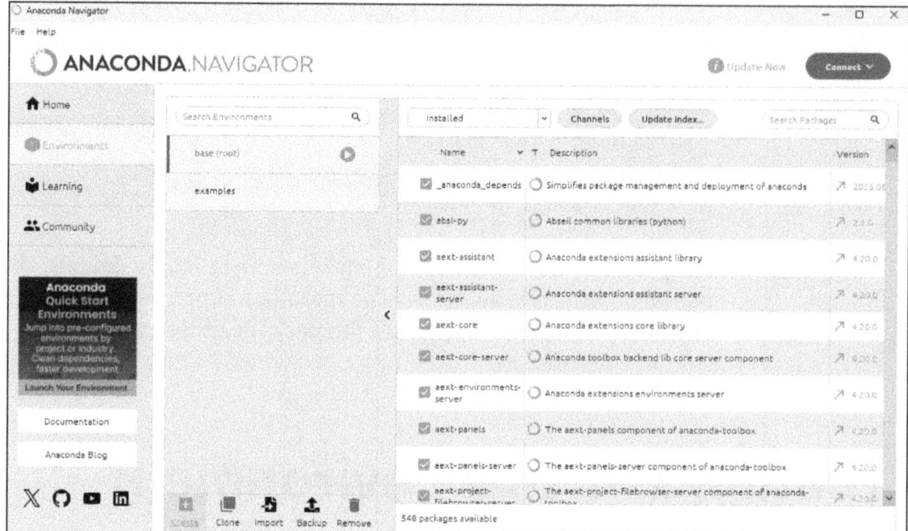

FIGURE 1-3: The Anaconda Navigator method of creating a new virtual environment.

Breaking Down the VS Code Interface

When you open VS Code for the first time after installing it, it will probably ask if you want to open a folder. Go ahead and choose a folder in your file system that you'll use to store project files for this book.

The layout for VS Code on startup is shown in Figure 1-4. To the left, you'll see the Explorer pane, which allows you to view the files located in your open folder. The icons to the extreme left allow you to switch between the Explorer pane, a Search pane, a Source Control pane, a Debugging pane, and an Extensions pane. We'll stick inside the Explorer pane for most of the book.

The top menu enables you to navigate several of the settings in VS Code. The welcome screen in the middle gives you some quick options for getting started in the IDE. Along the right is the option to chat with an AI Agent, which can help you debug, although we (ironically) won't be using it in the book.

Creating a new file

From the welcome menu, or in the Explorer pane using the + button on the file icon, create a new file. Call it **hello_world.py**. Figure 1-5 displays the view after creating the file; the file itself should be visible in the Explorer pane on the side of the screen, with the (empty) contents of the file in the middle of the screen.

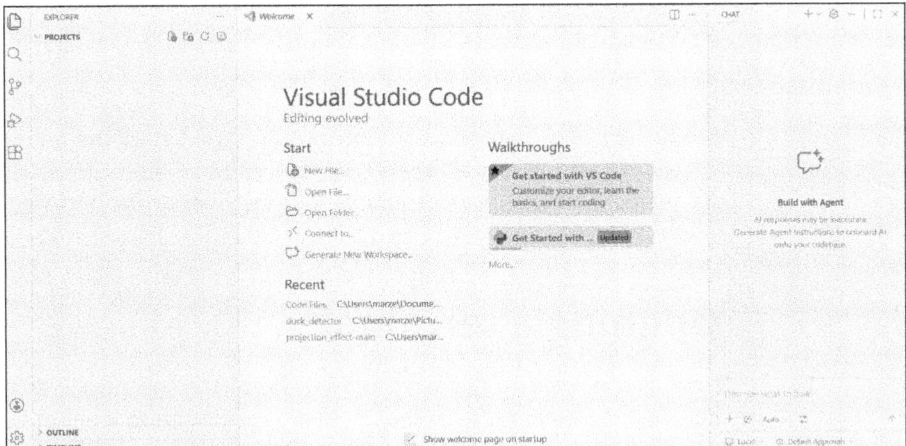

FIGURE 1-4: The VS Code start-up view.

FIGURE 1-5: View in VS Code after creating a new file.

Selecting the Python interpreter

The first thing you want to do is make sure VS Code knows that you want to use Anaconda as your Python interpreter. Press Control + Shift + P in Windows/Linux or Command + Shift + P to open the Command Palette, or select View from the top menu and then Command Palette.

This opens the searchable command palette. You are going to be looking for a command that says "Python: Select Interpreter." Start typing this text, and the matching command should show up (if it doesn't, you may need to install the Python Extension from the Extensions pane).

From the list of potential Python interpreters, select the one that matches your virtual environment name, `Python <version number> (examples)`. You should see your Python interpreter and version number at the bottom of the screen after selecting.

Opening a terminal

Now, you'll need to open a terminal. From the top menu, select Terminal (you may need to access it with the . . . menu continuation icon) and then New Terminal. This should open a new terminal at the bottom of your screen, as shown in Figure 1-6.

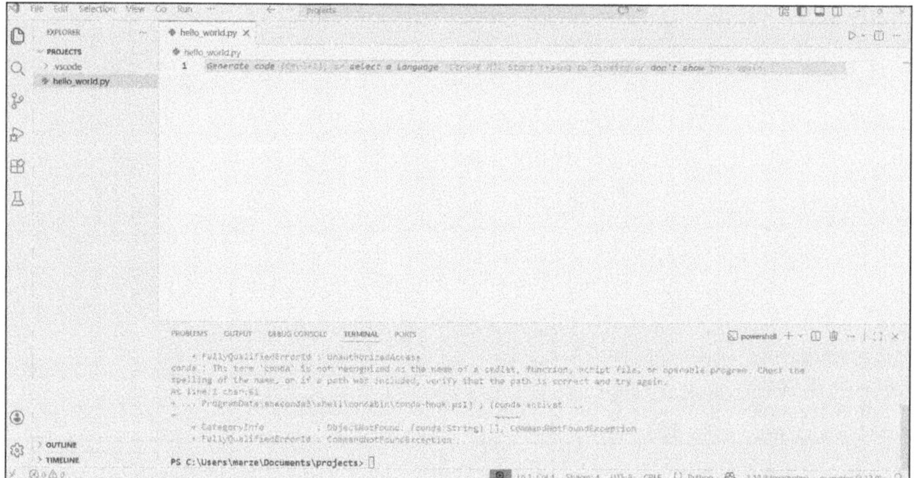

FIGURE 1-6: Opening a terminal in VS Code.

In Windows, this may open the PowerShell terminal by default, which doesn't always activate the correct Anaconda environment. If this is the case, click the down arrow by the + sign next to the PowerShell name at the top of the terminal window. Click Command Prompt. This should open the terminal and activate the correct environment (see Figure 1-7). If you see a warning about a missing temp file, you can ignore it.

Now, you're ready to start programming!

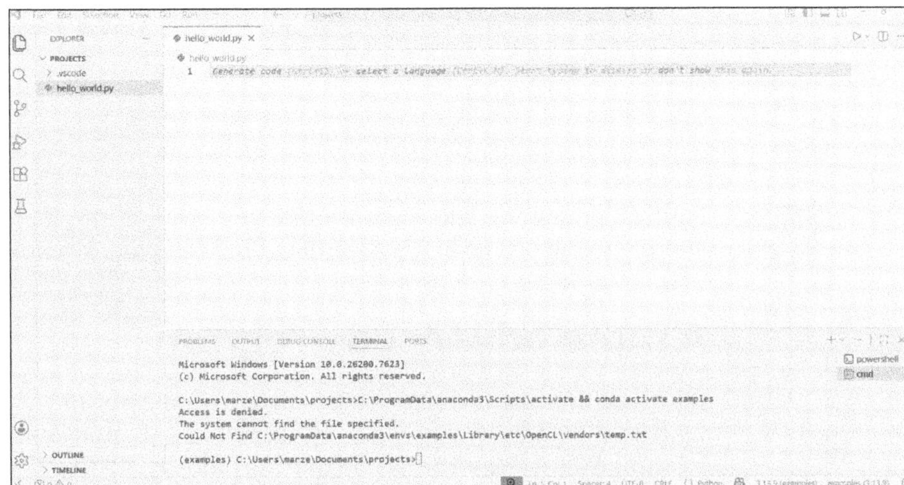

FIGURE 1-7: Using a Command Prompt terminal in VS Code.

Hello, World!

Your first Python program is incredibly simple. Listing 1-1 gives the program in its entirety.

LISTING 1-1: Your First Python Program (hello_world.py)

```
print("Hello, World!")
```

That's it! Remember, Python is case-sensitive, so capitalization matters — type the listing exactly as it is here. Press Control/Command + s to save the program, or click File ⇨ Save.

Run the program by typing:

```
python hello_world.py
```

into the terminal and press Enter. Remember, this tells your computer to use the `python` interpreter to run the commands stored in the file named `hello_world.py`.

The program only has one command — print "Hello, World." Figure 1-8 shows the terminal output you should see from running this program. Congratulations, you just commanded your computer to do something using Python!

```
(examples) C:\Users\marze\Documents\projects>python hello_world.py
Hello, World!

(examples) C:\Users\marze\Documents\projects>
```

FIGURE 1-8: Terminal output of running Listing 1-1.

TECHNICAL STUFF

Most programming languages courses start with a tutorial for printing "Hello, World!" to the terminal. It's a weird but fun computer science convention.

A more advanced program

Now, you'll create a slightly more advanced program to show off some Python functionality. Create a new file by using the + button on the file icon, or by selecting File -> New File. Name this file **more.py**. Listing 1-2 displays the commands that will be written in `more.py`, while Figure 1-9 gives the terminal output of running Listing 1-2.

LISTING 1-2: Example Python Functionality (more.py)

```
#Import a library
import random

#Use the library to access a function, and store the
#result in a variable
random_number = random.randint(3, 11)
#print the value of the variable
print("Random Number:")
print(random_number)

#Define a list
print("List")
list_of_numbers = [6, 5, 3, 4, 10]
#Access the first number in the list
print(list_of_numbers[0])

#Check a condition
print("Condition")
if random_number > 7:
    print("Greater than 7!")
else:
    print("Less than or equal to 7")

#Use a loop to print the numbers up to your random number
print("Loop")
```

```
for i in range(0, random_number):
    print(i)

#Define a function
def add_one(num):
    new_num = num+1
    return new_num

#Call the function
print("Call function")
returned_number = add_one(random_number)
print(returned_number)
```

```
(examples) C:\Users\marze\Documents\projects>python more.py
Random Number:
3
List
6
Condition
Less than or equal to 7
Loop
0
1
2
Call function
4
```

FIGURE 1-9: Terminal output of running Listing 1-2.

Following is a breakdown of the code, section by section:

```
#Import a library
```

This line starts with a pound sign (or hashtag, if you are from a slightly younger generation), which marks it as a comment. This means the line can be used as a note to yourself or whoever else might be reading your code — the computer won't execute it as a command.

```
import random
```

This line *imports* a package called "random" (which is installed in most Python distributions by default). It contains some handy Python code someone else has written that you can use in your project. The `import` statement allows you to import packages that you download with `pip` or `conda`, or even functions, variables, and classes inside other Python files in the same folder!

```
#Use the library to access a function, and store the
#result in a variable
random_number = random.randint(3, 11)
#print the value of the variable
print("Random Number:")
print(random_number)
```

This section starts with comments explaining what the code is doing. We use the `randint` function located inside the `random` library (we use dot notation to access this), and *call* the function with two number *arguments* inside the parentheses. This tells the function to give us a random number between 3 and 11 (the function is inclusive, meaning it could also return 3 or 11). The result returned by the function is stored in a variable called `random_number`, which is then printed to the terminal. As shown in Figure 1-9, this function gave us the random number 3.

```
#Define a list
print("List")
list_of_numbers = [6, 5, 3, 4, 10]
#Access the first number in the list
print(list_of_numbers[0])
```

This section defines a list, which is a type of structured data in sequence. We use brackets to enclose the items in the list, and commas to separate individual items in the list. After defining the list and storing it in a variable called `list_of_numbers`, we can access different items in the list by using brackets. In this case, we access the first item in the list, index 0 (which happens to be the number 6). In Python, like many programming languages, counting items starts at 0 rather than 1.

```
#Check a condition
print("Condition")
if random_number > 7:
    print("Greater than 7!")
else:
    print("Less than or equal to 7")
```

In this section, we use Python condition-checking. The first line after the print statement checks if the `random_number` variable has a value greater than 7. If that is true, it will execute all the code in the indented block below it — in this case, a command that prints "Greater than 7!". If this is not true, it will skip down to the else declaration and execute the commands indented under it, printing "Less than or equal to 7!". Since our random_number was given the value 3 earlier in the program, the output printed "Less than or equal to 7!". There are many possible conditions you can check in Python.

```
#Use a loop to print the numbers up to your random number
print("Loop")
for i in range(0, random_number):
    print(i)
```

This section creates a *loop*, which executes the code in the indented block multiple times. In this case, the statement creates an *iterator*, i, which will start at the value in the beginning of the range function (0) and stop one before the value at the end of the range function (random_number -1). Python is a little unusual in that the range function is exclusive of the second argument, meaning it will stop the loop before the iterator reaches this value. In this case, the indented block prints the value of the iterator. Since random_number is 3 in our case, the program prints the numbers 0, 1, and 2.

```
#Define a function
def add_one(num):
    new_num = num+1
    return new_num
```

This section defines a *function*, which is a reusable piece of code. The def keyword indicates that we're creating a new function. This is followed by the function name add_one, and open and closed parentheses which contain an argument, num (information given to the function when it is called). When the function is called, it will execute the code indented inside of it. In this case, it will take the num argument, add the number 1 to it, assign it to a variable called new_num, and return this value.

```
#Call the function
print("Call function")
returned_number = add_one(random_number)
print(returned_number)
```

The final section of code *calls* the function. It uses the function name (add_one) with the value we'll pass to it (random_number) inside the parentheses and returns the value of the function to a variable called returned_number. It then prints this returned_number. This takes our random_number, 3, and adds 1 to it to return a value of 4. We can call a function any time after it is defined.

TIP

Note that since we ask the program for a random number, we'll get a different number each time we run the program (if you are following along, you probably already noticed this).

These are some basic Python abilities to get you started, but many more resources for learning Python and testing its limits are available online. We highly encourage you to play around with it and see what's possible!

REMEMBER

Throughout this book, we provide a code listing followed by an explanation of the commands within the code. If you want to follow along on your own machine, you can find the source code for each chapter in the downloadable source code provided for this book. See the Introduction for details on how to find these source files.

USEFUL TIPS FOR WORKING WITH THE PYTHON PROGRAMMING LANGUAGE

Getting started in Python is fast, but getting comfortable with the language can take a little longer. Don't despair. This book will provide plenty of practice examples. Keep these tips in mind:

- **Be patient:** If code isn't running or a bug isn't being resolved, welcome to the programming club! A good programming practice is to never spend more than an hour or two at a time trying to solve a problem. If you're stuck, take a walk, eat a snack, or otherwise spend time giving yourself a little time off. Usually, the fix will be much faster when you're coming at it fresh.
- **Use online resources:** The Python community is a treasure trove of great libraries, excellent starter problems, and debugging help!
- **Check documentation:** If a library is behaving oddly, double-check its documentation. Sometimes a variable is supposed to be a different type than the one you're trying to use, or there are multiple similar function calls implementing different behavior.
- **Be curious:** There's no shortage of great Python projects in the wild. Read other people's code, explore different packages, and don't be afraid to implement something new!

In Chapter 2, we dive deeper into some fundamental AI concepts that you'll use in Python projects throughout the book.

Troubleshooting

It's rare to get a perfectly running program the first time around. Or the second time . . . or the third. It's okay! Persistence will pay off. Here are a few errors new programmers commonly encounter, but can be frustrating to debug:

- **File not saved:** Programs will only run saved commands. A white dot will appear on the top of the file name tab in VS Code if the file isn't saved. Make sure to save it before you try and run it!
- **Trapped inside Python terminal:** If you type the `python` command and then forget to type a file name after, you will run the interpreter directly inside the terminal. It will be expecting all subsequent commands to be in the Python language, rather than in your computer's language. Go ahead and type `exit()` and press Enter to exit this mode.
- **Syntax errors:** If you have an error with your written commands in the program, the terminal will not run your program fully. In this case, the interpreter program will generally print out the line on which the error occurred and what it thinks the error is. It can take some practice to get used to debugging these problems, but the provided information can be helpful!

IN THIS CHAPTER

» Defining AI and exploring the AI model taxonomy

» Using different types of machine learning models

» Defining a model

» Evaluating and improving a model

Chapter 2
Defining Fundamental AI Concepts

AI is currently one of the hottest topics internationally. It's difficult to interact with any sort of digital tool without coming across an AI component — whether it's a chatbot trying to help you figure out why you can't put a travel notice on your bank account, a predictive analytics package used for sales data at work, or a video-editing tool that lets you replace every building in a photo with a giant turtle. The use of AI tools today spans from completely groundbreaking to astonishingly frivolous. Inside this spectrum, it can be difficult to navigate the pros, cons, and limitations of technology, especially when it's not always clear which technology is being used where. This chapter is designed to give you a clearer picture of AI terminologies and how they relate to AI's use today.

Defining AI

What is AI, anyway? There are many definitions out there, but at its most basic, *AI is any technology that helps a computer make a decision.* That's a pretty broad scope! AI can be as simple as a series of if-then rules that help a maintenance operator troubleshoot equipment, or as complex as a large language model chatbot summarizing a text document for a meeting.

Many subfields exist within this definition, and the subfields have different expectations for data and capabilities. Figure 2-1 outlines the taxonomy of AI approaches and models. It should be noted that other taxonomies exist, but we like this one because it sorts the different techniques more by method of approach than use case. Note that the distinctions we make between models here aren't so clean in real life. There are many hybrid approaches or models that use more than one type of technique. The requirements for each of these models can also vary widely, even within a single subfield! However, this is a good starting introduction to the AI family as a whole.

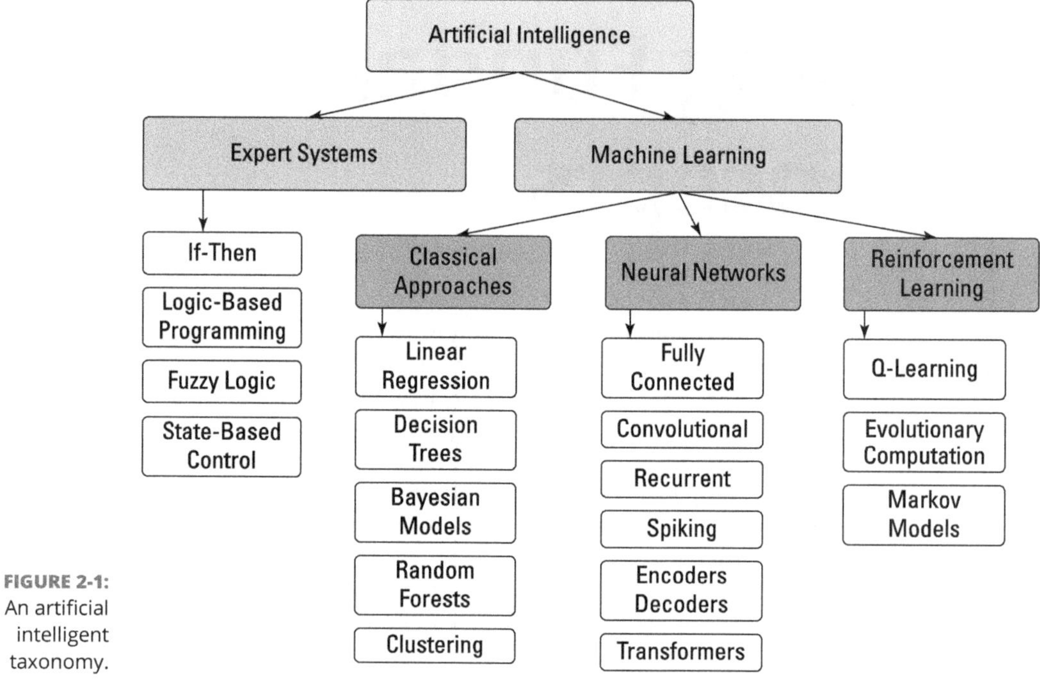

FIGURE 2-1: An artificial intelligent taxonomy.

In the taxonomy, AI is the broadest category, encompassing all approaches. There are two main subfields:

- Expert systems or rule-based approaches
- Machine learning

Expert systems or rule-based approaches

Expert systems or rule-based approaches typically try to encode human knowledge into some format that a computer can use. This is a specialized process with a clearly defined scope for a task at hand. It also often involves direct interfacing between the expert or experts and the programmer. For example, expert systems could include:

- Creating a series of if/then statements in a specialized program to help drill down on a decision or diagnose a problem at the time of use
- Using a logic-based programming language (like Prolog) to define rules and relationships, creating logical thinking patterns, and connecting patterns between entities
- Creating a fuzzy logic program to convert inputs and values into human-understandable decision spectrums
- Using state-based control to define sequences of steps or actions

REMEMBER

Expert systems can be very powerful, but they often take a lot of time and effort to create. They are not always easy to update, and are usually specific to a limited set of tasks. Initially, a lot of AI systems were expert systems. However, the advent of big data shifted the AI development focus from expert systems to machine learning.

Machine learning

The machine learning category of AI is what most people mean when they discuss AI. Likely 99 percent of the models you have run across in your life fall into this category. Machine learning models necessitate collecting data. The models are trained on and adjust their parameters based on the data's characteristics. Expert systems might use some data as inputs to their underlying logical schemes, but for machine learning systems, data collection is nonnegotiable.

The machine learning category can be further divided into three subcategories:

- Classical machine learning models
- Neural network approaches
- Reinforcement learning

Classical machine learning models

Classical machine learning models learn parameters from data, usually in a statistically based way. They don't use a neural network structure, and they tend to be simpler and more explainable than neural network approaches. However, this is a very broad category, and the complexity and usability of each depend a lot on the context and architecture of the model. Classical machine learning models include:

- Linear regression (Chapter 5)
- Decision trees (Chapter 6)
- Bayesian models
- Random forests (Chapter 7)
- Many clustering approaches

Classical machine learning approaches may have reduced in popularity with the advent of neural networks — but don't count them out! These models can outperform other approaches on a surprisingly broad set of problem cases — while maintaining a higher level of explainability, in many situations.

Neural network models

Remember when we said that 99 percent of the time, when someone discusses AI, they are talking about machine learning techniques? Well, 95 percent of the time, they are also talking about neural network approaches.

Many neural network approaches exist, and we spend a good portion of this book discussing them. Neural networks are the current state-of-the-art in AI. They all share the characteristics of forming an architecture loosely based on your brain wiring. Most neural networks use gradient descent parameter optimization and backpropagation to assign errors to parameters and update them. Following is a brief overview of some of the types of neural networks. Chapter 11 discusses the neural network family in more detail.

FULLY CONNECTED NEURAL NETWORKS

These networks are the "vanilla" flavor of the category, and usually take in structured tabular data into a fully connected setup to make a prediction or classify inputs.

CONVOLUTIONAL NEURAL NETWORKS

Convolutional neural networks incorporate image data and are structured so that they can understand matrix data for classifying, locating, and segmenting images. Chapter 14 covers convolutional neural networks in more detail.

RECURRENT NEURAL NETWORKS

Recurrent neural networks incorporate the time dimension for sequence data. These networks have a "memory" and can be used for tasks with time dependencies.

SPIKING NEURAL NETWORKS

Spiking neural networks are designed to mimic analog signals in the brain and are structured around accumulating signals. While not discussed in this book, they require specialized hardware and ideally improve sensory signal analysis.

ENCODERS AND DECODERS

These networks compress input into a different representation and turn it into new output. These networks are used in many tasks individually and can also form a component of a separate network.

TRANSFORMERS

Ninety percent of the time, when someone mentions AI, they are talking about a transformer. Transformers form the basis of generative AI, chatbots, and so on. While there are many, many versions of this model, their key characteristic is the incorporation of an attention mechanism. Chapters 15 and 16 cover transformers in more detail.

Reinforcement learning

Reinforcement learning encompasses a family of techniques that use a modified trial-and-error process to learn from past experiences and mistakes. Reinforcement learning techniques are often used to explore a solution space rather than make a single prediction or classification.

Classical reinforcement learning techniques include Q-learning and policy optimization. These techniques are covered more in Chapter 18. Another sub-field, evolutionary computation, uses a set of biologically-based approaches to find solutions and search areas efficiently. These techniques are covered more in Chapter 19. Markov models and Monte Carlo simulations also typically fall into the reinforcement learning category. These techniques are sometimes used for business scenario planning.

How Big Data Gave Rise to Machine Learning

Most of this book focuses on machine learning models, as these are the most widely implemented techniques in practice. But how did we get here? Why are these techniques so popular?

The machine learning explosion is probably the result of a few different simultaneous advancements. In the last 20 years, storage and database technology have improved to the point where it is feasible to store large amounts of organized data. Companies and organizations began collecting this data to analyze and study. The "big data" revolution provided the training material for machine learning models that, beforehand, could involve an arduous hand-collection process. The storage and use of big data is a major enabler of the technology — beginner AI students have their choice of online data repositories for many different tasks while learning the ropes. In this book, we'll be using some open datasets as well.

In addition to data and storage, compute power became more available and efficient. Specialized chips designed to complete highly parallel operations were invented for graphics processing — and then used for machine learning number crunching. Consumer-level processing hardware and memory improved. Machine learning — which needs a lot of data and compute cycles — suddenly became feasible to do on a laptop from a department store.

Machine learning is exciting both due to its advanced capabilities and its wide availability. You might not be able to run Grok on your desktop, but you can easily train a decision tree at home. You might not be able to develop an image generator on your own hardware, but you can use a mix of online tools and a webcam to create your own object detector. Machine learning is fun — and approachable!

REMEMBER

It would be unwise not to discuss the limitations of machine learning, however. Because of the data dependencies, machine learning models are typically only as good as the data they are fed. Messy data leads to garbage models. Another tricky issue with machine learning models is that sometimes they are a little too attached to their own training data — at the expense of being more generally usable. I might be able to bake a pretty fantastic huckleberry pie — but if that's all I focus on, I'm probably not going to be able to open a bakery. Machine learning models can get lost in optimizing for a very small subset of tasks instead of the broader set you are trying to train them on.

In this book, we look at methods for data preparation and model training that will try to avoid these issues.

Breaking Down Models

What is a model, anyway? Figure 2-2 provides a basic illustration.

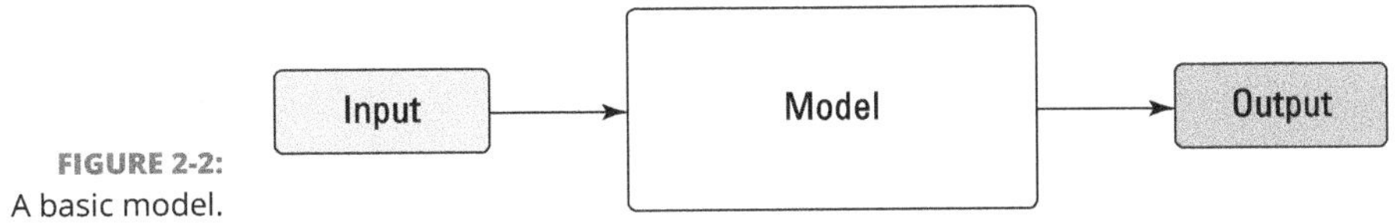

FIGURE 2-2: A basic model.

Models are simple. They take an input and give you an output. That's it! You could also say a function is a model. The input you give the model is the data you have. This can be:

- Sensor readings
- Sales figures
- A picture
- A text prompt
- The weather report
- Or anything else that can be represented digitally!

The output the model gives you back is some sort of answer you want. This can be:

- A time-to-failure prediction
- A sales forecast
- An object classification image
- A sentiment analysis
- A weather alert
- Or anything else that can be represented digitally!

There are even some models whose input and output are exactly the same. Typically, you build a model to either automate a task you don't want to do over and over again, or to find patterns in data you can't identify by yourself.

Highly capable models may seem magic, but they share a lot of simple characteristics. Machine learning models have:

- Input data
- Internal parameters
- Output data
- Correct answer
- Error

Figure 2-3 is a simple illustration of a machine learning model. The goal of model training is to adjust the internal parameters of the model to produce the output data that results in the minimum possible error. It's a simple enough goal — with sometimes a very complicated implementation!

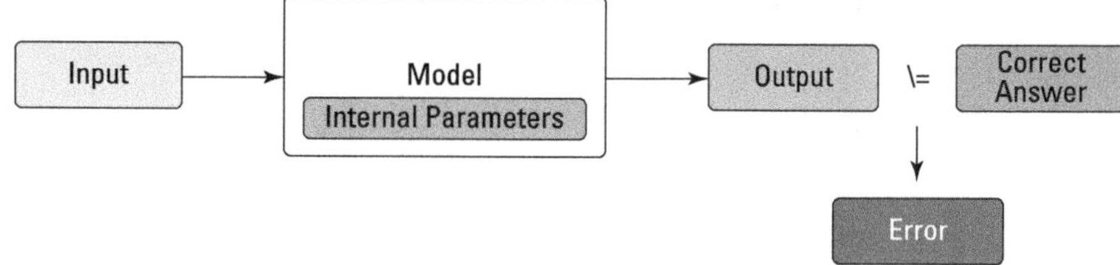

FIGURE 2-3: A machine learning model.

TECHNICAL STUFF

A simple model — linear regression, for instance — may have one parameter. The large language models you interact with have billions or trillions. However, both adjust their parameters based on the data they are given. The complexity of their implementations is quite different!

Input data

Input data is what the model receives. The model uses the input data in conjunction with its internal parameters to produce output data. The input data is often one of the most important aspects of the model decisions — well-optimized models can rarely make good outputs on bad data, but even mediocre models can often make good outputs on excellent data.

Input data may need to be formatted a particular way for model ingestion. Some models are more relaxed about data types and formats, and other types are very strict about what they can handle.

Internal parameters

The internal parameters of a model are what define the type of model you are using. Different models have different sets of internal parameters. Neural networks use weights and bias numbers within their structure to make decisions. Linear regression uses multiplicative coefficients. Decision trees use threshold splits on the data. The internal parameters change based on the training process. Models may have another set of parameters, called *hyperparameters*, which do not get adjusted during the training process. For hyperparameters, it is up to the machine learning engineer to set the best possible hyperparameters based on their resource constraints to help the model do its job.

Output data

Output data is the model's "answer" to the input data — the final information the model gives back. The goal of most model training is to get this output data to be as close as possible to 100 percent correct for the task at hand. Depending on the problem, the correctness of the output can be difficult to define or quantify. In supervised machine learning, all input training data is associated with labeled, correct, "ground-truth" data (correct answers) for comparison with the model's produced output data.

Correct answers

Along with the input data, you supply the model with correct answers (usually matched to a given input sample). The model uses these to calculate the error and have something to compare its performance to.

TIP

Getting the correct answer or ground-truth data can sometimes be the most difficult part of the data collection process, since you typically want to use real-world outcomes, events, or knowledge. It can be hard to come by individuals with sufficient knowledge to determine these, in many cases. If you are in charge of forming a model from start to finish it's important to note the time and resources involved in collecting the ground-truth outcomes of interest.

Error

The error of the model is the difference between the model's output and the correct answers for the given data. Usually, some sort of error function is used to determine the error. The error helps quantify how the model needs to adjust its internal parameters to improve its performance.

MODEL TRAINING

The process to train a machine learning model usually involves the following steps:

1. The input data is preprocessed for use by the model.
2. The model receives the input data.
3. The model uses the input data and its internal parameters to create output data.
4. The output data is compared to ground-truth data, and an error is created.
5. The model uses the error to adjust its internal parameters to create better output.
6. Steps 2–5 are repeated until the error is reduced or training must stop.

Minor differences may occur in these steps depending on the type of training. Sometimes the model receives input and creates outputs several times in a row before calculating error. Sometimes the amount of error is ill-defined and the model adjusts its parameters based on a best guess. Sometimes the best parameters can be calculated directly from the data without a lengthy adjustment process. For machine learning models, however, these steps hold true most of the time.

Evaluating and Improving a Model

The error function is usually the best method of evaluating a model. However, sometimes other metrics are useful. Methods of evaluating a model's performance include:

- Assessing the accuracy of classification
- Evaluating the feasibility of a solution
- Evaluating the optimality of a solution
- Determining the explainability of a solution
- Assessing if the model has provided new insights not previously known

These metrics may not always factor directly into the model training process. If they don't, but are very important to the actual use of the model, it's a good idea to investigate making them more directly influence the training process.

Models will pretty much always try to adjust themselves to meet the training goal you set. If that doesn't align with what you actually want, you'll wind up with useless models.

Different model types use different techniques to improve their ability to create the output you want. In machine learning, the data is used to "learn" the best model parameters. This is often a guided trial-and-error process. Often, the model will try some parameters, evaluate their performance, and make minor adjustments if the performance is lackluster. The error quantification can often help the model make better adjustments.

The model must investigate two major considerations when making a change:

- Which parameters were responsible for the mistakes?
- How much should the parameters be changed to improve?

Sometimes these questions can be answered directly from the training process. Sometimes they can be inferred from characteristics of the data. And sometimes the model just has to guess! This book covers many different model types and explains how parameters are chosen, used to make decisions, and changed.

Improving the model is usually the most time-consuming part of the model-creation process. Compute constraints may factor into how much you are able to improve the model after setting it up. Simple models can usually improve more quickly than complex models — but have lower capacity to solve the overall task. More complex models may have unbounded capacity to solve problems — but also unbounded potential training time!

When improving models, a lot of advancements in the machine learning field focus on making the model training process faster or more efficient. However, this is not the only area that can be improved. Better data pre-processing often makes a huge difference in overall model performance! Reducing bad or noisy data can also go a long way in getting better results.

Getting Started in the AI World

The information in this chapter may seem daunting — with so many models to choose from, how should you get started? Fortunately, you picked up this book!

Classical machine learning models tend to be easier to understand, both in terms of the mathematics behind them and the output they provide. We'll start with these model types in Part 2. Part 3 covers the neural network approaches. While more complicated, we'll spend some time together learning how they tick and what makes them so powerful. Neural network approaches aren't so unapproachable either — you'll be able to run examples directly on your machine. Part 4 focuses specifically on AI models for image tasks, and Part 5 covers the more advanced models. This is a good progression to follow if you are brand new to the AI world. If you've poked around in AI before, feel free to skip around or visit the techniques you want to learn more about!

IN THIS CHAPTER

» Exploring different types of data

» Working with a practice dataset

» Using the pandas library

» Filtering and processing data

» Visualizing data properties

Chapter 3
Working with Data

Working with data is fundamental in AI. There's not always a neat line between "data scientist" and "machine learning engineer," because many of the concepts, tips, and techniques overlap. In this chapter, you explore how to work with a dataset. You first look at the different types of variables found in tabular data by exploring an open dataset called Steel Plates Faults. You install the pandas data manipulation library and discover how to inspect and statistically analyze different features of your dataset. You access various columns and rows and learn how to filter the dataset into smaller views of the data with conditional selection. You get rid of pesky nonexistent data and discover how to create descriptive plots and charts with Matplotlib. Finally, you uncover the importance of working with an expert for any data project.

Preparing Data for a Machine Learning Model

This chapter is designed to get you up and running with some basic skills in working with and preparing data for a machine learning model. To do this, you'll work with an open dataset from the UC Irvine Machine Learning Repository called Steel Plates Faults (`https://archive.ics.uci.edu/dataset/198/steel+plates+faults`). The UCI Repository is a good place to find donated datasets for practice projects, and we highly recommend exploring some of their other options as you begin your AI journey. You can download the compressed version of the dataset on the repository site, and it is also available as part of the downloadable source code for the book as a .csv file for easier importing into your Python environment.

REMEMBER

You can find the source code for this chapter in the "programs" folder of the downloadable code file. See the Introduction for details on how to find this file as well as all the source code files for the code listings in the book. The dataset will be inside the "datasets_and_media" folder.

The Steel Plates Faults dataset is a *tabular* dataset, meaning it can be represented as a table. Columns in the dataset represent the different *features* of the data, while rows represent *instances* of the data. Features are different properties measured from a data instance. For example, in the steel dataset, each row is a different steel plate. The columns contain information about the steel plate's measurements and visual properties, as well as the presence or absence of any faults in the sample.

Explaining variable types

Variables in a dataset can be sorted into different types. Measurements are a type of data, as well as categorical classifications, images, and many more. For tabular data, variables tend to fall in the following categories:

- » Numeric
- » Categorical

As you might expect, *numeric* data types are made of numbers. These are often measurements or meaningful scales of values. A numeric feature might be a continuous variable, meaning it can take any fractional value in its range, or it might be an integer variable, meaning it can only take on a whole number value. In our dataset, there is a mix of continuous features (Edges_Index, LogOfAreas, Luminosity_Index, and so on) and integer features (X_Minimum, Y_Maximum, Pixels_Areas, and so on).

Categorical data types assign a feature to a category. This is pretty common with classification outcomes (for example, this instance is a "dog" or a "cat"). However, typically, such labels aren't used when working with AI. Categories are usually encoded by assigning them to a number, and there are a few ways to do this. The first is to create a different number for each category (for example, dog = 1, cat = 2, bird = 3, and so on), but keep all the categories in the same column. This is useful organizationally — but, depending on the model you picked, it can sometimes cause confusion. Because the computer is only seeing a number, it might assume there is a meaningful numeric difference of 2 between dog and bird (3-1 = 2), which is nonsense (Note: if that isn't nonsense to you, you might be operating on another intelligence plane than the authors).

Another way to split categories is to create binary outcomes for each potential variable value. In this case, dog, cat, and bird would each be split off to their own column, with a value of 1 if the instance belonged to that class and 0 otherwise. In our dataset, each of the seven potential outcome faults — Pastry, Z_Scratch, K-Scatch, Stains, Dirtiness, Bumps, and Other_Faults — are binary-encoded. Any steel plate with a particular fault will have a 1 in that column. Again, depending on your model, you may want to create a separate column called "faults" and encode each fault with a number from 0 to 6. It depends entirely on your implementation.

There are 27 "feature" column variables in the dataset, and 7 "outcome" variables, for a total of 34 columns. There are 1,941 total rows, meaning 1,941 different steel plates were recorded. Overall, 1,941 steel plates were analyzed on 34 different features and outcome values, meaning our dataset contains 65,994 individual pieces of information. For machine learning, this is actually considered a small dataset!

Cute and cuddly: Installing the pandas library

Okay, okay, the pandas library is not actually named after the cute bamboo-eating animal, but a contraction of "panel data" (tabular data), which is the type of data it's meant to help process. Pandas is a free Python library with many handy features and functions for exploring, filtering, cleaning, and using tabular data. For this book, pandas is our library of choice for data manipulation, and we'll spend most of this chapter exploring its handy properties to help us wrangle our information.

You can install the library by running:

```
conda install pandas
```

if you are running an Anaconda virtual environment, or by running:

```
pip install pandas
```

if you are running a native Python installation.

Now that you have a little bit of background on the dataset and the library, it's time to jump into using Python and pandas!

Describing the Data

To begin, we'll explore what is contained in our dataset. Listing 3-1 displays the code for these operations, and the output of running the listing is shown in Figure 3-1.

LISTING 3-1: Basic DataFrame Information (data_exploration_explore.py)

```
import pandas as pd

#Read the dataset into the "faults_df" variable
faults_df = pd.read_csv("faults.csv")

#Get an overview of the data
print("Dataset first 5 rows")
print(faults_df.head())

#Print the columns - method 1
print("Columns Index")
print(faults_df.columns)

#Print the columns - method 2
print("Columns as a List")
print(list(faults_df.columns))

#Describe the data
print("Describe the data")
print(faults_df.describe())
```

The code file does the following:

- Imports the pandas library and renames it pd. This is a handy alias you'll often see programmers use to shorten the library name.
- Reads in the faults.csv file using the pandas `read_csv()` function. This function takes in the name of the file and stores it as a DataFrame variable named `faults_df`. The DataFrame is a two-dimensional pandas object used to represent and manipulate tables.
- Uses the `head()` function of the `faults_df` DataFrame object to print the first five rows of the data. This gives us a good overview of the structure and columns of the data. Depending on your terminal size, some of the output columns might have been omitted in the display.

```
(examples) C:\Users\marze\Documents\Book\Code Files>python data_exploration_explore.py
Dataset first 5 rows
   X_Minimum  X_Maximum  Y_Minimum  Y_Maximum  Pixels_Areas  X_Perimeter  ...  Z_Scratch  K_Scatch  Stains  Dirtiness  Bumps  Other_Faul
ts
0         42         50     270900     270944           267           17  ...          0         0       0          0      0
 0
1        645        651    2538079    2538108           108           10  ...          0         0       0          0      0
 0
2        829        835    1553913    1553931            71            8  ...          0         0       0          0      0
 0
3        853        860     369370     369415           176           13  ...          0         0       0          0      0
 0
4       1289       1306     498078     498335          2409           60  ...          0         0       0          0      0
 0

[5 rows x 34 columns]
Columns Index
Index(['X_Minimum', 'X_Maximum', 'Y_Minimum', 'Y_Maximum', 'Pixels_Areas',
       'X_Perimeter', 'Y_Perimeter', 'Sum_of_Luminosity',
       'Minimum_of_Luminosity', 'Maximum_of_Luminosity', 'Length_of_Conveyer',
       'TypeOfSteel_A300', 'TypeOfSteel_A400', 'Steel_Plate_Thickness',
       'Edges_Index', 'Empty_Index', 'Square_Index', 'Outside_X_Index',
       'Edges_X_Index', 'Edges_Y_Index', 'Outside_Global_Index', 'LogOfAreas',
       'Log_X_Index', 'Log_Y_Index', 'Orientation_Index', 'Luminosity_Index',
       'SigmoidOfAreas', 'Pastry', 'Z_Scratch', 'K_Scatch', 'Stains',
        'Dirtiness', 'Bumps', 'Other_Faults'],
       dtype='object')
 Columns as a List
 ['X_Minimum', 'X_Maximum', 'Y_Minimum', 'Y_Maximum', 'Pixels_Areas', 'X_Perimeter', 'Y_Perimeter', 'Sum_of_Luminosity', 'Minimum_of_Lumi
 nosity', 'Maximum_of_Luminosity', 'Length_of_Conveyer', 'TypeOfSteel_A300', 'TypeOfSteel_A400', 'Steel_Plate_Thickness', 'Edges_Index',
 'Empty_Index', 'Square_Index', 'Outside_X_Index', 'Edges_X_Index', 'Edges_Y_Index', 'Outside_Global_Index', 'LogOfAreas', 'Log_X_Index',
  'Log_Y_Index', 'Orientation_Index', 'Luminosity_Index', 'SigmoidOfAreas', 'Pastry', 'Z_Scratch', 'K_Scatch', 'Stains', 'Dirtiness', 'Bu
 mps', 'Other_Faults']
 Describe the data
          X_Minimum    X_Maximum     Y_Minimum     Y_Maximum  ...       Stains    Dirtiness        Bumps  Other_Faults
 count  1941.000000  1941.000000  1.941000e+03  1.941000e+03  ...  1941.000000  1941.000000  1941.000000   1941.000000
 mean    571.136012   617.964451  1.650685e+06  1.650739e+06  ...     0.037094     0.028336     0.207110      0.346728
 std     520.690671   497.627410  1.774578e+06  1.774590e+06  ...     0.189042     0.165973     0.405339      0.476051
 min       0.000000     4.000000  6.712000e+03  6.724000e+03  ...     0.000000     0.000000     0.000000      0.000000
 25%      51.000000   192.000000  4.712530e+05  4.712810e+05  ...     0.000000     0.000000     0.000000      0.000000
 50%     435.000000   467.000000  1.204128e+06  1.204136e+06  ...     0.000000     0.000000     0.000000      0.000000
 75%    1053.000000  1072.000000  2.183073e+06  2.183084e+06  ...     0.000000     0.000000     0.000000      1.000000
 max    1705.000000  1713.000000  1.298766e+07  1.298769e+07  ...     1.000000     1.000000     1.000000      1.000000

 [8 rows x 34 columns]
```

FIGURE 3-1: Output of running Listing 3-1.

- Uses the `columns` property of `faults_df` to print out all the columns in their index form.
- Uses the `list()` function in Python to convert the columns to a `list` type and print them. This can sometimes be useful if you need to use list operations on the columns.
- Uses the `describe()` function of `faults_df` to describe the data. This prints more statistical information for each column, such as the overall count of the feature (number of rows it's included in), the mean, max, min, and standard deviation of feature values, and the values at the 25th, 50th, and 75th percentiles.

Accessing and Filtering the Data

Sometimes you may want to access individual rows or columns, or filter the amount of data you are looking at based on some feature condition. The code for handling these operations appears in Listing 3-2. The output of running Listing 3-2 is shown in Figures 3-2 and 3-3.

LISTING 3-2: Accessing and Filtering Data with Pandas (data_exploration_filter.py)

```
import pandas as pd

#Read the dataset into the "faults_df" variable
faults_df = pd.read_csv("faults.csv")

#Indexing
#Return a series with the 'X_Minimum' column of the dataset
X_Minimum_series = faults_df['X_Minimum']
print("X_Minimum series")
print(X_Minimum_series)

#Get a list of values from a column
X_Minimum_list = faults_df['X_Minimum'].values.tolist()
print("X_Minimum List - First 10 values")
print(X_Minimum_list[0:10])

#loc
#Get everything in X_Minimum
print("Entire X_Minimum column")
print(faults_df.loc[:,"X_Minimum"])

#Get the first value in X_Minimum
print("First X_Minimum value")
print(faults_df.loc[0,"X_Minimum"])

print("Second and up to 5th-indexed (4 total) X_Minimum values")
print(faults_df.loc[2:5,"X_Minimum"])

print("Everything before and up to the 3rd-indexed (4 total) X_
  Minimum values")
print(faults_df.loc[:3,"X_Minimum"])

print("Everything including and after the 1939th-indexed (2 total)
  X_Minimum values")
print(faults_df.loc[1939:,"X_Minimum"])

print("0 through 5th-indexed (6 total) X_Minimum and Pixels_
  Areas values")
print(faults_df.loc[0:5,["X_Minimum", "Pixels_Areas"]])

#Use iloc
print("Row indexes 1-2 and column indexes 1-4")
```

```
print(faults_df.iloc[1:3, 1:5])

print("4th row index, first column")
print(faults_df.iloc[4, 0])

print("All columns, row index 4")
print(faults_df.iloc[4, :])

#Selecting a row based on a condition
print("All rows where X_Minimum is above 500")
print(faults_df.loc[faults_df["X_Minimum"] > 500])
#How many rows is this?
print("How many rows is this?")
print(len(faults_df.loc[faults_df["X_Minimum"] > 500].index))

#Create a new dataframe based on a condition
print("All rows where X_Minimum is above 500 and Pixels_Areas is
  equal to 176")
sub_df = faults_df.loc[(faults_df["X_Minimum"] > 500) & (faults_
  df["Pixels_Areas"] == 176)]
print(sub_df.head())
print("How many rows is this?")
print(len(sub_df.index))
```

The code performs each task outlined as follows.

Provides basic column access:

- Imports pandas and reads in the faults dataset to a DataFrame object named `faults_df`.
- Accesses just the "X_Minimum" column of the DataFrame by using a bracket indexer and stores it in variable `X_Minimum_series`. This returns a `Series` object from the pandas library, which is essentially one column of a DataFrame (a one-dimensional object). It prints the series to the terminal.
- Accesses the same column using the same notation, but uses the `values.tolist()` property and function call to convert this series to a list instead. This can be useful if you need to perform operations on a list of column values rather than use the underlying `Series` datatype. It prints the first ten values of this list to the terminal.

```
(examples) C:\Users\marze\Documents\Book\Code Files>python data_exploration_filter.py
X_Minimum series
0        42
1       645
2       829
3       853
4      1289
       ...
1936    249
1937    144
1938    145
1939    137
1940   1261
Name: X_Minimum, Length: 1941, dtype: int64
X_Minimum List - First 10 values
[42, 645, 829, 853, 1289, 430, 413, 190, 330, 74]
Entire X_Minimum column
0        42
1       645
2       829
3       853
4      1289
       ...
1936    249
1937    144
1938    145
1939    137
1940   1261
Name: X_Minimum, Length: 1941, dtype: int64
First X_Minimum value
42
Second and up to 5th-indexed (4 total) X_Minimum values
2     829
3     853
4    1289
5     430
Name: X_Minimum, dtype: int64
Everything before and up to the 3rd-indexed (4 total) X_Minimum values
0     42
1    645
2    829
3    853
Name: X_Minimum, dtype: int64
Everything including and after the 1939th-indexed (2 total) X_Minimum values
1939    137
1940   1261
Name: X_Minimum, dtype: int64
0 through 5th-indexed (6 total) X_Minimum and Pixels_Areas values
   X_Minimum  Pixels_Areas
0         42           267
1        645           108
2        829            71
3        853           176
4       1289          2409
5        430           630
Row indexes 1-2 and column indexes 1-4
   X_Maximum  Y_Minimum  Y_Maximum  Pixels_Areas
1        651    2538079    2538108           108
2        835    1553913    1553931            71
```

FIGURE 3-2: The first part of the output of running Listing 3-2.

Uses the "loc" indexer:

» Uses the `loc` property of the DataFrame. The `loc` property allows you to use slicing to specify rows and provide a column label or labels to return the appropriate value. Slicing involves using the `:` symbol and providing a number before and after the `:` to indicate a range of values. The `loc` indexer includes the second slice value in its range, unlike `iloc`, which we will get to later. The first call returns *all* rows (using just the colon indexer `:`) in the "X_Minimum" column.

```
4th row index, first column
1289
All columns, row index 4
X_Minimum                1289.0000
X_Maximum                1306.0000
Y_Minimum              498078.0000
Y_Maximum              498335.0000
Pixels_Areas             2409.0000
X_Perimeter                60.0000
Y_Perimeter               260.0000
Sum_of_Luminosity      246930.0000
Minimum_of_Luminosity      37.0000
Maximum_of_Luminosity     126.0000
Length_of_Conveyer       1353.0000
TypeOfSteel_A300            0.0000
TypeOfSteel_A400            1.0000
Steel_Plate_Thickness     185.0000
Edges_Index                 0.0695
Empty_Index                 0.4486
Square_Index                0.0662
Outside_X_Index             0.0126
Edges_X_Index               0.2833
Edges_Y_Index               0.9885
Outside_Global_Index        1.0000
LogOfAreas                  3.3818
Log_X_Index                 1.2305
Log_Y_Index                 2.4099
Orientation_Index           0.9338
Luminosity_Index           -0.1992
SigmoidOfAreas              1.0000
Pastry                      1.0000
Z_Scratch                   0.0000
K_Scatch                    0.0000
Stains                      0.0000
Dirtiness                   0.0000
Bumps                       0.0000
Other_Faults                0.0000
Name: 4, dtype: float64
All rows where X_Minimum is above 500
      X_Minimum  X_Maximum  Y_Minimum  Y_Maximum  Pixels_Areas  ...  K_Scatch  Stains  Dirtiness  Bumps  Other_Faults
1           645        651    2538079    2538108           108  ...         0       0          0      0             0
2           829        835    1553913    1553931            71  ...         0       0          0      0             0
3           853        860     369370     369415           176  ...         0       0          0      0             0
4          1289       1306     498078     498335          2409  ...         0       0          0      0             0
11          505        515     106604     106668           284  ...         0       0          0      0             0
...         ...        ...        ...        ...           ...  ...       ...     ...        ...    ...           ...
1916        767        788     566837     566850            83  ...         0       0          0      0             1
1926       1053       1063     173208     173226            68  ...         0       0          0      0             1
1928       1303       1344      33298      33323           452  ...         0       0          0      0             1
1931        523        567     266325     266337           209  ...         0       0          0      0             1
1940       1261       1281      87951      87967           103  ...         0       0          0      0             1

[921 rows x 34 columns]
How many rows is this?
921
All rows where X_Minimum is above 500 and Pixels_Areas is equal to 176
     X_Minimum  X_Maximum  Y_Minimum  Y_Maximum  Pixels_Areas  X_Perimeter  ...  Z_Scratch  K_Scatch  Stains  Dirtiness  Bumps  Other_Fa
ults
3          853        860     369370     369415           176           13  ...          0         0       0          0      0
   0
883        699        740    1503538    1503546           176           44  ...          0         0       0          0      1
   0

[2 rows x 34 columns]
How many rows is this?
2
```

FIGURE 3-3: The output of running Listing 3-2, continued.

- Uses the `loc` property with 0 as the row argument and "X_Minimum" as the column label to get the first row value in the `X_Minimum` column.
- Uses the `loc` property and slicing to return rows 2 to 5 in the `X_Minimum` column.
- Uses the `loc` property and slicing to return everything before and including the third-indexed row in the `X_Minimum` column.
- Uses the `loc` property and slicing to return everything including and after the 1,939th-indexed row in the `X_Minimum` column.

- Uses the `loc` property and slicing to get rows 0 to 5 and both the `X_Minimum` and `Pixel_Areas` column values.

Uses the "iloc" indexer:

- Uses the `iloc` property. This allows you to specify a slicing indexer for both rows and columns, rather than using a column label name. Unlike `loc`, `iloc` excludes the final value in the slicing notation. The first call provides arguments `1:3` for the rows and `1:5` for columns, meaning it will return rows 1 and 2 and column values 1, 2, 3, and 4. These correspond to the `X_Maximum`, `Y_Minimum`, `Y_Maximum`, and `Pixels_Areas` columns.
- Uses `iloc` to get the row index 4, column index 0 (`X_Minimum`) value.
- Uses `iloc` to get all column values at row 4.

Filters the DataFrame:

- Filters the DataFrame based on a condition. This involves using `loc` or `iloc` and providing a comparison statement. Interestingly, you have to provide the DataFrame name even inside of the `loc` search. The first call uses `loc` to see if the value of "X_Minimum" value in `faults_df` is above 500, and returns only the rows that meet this condition.
- Prints the number of rows meeting the above condition by calling the `len()` (length) function of the `index` property on `faults_df`.
- Creates a new DataFrame by filtering on two conditions: whether or not `fault_df`'s `X_Minimum` column is above 500 *and* `fault_df`'s `Pixels_Areas` column is equal to 176. The returned DataFrame is stored in `sub_df`.
- Prints the rows of `sub_df` using the `head()` function and also prints the length of the `index` to get the overall row count.

Handling Missing Data

One of the trickiest aspects of working with data is finding missing values, since many machine learning models can't handle a NaN (Not a Number) value. (NaN is the default code for missing data in pandas.) Listing 3-3 gives the code for finding and handling NaN data, and Figure 3-4 shows the output of running the listing. In this code file, we are removing any rows with missing data.

TECHNICAL STUFF

Removing rows with missing data is not the only way to handle NaN values. In time series data manipulation, for instance, it's common to *interpolate* missing values by filling them with the last valid value for the column (forward fill), or the next valid value for the column (backward fill), or even averaging the last and next value together.

LISTING 3-3: Finding and Handling Missing Data (data_exploration_missing_data.py)

```
import pandas as pd

#Read the dataset into the "faults_df" variable
faults_df = pd.read_csv("faults.csv")

##Find and Handle NaNs
print(faults_df.isna().value_counts())

#Insert an NaN value
print("Value before setting to NaN")
print(faults_df.loc[0, 'X_Minimum'])
new_df = faults_df
new_df.loc[0, 'X_Minimum'] = None
print("Value after setting to NaN")
print(new_df.loc[0, 'X_Minimum'])

#Drop the na value
print("Number of rows before dropping NaN")
print(len(new_df.index))
cleaned_df = new_df.dropna()
print("DataFrame after dropping NaN value - note the index")
print(cleaned_df.head())
#Reset the index
cleaned_df.reset_index(inplace=True)
print("Number of rows after dropping NaN")
print(len(cleaned_df.index))
print("Value at previously-NaN index")
print(cleaned_df.loc[0, "X_Minimum"])
print("DataFrame after resetting NaN value - note the index")
print(cleaned_df.head())
```

```
(examples) C:\Users\marze\Documents\Book\Code Files>python data_exploration_missing_data.py
X_Minimum  X_Maximum  Y_Minimum  Y_Maximum  Pixels_Areas  X_Perimeter  Y_Perimeter  Sum_of_Luminosity  Minimum_of_Luminosity  Maximum_of
_Luminosity  Length_of_Conveyer  TypeOfSteel_A300  TypeOfSteel_A400  Steel_Plate_Thickness  Edges_Index  Empty_Index  Square_Index  Outs
ide_X_Index  Edges_X_Index  Edges_Y_Index  Outside_Global_Index  LogOfAreas  Log_X_Index  Log_Y_Index  Orientation_Index  Luminosity_Ind
ex  SigmoidOfAreas  Pastry  Z_Scratch  K_Scatch  Stains  Dirtiness  Bumps  Other_Faults
False      False      False      False      False       False       False       False             False                 False
           False            False          False          False               False      False      False      Fals
e          False      False      False             False      False      False      False            False
   False         False  False     False     False  False     False  False        1941
Name: count, dtype: int64
Value before setting to NaN
42
Value after setting to NaN
nan
Number of rows before dropping NaN
1941
DataFrame after dropping NaN value - note the index
   X_Minimum  X_Maximum  Y_Minimum  Y_Maximum  Pixels_Areas  X_Perimeter  ...  Z_Scratch  K_Scatch  Stains  Dirtiness  Bumps  Other_Faul
ts
1      645.0        651    2538079    2538108           108           10  ...          0         0       0          0      0
 0
2      829.0        835    1553913    1553931            71            8  ...          0         0       0          0      0
 0
3      853.0        860     369370     369415           176           13  ...          0         0       0          0      0
 0
4     1289.0       1306     498078     498335          2409           60  ...          0         0       0          0      0
 0
5      430.0        441     100250     100337           630           20  ...          0         0       0          0      0
 0

[5 rows x 34 columns]
Number of rows after dropping NaN
1940
Value at previously-NaN index
645.0
DataFrame after resetting NaN value - note the index
   index  X_Minimum  X_Maximum  Y_Minimum  Y_Maximum  Pixels_Areas  ...  Z_Scratch  K_Scatch  Stains  Dirtiness  Bumps  Other_Faults
0      1      645.0        651    2538079    2538108           108  ...          0         0       0          0      0             0
1      2      829.0        835    1553913    1553931            71  ...          0         0       0          0      0             0
2      3      853.0        860     369370     369415           176  ...          0         0       0          0      0             0
3      4     1289.0       1306     498078     498335          2409  ...          0         0       0          0      0             0
4      5      430.0        441     100250     100337           630  ...          0         0       0          0      0             0

[5 rows x 35 columns]
```

FIGURE 3-4: The output of running Listing 3-3.

This code does the following:

- Imports the pandas library and reads in the faults dataset to `faults_df`.
- Uses the `isna()` and `value_counts()` properties of `faults_df` to find and report the number of NaN values for each column. This will display the counts for `True` (there was an NaN value) and `False` (no NaN value). You can see in Figure 3-4 that this dataset contains no NaN values (all counts are `False`). That's a good thing! But realistically, many real datasets are messier than this. So let's add one!
- Uses the `loc` property to print the value in the `X_Minimum` column in row 0. This is our "before" value.
- Creates a copy of the `faults_df` DataFrame and stores it in a new DataFrame called `new_df`.
- Uses `loc` to grab the same value and set it equal to `None`.

* Prints the value after setting it to None. This is the "after" value and should now read nan in the output.
* Counts the number of rows in the DataFrame before dropping values by using the `len()` function and `index` property of `new_df` and prints this number.
* Drops the NaN values using the `dropna()` function on `new_df` and sets it to a new DataFrame called `cleaned_df`.
* Prints the first five rows of `cleaned_df` using the `head()` function. You'll note that this kept the old index number from before the drop — so you have no row 0 and the DataFrame starts at row 1. This might cause issues down the line, so you may want to reset the index.
* Uses the `reset_index()` function on `cleaned_df` to reset the index to start at 0. This passes the argument `inplace=True` to the function, so you don't have to reset it back to the `cleaned_df` variable.
* Prints the new length of the `cleaned_df`. It now has one row less than before. It also prints the new value at index 0 and the first five rows of the DataFrame. You can see that the index is back to normal.

Visualizing the Data

It's a good idea to create some data visualizations when exploring a new dataset to understand variable distributions and identify any patterns. Matplotlib is a great library for creating graphs and charts. You can install the library with:

```
conda install matplotlib
```

in a virtual environment, or with:

```
pip install matplotlib
```

if you are running Python natively. Matplotlib could have a chapter all to itself, but we'll create some basic charts to get you started. Listing 3-4 displays the code for three visualizations, while Figures 3-5, 3-6, and 3-7 give the visual output of running Listing 3-4.

LISTING 3-4: Visualizing the Data (data_exploration_visualize.py)

```
import pandas as pd
import matplotlib.pyplot as plt

#Read the dataset into the "faults_df" variable
faults_df = pd.read_csv("faults.csv")

#Plot - 1 Variable
plt.plot(faults_df["X_Minimum"])
plt.show()
plt.clf()

#Scatter Plot - 2 Variables
plt.scatter(faults_df["X_Minimum"], faults_df["X_Maximum"])
plt.show()
plt.clf()

#Histogram of Counts
plt.hist(faults_df["Pastry"])
plt.show()
plt.clf()
```

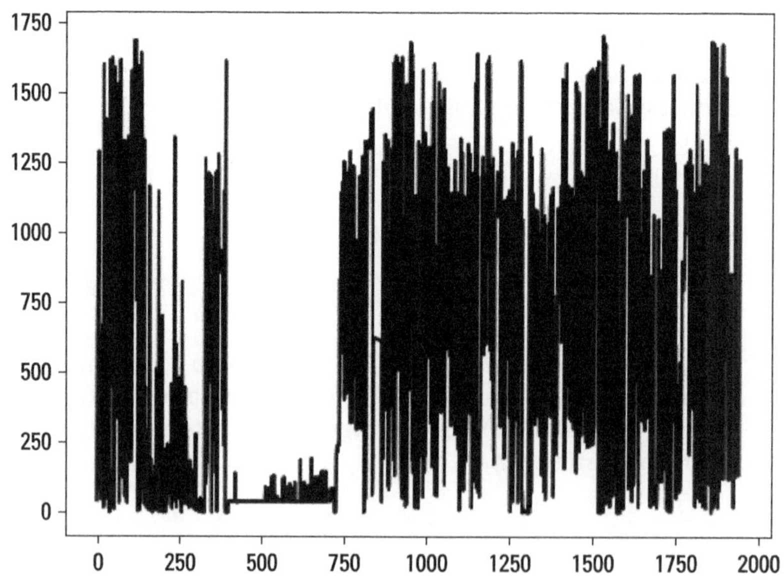

FIGURE 3-5: Basic, one-variable plot output of Listing 3-4.

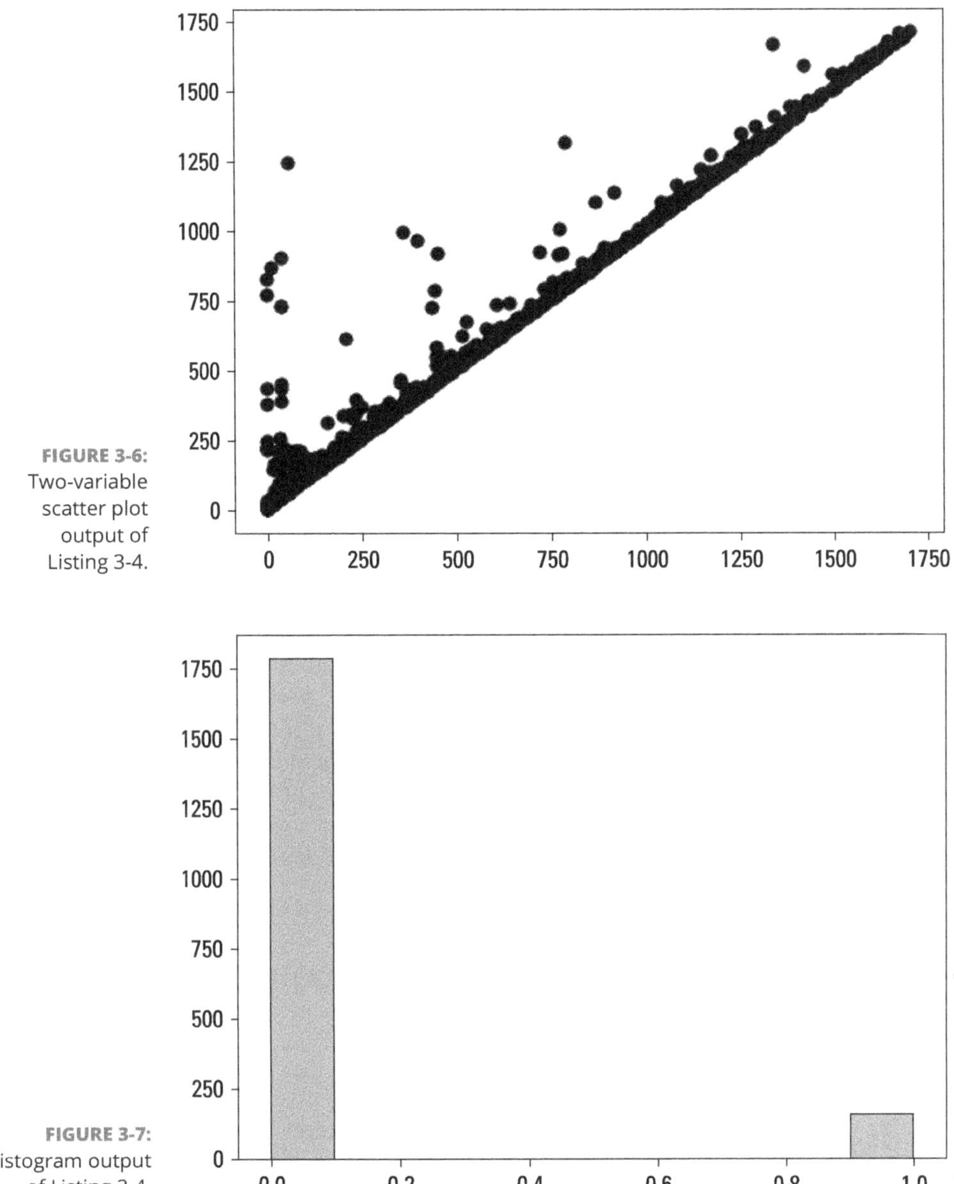

FIGURE 3-6: Two-variable scatter plot output of Listing 3-4.

FIGURE 3-7: Histogram output of Listing 3-4.

The code does the following:

- Imports the `pandas` library as `pd` and the `matplotlib.pyplot` library module as `plt`.
- Reads in the faults dataset and sets it to the `faults_df` DataFrame object.

- Creates the first plot, using the `plot()` function of the `plt` library. This uses the `X_Minimum` column of `faults_df` to create a line plot showing the different values across the instances. Note that because these are discrete rows, a line plot is probably not the best visualization, since there isn't a time component in the data. The `show()` function is used to display the plot in a window, and the `clf()` (clear figure) function clears out the display for the next chart.
- Creates the second plot, using the `scatter()` function of the `plt` library. This takes in two variables, the `X_Minimum` and `X_Maximum` columns of `faults_df`, and plots them against each other. You can see from the chart that these are highly correlated with one another. The `show()` and `clf()` functions are called again.
- Uses the `hist()` function to create the final plot: a histogram of the `Pastry` fault column in `faults_df`. This plot displays the number of rows with each possible value. You can see that most rows (around 1,780 of them) do not have the "Pastry" fault present (value is 0) while about 150 of the rows do have this fault (value is 1). The `show()` and `clf()` functions are called a final time.

TIP

Don't be afraid to play around with the different visualizations by swapping out the various columns! It's a good idea to do a thorough investigation of your data's behavior before you pass it into a machine learning model. Visualizations can help you catch potential outliers that you may want to remove before model training. Visualizations can also help you determine if your data shows correlations (which you may or may not want), is incorrectly typed, or contains surprising distributions. Data exploration is a very important step in ensuring your machine learning model has the proper resources to make good decisions.

Trusting the Experts: The Importance of Domain Knowledge

Manipulating and wrangling a dataset from a free repository is a lot of fun. However, data can be hard to interpret if you weren't the original source that collected it. If you aren't an expert in the domain where the data originated, you might not know:

- The valid range for the data to be in (which is useful for finding outliers).
- What a column name means.
- Whether or not a correlation between features is true or a "spurious" correlation.

These aspects are important when cleaning and preparing data for a model, because the model is generally only as good as the data you give it. Mistakes in a dataset will show right back up in the model! For example, Marz has a family member who works as a fish biologist, and he mentions that a common mistake in their data collection is mixing up the length and weight columns for steelhead salmonids. It might not be immediately obvious to the layperson that a 6-inch, 23-pound steelhead doesn't exist, but he can spot the mistake from a mile away. We highly recommend working with an expert in the data's domain whenever you are working on a machine learning project. They are vital for determining whether your data preparations make sense and for interpreting the output of your investigations. If you don't understand the problem like a 20-year veteran of the field, that's okay! But make sure to have one on speed dial when your model starts outputting impossible fish.

With fundamental Python, AI, and data manipulation skills under your belt, you're ready for the big time. In the next chapter, you'll explore the scikit-learn library and how to use it to run machine learning models.

2 Fundamental Machine Learning Models

IN THIS PART . . .

Explore the scikit-learn library — the Swiss Army Knife of AI libraries — and implement useful preprocessing functions and discover the difference between training, test, and validation sets.

Understand the relationship between independent variables and outcomes and how they are modeled with the equation of a line.

Implement a linear regression model using shortcut formulas and using the scikit-learn library.

Review fundamental information-theory concepts such as surprise, information, entropy, and the Gini index, and apply these concepts to building a decision tree.

Create ensemble models and discover the power of using multiple models together.

IN THIS CHAPTER

» Installing the scikit-learn library

» Preprocessing data for models

» Splitting data into training and test sets

» Understanding classification, regression, and clustering models

Chapter 4 Working with the scikit-learn Library

Now that you have some experience with Python and pandas, it's time to play around with your first AI library. In this chapter, you learn all about the scikit-learn library, a machine learning powerhouse. Plenty of libraries are available in Python to help you accomplish AI tasks, and different codebases are better suited to different problems. But if AI libraries are tools, scikit-learn is your Swiss Army Knife.

In this chapter, you install the scikit-learn library and learn how the submodules are broken down into logical groups. You implement some useful preprocessing functions, such as one-hot encoding and min-max scaling. You discover the difference between training, test, and validation sets and program these splits using the library. You also get a sense for how classification problems differ from regression problems, and clustering forms its own group (literally). Finally, you use the library's model API to implement a poetically-named "Dummy Classifier" on the Steel Plates Faults dataset from Chapter 3.

An Overview of scikit-learn

The scikit-learn library is an open-source community machine learning package. While scikit-learn doesn't implement every single model out there, it's fantastic for:

- Preparing data to be in the format(s) expected by a model
- Implementing non-deep learning statistical models
- Evaluating models with different metrics

The library is split up into several submodules, which is very helpful. Because it's a large project, this structure helps you import only the things you need for your specific script. We encourage you to check out the library's application programming interface (API) to learn about all of these great modules, but some of the particularly useful ones include:

- **sklearn.datasets:** Lets you load some preexisting open datasets, which are useful for practicing your machine learning chops or experiencing different classes of AI problems.
- **sklearn.dummy:** Lets you create a "dummy" model, which we'll use to practice the model API later in this chapter.
- **sklearn.ensemble:** Lets you create ensemble models, including bagging and boosting classifiers and random forests — more on those in Chapter 7.
- **sklearn.linear_model:** Lets you create models that are — (surprise, surprise!) — linear. This includes regression models, which we cover in Chapter 5.
- **sklearn.metrics:** Lets you create metrics and reports useful for determining how well a model performed on your data.
- **sklearn.model_selection:** Helps you split data into different sets and formats. Different choices made with these functions depend on the best practices for the model you picked.
- **sklearn.preprocessing:** Helps you preprocess data. This can be a very important step if your model has a specific format your data must conform to.
- **sklearn.tree:** Lets you create tree models, such as decision trees. More on those in Chapter 6.
- **sklearn.utils:** Contains some handy functions for general machine learning tasks that don't fit nicely into the other categories.

Installing scikit-learn

If you are using an Anaconda environment, chances are good you already have scikit-learn installed. You can check this by running the following (with your environment active):

```
pip show scikit-learn
```

This should output the package name, version, and summary to your terminal. If you see that, you should be good to go! Otherwise, you should be able to run (with Anaconda):

```
conda install scikit-learn
```

or:

```
conda install conda-forge:scikit-learn
```

to get the package. If you are running Python natively, try:

```
pip install scikit-learn
```

Once you have the package installed, you are ready to get cracking!

Preprocessing Data with scikit-learn

In Chapter 3, you reviewed some basic data wrangling steps like loading in a dataset, filtering data, getting rid of missing data, and visualizing data to look for outliers. Scikit-learn comes with a preprocessing module as well, but it's more focused on tasks that help prepare your data for a specific model. This module is a lifesaver in particular for two common machine learning tasks: encoding outputs and scaling data.

Encoding outputs

In Chapter 3, you practiced data manipulation with the Steel Plates Faults dataset, which we'll continue to use for this chapter. This dataset has 27 input features that lead to one of seven types of fault classification per row.

In the dataset, seven different columns are used to indicate the type of fault we're dealing with (if it's a member of that fault class, the entry under that particular column will include a "1"). Depending on the model, you may want one output column with a number corresponding to the type of output, or you may want a *one-hot encoded vector* indicating the type of fault. Instead of encoding the type of fault as a number, this would change each sample's outcome to an array of seven numbers. Every position in the array includes a "0" entry, except for the fault class, which has a "1." We discuss one-hot encoded vectors more in Chapter 10, but the scikit-learn preprocessing section has many useful classes that help encode data into one form or another.

Listing 4-1 illustrates an example of using one-hot encoding in scikit-learn. It first consolidates the outcome data into one column and then performs the encoding on that column. Figure 4-1 displays the output of running the listing.

LISTING 4-1: One-Hot-Encoding Dataset Outcomes (using_scikit_learn_one_hot.py)

```
import pandas as pd
from sklearn.preprocessing import OneHotEncoder

faults = ["Pastry", "Z_Scratch", "K_Scatch", "Stains", "Dirtiness",
  "Bumps", "Other_Faults"]

def read_in_dataset(faults):
    df = pd.read_csv("faults.csv")
    df['fault'] = 0
    #Lets create a categorical variable for each fault
    #In the new "fault" column
    for i in range(0, len(faults)):
        #index list
        true_fault_indexes = df.loc[df[faults[i]] ==
  1].index.tolist()
        df.loc[true_fault_indexes, "fault"] = i+1
        #Create our dataset
    return df

df = read_in_dataset(faults)
print("Before One-Hot Encoding:")
print(df["fault"])
encoder = OneHotEncoder()
encoder.fit(df[["fault"]])
print(encoder.categories_)
```

```
one_hot_encoded_outcomes = encoder.
  transform(df[["fault"]]).toarray()
print("After One-Hot Encoding:")
print(one_hot_encoded_outcomes)
```

```
(examples) C:\Users\marze\Documents\Book\Code Files>python using_scikit_learn_one_hot.py
Before One-Hot Encoding:
0       1
1       1
2       1
3       1
4       1
       ..
1936    7
1937    7
1938    7
1939    7
1940    7
Name: fault, Length: 1941, dtype: int64
[array([1, 2, 3, 4, 5, 6, 7])]
After One-Hot Encoding:
[[1. 0. 0. ... 0. 0. 0.]
 [1. 0. 0. ... 0. 0. 0.]
 [1. 0. 0. ... 0. 0. 0.]
 ...
 [0. 0. 0. ... 0. 0. 1.]
 [0. 0. 0. ... 0. 0. 1.]
 [0. 0. 0. ... 0. 0. 1.]]
```

FIGURE 4-1: Output of running Listing 4-1.

The code does the following:

- Imports pandas as pd and then imports the `OneHotEncoder` module from `sklearn.preprocessing`.
- Creates a list named `faults` that outlines each fault column name in the dataset.
- Creates a function called `read_in_dataset`, which takes in the `faults` list. This function reads in the `faults.csv` file to a DataFrame named `df`, and creates a new column in `df` called "fault." For every fault type in the passed-in list, the `fault` column is assigned an integer (whole number) to match where that particular fault is present. The function then returns `df`.
- Calls the `read_in_dataset` function with the `faults` list and assigns the output to `df`.
- Prints the `fault` column in `df` before one-hot encoding.

» Creates an instance of the `OneHotEncoder` class and assigns it to the `encoder` variable.

» Calls the `fit` function on `encoder`, passing it the `fault` column. Due to datatype expectations, the column is wrapped in additional brackets.

» Prints the created `encoder` categories using the `categories_` property.

» Uses the `transform` function on the encoder along with the `toarray()` function to create the one-hot vectors and assigns them to `one_hot_encoded_outcomes`.

» Prints the `one_hot_encoded_outcomes` variable to compare it to the regularly encoded values. In Figure 4-1, notice that these outcomes are now a list of numbers where the presence of a "1" indicates the class type.

Scaling data

Another common preprocessing technique involves manipulating the data to fall within a certain scale. For example, in the Steel Plates Faults dataset, the `X_Minimum` feature has a minimum value of 0 and a maximum value of 1,705, while the `Pixels_Areas` feature has a minimum value of 2 and a maximum value of 152,655. These features exist on pretty different scales!

REMEMBER

Some models have difficulty handling features with wildly different ranges of values. Depending on how the model is architected, sometimes a model will start favoring a feature that has larger numbers in it, even if the relative importance of that feature is the same as one with a smaller scale. For example, when making chocolate chip cookies, flour and chocolate chips are equally important ingredients. However, you tend to use a lot more flour in the recipe than chocolate chips (Marz's sugar-crazed family's recipe aside). If you have an outside contractor ordering food for your bakery with no idea what you plan to sell, they might consider your flour order much more important than the chocolate chip order since it's three times the size. If they accidentally miss the chocolate chips because they were focused on the flour, they won't realize that this spells disaster for your star cookie attraction.

Some models fall into this same trap, so resizing features to exist on similar scales can help the algorithm balance their initial importance.

Scikit-learn comes with several methods of accomplishing this. One is the `MinMaxScaler` module, which takes every data point in a feature column, subtracts the minimum value, and divides by the range (maximum minus minimum value). This remaps every point to a scale between 0 and 1 while retaining the relative distance between values. The `RobustScaler` uses similar tricks but scales by quantile (which helps with outliers). In the bakery illustration, instead of your order reading "I need 300 pounds of flour and 20 pounds of chocolate chips," your request becomes "I need 50 percent of my largest order of flour and 50 percent of my largest order of chocolate chips." Equal importance, same scale!

Listing 4-2 gives a code example of using `MinMaxScaler` on one of the feature columns. Figure 4-2 displays the output of running Listing 4-2.

LISTING 4-2: Min-Max Scaling Data (using_scikit_learn_scaling.py)

```
import pandas as pd
from sklearn.preprocessing import MinMaxScaler

faults = ["Pastry", "Z_Scratch", "K_Scatch", "Stains", "Dirtiness",
  "Bumps", "Other_Faults"]

def read_in_dataset(faults):
    df = pd.read_csv("faults.csv")
    df['fault'] = 0
    #Lets create a categorical variable for each fault
    #In the new "fault" column
    for i in range(0, len(faults)):
        #index list
        true_fault_indexes = df.loc[df[faults[i]] ==
  1].index.tolist()
        df.loc[true_fault_indexes, "fault"] = i+1
        #Create our dataset
    return df

df = read_in_dataset(faults)
print("Before MinMaxScaling")
print(df["X_Minimum"])
scaler = MinMaxScaler()
scaled_x_min = scaler.fit_transform(df[["X_Minimum"]])
print("After MinMaxScaling:")
print(scaled_x_min)
```

```
(examples) C:\Users\marze\Documents\Book\Code Files>python using_scikit_learn_scaling.py
Before MinMaxScaling
0         42
1        645
2        829
3        853
4       1289
        ...
1936     249
1937     144
1938     145
1939     137
1940    1261
Name: X_Minimum, Length: 1941, dtype: int64
After MinMaxScaling:
[[0.02463343]
 [0.37829912]
 [0.48621701]
 ...
 [0.08504399]
 [0.08035191]
 [0.73958944]]
```

FIGURE 4-2: Output of running Listing 4-2.

The code does the following:

- imports pandas as pd and then imports the `MinMaxScaler` module from `sklearn.preprocessing`.
- Uses the same `read_in_dataset` function to read in the Steel Plates Faults dataset and assigns the output to `df` as in Listing 4-1.
- Prints the value of the "X_Minimum" column in `df` before scaling.
- Creates an instance of the `MinMaxScaler` module and assigns it to the `scaler` variable.
- Calls the `fit_transform` function on `MinMaxScaler` to fit the scaler and manipulate the data in one call, applied to the `X_Minimum` column of `df`. This stores the output in the `scaled_x_min` variable.
- Prints the `scaled_x_min` variable to compare the data after scaling. You can see in Figure 4-2 that the data now exists entirely in the range of 0 to 1.

Dividing Data into Training, Validation, and Test Sets

In addition to changing the underlying data representation, data is often split into different subsets before it is passed to a model. While the sets you might want to use depend on the type of model, one of the most common machine learning paradigms uses training, validation, and test sets.

- **Training set:** This is the data your model will act upon during the training phase. The training set is the only subset that causes a direct change in model parameters to improve performance.
- **Validation set:** This acts like a mini-test set the model will use to spot-check its performance after one or more training phases. While the model isn't allowed to directly change its parameters based on the validation set, if the model trains long enough, it can start to meta-train on the validation set. The validation set is often used to help determine whether the model is overfitting (more on overfitting in Chapter 10).
- **Test set:** This is the actual measure of model performance on new, unseen data. The test set isn't used in any part of the training process, which gives you a good idea of how the model would "generalize" to new information.

TIP

A validation set is often used for training neural networks. Because these architectures tend to be computationally-intensive, the validation set can help determine whether you can stop training early. For scikit-learn models, it's a little less common to use a validation set, and most of our examples for this library will just use a training and test set.

How much data you want to set aside for each set is up to you, but common splits use 90 percent of the data for the training set and 10 percent for the test set, or 80 percent for training and 20 percent for testing. These numbers are typical but a little bit arbitrary — the real trick is figuring out how much data your model needs to train effectively while withholding enough data to get a good idea of how the model might perform "in the wild." This is not always a trivial determination! Models tend to perform better with more data, so this usually boils down to figuring out how much data you can sacrifice to your test set to ensure you can evaluate the model correctly while giving your model the best possible training toolkit. If you are using a validation set, it's common to take that as an additional 10 to 20 percent of the training set.

Sciki-learn comes with a handy function in its `model_selection` module to make these splits painless. The `train_test_split` function allows you to pass in your data and specify the sizes of the sets. It has the following arguments:

- **Data:** The only non-keyword argument. This is the dataset to split into subsets.
- **test_size:** The percent size of the test set. It defaults to 0.25 or 25 percent. You can also provide an integer to specify exactly how many samples to include in the test set.

- **train_size:** The percent size or number of samples in the training set. It will be determined based on the test size if that isn't provided.
- **random_state:** This allows you to pass an integer to seed the randomness of the split. If you do, it will split the dataset the same way each time.
- **shuffle:** This defaults to True and will shuffle the data before splitting. This is handy to ensure you get a mix of the classes in your training and test set. For example, in the Steel Plates Faults dataset, the examples are listed in order of defect class. If you didn't shuffle the dataset before splitting, you would likely miss classes in the training and test sets.
- **stratify:** This performs a stratified split of the dataset based on the class labels. This is helpful if you have imbalanced classes in the dataset (which is common in many real-world problems).

The function returns your training and test set, in that order.

The code for implementing a training and test set split is shown in Listing 4-3, and Figure 4-3 displays the output of running this code.

LISTING 4-3: Splitting the Data into Training and Test Sets (using_scikit_learn_data_splits.py)

```
import pandas as pd
from sklearn.model_selection import train_test_split

faults = ["Pastry", "Z_Scratch", "K_Scatch", "Stains", "Dirtiness",
  "Bumps", "Other_Faults"]

def read_in_dataset(faults):
    df = pd.read_csv("faults.csv")
    df['fault'] = 0
    #Lets create a categorical variable for each fault
    #In the new "fault" column
    for i in range(0, len(faults)):
        #index list
        true_fault_indexes = df.loc[df[faults[i]] ==
  1].index.tolist()
        df.loc[true_fault_indexes, "fault"] = i+1
        #Create our dataset
    return df

df = read_in_dataset(faults)
print("Full Dataset Size")
print(len(df.index))
```

```
train_set, test_set = train_test_split(df, test_size=0.1)
print("Train Set Size")
print(len(train_set.index))
print("Test Set Size")
print(len(test_set.index))
```

```
(examples) C:\Users\marze\Documents\Book\Code Files>python using_scikit_learn_data_splits.py
Full Dataset Size
1941
Train Set Size
1746
Test Set Size
195
```

FIGURE 4-3: Output of running Listing 4-3.

The code does the following:

- Imports pandas as pd and then imports the `train_test_split` function from `sklearn.model_selection`.
- Uses the same `read_in_dataset` function to read in the Steel Plates Faults dataset and assigns the output to `df` as in Listing 4-1.
- Prints the full dataset size by using the `len()` function on the `index` property of `df`.
- Calls the `train_test_split` function on `df`, with `test_size` set to 0.1. This splits the dataset into 90 percent for the training set and 10 percent for the test set. The output of the function is assigned to `train_set` and `test_set`.
- Prints the `train_set` and `test_set` sizes. Notice in Figure 4-3 that the test set is approximately 10 percent of the overall size.

Classification, Regression, and Clustering, Oh My!

While the models provided by scikit-learn are too numerous to list in this book, they can be broadly sorted into three categories:

- Classification
- Regression
- Clustering

Classification models sort data into different classes or assign them to different labels. Trying to determine if that thing you heard rustling around in the bushes is a wolf or a robin is a classification problem. Sorting your possible actions into "run," "hide," or "fight" is a classification problem. There is also a special kind of classification problem called binary classification, where there are only two possibilities, usually represented by 0 or 1 or the presence/absence of something. The responding EMT declaring you "dead" or "alive" is using a binary classification system. Classification problems attempt to output the most accurate categorization or label for a given data sample.

On the other hand, regression problems try to output a specific number, usually predicting or forecasting some sort of value. Determining how many people will be attacked by wolves in the forest this year would be a type of regression problem. Forecasting the number of minutes it would take to run from the forest back to the lodge is also a regression problem. In general, regression problems are trickier to get 100 percent accurate than classification problems. Results that are close to the real value are usually still actionable, however. For example, if you predict it will take you 5 minutes to run away from a wolf when it actually takes you 15 minutes, your time would be better spent writing out your last will and testament. If you predict it will take you 5 minutes to run away and it actually takes you 5.2 minutes, you're still in the clear.

Clustering problems are unique in that they try to figure out which data points belong in the same group, rather than try to assign a specific number or label to a data point. In a clustering problem, you are generally not trying to figure out a specific outcome for the data sample, but rather trying to explore which data samples belong together based on one or more properties. This is useful for exploring properties or subgroups in a dataset, or trying to figure out related event sequences in time-series data.

Many scikit-learn models are implemented as both a classification model and a regression model. The outputs of the models will be different depending on what class of problem they belong to. For the Steel Plates Faults dataset, we are trying to assign data samples to a specific defect, so we'll use classification models to accomplish this. In Chapter 5, we'll use a different dataset to illustrate working with a regression model on a regression problem. Clustering models are contained in their own submodule in scikit-learn, `sklearn.cluster`. We won't cover these types of models as extensively in this book, but we encourage you to check out the options offered in the library!

Using the scikit-learn Model API

Most of the models provided by scikit-learn share a similar API. This is handy if you are trying out more than one type of model, but don't want to completely restructure your code when you swap out one for another. Models are initialized using their class name, and the initialization process will let you pass in properties and parameters specific to that particular model. However, most models share the following functions:

- `fit`: This function takes in the feature and output data, and performs the actual model training.
- `predict`: After training, this function takes in feature data and outputs the model predictions.
- `score`: Also used after training, this function takes in both feature data and output data. It predicts the feature data and compares that with the actual outcomes, and returns the accuracy (classification) or R^2 value of the model (regression).

TECHNICAL STUFF

Classification models in scikit-learn typically also have a `predict_proba` function, which takes in feature data and outputs the prediction probabilities for each class in the dataset, rather than a classification itself. The method to obtain these probabilities will vary by the type of model used.

In the true *For Dummies* spirit, you now take a look at scikit-learn's `DummyClassifier` model to get an idea of how this API works. This model doesn't use any kind of AI to make informed decisions, but lets you select a "strategy" to use as a comparison for other models. In this case, we'll use the `"most_frequent"` strategy to have the model always predict the class most often seen in the dataset.

The code for running the dummy model example is shown in Listing 4-4. Figure 4-4 displays the output.

LISTING 4-4: Using the Model API on a Dummy Classifier (using_scikit_learn_dummy_model.py)

```
import pandas as pd
from sklearn.model_selection import train_test_split
from sklearn.dummy import DummyClassifier

faults = ["Pastry", "Z_Scratch", "K_Scatch", "Stains", "Dirtiness",
  "Bumps", "Other_Faults"]
```

(continued)

LISTING 4-4: *(continued)*

```
def read_in_dataset(faults):
    df = pd.read_csv("faults.csv")
    df['fault'] = 0
    #Lets create a categorical variable for each fault
    #In the new "fault" column
    for i in range(0, len(faults)):
        #index list
        true_fault_indexes = df.loc[df[faults[i]] ==
   1].index.tolist()
        df.loc[true_fault_indexes, "fault"] = i+1
        #Create our dataset
    return df

df = read_in_dataset(faults)
train_set, test_set = train_test_split(df, test_size=0.1)
train_features = train_set.drop(columns=faults+["fault"])
test_features = test_set.drop(columns=faults+["fault"])
train_outcomes = train_set["fault"]
test_outcomes = test_set["fault"]
model = DummyClassifier(strategy="most_frequent")
model.fit(train_features, train_outcomes)
avg_accuracy = model.score(test_features, test_outcomes)
print("Average model accuracy")
print(avg_accuracy)
predictions = model.predict(test_features)
print("Predictions")
print(predictions)
```

```
(examples) C:\Users\marze\Documents\Book\Code Files>python using_scikit_learn_dummy_model.py
Average model accuracy
0.3435897435897436
Predictions
[7 7 7 7 7 7 7 7 7 7 7 7 7 7 7 7 7 7 7 7 7 7 7 7 7 7 7 7 7 7 7 7 7 7 7 7 7
 7 7 7 7 7 7 7 7 7 7 7 7 7 7 7 7 7 7 7 7 7 7 7 7 7 7 7 7 7 7 7 7 7 7 7 7 7
 7 7 7 7 7 7 7 7 7 7 7 7 7 7 7 7 7 7 7 7 7 7 7 7 7 7 7 7 7 7 7 7 7 7 7 7 7
 7 7 7 7 7 7 7 7 7 7 7 7 7 7 7 7 7 7 7 7 7 7 7 7 7 7 7 7 7 7 7 7 7 7 7 7 7
 7 7 7 7 7 7 7 7 7 7 7 7 7 7 7 7 7 7 7 7 7 7 7 7 7 7 7 7 7 7 7 7 7 7 7 7 7
 7 7 7 7 7 7 7 7 7 7]
```

FIGURE 4-4: Output of running Listing 4-4.

TIP

Note in Figure 4-4 that because the classifier is a dummy, it will predict the class most often in the dataset regardless of the input. This happens to be class "7."

The code does the following:

- » imports pandas as pd and then imports the train_test_split function from sklearn.model_selection and DummyClassifier from sklearn.dummy.
- » Uses the same read_in_dataset function to read in the Steel Plates Faults dataset and assigns the output to df as in Listing 4-1.
- » Uses the train_test_split function to divide df into the train_set and test_set as in Listing 4-3.
- » Creates train_features and test_features by using the drop() function on train_df and test_df. This drops the passed-in faults list and fault column of the DataFrames, which ensures only feature data is left.
- » Creates train_outcomes and test_outcomes by taking just the fault column of train_df and test_df. This is the only outcome variable we care about to fit the model for this dataset, since it contains the encoding for all variables. For other model types, you may need to use separate columns or one-hot encoding.
- » Creates an instance of DummyClassifier using the "most_frequent" strategy and assigns it to the model variable.
- » Calls the fit() function of model and passes in the train_features and train_outcomes to "train" the dummy model.
- » Calls the score() function of model and passes it the test_features and test_outcomes. This returns the average accuracy and stores it in avg_accuracy.
- » Prints the average accuracy of the model. In Figure 4-3, this is about 34 percent. This may change slightly for your own run, since the training and test sets are randomly split, and this will depend on how often the most frequent class is contained in your test set.
- » Calls the predict() function of model to predict the test_features and stores this in the predictions variable.
- » Prints out the predictions. These are all predicted as the most frequent class ("7," which is "Other Faults"). Because only a dummy classifier is used, it will completely ignore the input features and output the encoding for the most frequent class. In this case, the Steel Plates Faults dataset has the most samples belonging to the "Other Faults" class, encoded as "7."

Now that you've worked with the scikit-learn's model API, you're ready to implement some AI techniques! Chapter 5 starts out with a tried-and-true classic: linear regression.

IN THIS CHAPTER

» Reviewing linear relationships between data and outcomes

» Evaluating a model with the coefficient of determination

» Implementing a linear regression model manually in Python

» Implementing a linear regression model in scikit-learn

Chapter 5

The Plot Thickens: Regression Models

In the wild world of AI models, it's tempting to pick the shiniest new offering on the market. Sometimes, of course, the latest is truly the greatest for the task at hand. This chapter covers a more humble model with a long, storied history of use: linear regression. However, you probably won't find many practitioners who consider linear regression a true AI model. We include it in the book for a few reasons:

- Linear regression is trained by learning parameters from existing data, which fits the mold for supervised machine learning models.
- Linear regression is simple to implement, understand, and use.
- In actual analytical practice, linear regression is very popular!

In this chapter, you dive into the relationship between independent variables and outcomes and how they are modeled with the equation of a line. You look at linear regression model parameters and how these are extended for multiple variables. You explore the ordinary least squares method of finding these model parameters and evaluating the overall model's performance with the coefficient of determination. You then implement a linear regression model in two ways: manually, using shortcut formulas, and using the scikit-learn library. Finally, you explore some other regression models and what they are used for.

Taking a Look at a Classic: The Linear Regression Model

The math behind linear regression is pretty straightforward, making it a good starting point for many into the world of machine learning. It all starts with the equation of a line.

Reviewing the equation of a line

Back in elementary school, you may have learned the equation of a line when plotting data on a graph. It is shown in Equation 5-1 in case you forgot.

Equation 5-1: The equation of a line

$$y = mx + b$$

Where:

y is the dependent variable, or outcome. The value of *y* depends on the values of *m*, *x*, and *b*.

m is the slope or the multiplicative coefficient. It is multiplied by *x* and controls the angle of the line.

x is the independent variable. It's a measure you typically don't have control over, and it is usually something recorded or observed.

b is the slope-intercept. It shifts the graph of your line up or down and is added to the *mx* term.

In supervised machine learning, you typically have data features and outcomes. The x term (or terms) will relate to the observed features, and the y term will correspond with an outcome of interest.

Because we can (and often do) extend linear regression models for more than one x variable, sometimes the equation is represented with different labels, as shown in Equation 5-2.

Equation 5-2: More general linear model representation

$$y = b_0 + b_1 x_1 + \ldots + b_n x_n$$

Where:

b_0 is the slope-intercept

$b_1 \ldots b_n$ are the coefficients for independent variables $x_1 \ldots x_n$

The independent x variables and the outcome y variable are provided by the dataset. The job of model training is to find the *b* coefficients and b_0 parameter to relate the variables to the outcome.

Linear regression, of course, assumes that the variables are independent of one another and that the relationship between the independent variables and the outcome variable is linear. Usually, both assumptions are wrong when it comes to real-world data. Despite this, linear regression is a useful model to describe the broad importance of variables to an outcome.

TIP

You can model a Celsius to Fahrenheit calculation with linear regression. The dependent y variable is the degrees Fahrenheit, the coefficient is 1.8, and the intercept is 32. Therefore, 0 degrees Celsius is 32 degrees Fahrenheit, and 10 degrees Celsius is 50 degrees Fahrenheit.

Modeling linear regression

Linear regression typically starts with a set of data. Let's look at a simple graph of price and sales data from a pretend company. Figure 5-1 displays price, the independent variable, on the x-axis, and sales, the dependent variable, on the y-axis.

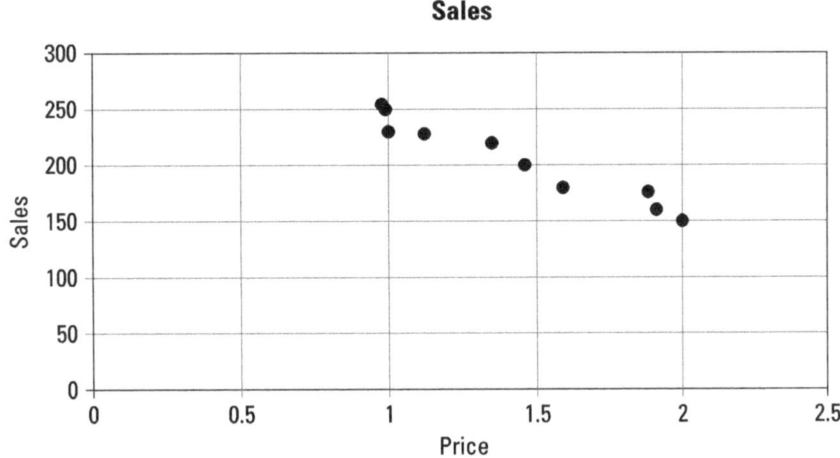

FIGURE 5-1: Price versus sales data for a fictional company.

In Figure 5-1, you can see a clear downward trend: higher prices lead to fewer sales. However, it would be more useful to us as managers if we could predict the sales quantity at a given price point, in case we want to explore the profit margin. For this, we need a model that spits out a sales forecast for any given price.

Figure 5-2 illustrates the model we want to create: a continuous line that fits our data best. Once we have the equation of the line, we can predict the sales at any point on it.

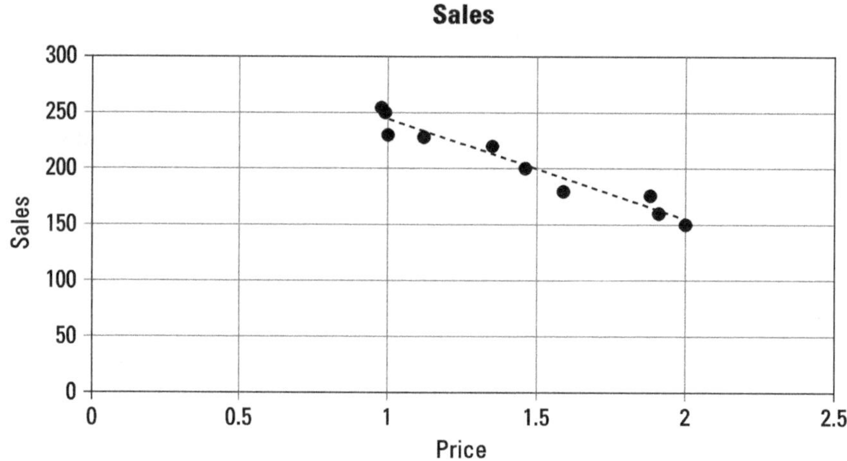

FIGURE 5-2: Scatter plot of price versus sales with a trendline.

Exploring ordinary least squares

How do you find the best linear regression model for our data? Well, one way to look at the quality of the line is to look at how much error the linear regression model has in predicting data. To calculate the error, take the sum of the squared differences between the model prediction and the actual value. This is called the *residual sum of squares*. The job of the linear regression model is to find its parameters to minimize the residual sum of squares as much as possible.

TECHNICAL STUFF

The differences between the model output and the actual data are squared because these differences could be either positive or negative. You don't want to accidentally have differences cancel each other out and make the model pretend it's better than it is!

Ordinary least squares is the method to obtain these parameters. While the math behind this method is a little out of scope for this chapter, it essentially manipulates the residual squares function to be in terms of the coefficients, sets them equal to zero to minimize, and then solves with partial derivatives. You can get the final results with some shortcut functions by using Equations 5-3 and 5-4.

Equation 5-3: The b_1 coefficient calculation

$$b_1 = \frac{\sum_{i=1}^{n} x_i y_i - \left(\left(\sum_{i=1}^{n} x_i * \sum_{i=1}^{n} y_i\right)\frac{1}{n}\right)}{\sum_{i=1}^{n} x_i^{\,2} - \left(\left(\sum_{i=1}^{n} x_i * \sum_{i=1}^{n} x_i\right)\frac{1}{n}\right)}$$

Where:

n is the number of samples

x is the independent variable (feature values)

y is the dependent variable (outcome)

Equation 5-4: The b_0 term calculation

$$b_0 = y_{mean} - b_1 * x_{mean}$$

Where:

y_{mean} is the mean of all *y* values

x_{mean} is the mean of all *x* values

Calculating the coefficient of determination

The *coefficient of determination*, often called the R^2 term, gives you an idea of how "good" your final linear regression model is. It measures how much of the outcome's variance is explained by your model versus random chance. In general, the higher the R^2 term, the better your model. The coefficient of determination calculation is shown in Equation 5-5.

Equation 5-5: The coefficient of determination calculation

$$R^2 = 1 - \frac{\sum_{i=1}^{n} (y - y_{pred})^2}{\sum_{i=1}^{n} (y - y_{mean})^2}$$

Where:

y_{pred} is the model-predicted value of *y*

y_{mean} is the mean value of *y*

n is the number of samples

A coefficient of determination that marks a "good" model depends entirely on the problem at hand and the industry you work in. A rule of thumb that is often used in statistics is to shoot for 0.8 or above, but the metric you want to hit is usually defined by your specific problem.

Implementing Linear Regression Manually in Python

Linear regression is one of the models you can actually implement without needing a library! Listing 5-1 displays the code for running a small linear regression model. Figure 5-3 shows the terminal output of the program.

LISTING 5-1: Manually Implementing Linear Regression (linear_regression_manual.py)

```
#Data
price = [0.98, 0.99, 1, 1.12, 1.35, 1.46, 1.59, 1.88, 1.91, 2]
sales = [254, 250, 230, 228, 220, 200, 180, 176, 160, 150]

#Manual regression
n = len(price)
sum_x =sum(price)
sum_y = sum(sales)
x_mean = sum_x/n
y_mean = sum_y/n
sum_x_times_y = sum([a*b for a, b in zip(price, sales)])
sum_x_squareds = sum([a*a for a in price])
print(f"n: {n}")
print(f"Sum of x values {sum_x}")
print(f"Sum of y values {sum_y}")
print(f"x mean value {x_mean}")
print(f"y mean value {y_mean}")
print(f"Sum of x times y {sum_x_times_y}")
print(f"Sum of squared x values {sum_x_squareds}")

#Calculate our numerator and denominator for m
Sxy = sum_x_times_y - (sum_x*sum_y)/n
Sxx = sum_x_squareds - (sum_x*sum_x)/n
print(f"Sxy: {Sxy} Sxx: {Sxx}")
```

```
#Get our line variables
m = Sxy/Sxx
b = y_mean - m*x_mean
print(f"Regression Equation: y = {m}x + {b}")

#Predict a value
row = 5
price_val = price[row]
sales_val = sales[row]
predicted_sales = price_val*m + b
print(f"For price value {price_val}, the predicted sales value was
  {predicted_sales} and the actual value was {sales_val}")

#Coefficient of determination
predictions = [a*m + b for a in price]
residual_squares = sum([(a-b)*(a-b) for a, b in zip(sales,
  predictions)])
total_squares = sum([(a-y_mean)*(a-y_mean) for a in sales])
r_squared = 1- residual_squares/total_squares
print(f"Coefficient of determination: {r_squared}")
```

```
(examples) C:\Users\marze\Documents\Book\Code Files>python linear_regression_manual.py
n: 10
Sum of x values 14.28
Sum of y values 2048
x mean value 1.428
y mean value 204.8
Sum of x times y 2793.46
Sum of squared x values 21.8596
Sxy: -131.08399999999983 Sxx: 1.4677600000000002
Regression Equation: y = -89.30887883577674x + 332.3330789774892
For price value 1.46, the predicted sales value was 201.94211587725516 and the actual value was 200
Coefficient of determination: 0.9482702398675632
```

FIGURE 5-3: The terminal output of running Listing 5-1.

The program does the following:

- Creates two lists of data: `price` (the independent variable) and `sales` (the dependent variable), each with ten entries.
- Gets the length of the samples and stores it in a variable, `n`.
- Gets the sum of the x values and y_values and stores it in variables `sum_x` and `sum_y`.
- Gets the mean of the x and y values and stores it in variables `x_mean` and `y_mean`.

- Gets the sum of the x values times the y values and stores it in variable `sum_x_times_y`.
- Gets the sum of the x values squared and stores it in variable `sum_x_squareds`.
- Prints the variable values as a sanity check.
- Calculates the numerator for the b_1 coefficient and stores it in variable `Sxy`.
- Calculates the denominator for the b_1 coefficient and stores it in variable `Sxx`.
- Calculates the b_1 coefficient and stores it in variable `m`.
- Calculates the b_0 coefficient and stores it in variable `b`.
- Prints the final regression equation.
- Picks an index for a sample with the `row` variable and grabs the `price` and `sales` values for that instance.
- Calculates the model prediction for the instance and stores it in the `predicted_sales` variable.
- Prints the price value, predicted sales value, and actual sales values.
- Applies the model to all values of `price` and stores it in the `predictions` variable.
- Calculates the residual squares and stores the value in the `residual_squares` variable.
- Calculates the total squares and stores the value in the `total_squares` variable.
- Calculates the coefficient of determination from the `residual_squares` and `total_squares` variables and stores the value in the variable `r_squared`.
- Prints the coefficient of determination value.

Note that in Figure 5-3, we take a price value, multiply it by -89.31, and add 332.33 to arrive at a final sales value. Our coefficient of determination is also 0.95 — not bad!

TIP

If you are getting different output in your program, double-check the equations that sum list elements. It is very easy to accidentally introduce bugs in these sections!

Now that you've seen it done the hard way, let's use the scikit-learn library.

Implementing Linear Regression in scikit-learn

You can use the typical model API to create a linear regression model in scikit-learn. Listing 5-2 displays the code for running the regression model. Figure 5-4 illustrates the terminal output, and Figure 5-5 shows the graphical output.

LISTING 5-2: Implementing Linear Regression with scikit-learn (linear_regression_library.py)

```
from matplotlib import pyplot as plt
from sklearn.linear_model import LinearRegression
from sklearn.model_selection import train_test_split

#Data
price = [0.98, 0.99, 1, 1.12, 1.35, 1.46, 1.59, 1.88, 1.91, 2]
sales = [254, 250, 230, 228, 220, 200, 180, 176, 160, 150]

#Linear Regression with Scikit Learn Model
linear_regression_model = LinearRegression()
price_format = [[a] for a in price]
sales_format = [[a] for a in sales]
linear_regression_model.fit(price_format, sales_format)
model_m = linear_regression_model.coef_[0][0]
model_b = linear_regression_model.intercept_[0]
print("Scikit Learn Regression Model")
print(f"Regression Equation: y = {model_m}x + {model_b}")

#Predict a value
row=5
predicted_model_quality = linear_regression_model.
  predict([price_format[row]])
print(f"For price value {price[row]}, the predicted sales value was
  {predicted_model_quality[0][0]} and the actual value was
  {sales[row]}")

#Get the Coefficient of determination
score = linear_regression_model.score(price_format, sales_format)
print(f"Coefficient of determination: {score}")
```

(continued)

LISTING 5-2: *(continued)*

```
#Plot best fit line
predictions = linear_regression_model.predict(price_format)
plt.scatter(price, sales)
plt.plot(price, predictions, linestyle="solid")
plt.xlabel("price")
plt.ylabel("sales")
plt.title("Price vs Sales")
plt.show()
```

```
(examples) C:\Users\marze\Documents\Book\Code Files>python linear_regression_library.py
Scikit Learn Regression Model
Regression Equation: y = -89.30887883577697x + 332.3330789774895
For price value 1.46, the predicted sales value was 201.94211587725513 and the actual value was 200
Coefficient of determination: 0.9482702398675632
```

FIGURE 5-4: Terminal output of running Listing 5-2.

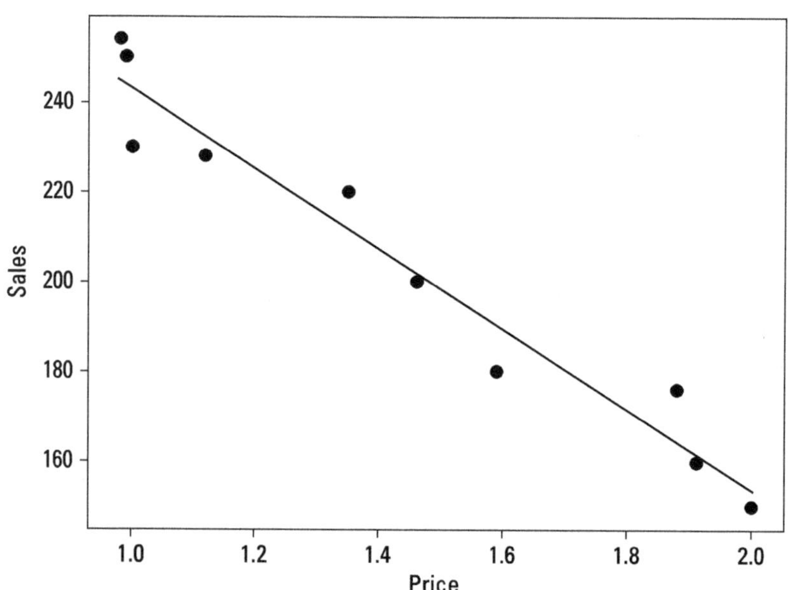

FIGURE 5-5: Graphical output of running Listing 5-3.

The program does the following:

» Imports the necessary libraries. Matplotlib's `pyplot` is used to plot the line of best fit, and the `LinearRegression` and `train_test_split` modules of scikit-learn are used to prepare the data and implement the model.

- Creates variables for `price` and `sales` data, as in Listing 5-1.
- Creates a linear regression model, `linear_regression_model`, using the `LinearRegression` module.
- Formats the price and sales variables for scikit-learn by wrapping each element in its own list and storing in variables `price_format` and `sales_format`.
- Fits the linear regression model with the `price` and `sales` data.
- Grabs the b_0 and b_1 terms from the trained model and prints the regression equation.
- Predicts a sample sales forecast from a price value using the `predict` method of the `linear_regression_model` and prints the prediction.
- Gets the coefficient of determination using the `score` method of the `linear_regression_model` and prints it.
- Gets all predictions from the price data using the `predict` method of the `linear_regression_model` and stores them in the variable predictions.
- Plots the data and the best-fit line through it using `pyplot`.

You can see from Figure 5-4 that we take a price value, multiply it by -89.31, and add 332.33 to arrive at a final sales value. Our coefficient of determination is also 0.95. We got the same values as our manual regression exercise — nice!

Not Forgetting Other Regression Models

Linear regression is an old standby for many number-crunchers, but not the only regression-type model out there. Other regression models include:

- Multiple regression
- Logistic regression
- Ridge and lasso regression
- Polynomial regression

Multiple regression

Multiple regression is the same as normal linear regression, but with more than one independent variable. For example, if you added a second variable to our code in the previous section, say, the number of stores, you could run a multiple linear regression to determine how much each of these variables — price and number of stores — contributes to the sales forecast. Scikit-learn allows for multiple regression, which is why independent variables are expected to be formatted as a list (the program can handle multiple).

Logistic regression

Logistic regression is useful for variables with binary outcomes: 0 or 1. It uses a sigmoid curve to fit the data, and is best for large datasets where the two outcomes are balanced (the 0 case and 1 case occur about the same number of times). Logistic regression is one way to use a regression model for binary classification.

Ridge and lasso regression

Ridge and lasso regression are useful when your variables are highly correlated with each other, which violates the typical linear regression assumptions. These methods use some regularization techniques to reduce the impact of overfitting models.

Polynomial regression

Polynomial regression fits a polynomial line to a regression problem. While this is much more flexible, it is also much more prone to overfitting, and you may end up with some undesirable predictions, especially if the data is noisy.

TECHNICAL STUFF

If feature data used for linear regression models is too highly correlated with other features, a technique called principal component analysis (PCA) can be used to reduce this problem. It takes combinations of the features to create new ones and then uses these new features in the models. While the new features — principal components — don't have a lot of intrinsic meaning on their own, they help reduce the collinearity problem.

IN THIS CHAPTER

» Understanding flowcharts and trees

» Using information theory to build trees

» Programming a decision tree

» Exploring decision-tree parameters

Chapter 6
Making Decisions with Trees

Decision trees are some of the most powerful model types in classical machine learning. They often form the basis for other models, like bagging and boosting ensembles (discussed in Chapter 7), and as such, are very useful models to become familiar with.

In this chapter, you spend time admiring flowcharts as efficient decision-making tools and how they form the basis for decision trees. You explore fundamental information-theory concepts such as surprise, information, entropy, and the Gini index, and apply these concepts to build a decision tree, feature by feature. You use the scikit-learn library to program your own decision tree and evaluate its performance. You then explore different decision tree parameters provided by the library and learn how constructing your tree provides trade-offs between usability and accuracy.

Exploring the Beautiful Flowchart of a Decision Tree

When you make a decision, you usually take several factors into account. For example, if you're deciding whether or not to go surfing, you probably want to look at the weather forecast, the swell forecast, and the shark population. If you're thinking about eating a mushroom you picked in the forest, you look at the size, coloration, shape, and texture of the mushroom, as well as the suspicious number of sick animals walking dizzily away from the area.

It's often helpful to make decisions using a flowchart. Flowcharts are diagrams where features or decision points are evaluated one at a time, with the more important features near the top. Some features are so impactful that they can help you make a decision immediately, which saves you time when traversing the flowchart.

Figure 6-1 displays a handy flowchart for deciding whether or not to explore a mysterious ruin. (We can't tell you how many times this flowchart has come in handy!)

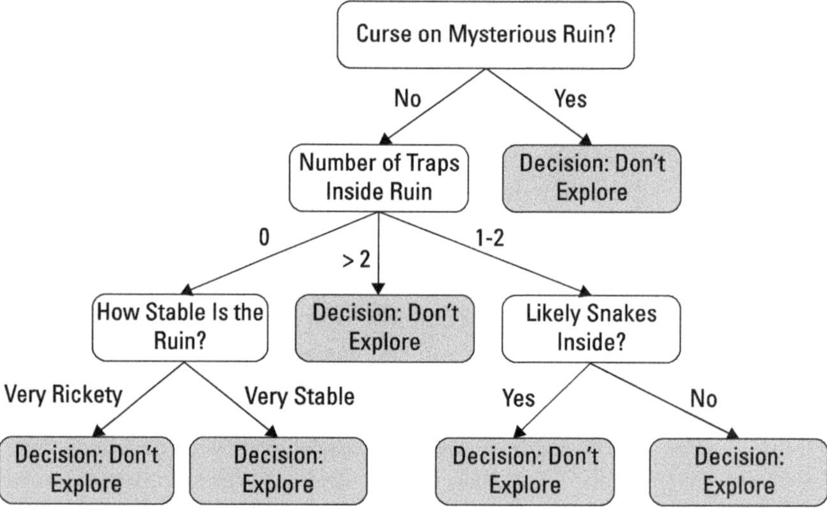

FIGURE 6-1: A useful flowchart layout with features relevant to making a decision about exploring a mysterious ruin.

As indicated in Figure 6-1, the most important feature in making the decision is whether or not the ruin is cursed. If it is, obviously, you shouldn't explore it. If the ruin isn't cursed, you move on to the next factor: How many traps are in the ruin? This creates different branches of the flowchart depending on the situation, and in this case, different branches require different features to make the right call. If there are more than two traps in the ruin, you arrive at a decision again: Don't explore. If there are no traps, you need to know how stable the ruin is. Are there no traps because the ruin is structurally unsound? If so, don't explore. If it looks stable, go for it! If, however, there were one or two traps in the ruin, you can assume it must be somewhat stable for the traps to survive. In this case, you need to decide whether the number of snakes in the ruin will make your adventure worth your time.

A decision tree creates a very similar flowchart to this one, although the decision points are usually quantified by a specific number or the presence or absence of a value. The tree is created from an existing dataset using information theory to determine what features and values are most important.

TIP

Classic flowcharts and decision trees are quite similar. While there aren't clearly defined differences (certain flowcharts could easily be decision trees, and all decision trees can be used as flowcharts), flowcharts might use more subjective and human-understandable terms (for example, "a lot," "medium warm," "tiny"), while decision trees usually quantify the decision criteria (for example, >10, True, <= 2.5).

A few terms from the scikit-learn documentation are useful for describing a decision tree. These are:

- **Nodes:** Nodes are decision points on the tree. In Figure 6-1, the "Curse on Mysterious Ruin?", "Number of Traps Inside Ruin," "How Stable Is the Ruin?", and "Likely Snakes Inside?" boxes are nodes.
- **Leaf nodes:** Leaf nodes are terminal nodes inside the tree that represent the decisions. In Figure 6-1, the "Decision: Explore" and "Decision: Don't Explore" boxes are leaf nodes. Once you hit one of these boxes, you have your answer, and you stop exploring the tree.
- **Depth:** Depth is how far down the tree goes. Of course, there are different paths through the tree that might kick you out earlier. Generally, depth refers to how many levels down you can go in the longest scenario. In the case of Figure 6-1, the most nodes you could encounter before a decision is three, so the depth of the tree is three.
- **Split:** The split of a node is the value threshold used to explore different branches. In Figure 6-1, the "Curse" node was split into Yes or No pathways. In the "Number of Traps Inside Ruin" node, the split was 0, 1–2, and greater than 2.

In Figure 6-1, a node could have multiple splits, as in the "Number of Traps Inside Ruin" case. In general, most implementations will only split the node into two cases, and that split is usually based on a threshold value or on the presence or absence of a value. Reusing the feature node further down in the tree helps create more splits on one feature, if needed.

The decision-tree method looks at labeled data and creates nodes and their splits based on their relevance to an outcome of interest. The next section explores the information theory concepts that make the algorithm work.

Understanding Information Theory

Information theory helps quantify the information of a given variable, which is useful when you want to use that variable to make decisions. Sometimes it's helpful to look at a variable or statement in terms of how surprising it is. For example, consider these pronouncements:

- Tomorrow, the sun will rise.
- Tomorrow, it will be cloudy.
- Tomorrow, you will be attacked by a wolverine.

The first statement isn't very surprising — barring the apocalypse, it is pretty much guaranteed to happen. The second statement could be surprising depending on the time of year and the climate where you live. The final statement is very surprising — in fact, you'll probably be on the front page of the newspapers. (As a side note, if that last statement is not at all surprising for you, we wish you well.)

The unsurprising statement contains basically no information. You're assuming the sun will rise in order to carry out your day. The second statement has some useful information for you and may influence your decision to pack a sweater. The last statement has the most information. In fact, your day might be rearranged around avoiding this wolverine attack, or at the very least packing your sturdiest pair of pants.

You can see that the probability of an event and the information of an event are related. Equation 6-1 outlines the relationship specifically.

Equation 6-1: The information of an event *x*

$$x = -\log_2 p(x)$$

Where:

x is the event of interest

p(x) is the probability of event *x*

You can see that there is an inverse relationship between the information of an event and the probability of the event. If the statement "Tomorrow, the sun will rise" has 100 percent probability, then its information is 0. If the statement "It will be cloudy tomorrow" has 50 percent probability, its information is 0.301. If you have a one in a million chance of being attacked by a wolverine, then that statement's information is 6.

Outlining entropy

Another important calculation for decision trees is entropy. *Entropy* is the measure of how much information is contained in a random variable, which has a lot to do with the variance of the variable. The entropy calculation is shown in Equation 6-2.

Equation 6-2: The entropy calculation

$$x = -\sum_{k}^{n} p(k)\log_2 p(k)$$

Where:

x is the event in question

There are *k* different values *x* can take

There are *n* instances of event *x*

For example, if you are trying to make a decision to swim in the ocean, you might have an event or feature called *Shark Attack?*. This event can take two different values: *Yes* or *No*.

Say that in the past, you went swimming nine times and were attacked by a shark three of those times. Therefore, x = Shark Attack?, k=2 (Yes or No), and n=9. Your entropy would be 0.92 since your "Yes" probability is 0.33 (3 out of 9) and your "No" probability is 0.66 (6 out of 9).

REMEMBER

The greater the entropy of a feature, the more surprising it is. Unsurprising distributions have low entropy; surprising distributions have high entropy.

TIP

To make the actual tree, you want to pick features to split on that remove the most entropy. This calculation is called *information gain*. When you pick a feature to help classify part of the dataset, you want to remove the most uncertainty as soon as possible.

Gaining more information through entropy

Information gain is calculated as the entropy of the current dataset based on the outcome of interest minus the entropy of a particular feature, weighted by its value occurrences. This calculation is repeated for all features, and the features with the highest information gain are chosen for the split.

Creating a decision tree involves:

- Calculating the entropy of the entire dataset based on the outcome of interest.
- Calculating the entropy of each individual dataset feature based on the feature value's relation to the outcome of interest.
- Subtracting the entropy of the feature from the entropy of the entire dataset to get the information gain.
- Choosing to split the data on the feature with the highest information gain.
- Repeating the process with the subsets of data on each branch until all data is classified or a stopping criterion is reached.

Figure 6-2 illustrates a worked-out example for the first split in deciding whether or not a berry is poisonous.

In Figure 6-2, the entropy is first calculated based on the number of poisoned berries and normal berries. Then, the entropy is calculated for the color feature based on how often the feature values of "red" and "blue" correspond to a poisoned or normal berry. These entropy values are weighted by how often a red or blue berry occurs in the first place. Finally, this weighted entropy is subtracted from the overall entropy. The process is repeated with the "length" variable (split on 10cm) to arrive at the information gain of the feature.

The figure shows that the information gain of the color feature is 0.47 while the information gain of the length feature is only 0.08. In this case, we would definitely pick the color feature to split on first. If you look at the table, this makes sense — in our dataset, red berries are always poisonous!

Attempt	Color	Length	Poison?
1	Red	10cm	Yes
2	Blue	5cm	No
3	Red	15cm	Yes
4	Blue	10cm	No
5	Blue	2cm	Yes
6	Blue	7cm	No

Entropy: (Whole Distribution):
Probability of poison berry: 0.5
Probability of normal berry: 0.5

Entropy of whole:
–0.5*log(0.5) – 0.5*log(0.5) = **1**

Entropy (Color):
Blue:
Poison Blue Berry Probability: 0.25
Normal Blue Berry Probability: 0.75
Entropy of Blue Berries: 0.81

Red:
Poison Red Berry Probability: 1
Normal Red Berry Probability: 0
Entropy of Red Berries: 0

Probability of Blue Berries: 0.66
Probability of Red Berries: 0.33

Weighted Entropy of Color:
0.66*0.81 + 0.33*0 = 0.53

Information Gain of Color:
1 – 0.53 = **0.47**

Entropy (Length):
>= 10cm:
Poison Long Berry Probability: 0.66
Normal Long Berry Probability: 0.33
Entropy of Long Berries: 0.92

< 10cm:
Poison Short Berry Probability: 0.33
Normal Short Berry Probability: 0.66
Entropy of Short Berries: 0.92

Probability of Long Berries: 0.5
Probability of Short Berries: 0.5

Weighted Entropy of Length:
0.5*0.92 + 0.5*0.92 = 0.92

Information Gain of Length:
1 – 0.92 = **0.08**

FIGURE 6-2: A worked-out example for choosing which feature to split on first in a decision tree.

REMEMBER

High information means high surprise and high entropy, which correlates with low probability. Low information means low surprise and low entropy, which correlates with high probability. Information gain involves removing entropy — essentially, removing the maximum amount of "surprise" possible in our data to create higher-quality predictions.

Gini in a bottle

Entropy isn't the only possible measure used in a decision tree. The Gini index is also a popular measure of impurity in a dataset. Equation 6-3 gives the Gini index calculation.

Equation 6-3: The Gini index calculation

$$Gini\ Index = 1 - \sum_{i=1}^{k} (p(i))^2$$

Where:

k is the number of classes

$p(i)$ is the probability of a given class

The Gini index is sometimes used instead of entropy, as it is straightforward to calculate and measures the impurity of a distribution. Unlike information gain, a decision tree would take the minimum value of the Gini index to choose a feature to split on. The Gini index also only works for binary splits.

Now that you understand how a decision tree is built, it's time to see one in action!

Programming a Decision Tree

To program a simple decision tree, you'll use the scikit-learn library with the Steel Plates Faults dataset. Listing 6-1 displays the code, and the terminal output of the program is shown in Figure 6-3. Figure 6-4 shows the graphical display output.

LISTING 6-1: Creating a Decision Tree with scikit-learn (decision_tree.py)

```
import pandas as pd
from sklearn.tree import DecisionTreeClassifier, plot_tree
from sklearn.model_selection import train_test_split
import matplotlib.pyplot as plt

faults = ["Pastry", "Z_Scratch", "K_Scatch", "Stains", "Dirtiness",
  "Bumps", "Other_Faults"]

def read_in_dataset(faults):
    df = pd.read_csv("faults.csv")
    df['fault'] = 0
    #Lets create a categorical variable for each fault
    #In the new "fault" column
    for i in range(0, len(faults)):
        #index list
        true_fault_indexes = df.loc[df[faults[i]] ==
  1].index.tolist()
        df.loc[true_fault_indexes, "fault"] = i+1
        #Create our dataset
    return df

df = read_in_dataset(faults)
#Create the training and test set
drop_features = ["fault"] + faults
features = df.drop(drop_features, axis=1)
outcomes = df["fault"]
training_features, test_features, training_outcomes, test_outcomes =
  train_test_split(features, outcomes, test_size=0.1)

model = DecisionTreeClassifier()

model.fit(training_features, training_outcomes)
test_accuracy_score = model.score(test_features, test_outcomes)
```

```
training_accuracy_score = model.score(training_features,
  training_outcomes)
print(f"Training accuracy {training_accuracy_score}")
print(f"Test accuracy {test_accuracy_score}")
plot_tree(model)
plt.show()
plt.clf()
```

FIGURE 6-3: Terminal output of Listing 6-1.

```
(examples) C:\Users\marze\Documents\Book\Code Files>python decision_tree.py
Training accuracy 1.0
Test accuracy 0.6461538461538462
```

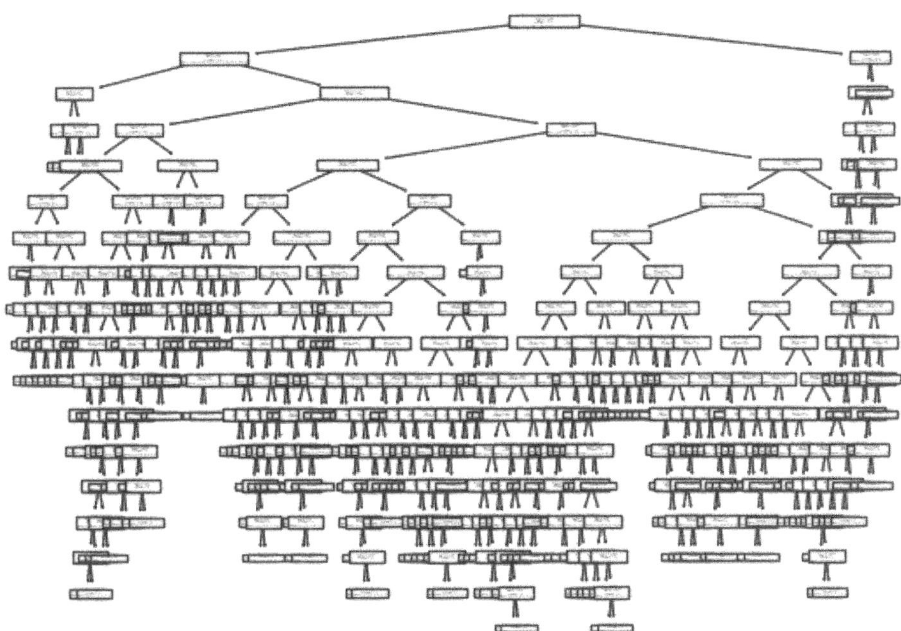

FIGURE 6-4: Graphical display output of Listing 6-1.

The code listing does the following:

- Imports the necessary libraries for the program. The pandas library reads in the dataset, while the `DecisionTreeClassifier` and `plot_tree()` modules from scikit-learn create and visualize the decision tree. The `train_test_split()` function from scikit-learn prepares the dataset, while Matplotlib's `pyplot` module helps visualize the tree.

- Reads in the dataset. The faults list describes the different steel plate faults to classify, and the `read_in_dataset()` function creates a new `fault` variable to store each category of fault. The program drops all the outcomes except the final `fault` variable.
- Creates the dataset splits. The `train_test_split()` function splits the dataset into training and test features and outcomes.
- Creates the model. The `DecisionTreeClassifier()` module creates a new decision tree model.
- Fits the model. The `fit()` function of the model class receives the training features and outcomes to create the decision tree.
- Scores the model. The `score()` function of the model class is used to get an overall accuracy score for the training and test set, which are printed to the terminal.
- Visualizes the tree model with the `plot_tree()` function and the `pyplot show()` function.

You can see from the output that the training set accuracy was 100 percent while the test set accuracy was 65 percent (Remember, there is some randomness in the data split, so your values might be slightly different than the ones listed here). However, the tree is absolutely enormous. Maybe too large to fully understand. In the next section, we review parameters to make the decision tree a little more manageable.

Explaining Important Decision-Tree Parameters

Scikit-learn provides several useful parameters for controlling decision-tree behavior. The following are some helpful ones to consider:

- `criterion`: You choose whether you want to use the Gini index or entropy to split the nodes. The default value is the Gini index.
- `max_depth`: You set a limit on how deep you want the tree to grow. By default, there is no max depth, which can sometimes make the tree become unmanageably deep.

- » `min_samples_split`: You specify whether to require a minimum number of samples to split a node. By default, this value is 2. You could set the value higher if the model is overfitting too much.
- » `min_samples_leaf`: You specify whether a leaf node requires a certain number of samples associated with it to be created. By default, this value is 1.
- » `max_features`: You specify the maximum number of features the tree should consider at each split. By default, it uses all features.
- » `max_leaf_nodes`: You specify the maximum number of leaf decision nodes.

We'll manipulate some of these parameters to see how they affect our output. Listing 6-2 presents a new decision-tree program with a few of the parameters changed to make the tree smaller. The terminal output of Listing 6-2 is shown in Figure 6-5, and Figure 6-6 shows the graphical output.

LISTING 6-2: Manipulating Decision-Tree Parameters (decision_tree_parameters.py)

```
import pandas as pd
from sklearn.tree import DecisionTreeClassifier, plot_tree
from sklearn.model_selection import train_test_split
import matplotlib.pyplot as plt

faults = ["Pastry", "Z_Scratch", "K_Scatch", "Stains", "Dirtiness",
  "Bumps", "Other_Faults"]

def read_in_dataset(faults):
    df = pd.read_csv("faults.csv")
    df['fault'] = 0
    #Lets create a categorical variable for each fault
    #In the new "fault" column
    for i in range(0, len(faults)):
        #index list
        true_fault_indexes = df.loc[df[faults[i]] ==
  1].index.tolist()
        df.loc[true_fault_indexes, "fault"] = i+1
        #Create our dataset
    return df

df = read_in_dataset(faults)
#Create the training and test set
```

(continued)

LISTING 6-2: *(continued)*

```
drop_features = ["fault"] + faults
features = df.drop(drop_features, axis=1)
outcomes = df["fault"]
training_features, test_features, training_outcomes, test_outcomes =
  train_test_split(features, outcomes, test_size=0.1)

model = DecisionTreeClassifier(criterion="entropy", max_depth=3,
  min_samples_leaf=4)

model.fit(training_features, training_outcomes)
test_accuracy_score = model.score(test_features, test_outcomes)
training_accuracy_score = model.score(training_features,
  training_outcomes)
print(f"Training accuracy {training_accuracy_score}")
print(f"Test accuracy {test_accuracy_score}")
plot_tree(model, fontsize=8, filled=True)
plt.show()
plt.clf()
```

```
(examples) C:\Users\marze\Documents\Book\Code Files>python decision_tree_parameters.py
Training accuracy 0.5532646048109966
Test accuracy 0.5846153846153846
```

FIGURE 6-5: Terminal output of Listing 6-2.

This code listing is the same as the previous except:

- » The `criterion` changes to entropy, the `max_depth` of the tree is set to 3, and the `min_samples_leaf` is set to 4.
- » The `plot_tree()` function changes the font size to 8 and fills the boxes with color.

You can also see in the terminal output that by manipulating the parameters, we took a hit in the overall accuracy (58 percent). There is often a trade-off between the accuracy of the model and its usability. Simpler, shorter decision trees are much easier for a human to understand, but may not make predictions as high-quality as others.

TECHNICAL STUFF

Like other scikit-learn models, the decision tree model can be implemented as either a classifier or a regressor. A classifier sorts data into categorical class designations, while a regressor outputs a final number. The `DecisionTreeRegressor` module would be used in place of `DecisionTreeClassifier`.

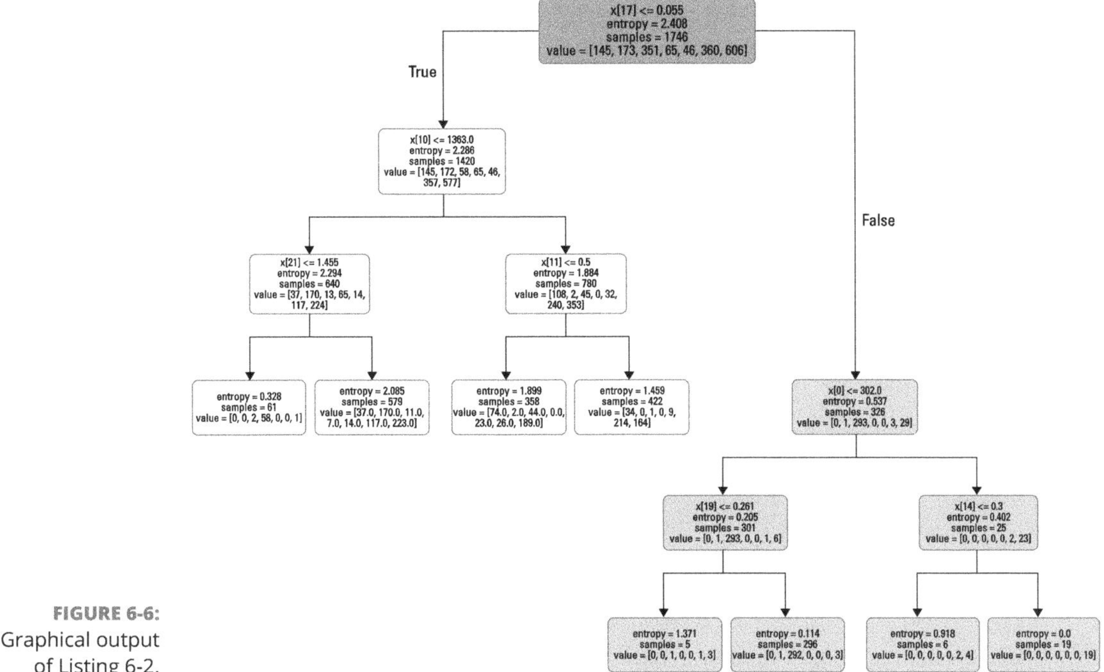

FIGURE 6-6: Graphical output of Listing 6-2.

IN THIS CHAPTER

» Creating ensemble models from multiple base models

» Increasing your base models' performance with bagging and boosting

» Leveling up a decision tree into a random forest

» Overfitting and explainability trade-offs

Chapter 7

Better Together: Boosting, Bagging, and Random Forests

For complicated problems, sometimes a single AI model isn't cut out to solve the whole thing by itself. Sometimes the underlying problem has multiple potential causes, and an AI model may only be capable of covering one or two of them. Or, depending on the split of the training and test data, one AI model might emphasize a particular aspect of the problem at the expense of another, equally important aspect.

In this chapter, you discover the power of using multiple models together to create ensemble models. You first explore what an ensemble model is and how it is created under two different algorithms: *bagging*, which leverages the knowledge of the crowd, and *boosting*, which uses its past mistakes to make better future predictions. You then explore how to take a basic decision tree and multiply it into a random forest powerhouse. This chapter provides examples on how to use these models and tweak the parameters to get the best possible outcome with the scikit-learn library.

Two Heads Are Better than One: Ensemble Models

If you've ever listened to a piece of orchestral music — say, Tchaikovsky's *1812 Overture* — you may have appreciated the fact that multiple instruments working together can be greater than the sum of their parts. You might get the gist of the melody with one single trumpet, but it's hard to get the full experience without also hearing the flutes, clarinets, drums, and trombones. (Also, the cannons. Especially the cannons!)

Ensemble models, at their core, are multiple models working together to create an output. Just as two heads can be better than one, an ensemble model assumes that more than one model working on the task will come up with a better solution than a single model.

Of course, if you have ever been in a group project, you know that multiple people working on the same problem need structure to agree on the solution. Ensemble models are no different. One of the most important aspects of working with ensemble models is determining how they are going to work together.

TECHNICAL STUFF

In the AI world, an *ensemble* model refers to multiple models working together. However, you may run across other terms. *A hybrid* model, for instance, also usually refers to more than one model working on a problem, but in a hybrid structure, it is usually assumed that at least one of the underlying models is of a different type. Ensemble models more typically use multiple models of the same type. For example, an ensemble model might use three decision trees applied to one problem, where a hybrid model might use one decision tree together with a linear regression model.

The most straightforward way to get a team of models working together is also the most democratic: voting. In this scheme, all the models in the ensemble work on the problem separately to come up with an answer to the problem. Each model gets one "vote" to contribute to the overall system. The answer (often a classification) with the most votes wins. However, this isn't the only way to get your all-star model team to come up with a solution; we explore alternative methods in the Boosting section of this chapter.

When designing your ensemble model, there are several things you'll want to think about:

- What base model do you want to use?
- How many models should be on your team?
- Do all the models get to train on the entire dataset? Or, should they each get a subset of the dataset samples?
- Do all the models get to train on all the data features? Or, should they each get a subset of the features?

Implementing the best team of models for a problem depends a lot on the problem itself. Fortunately, scikit-learn has many built-in model classes (located in the Ensemble module of the library) that make trying different types of ensemble models a simple task.

TIP

In this chapter, you explore working with Bagging, Boosting, and Random Forest ensemble classifiers. However, the scikit-learn library has many other types of ensemble models, including Voting Classifiers and Regressors, Stacking Classifiers and Regressors, and Isolation Forests. We recommend checking the scikit-learn library documentation (`https://scikit-learn.org/stable/api/sklearn.ensemble.html`) for more information on how each model works.

Bragging about Your Bagging Model

Bagging ensemble models use multiple models working on different subsets of the data. Essentially, each model in the team gets assigned a random set of samples out of the entire dataset and trains on only that subset to create the best possible prediction they can. When all models have finished training, they put their answers together. The final answer is chosen by voting on each prediction or averaging them together. A diagram of a bagging model is shown in Figure 7-1.

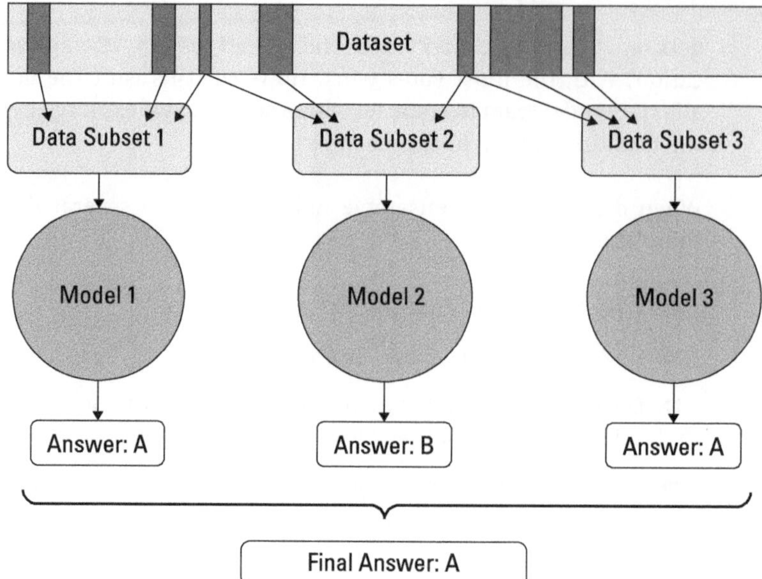

FIGURE 7-1: A diagram of a bagging ensemble model using subsets of data.

Choosing data subsets

According to the scikit-learn library documentation, there are multiple ways of dividing up the data for each model to use. When we discuss these methods, it's important to remember the distinction between dataset samples and dataset features. A dataset *sample* is a distinct individual or event in your data, which has associated *features*. For example, if you have a dataset made up of different dogs, a single sample might be the dog named Fluffy with associated features of "weight: 40 pounds," "color: brown," and "breed: collie." The features "weight," "color," and "breed" are shared across multiple samples, with different values for each. Data subsets can be created from samples, features, or both.

- **Pasting** takes random subsets of the dataset samples. For example, one model might train on the dogs Spike, Spot, Fluffy, and Rex, while the other model trains on Fido, Daisy, Max, and Buster.
- **Bagging** takes random subsets of the dataset samples, but draws these samples with replacement (puts the chosen sample back in the pool for the next draw). In this case, the same dataset sample might end up in more than one model. For example, one model might train on Fido, Rex, and Daisy, one model might train on Max, Buster, and Fido, and one model might train on Spot, Spike, and Max.
- **Random subspaces** use subsets of the features. For example, all the models might have access to every dog sample, but Model 1 only uses the "weight" features, while Model 2 uses the "color" and "breed" features.

- **Random patches** takes subsets from both the dataset samples and the dataset features. In this case, one model might use just the "breed" feature of Fido, Max, and Daisy, while another model uses the "weight" feature of Spot and Spike.

Bagging model parameters in scikit-learn

In the scikit-learn library, bagging models are implemented as `BaggingClassifier` or `BaggingRegressor` in the ensemble module. The model API is the same as other classification and regression models in scikit-learn, making it easy to swap in and out different models as you experiment with data.

TIP

Most classification models in scikit-learn have a corresponding regression model. Remember, classification models usually output distinct categories or labels, while regression models usually output a continuous number.

Most ensemble models in scikit-learn will ask you to set a base estimator, which is the type of underlying model used in the overall team. You can also usually control the overall number of estimators in the team. (There is a different default number of estimators depending on the particular ensemble model. For the `BaggingClassifer`, the default is 10.) The following parameters help you control the specific dataset subsets you want to implement for a model:

- `max_samples`: This is the number of samples to give each model. If you provide an integer, it will draw that number of samples for each underlying model. If you provide a float (decimal number), it will multiply that number by the total number of samples.
- `max_features`: This is the number of features to give each model. If you provide an integer, it will draw that number of features. If you provide a float, it will multiply that number by the total number of features to arrive at the feature number.
- `bootstrap`: If this is true, it will take dataset samples with replacement for each model.
- `bootstrap_features`: If this is true, it will take dataset features with replacement for each model.

By default, the bagging classifier is implemented with `max_samples` and `max_features` set to 1.0 (meaning all dataset samples and features are fair game). The bootstrap feature is set to True by default, while `bootstrap_features` is set to False. This implements the true "bagging" dataset subspace. To implement pasting, bootstrap must be set to False. To implement random subspaces or patches, you would set `bootstrap_features` to True.

One parameter you will see on several ensemble models, including the `BaggingClassifier`, is `oob_score`. This stands for "out-of-bag" score, and is used to estimate the error of the ensemble models. "Out-of-bag" samples are samples that might be used in the training data generally, but aren't used in a specific model inside the ensemble. These scores can be averaged across all the ensemble models to get an idea of the overall error, which is another handy way to check how well your model is generalizing outside of using a validation/test set.

Implementing a bagging model in Python

Listing 7-1 displays the code for implementing a bagging model in Python using the scikit-learn library. Note that the code file uses the "faults" dataset of Steel Plates Faults from Chapter 3.

Figure 7-2 displays the output. Note that your output might be different based on the random data chosen for training and test sets.

LISTING 7-1: Bagging Model in Python with scikit-learn (bagging_model.py)

```
import pandas as pd
from sklearn.model_selection import train_test_split
from sklearn.ensemble import BaggingClassifier

faults = ["Pastry", "Z_Scratch", "K_Scatch", "Stains", "Dirtiness",
  "Bumps", "Other_Faults"]

def read_in_dataset(faults):
    df = pd.read_csv("faults.csv")
    df['fault'] = 0
    #Lets create a categorical variable for each fault
    #In the new "fault" column
    for i in range(0, len(faults)):
        #index list
        true_fault_indexes = df.loc[df[faults[i]] ==
  1].index.tolist()
        df.loc[true_fault_indexes, "fault"] = i+1
        #Create our dataset
    return df

df = read_in_dataset(faults)
#Create the training and test set
```

```
drop_features = ["fault"] + faults
features = df.drop(drop_features, axis=1)
outcomes = df["fault"]
training_features, test_features, training_outcomes, test_outcomes =
  train_test_split(features, outcomes, test_size=0.1)

model = BaggingClassifier()

model.fit(training_features, training_outcomes)
test_accuracy_score = model.score(test_features, test_outcomes)
training_accuracy_score = model.score(training_features,
  training_outcomes)
print(f"Training accuracy {training_accuracy_score}")
print(f"Test accuracy {test_accuracy_score}")
```

```
(examples) C:\Users\marze\Documents\Book\Code Files>python bagging_model.py
Training accuracy 0.9925544100801833
Test accuracy 0.764102564102564
```

FIGURE 7-2: Output of the bagging model example.

The code listing does the following:

- Imports the necessary libraries: pandas, the `train_test_split` class from the scikit-learn `model_selection` module, and the bagging classifier from the scikit-learn ensemble module
- Creates a list of `outcomes` (the faults of interest)
- Defines a function (`read_in_dataset`) for processing the dataset for the model, as in Chapter 6. This creates a new column, "faults," with a number corresponding to each fault category you want to classify:
  - Creates the dataframe by calling the `read_in_dataset` function
  - Creates the `features` and `outcomes` sub-dataframes
  - Splits the dataset into training and test sets
  - Initializes the `BaggingClassifier` model
  - Fits the model with the training data
  - Scores the model on both the training and test data

Boosting Your Models for Liftoff

Having one person working on a problem is great. Having a team of people working on the same problem is often even better. Having a team of people work on a problem — and having that same team talk to each other and learn from each other's mistakes — is often the best-case scenario for getting that problem solved.

For example, suppose that you have an ensemble model working on a complicated problem — how to conduct a daring and elaborate heist of the stolen jewels from the super villain's lair (a typical ensemble model use-case). This is a tricky issue, since the super villain in question has all the standard tools of the trade, like electric fences, shark moats, and laser webs. Obviously, you decide you need a heist team with the usual specialties — a locksmith, a master of disguise, and a gymnast. If you were implementing a simple bagging-type model, you might assign each expert a different point of entry into the villain's lair — the locksmith gets the vault, the gymnast gets the garden, and the master of disguise gets to infiltrate the gala. But in a bagging ensemble, each model works independently on their own data to come up with a solution. After they work on their own task, they report back — and that's about it.

No good heist has ever come off without the all-important earpiece letting each team member know what the others have accomplished. What makes boosting effective as an ensemble model technique is that it allows the individual models to work off each other to come up with the ultimate solution. Often, this is implemented by having subsequent models learn from other models' mistakes. In the heist example, maybe the locksmith got the back door open, but couldn't go any further because they ran into the laser web. Finding this, they call in the gymnast, who navigates the lasers with ease. Boosting creates sequential, specialized models to improve the overall prediction performance.

Boosting models start with a base model (usually just a single base model rather than a group of them). It trains on the data and then makes a note of the dataset samples it misclassified. From there, the ensemble system creates another model that trains, with special attention paid to samples that were misclassified. This process is usually repeated until everything is classified correctly or a certain total number of models is reached. A diagram of a boosting model is shown in Figure 7-3.

Types of boosting

Boosting models can be implemented in several ways, but two popular methods are the AdaBoost algorithm and Gradient Boosting. Both methods focus on the misclassified dataset samples when creating subsequent models.

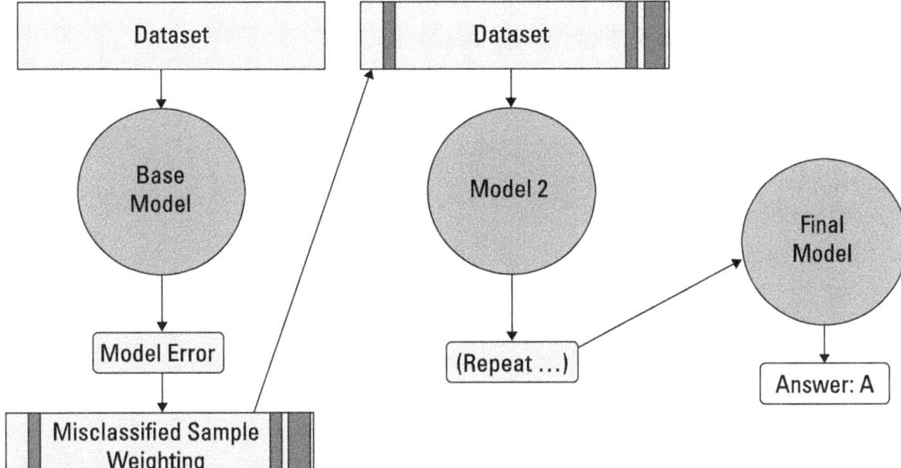

FIGURE 7-3: A boosting model implementing misclassified sample weighting.

The AdaBoost algorithm uses the following method:

1. The ensemble creates an initial model and calculates its error.
2. The initially misclassified examples are assigned higher weights than the correctly classified examples.
3. Another model is created and trained on the data. The higher-weighted samples get more consideration when calculating the overall model error.
4. The process is repeated until a certain accuracy is reached or a certain number of models is created.

Gradient Boosting works similarly, except instead of weighting the misclassified samples differently, it takes the gradient of the loss of the models with respect to a given sample. This gives an idea of how much of the overall loss the specific sample was "responsible" for.

TECHNICAL STUFF

Gradient Boosting uses the concept of gradient descent to appropriately consider misclassified training samples. *Gradient descent* is a popular technique in machine learning models to appropriately assign the "blame" of a given system component to the overall error of the system. Gradient descent is discussed in much more detail in Chapter 9.

Implementing a boosting model in Python

Listing 7-2 displays the code for implementing a Gradient Boosting model in Python. Note that the only difference from Listing 7-1 is that the `GradientBoostingClassifier` model is imported and initialized from the ensemble model rather than the `GradientBoostingClassifier`. The output of the model is shown in Figure 7-4. Note that your own output might vary based on randomness in the training and test set data selection.

LISTING 7-2: Boosting Model in Python with scikit-learn (boosting_model.py)

```
import pandas as pd
from sklearn.model_selection import train_test_split
from sklearn.ensemble import GradientBoostingClassifier

faults = ["Pastry", "Z_Scratch", "K_Scatch", "Stains", "Dirtiness",
  "Bumps", "Other_Faults"]

def read_in_dataset(faults):
    df = pd.read_csv("faults.csv")
    df['fault'] = 0
    #Lets create a categorical variable for each fault
    #In the new "fault" column
    for i in range(0, len(faults)):
        #index list
        true_fault_indexes = df.loc[df[faults[i]] ==
  1].index.tolist()
        df.loc[true_fault_indexes, "fault"] = i+1
        #Create our dataset
    return df

df = read_in_dataset(faults)
#Create the training and test set
drop_features = ["fault"] + faults
features = df.drop(drop_features, axis=1)
outcomes = df["fault"]
training_features, test_features, training_outcomes, test_outcomes =
  train_test_split(features, outcomes, test_size=0.1)

model = GradientBoostingClassifier()

model.fit(training_features, training_outcomes)
test_accuracy_score = model.score(test_features, test_outcomes)
training_accuracy_score = model.score(training_features,
  training_outcomes)
print(f"Training accuracy {training_accuracy_score}")
print(f"Test accuracy {test_accuracy_score}")
```

FIGURE 7-4: Output of the boosting model example.

```
(examples) C:\Users\marze\Documents\Book\Code Files>python boosting_model.py
Training accuracy 0.9684994272623139
Test accuracy 0.8512820512820513
```

Random Forest: Your scikit-learn Powerhouse

When it comes to machine learning models, it would be hard to overstate the popularity of a random forest. Perhaps machine learning engineers need to go camping more often? Whatever the reason, random forests are common implementations of ensemble models and are beloved for their typical performance gain over a standard decision tree. But what's a random forest?

Random forests are ensemble models of decision trees. That's it! Well, okay, there's a little more to it than that, but at its core, a random forest is an ensemble model made of multiple decision trees working together.

There are many ways to implement a random forest classifier, but individual models are usually created with subsets of the dataset samples (similar to a bagging model). In fact, a bagging model and a random forest model could be implemented the same way. However, a random forest model assumes an underlying decision tree model, while a bagging model will let you swap in a base model of your choice. A diagram of a random forest model is shown in Figure 7-5.

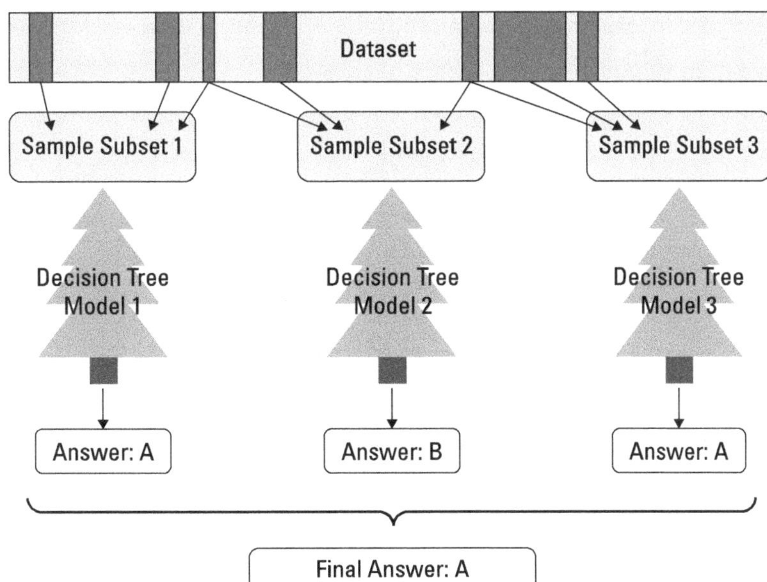

FIGURE 7-5: A random forest model. Note the similarity to the bagging model in Figure 7-1, but with a decision tree as the base.

TIP

Most ensemble models in the scikit-learn library assume a base model of a decision tree classifier. You can usually swap this using the "estimator" parameter.

Implementing a random forest model in Python

Listing 7-3 displays the code for implementing a random forest model in scikit-learn. Note that the only difference between this code and the code in Listings 7-1 and 7-2 is the import and initialization of the `RandomForestClassifier` rather than the `BoostingClassifier` or `GradientBoostingClassifier`. The model output is shown in Figure 7-6. Note that your own output might be different depending on the random selection of your training and test data.

LISTING 7-3: Random Forest Model in Python with scikit-learn

```
import pandas as pd
from sklearn.model_selection import train_test_split
from sklearn.ensemble import RandomForestClassifier

faults = ["Pastry", "Z_Scratch", "K_Scatch", "Stains", "Dirtiness",
  "Bumps", "Other_Faults"]

def read_in_dataset(faults):
    df = pd.read_csv("faults.csv")
    df['fault'] = 0
    #Lets create a categorical variable for each fault
    #In the new "fault" column
    for i in range(0, len(faults)):
        #index list
        true_fault_indexes = df.loc[df[faults[i]] ==
  1].index.tolist()
        df.loc[true_fault_indexes, "fault"] = i+1
        #Create our dataset
    return df

df = read_in_dataset(faults)
#Create the training and test set
drop_features = ["fault"] + faults
features = df.drop(drop_features, axis=1)
outcomes = df["fault"]
```

```
training_features, test_features, training_outcomes, test_outcomes =
  train_test_split(features, outcomes, test_size=0.1)

model = RandomForestClassifier()

model.fit(training_features, training_outcomes)
test_accuracy_score = model.score(test_features, test_outcomes)
training_accuracy_score = model.score(training_features,
  training_outcomes)
print(f"Training accuracy {training_accuracy_score}")
print(f"Test accuracy {test_accuracy_score}")
```

FIGURE 7-6: Output of the random forest model example.

```
(examples) C:\Users\marze\Documents\Book\Code Files>python random_forest_model.py
Training accuracy 1.0
Test accuracy 0.7538461538461538
```

Important random forest parameters

Because random forests assume an underlying decision tree model, they can tweak more parameters directly compared to some other ensemble models. The scikit-learn library implementation includes:

- `criterion`: As with the decision tree (see Chapter 6 for more details), this parameter lets you choose what information theory concept you prefer for your individual tree implementation.
- `max_depth`: This lets you choose how deep you want each tree in the forest to get.
- `min_samples_split` and `min_samples_leaf`: If these are set to a number, there must be at least that number of samples corresponding to splitting at a node or creating a tree leaf node.
- `max_features` and `max_leaf_nodes`: If these are set to a number, they enforce limits on the overall number of features allowed to be considered for a split or the total number of leaf nodes allowed per tree.

TECHNICAL STUFF

In most ensemble models, you can pass in the base estimator model as a model of your choice, so long as it follows the scikit-learn API. You can set most of the parameters noted in the `RandomForestClassifier` class as properties of the underlying estimator for a different ensemble model if you want to make the same customizations.

When 100 Percent Accuracy Is 100 Percent Wrong

Ensemble models are powerful tools that combine the strengths of individual models to create predictions that are often more accurate than a single model by itself. As a consequence, however, ensemble models can have a problem with unchecked growth — that is, an ensemble system may keep adding more and more models to its team until all samples in a dataset are classified correctly, at the expense of learning more robust skills to classify samples in the first place.

If you own a major league baseball team, you want nine players with specialized skills — running, throwing, catching, pitching — to successfully win a game. Let's look at one specific task in baseball: catching a fly ball in the outfield to successfully get a batter out. For this, we use three people with specialized skills: a right-fielder, a center-fielder, and a left-fielder. These people have practiced and honed their skills in running to the correct location in the field, finding the ball, and catching it in their mitt.

Of course, this isn't the only way we could catch fly balls. If we filled the entire outfield so every square inch of it was covered with people, and every person had a baseball mitt glued to the top of their hat, then chances are good that every fly ball would be caught. However, none of the players would have learned anything about playing baseball.

This is a silly example, but one that ensemble models are particularly prone to: creating a model that focuses on very specific examples in order to classify them correctly, rather than learning more generalized skills needed for the classification problem. This is model overfitting 101!

For many AI models, it's a good idea to withhold a portion of your data as a test and/or validation set to make sure your model is learning useful skills, rather than just memorizing training examples. If you have a high-dimensional, complex dataset and you see 100 percent training accuracy after training your model, you might consider this a red flag. In many cases, real-world data is noisy and very difficult to predict with 100 percent accuracy. These results may look attractive, but they are probably hiding the fact that your model decided it was easier to memorize than learn. In any case, treat 100 percent accuracy with extreme suspicion.

TIP

For ensemble models, we highly recommend using a test and/or validation subset of your data to track the general performance of the model with data it's never seen before. Ensemble models are particularly prone to overfitting compared to baseline models.

REMEMBER

Model parameters can be changed inside the scikit-learn library to help control the amount of overfitting. In general, reducing the overall number of model parameters can force models to be more general. For example, limiting the overall number of models in your team can help prevent dataset sample memorization.

It Works Well, But I Have No Idea Why

Adding more models means adding more trainable parameters to your AI system. This often comes with a performance increase, which is great! However, more overall parameters mean more overall things to keep track of when evaluating your model. And if humans are known for anything, it's for their incredible ability to keep track of a lot of different complicated math functions in their head at the same time.

Ensemble models are classic examples of the performance versus explainability trade-off. While more models attacking your problem will hopefully lead to better results, it will probably come at the cost of the problem being solved with less clarity. If you think of AI as a food system, a base model is like a family farm. You can travel to the farm stand, pick up a tomato, and feel pretty confident about the way it was grown. On the other hand, if you are craving a more complicated food like a frozen pizza, you would have to track down multiple suppliers in the chain and trace ingredients to several facilities and locations to understand how the pizza got from the ground into your stomach. Complexity comes at an explainability trade-off. You can print off the nice decision tree flowchart, but it's going to be tricky to visualize a random forest without some serious constraints.

Depending on your problem, you might have more or less tolerance for explainability. If you are implementing an AI program on a high-stakes problem, you might think twice before using a model that isn't completely transparent. If you have a lower-stakes problem or if you are using multiple methods of validation, using an ensemble model might be better suited to your needs.

Ensemble models aren't the only models with unclear behavior. Usually, any model of a certain size (typically a function of the number of trainable parameters) is going to be too hard to understand for the average human. In Part 3 of this book, you'll see that neural networks have similar considerations with size versus explainability.

A model whose behavior cannot be easily explained is called a "black-box" model in industry jargon. In some cybersecurity circles, however, a "black-box" model refers to an AI model whose trainable parameters you don't have access to. A "white-box" model refers to an AI model whose trainable parameters you do have access to, regardless of how easy they are to understand. In general, this book refers to "black-box" models from an explainability standpoint rather than a cybersecurity one.

3 The Neural Network Family

IN THIS PART . . .

Understand the fundamental building blocks of a neural network — neurons, weights, biases, and activation and error functions.

Explore how to train a neural network to get the best possible performance.

Break down the math behind the backpropagation algorithm and discover that it isn't as complicated as it may seem.

Review neural network model and architecture choices, and build a neural network first with Keras and then with PyTorch.

Check out convolutional neural networks and how they relate to image processing and object detection.

Discover how different neural networks can work together to improve AI results.

IN THIS CHAPTER

» **Exploring your brain's neural network architecture**

» **Defining important parts of a neural network model**

» **Using a neural network to make a prediction based on data**

» **Breaking down complications with neural network notation**

Chapter **8**

Meeting Your Brain: Neural Network Architectures

If you're reading this, you already have everything you need to understand the concepts of this chapter — a brain! In fact, you have a pretty impressive brain. You're currently operating a machine that converts milkshakes and salads into a general-purpose object detector, environment manipulator, and multisensory powerhouse. You're doing all this with less energy than it takes to light up a lightbulb. Neat stuff! Try to remember this next time you lock the keys inside your house.

In this chapter, you explore the power of your own brain's fascinating and powerful neural network architecture. You discover the biological reasons your brain is so great and how these transfer to a computational model. You define the fundamental building blocks of a neural network — neurons, weights, biases, and activation and error functions. You see all of these components in action as we break down how the network accepts data and turns it into a useful prediction. The chapter ends with a note on the complexity of neural network notation and how you can avoid getting lost in the numbers.

Examining the Biological Concepts of Neural Networks

Human brains are incredibly powerful and efficient. Your ability to learn and adapt is unsurpassed in the animal kingdom. It was a logical step for computer scientists to seek inspiration for AI from the best natural intelligence — our own minds. This section covers the biological concepts behind neural networks as they relate to your physical brain infrastructure.

Neurons: The basic building blocks

Figure 8-1 shows a picture of a neuron, the basic unit of your neural network, which is the underlying structure of your brain. It kind of looks like a fried egg, if a fried egg grew legs and decided to conduct electricity. The small objects that look like legs or branches are called *dendrites*. The dendrites of a neuron receive connections from other neurons and send out signals to still more neurons via *synapses* at the end of the axon terminals (located on the long tail branch).

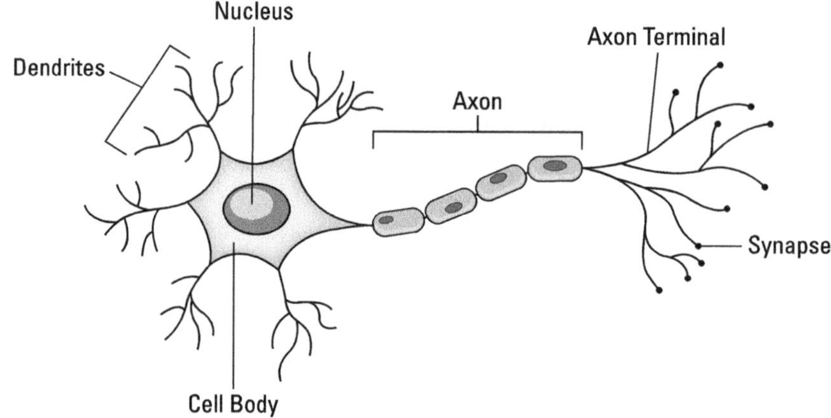

FIGURE 8-1: A diagram of a neuron in a biological neural network.

Your brain neurons are all about sending signals, receiving signals, and transforming signals. The signals are the result of biochemical reactions that produce electricity in your mind. You are truly electric!

When a neuron sends a signal to another neuron, the neuron is considered to be "firing." Neurons have different thresholds to fire — they usually accumulate signals in some pattern before sending their own signal off. At the most basic level, neurons are designed to receive input, transform the input, and send it off again.

Neural network: Sensory architecture

The way neurons form structures creates your neural network. The architecture is extremely important to the system's overall functioning. Your neurons receive sensory input from all areas of your body. They transform this input into information you use to think, take action, and make decisions. Every time you burn your hand on the oven, your neural network is there to interpret (maybe with a little too much enthusiasm) that your body just put itself in danger. Every time you can't decide between ordering takeout or eating inside a restaurant, your neural network is weighing your options.

TECHNICAL STUFF

We often refer to our sensory system as "the five senses" — taste, touch, smell, hearing, and vision. However, your body is receiving sensory input from far more than five senses. You also have a sense of balance, temperature, pain, and skin "stretchiness," to name a few. Incorporating all this information at once is no small task, and the efficiency with which your brain processes the wide variety and resolution of its inputs makes it a biological wonder.

How exactly is your neural network accomplishing this? For starters, with a lot — and we mean, *a lot* — of neurons. It's hard to get an exact count even with modern technology, but some studies hypothesize that you have billions of neurons set apart to handle all this information.

The structure of your neural network is important, too. Neuroscientists currently believe that neurons are organized into functional groups, with different subsections of neurons responsible for different tasks. If you've ever seen the map of the brain's function areas, this is roughly what they believe some of the higher-level organizations of neurons correspond to. The human brain is thought to have specific areas for:

- Vision processing (one of the largest areas of the sensory processing network for seeing humans)
- Facial recognition
- Emotions
- Breathing
- And many more

In fact, while we tend to think of your neural network as your brain, your neural network also exists in your spinal cord. It's even theorized that tasks like walking are computed closer to where they are used — that is, your spine is actually doing the hard thinking to make sure you can put one foot in front of the other.

In different animals, this is more extreme. A lot of thinking for an octopus is done by the neural networks that exist in its arms. In general, for creatures with a neural network, it's thought that more neurons are allocated to tasks more important for that creature. For seeing humans, a fair amount of brain power is allocated to processing visual input, since this is the sense we tend to rely on by default. For dogs, the sense of smell is the clear winner in terms of brain real estate.

Neural connections: Training your brain

In addition to the structure (which neurons are connected to which other neurons), the strength of the connection between connected neurons is impactful for thinking. In fact, one theory says that while the structure of a neural network is set more or less from birth, the strength of the connections between the network changes throughout your life. When you learn a task, you rewire your brain. While much of this connection process happens when you are younger, it continues for life. By reading this book and learning about neural networks, you are changing the strength of pathways in your brain right now. If you are feeling tired today, no wonder — brain surgery is hard work.

Brain plasticity is the concept of changing your neuron connections over time. Your ability to make these changes lets you learn new things and apply new skills. Your brain will automatically make the changes it believes are necessary to incorporate the things you practice more often. Brain plasticity is an enormously powerful tool — if you had a chunk of your brain removed right now, the rest of your brain would rewire itself to compensate. If you lose an ability — for instance, if you were to suddenly lose your vision or hearing — your brain would fill in the newly inactivated areas of your neural network with something else.

Of course, brain cells aren't an unlimited resource, and brain wiring can cause issues. Sometimes there are too many or too few connections in functional areas that can cause differences in cognition. This can be an advantage or a disadvantage, depending on what functions your brain decides to prioritize.

TIP

Using information from the field of neuroscience is helpful to understand the basic processes behind brain development. However, no models are perfect. When concepts from neuroscience translate to the computer science AI domain, remember that there isn't always a 1-to-1 correspondence between our brain model and the computer's brain model.

REMEMBER

Neurons are the basic building blocks of your body's signal transmission and processing. Neurons group together to form functional areas that handle certain tasks. The strength of connections between these groups helps you learn new information or complete tasks more efficiently. Great! Now — how do we model this with a computer?

Exploring the Computer Science Model of Neural Networks

Three principal components of neural networks come from our own biology:

- A neuron
- How neurons are grouped together
- How neurons are connected together

Now these biological model components need to be translated into something that can be represented with a computer.

Figure 8-2 displays a diagram of a computer neuron. It's represented here as a circle. The neuron receives input, just like your biological neurons receive sensory signals from your body. In the computer model, the neuron's input could be anything — a picture, a table, or even output from other neurons. However, by the time the input gets to the neuron, it needs to be represented by numbers.

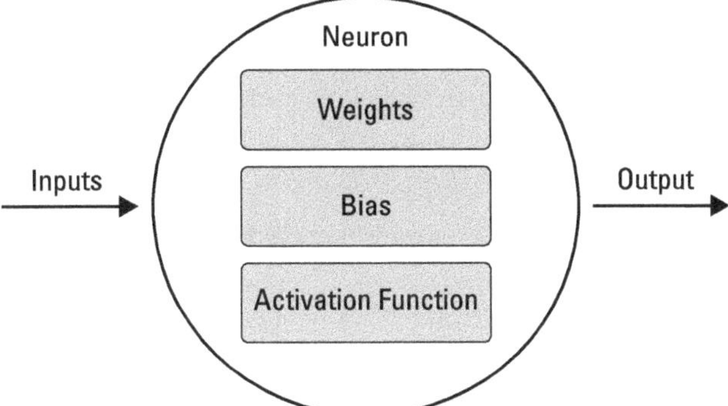

FIGURE 8-2: A diagram of the computational neuron model.

The neuron also has internal parameters. Some of these parameters are unique to each neuron, and some of them can be shared by other neurons. These parameters are:

- **Weights:** Weights are numbers that are associated with the input. Every input the neuron receives has a corresponding weight. If a neuron has two inputs coming in, it also has two weights. If a neuron has 332,965 inputs, it has — you guessed it — 332,965 weights. The weight values are completely unique to this particular neuron.

- **Bias:** The bias term, or bias, is also a number, but each neuron has only one bias. It's not associated with a particular input. The bias value is also completely unique to this particular neuron.
- **Activation function:** The activation function is the main reason a neural network can model nonlinear functions. This component takes in information (we discuss the intricacies in the next section) and turns it into different information by applying a function to it. The choice of activation function is up to the neural network designer. The activation function selection can be shared — and often is — by multiple neurons in the network.

TECHNICAL STUFF

Weights and biases tend to be represented as vectors — lists of numbers where the location in the list is important. Inputs are generally also represented as vectors, where the location of a given input in its vector corresponds to the location of a given weight in its vector. Rather than handle two separate vectors for weights and biases, sometimes the weights and bias are represented as one vector — the weights first, with the bias tacked on at the end. In order to solve the input/weight vector size mismatch, an additional input is created with a value of 1 and tacked on to the end of the input vector. Because the inputs and weights will be multiplied together, using an input with a value of 1 won't affect the bias number. This is generally a more efficient way to structure the neuron's parameters but can sometimes cause confusion when implementing.

The neuron's internal parameters, together with its input, will be transformed by an operation (discussed in the next section) and the activation function to create the neuron's output.

Grouping neurons together

Neurons in a neural network are stacked together to form layers. You can put as many neurons in a neural network layer as you want — just know that the more neurons you use, the more computation time and memory your model will require.

TIP

Neuron is the term we use in this chapter to refer to both a biological neuron and a computational neuron. In the computational world, *node* is also a popular term for a modeled neuron. You may hear it called a *unit* as well.

The number of layers you want in your neural network is up to you. Each layer can have a different number of neurons, or every layer could have the same number. As the architect, you decide how you want your neural network to be structured, hopefully giving it the best chance of solving the task.

Figure 8-3 displays a diagram of a three-layer neural network. The first layer has two neurons, the second layer has three, and the last layer has two.

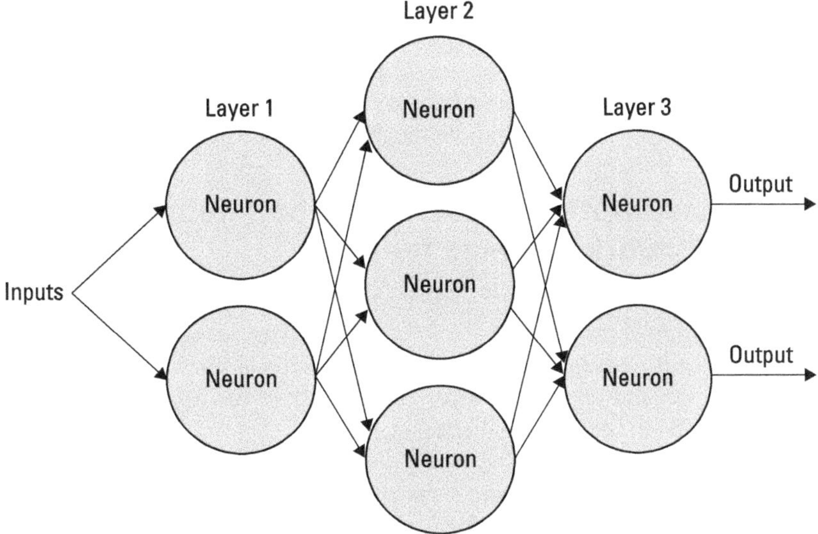

FIGURE 8-3: A diagram of a three-layer neural network.

The number of layers in the network also impacts the computational complexity of your overall model. Interestingly enough, when someone talks about the depth or complexity of a neural network, they are almost always referring to the number of layers, rather than the number of neurons in each layer. Both contribute to how much "math" happens in your neural network, but layers have more to do with the phases of computation, which we discuss more in Chapter 9.

Neural network models are often implemented on specific, optimized hardware that allows certain math steps to happen in parallel. If neurons are in the same layer, the math operations they require can often run on all neurons simultaneously if the computer has enough memory. However, operations that happen layer-to-layer happen in sequence. Because of this, the number of layers tends to be more of a computational constraint than the number of neurons in each layer.

How do you decide how many layers you need, and how many neurons go in each layer? Good thing there is a tried-and-true, fail-safe, foolproof method that works 100 percent of the time!

Just kidding. If you don't know where to begin, it's okay. In fact, you deserve a congratulations — you've officially completed the rite of passage for every neural network designer. The fact of the matter is that designing a neural network structure is much more of an art than a science. For a given problem domain, it's very tricky to know how much computational power and what form it should take to get good results.

Some basic assumptions can serve as a starting point for neural network design to inform our architecture. Note that these assumptions are almost always wrong in some respect — but can be useful as a baseline. From your starting point, you can analyze, refine, and change your network structure to get better results.

Assumption 1: Each layer of a neural network extracts features

When you are trying to solve a problem, you are often turning data into information in certain phases. For example, if you are walking in the woods one day, you might pause to appreciate the view. After a few seconds, you might start moving again and appreciate a very brisk walk in the opposite direction. How might this decision have come about?

For starters, you might have a functional vision system and, therefore, the ability to note contrasts in the environment. Your ability might even be advanced enough to recognize different objects in the environment. One of those objects might be a moose. You also might have learned that a big moose might be a mother and a small moose might be a calf. This information may have complemented other information you have about moose aggressiveness, and finally, you made the realization that you are in a perilous position.

If you create a neural network to determine danger in the forest, one of the assumptions often used is that a neural network is learning different features in different layers. For this example, suppose that the input to the network is just an image of the environment. Layer 1 might be responsible for figuring out lines in the image — horizontal, vertical, and diagonal. Layer 2, then, is responsible for shapes like squares, rectangles, circles, and diamonds. Layer 3 puts shapes together with contrasts and starts separating the foreground from the background. Layer 4 is an object detector, able to tell how many separate things are in the scene. Layer 5 is the object classifier, which understands which things are trees, which things are trails, and which things are moose. Layer 6 has learned that moose are not the safest animal to encounter in close quarters. Finally, layer 7 suggests you beat feet on the back trail before the mother moose sees you. Each layer is putting together different information ("features") from the input and the previous layers in a progressive manner to reach the final recommendation (Run!).

Layers in the neural network extract different features needed for the ultimate decision — though in reality, the actual features extracted are rarely so neat or straightforward as described in the example. Since the layers are synthesizing information to create new insights, you can assign the number of neurons to a layer that you think adequately covers the features it needs to extract.

Assumption 2: More neurons in the beginning layers are more useful than in later layers

Sticking with the forest example, note that there are probably more horizontal lines in a given image than moose. It is often assumed that there are more "lower-level features" the network needs to learn first to understand the input correctly. Lower-level features in our example would be lines, shapes, and contrast. The higher-level features are more complex bits of information, but perhaps more limited in scope — how to tell a moose from a tree, and which of these things is dangerous to our health.

We often put more neurons in the early layers of a neural network, assuming that there is some significant legwork the network must do in comprehending basic information before it gets to the decision-worthy stuff. This assumption is not always true, but it has proven useful in transfer learning, which we cover in Chapter 14.

Assumption 3: More neurons and layers give higher learning capacity

With our layer feature hierarchy, you can assume that the more layers the network has (the deeper it is, remember), the more the network is capable of learning. In theory, the network picks out more advanced patterns at every layer. For a very complex task, you probably need more layers. If a network is not solving a problem correctly, you may want to add more layers or more neurons.

This can cause other issues regarding overfitting. If you give a model too much capacity to learn, it may have the ability to simply memorize training examples rather than extract useful features in the first place. This particular problem is a headache for machine learning engineers everywhere.

TIP

When designing neural networks, machine learning engineers will often start with more neurons and layers than they think they need and prune the network until they get to an acceptable performance and complexity trade-off for their application. However, it's important to keep the computational constraints of your own application in mind when designing the neural network. If you need to train it on a laptop from 2003, you might want to keep the architecture simple.

Connecting your neural network

The final component of the computer-brain analogy has to do with neural network connections. While actual connection schemes can vary based on the type of neural network you're implementing, for the most basic, vanilla, standard neural network (also called a feed-forward neural network, a multi-layer perceptron, an artificial neural network, and about ten other names), it is assumed every individual neuron in a layer is connected to every neuron in the layer before it and every neuron in the layer after it.

A diagram of the neural network connections is shown in Figure 8-4. The first layer is connected to the input of the network. The first neuron is connected to both inputs, and the second neuron is connected to both inputs. The connections are in the form of the weights: The first neuron has two weights, one for each input, and the second neuron has two weights, one for each input. The weights have different values between the neurons, but every neuron in layer 1 has exactly two weights, to connect to exactly two inputs.

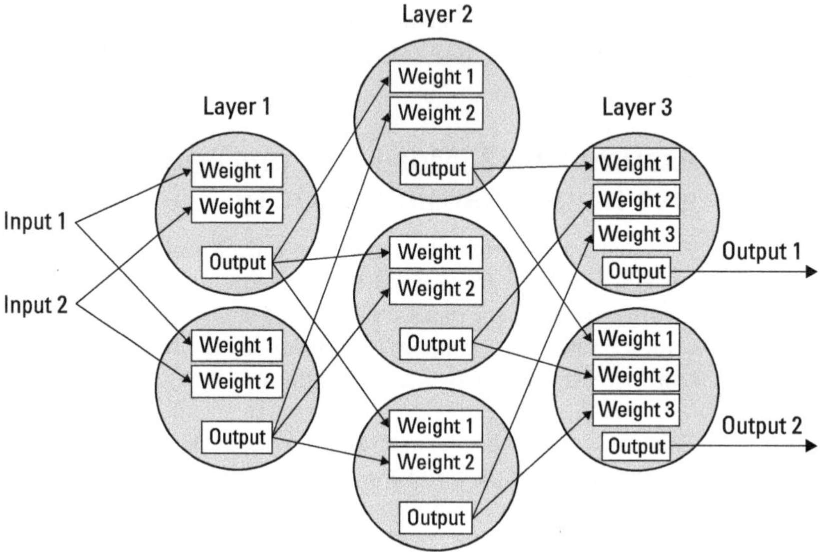

FIGURE 8-4: A connection diagram of a three-layer neural network.

Each neuron will transform the data it has been given into exactly one output value per neuron. This will become the input for the next layer. The next layer (layer 2) has three neurons in it. Each of the three neurons will have exactly two weights to connect to each of the two neurons in layer 1. Layer 2 will transform the data and have exactly one output per neuron. Layer 3 has two neurons. Each of the two neurons has exactly three weights to connect to each of the three neurons in layer 2. Layer 3 is the output layer, so each of the two neurons will create exactly one output, which will be the overall output (two different values) of the entire network.

REMEMBER

Neurons share the same number of weights as every other neuron in the same layer. However, the weights will not have the same values. So, every neuron in layer 2 has two weights. However, the first neuron might have weight values of 5 and 7, while the second neuron has weight values of 26 and 11.

We generally think of the connections in terms of the weights, but it's important to note that the bias and activation function are also important in transforming the data. These will affect the upstream learning, which is important to the backpropagation algorithm covered in Chapter 9.

Transforming data in the feed-forward phase

We've got the parts of a neural network down — the neurons, how they are grouped into layers, and how they are connected to each other — but how, specifically, do you get from an input to a decision?

Well, as usual, with an example! We're going to create a neural network that recommends whether to swim outside in a lake this morning. We are going to use four different inputs:

- Air temperature
- Water temperature
- Wind direction
- Wind speed

We'll design a neural network with three layers. The first layer will have three neurons, the second layer will have two neurons, and the final layer will have only one.

Figure 8-5 displays a diagram of this neural network. We are going to assume that each layer is responsible for a different set of features. The sheer amount of numbers you need to keep track of in a neural network — layer index, neuron index, weight value, and so on — can make the math in the feed-forward phase a bit tricky to follow. To help with this, we will refer to the layers by the feature we assume they extract. Layer 1 is the "comfort level" layer. Layer 2 is going to figure out "swimmer danger" levels. The final "decision" layer will be responsible for telling us whether or not we should swim.

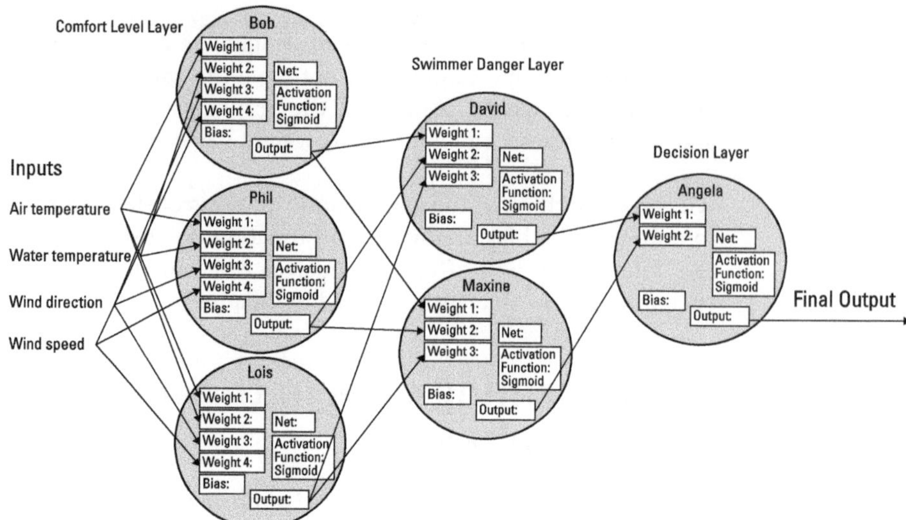

FIGURE 8-5: A diagram of a three-layer neural network for deciding whether or not to swim in a lake.

We'll also name the neurons instead of indexing them. The comfort layer will be staffed by the Bob, Phil, and Lois neurons. The danger level will be composed of David and Maxine. Angela will make the final decision for the network.

The feed-forward phase begins with the input. The transformation process is simple: Every input is multiplied by every weight in each neuron, added together within the neuron along with the bias term, and fed through the activation function to create the neuron's output. Equation 8-1 (the net equation) details the process of tying together the weights, input, and bias. It's explained here mathematically, but we are going to restate it in more approachable terms using the neuron names in the diagram.

Equation 8-1: Creating the neuron's net

$$net = b + \sum_{n=1}^{i}(w_n i_n)$$

Where:

b is the bias term of the neuron

There are i total inputs

w_n is a given weight of a neuron

i_n is the corresponding input

Equation 8-2 lists the sigmoid activation function we are choosing to use in this example. Sigmoid is a handy function to use because it always gives an output between 0 and 1. Equation 8-3 shows how it works on the neuron's net to create the neuron's output.

Equation 8-2: Sigmoid activation function

$$f(x) = \frac{1}{1+e^{-x}}$$

Where:

e is a constant, Euler's number

x is the input to the function

Equation 8-3: Creating the neuron's output

$$output = \frac{1}{1+e^{-net}}$$

Where:

output is the neuron's final output

net is the net of the neuron

Explained more simply, Bob, Phil, and Lois all have four weights to connect to four of the inputs. Bob takes each of his four weights and multiplies them by the corresponding input. Bob's first weight is multiplied by the air temperature, his second weight by the water temperature, his third weight by the wind direction, and his fourth weight by the wind speed. These are added together, along with the bias term. This sum (often called the "net," as in Equation 8-1) is then fed to an activation function (Equation 8-2). The output of the activation function (Equation 8-3) is Bob's total output.

Phil and Louis do the same with their own unique weights, acting on exactly the same input. At the end of layer 1's computational phase, Bob, Phil, and Lois each have an output.

In the next layer, David and Maxine both receive information from Bob, Phil, and Lois. David's first weight is multiplied by Bob's output, his second weight by Phil's output, and his third weight by Lois's output. These are added together, along with David's bias term, and fed through the activation function to create David's output. Maxine received the same information from Bob, Phil, and Lois, but uses her unique weight values and bias terms to create her own output.

Angela receives both David and Maxine's information. Her first weight is multiplied by David's output, and her second weight by Maxine's output. These are added together and fed through the activation function to create Angela's output — which is also the output of the network.

Angela's output may be right, or it may be wrong. We'll have to use an error function to determine how far off base we were. We'll go into this more in Chapter 9. But the basic feed-forward phase is essentially one big game of telephone where each neuron learns specific information and passes it on to the next until it's time to make a final choice.

Figure 8-6 illustrates a worked example of the feed-forward phase.

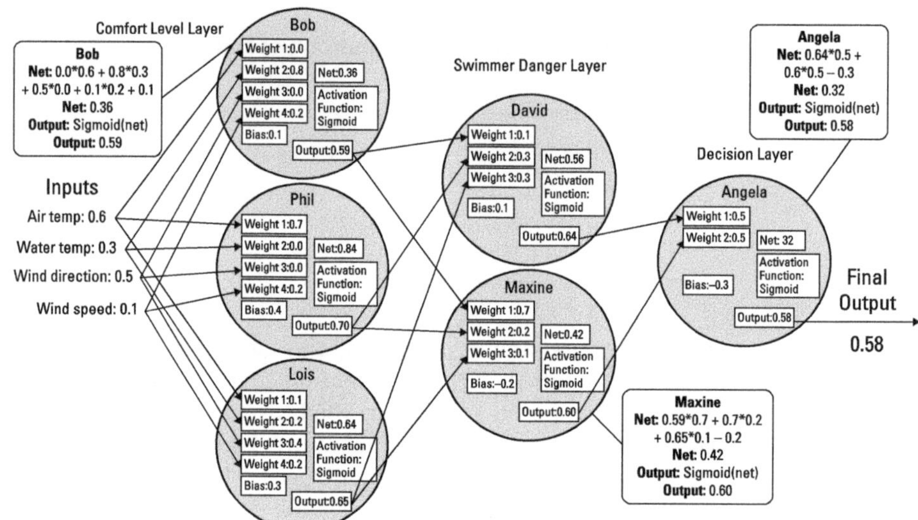

FIGURE 8-6: A worked example of the neural network feed-forward phase, from input to output.

We hope each neuron picks out a specific feature of relevance to the network's decision. In the comfort layer, Bob might be responsible for looking at the water temperature and wind speed to determine the water comfort level. Phil might be trained to look at the air temperature and wind speed to determine the air comfort level. Lois might care about all inputs to determine the shoreline comfort level. In the danger layer, David might be responsible for determining if the three comfort levels pose a storm danger. Maxine, on the other hand, looks at the three comfort levels to determine swimmer hypothermia danger. Angela might look at the storm and hypothermia danger levels and only recommend a swim if they are both low.

A NOTE ON NOTATION

We can describe the basic feed-forward phase of a neural network without getting too far into the weeds on notation. However, most online resources and worked examples you'll encounter in the wild will be more rigorous when it comes to using standard notation. There are a few different ways to annotate parts of the neural network, but usually, the following information is provided:

- A neuron has an associated layer number and an associated index number.
- A weight has an associated layer number, neuron number, and index number.
- A raw input has an associated index number.
- Neurons have weights associated with the inputs or previous layers. The index of the weight of a neuron should correspond to the previous input weight. So, weight index 5 should correspond to input 5 on every neuron in that layer.
- Outputs of a layer become inputs of the next layer. Don't be confused when the information multiplied by weights is referred to as an input, even if it's the output of a previous layer.
- Neural networks use labeled data (ground truth) to evaluate their predictions. If the label is a vector of information (which is fairly common), the index of a given label value should correspond with the index of the output node. Output node index 5 should correspond with ground truth index 5.

Notation, more often than not, is the most difficult thing to comprehend when learning about neural networks. Don't get bogged down in the numbers, subscripts, or superscripts — this book will focus more on the fundamental concepts than the mathematical formalities behind implementing them. If it's frustrating at first, don't give up! Neural networks often take a couple of passes through the information before completely grasping.

IN THIS CHAPTER

» Selecting error and activation functions

» Exploring error spaces with the gradient descent algorithm

» Breaking down the backpropagation algorithm

» Updating neural network parameters while learning

Chapter 9
The Not-So-Scary Math That Powers Neural Networks

Under the hood, neural networks are a lot of math. At every stage, you're transforming data into outputs, outputs into error, and error into model parameter changes. The individual calculations to do all of this processing aren't very complex, but repeating these over many neurons can be a little hard to comprehend. Getting more comfortable with the equations that power these models helps you understand why these techniques are so effective.

In this chapter, you explore how to train a neural network to get the best possible performance. You first break down different error and activation function choices and discover how they affect the network's performance. You learn what an error space is and how to walk around it efficiently with the gradient descent algorithm. You break down the backpropagation algorithm — the boogeyman of beginning neural network designers — into its essential components and discover that the math behind it isn't as complicated as it seems. Finally, you update the neural network parameters to make a better, brighter model.

Choosing the Right Activation and Error Functions

Designing neural networks involves many design choices, and two of the important ones are selecting an appropriate activation function (at the neuron level) and an appropriate error function (at the network level).

Activation functions

In Chapter 8, the feed-forward neural network example used the sigmoid activation function. This function has the handy property of always outputting a number between 0 and 1. However, other activation functions exist, including:

- Hyperbolic tangent (tanh)
- Rectified linear unit (ReLU)
- Leaky rectified linear unit (leaky ReLU)
- Softmax

TIP

Many, many activation functions exist for neural network designers — this is only a sample of some popular ones. Most neural network libraries in Python will let you design and implement a custom activation function if that suits your problem better.

Hyperbolic tangent (tanh)

The tanh function (Equation 9-1) is similar to the sigmoid function, but keeps outputs between -1 and 1. Sigmoid and tanh are relatively simple to implement in a neural network, and have the handy property of being differentiable. This will be important when you implement backpropagation later in the chapter. However, sigmoid and tanh both saturate quickly — which means a lot of the values plugged into the function will result in an output very close to the bounds (-1, 1, or 0). There are fewer possible values that will give a meaningful output that your network can use.

Equation 9-1: The tanh function

$$f(x) = \frac{(e^{2x} - 1)}{(e^{2x} + 1)}$$

This gives the neural network a little less theoretical learning capacity, since values that could be very different (10 and 1,000, for instance) will both output a very similar value (1). Depending on the application, this might be a problem. If you have a 10 micrometer measurement in one input sample and a 1,000 micrometer measurement in another, each with a tolerance of 2 millimeters, this might not be a big deal. However, if you have an input sample measuring 10 goats and another measuring 1,000 goats, the difference might possibly be more significant (and smellier).

Rectified linear unit (ReLU)

On the other hand, the ReLU function (Equation 9-2) returns the same input if the value is positive, and 0 otherwise. This function is unbounded for positive numbers, which helps with saturation. If the net input is negative, the ReLU activation essentially zeroes out the entire contribution of the neuron.

Equation 9-2: The ReLU function

$$f(x) = \begin{Bmatrix} x \ if \ x > 0 \\ 0 \ if \ x \leq 0 \end{Bmatrix}$$

TIP

ReLU is no longer differentiable since it is piecewise, but the derivative is easily broken into two parts for the backpropagation algorithm.

Leaky rectified linear unit (leaky ReLU)

Leaky ReLU (Equation 9-3) is similar to ReLU, but allows some small-value negative numbers. Both ReLU and leaky ReLU are popular choices for neural network activation functions you'll come across in the wild.

Equation 9-3: The leaky ReLU function

$$f(x) = \begin{Bmatrix} x \ if \ x > 0 \\ 0.01 * x \ if \ x \leq 0 \end{Bmatrix}$$

Note that the constant in front of x in the negative case can be changed to another small number.

Softmax

The last activation function is softmax. Softmax (Equation 9-4) is almost always used exclusively in the last (output) layer of a neural network for a classification problem. Softmax takes any number of inputs and turns them into a probability between 0 and 1. If you have the same number of output neurons as classes in a classification problem, softmax makes them output the percent probability of the sample being an instance of the class associated with the neuron. This is a very handy way for the network to measure its confidence in identifying a given output. It also allows you to pick the highest probability neuron overall to assign to a class identity.

Equation 9-4: The softmax function

$$f(x)_i = \frac{e^{x_i}}{\sum_k e^{x_k}}$$

Where *i* is a given output and there are *k* total outputs.

Error functions

When you submit a strawberry pie for the county fair, you might get a blue ribbon (first place), a red ribbon (second place), a white ribbon (third place), or nothing (you ate the pie on the way to the entry counter. Understandable. It was, after all, strawberry). This is a form of feedback. A blue ribbon suggests that if your submission wasn't perfect, it was pretty close. A white ribbon tells you that there is room for improvement (maybe you shouldn't put your sugar and salt in such similar containers). And no ribbon suggests you might want to start eating dinner a little earlier.

The county fair ribbon system gives you some pointers for how to get better, although they might not be very detailed. That third-place ribbon could have been due to the sugar/salt mishap, or you might have burned the crust. You know something needs to change, but you may not know where to start.

On the other hand, if you are writing an article for a newspaper, you probably have a copy editor giving you a lot of detailed feedback before the words are printed. They could tell you, for instance, that you misspelled the word "squirrel" 27 times in one paragraph, that the photo attached to the article is upside-down, and that you aren't allowed to count an interview with a poodle as a credible source. You might have a lot to change, but you certainly know what parts are causing the problem.

When training a neural network, it is important to give the neural network the ability to understand where it missed the mark. But it's a lot more helpful to the network to explain how close or far away it was from the mark in the first place. Choosing the right error function helps the neural network quantify exactly how much it went wrong.

TECHNICAL STUFF

For a classification problem, the neural network's performance could also be monitored by accuracy. However, accuracy is a binary outcome — a training instance is either a cat or it isn't. Using pure accuracy misses some nuance that would be helpful in guiding the training process. If the sample was actually a raccoon, the network isn't perfect, but probably only needs a small parameter change. If the training sample was actually a snowblower, you have a bigger issue.

Like activation functions, your choice of error function will affect how the neural network performs. Error functions can vary a lot by the problem type. Some popular examples include:

- Mean squared error (MSE)
- Mean average error (MAE)
- Root mean squared error (RMSE)
- Cross-entropy loss

Mean squared error (MSE)

The MSE function (Equation 9-5) takes the differences between the output neuron values and the labeled training examples (the targets, or the ground-truth) and squares them. It then takes the average value of these squared differences across the number of outputs/targets. MSE penalizes large errors more than small ones as a consequence of the exponential. This can be a handy property if you need to be in the ballpark area around a particular value.

Equation 9-5: The MSE function

$$f(x) = \frac{1}{n}\sum_{i=1}^{n}(Prediction_i - Target_i)^2$$

Where n is the number of predictions/targets.

Mean average error (MAE) and root mean squared error (RMSE)

The MAE function (Equation 9-6) and the RMSE function (Equation 9-7) usually get closer to the "real" error value, but the MAE takes a direct average error (usually the absolute value of the differences between outputs and targets), and the RMSE takes the square root of the squared errors (which is sometimes easier to work with on computers than the absolute value function). These might be better to implement if you need the neural network to be more precisely on target — although sometimes they will bounce the error around more sporadically.

Equation 9-6: The MAE function

$$f(x)=\frac{1}{n}\sum_{i=1}^{n}|Prediction_i - Target_i|$$

Where *n* is the number of predictions/targets.

Equation 9-7: The RMSE function

$$f(x)=\sqrt{\frac{\sum_{i=1}^{n}(Prediction - Target_i)^2}{n}}$$

Where *n* is the number of predictions/targets.

Cross-entropy loss

The cross-entropy loss function (Equation 9-8) is useful when comparing distributions of outputs. The function, which comes from information theory, is a popular choice for classification problems.

Equation 9-8: The cross-entropy loss function

$$f(x)=-\sum_{i=1}^{n}Target_i \log(Prediction_i)$$

Where *n* is the number of predictions/targets.

REMEMBER

Whatever error function you choose, it will allow you to measure the deviance of the neural network from the correct answer. This will help the gradient descent algorithm guide the neural network in the right direction to improve its performance.

DIFFERENT PROBLEMS, DIFFERENT FUNCTIONS

Understanding roughly the distribution of your outputs might help you pick the correct error function. But don't be surprised if your first choice isn't the perfect choice. A lot of neural network design is trying something, figuring out where you went wrong, and trying something else.

Creating Meaningful Change with Gradient Descent

You have a neural network answer. You have the target ground-truth answer. You compare them to the error function and you find that your neural network is . . . dead wrong.

The point of training the neural network is to make it solve the problem correctly. How do you make it change for the better?

It's important to understand that a lot of factors contribute to the overall error of the neural network. The data in the input sample might have been corrupted. The structure of the neural network might be wrong. The weight or bias value might be off.

All of these might need to be changed to get a perfect neural network. However, during the training phase, not all of these can be modified. An inherent property of a model that is updated during training is called a *parameter*. For a neural network, training parameters are weights and biases. An inherent property of a model that is not adjusted during training is a *hyperparameter*. For a neural network, this includes other properties like the number of neurons, the number of layers, and the choice of activation and error functions.

TIP

Often, *parameter* is used as the more general term when referring to a property of a neural network. Sometimes, when someone is referring to a parameter, they are referring to both the trainable parameters and hyperparameters together. This is the bane of Marz's students' existence when it comes to review questions. She has to make her course material *very* clear as to which type of parameter a problem is referring to. Just know that the trainable parameters are those that are changed during the training phase. Straightforward enough!

Gradient descent is an algorithm used to train a neural network in order to improve (minimize) its overall error. It will only adjust the trainable parameters of the neural network — the weight and bias terms used in the feed-forward phase (see Chapter 8 for a feed-forward implementation). Gradient descent's goal is to determine how much "blame" an individual parameter is responsible for in the overall error. To do this, the algorithm needs to understand the error surface.

Error surfaces

In a perfect world, your error would be zero. Your neural network would output the correct answer every time, no issues. In a realistic world, you shoot for the minimum possible error.

When the neural network's parameters take on specific values (often somewhat random when the network first begins training), they create a specific error value. When you change the parameters, you get another error value (usually somewhat different). If you repeat the process several times, you might be able to start visualizing the error surface.

If you have a model with two parameters — we'll call them w1 and w2 (for a very, very simple neural network, perhaps) — you could plot the error of the model at different values of w1 and w2. Figure 9-1 displays this graph.

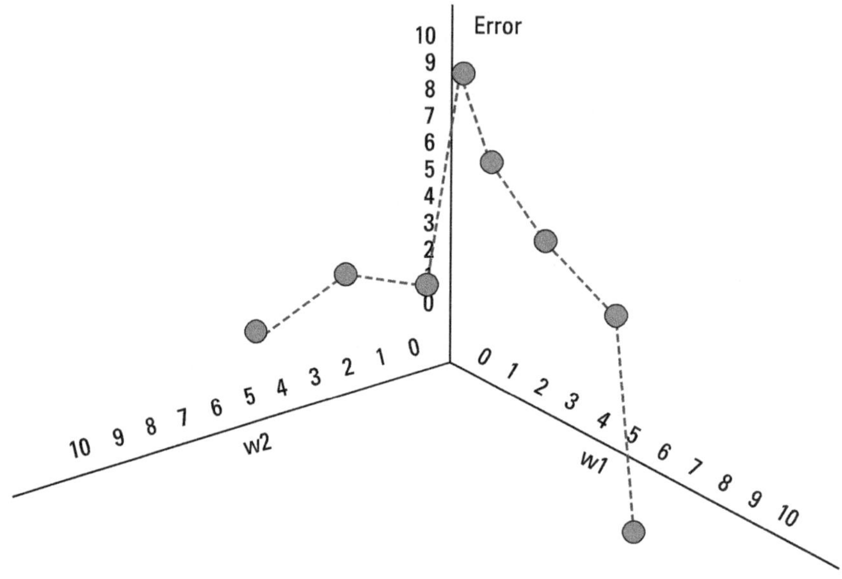

FIGURE 9-1: The error surface of a model with respect to its parameters, w1 and w2.

As you look at the error surface in Figure 9-1, notice that the lowest error occurred approximately when parameter w1 had the value 6.5 and parameter w2 had the value 1. For this set of experiments, you would want to use the model with these w1 and w2 values since they performed the best.

In most real-world problems, it would be impossible to explore all values of all parameters in trial-and-error combinations to find the best model. How do you make a smart search of parameter values to try to approximate a good model, even if you can't find the best one?

The answer lies in the *error surface*. As you can see in Figure 9-1, different values of w1 and w2 create an error curve — that is, the overall shape of the model error changes at different parameter values.

The example in Figure 9-1 uses a 3D surface (two input dimensions and one output dimension). However, the error surface can be extended for an arbitrary number of dimensions — and usually is, as most models have more than two parameters. Things get tough to visualize for humans outside of three dimensions!

Gradient descent uses some clever mathematics to try to move the model toward a lower point on the error surface as different parameter values are experimented with. The algorithm figures out the rate of change of a given parameter to the overall model error. This tells how much an individual parameter contributed to the overall error compared to the other parameters. This is the "blame" of the parameter — essentially, finding the rate of change lets gradient descent identify which parameter is moving the error most dramatically. When you want to move downhill on the error surface, toward the lowest possible error, this information lets you find the steepest path to get there.

If you are an explorer tasked with finding the lowest point in a mountainous valley, you understand that wandering around in a flat meadow is unlikely to get you very far in your goal. Instead, you'll pick a spot and start heading downhill. Gradient descent works similarly, trying to find the downhill slopes that will give the lowest error and therefore the best model.

Gradient descent makes a lot of intuitive sense when training a model by adjusting its parameters. But how do you figure out the rate of change in the first place?

Typically, this is solved by taking a partial derivative of the model error with respect to the individual parameter. A *derivative* is a rate of change (you may remember from calculus class). The mechanics of making this calculation are discussed in more detail in the backpropagation section of this chapter.

Local and global minimums

If you have done any mountaineering (or if you read about mountaineering instead of getting wet and cold), you might be familiar with the concept of a false summit. Initially, you identify a peak as the tallest in the area and begin to climb. When you reach the top, however, you realize that your view was blocked, and there was a much taller peak hiding behind it. Bad news for your crampons.

In gradient descent, the algorithm has similar issues with false minimums — lower areas in the error surfaces that aren't the absolute lowest. The more common name for these spots is "local minimums," while the goal is to find the overall lowest possible place — the "global minimum."

Figure 9-2 illustrates a 2D display of local minimums versus the global minimum. It can be easy for a model to be stuck in a local minimum, because on either side of the point, the steepest areas direct you back downhill. A lot of discussion in neural network training involves "escaping" a local minimum to get the model to explore a better slope. The learning rate, covered a little later in the chapter, is an important tool to help navigate local minimums.

Other AI techniques have similar issues with global versus local minimums. Escape strategies vary. In the AI class Marz teaches, she has students try to configure the optimal chocolate factory. The difference between the local and global minimum is only a few brands of candy.

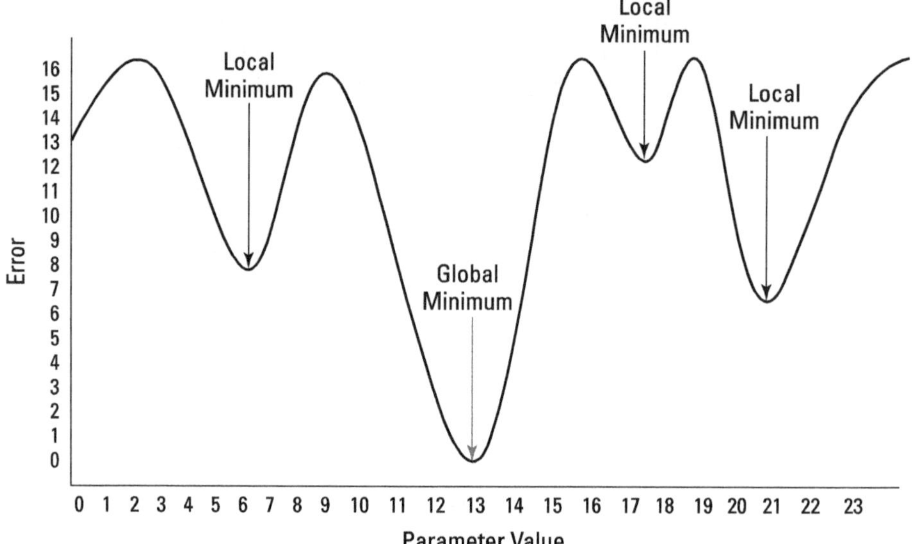

FIGURE 9-2: Local and global minimums in an error surface.

Types of gradient descent

You might run across three types of gradient descent in the wild. These are:

- Batch gradient descent
- Stochastic gradient descent
- Mini-batch gradient descent

Batch gradient descent averages the error across all training examples. The model sees every single training instance, calculates the error, and then updates the parameters from the average error after all data has passed through. While this results in fewer parameter update steps, averaging error across an entire dataset is often not a very efficient way of adjusting the parameters.

Stochastic gradient descent calculates the error of each individual sample in a dataset and updates the parameters of the model, then and there. This is a very detailed error process, but it requires many more calculations in the parameter updates and often results in very sporadic movement of the parameter values. If you implement this, you'll see your error value zig-zag around like crazy!

Mini-batch gradient descent is often used as a happy medium. A certain mini-batch size is designated, and that number of samples is run through the network. The average error is calculated across the mini-batch, and the parameters are updated after the mini-batch is complete.

In practice, mini-batch gradient descent is probably the most common implementation of gradient descent in a neural network. It allows a little more error smoothness in the update step, while also giving the network enough information to adjust itself in a useful way.

TIP

Since the feed-forward loop operation can be parallelized across the samples in a mini-batch, the mini-batch size is often chosen based on the amount of memory available in a computer. Mini-batch sizes, as a consequence, are often selected as powers of 2. 32, 64, and 128 samples are all popular mini-batch sizes.

Demystifying Backpropagation

Gradient descent is the fundamental training algorithm for neural networks. The networks start with weight and bias parameters, and then the network looks at the rate of change of these parameters with regard to the overall model error to adjust them and make the model better.

In theory, this is simple. In practice, taking the derivative is not always straightforward. Backpropagation is the main villain in many an early neural network designer's origin story. A lot of this has to do with our old friend and complicated friend, *notation*. Neural networks function better when their operations run in parallel. Parameters are often reformatted as matrices, and keeping track of the individual weight index, neuron index, and layer index gets messy quickly. For this section, we present the fundamental steps of taking the derivative first, and afterward break it up into a more mathematical example.

Note: We will be talking mostly about the parameters relating to a neural network's weights. Remember, the bias of a neural network can also be modeled as a weight with an input value that is always 1. For simplicity, we'll discuss the calculation with just the weight values.

A weight's magical journey to error

The first step in taking the derivative of the error with respect to a given weight is to understand how a weight value gets turned into an error in the first place. From the feed-forward step, you know that this involves three distinct phases:

- The weight is multiplied by an input and added to the other weight combinations to create the **net** input of the neuron.
- The net is sent through an activation function to become an **output**.
- The output of the overall network is sent through an error function to become the **error**.

In phase 1, a simple weighted-sum process turns a given weight into a net input. In phase 2, that net becomes an output by the activation function process. Finally, in phase 3, an error function process turns the output of the overall network into the error term.

Three phases. Three processes. Now, how do you get the derivative of just the error with respect to the weight?

The chain rule from calculus comes in clutch here: You find the derivative of each of the distinct processes and multiply them together.

The Three Musketeers of backpropagation

The chain rule leaves us with three calculations:

- The derivative of the error function (with respect to the output). We'll call this the **error** phase.
- The derivative of the output (with respect to the net input). We'll call this the **activation** phase.
- The derivative of the net input (with respect to the weight). We'll call this the **information** phase.

When these values are multiplied together, you end up with the derivative of the error with respect to the weight. Great!

REMEMBER

Backpropagation implementation is always going to come back to these three components — an error phase derivative, an activation phase derivative, and an information phase derivative. If you get stuck, it might be helpful to remember what phase you're currently trying to calculate.

Calculating the derivative in the activation phase is simple, as it's the derivative of the activation function. Calculating the derivative of the information phase is also simple, as this will end up being just the derivative of the weighted sum, which is the input value. Calculating the derivative of the error phase is simple — but only for output neurons (because it's the derivative of the error function). For neurons in the hidden layers, this is a more difficult calculation, because you don't have a ground truth value to compare the intermediate neurons with. We'll end up having to do some serious thinking about how each neuron contributes to the overall output neurons. This is a major task of backpropagation.

TECHNICAL STUFF

At this point, you can see the advantage of having an activation function that is differentiable. The activation phase of backpropagation will end up directly taking the derivative of the activation function.

A mathematical backpropagation example

Figure 9-3 illustrates an example of a simple neural network with two inputs, two hidden-layer neurons, and two output-layer neurons. Because a lot of backpropagation involves understanding proper indexes, we'll describe our indexing scheme up front:

- The index *i* will refer to the individual weight number in a given neuron.
- The index *j* will refer to the individual neuron in a given layer.
- The index *l* will refer to the individual layer in the network.

We'll also label the components of the network:

- *w* will refer to a weight.
- *o* will refer to a neuron's output.
- *t* will refer to the ground truth label matching an output.
- *x* will refer to a neuron's input.
- *err* will refer to the overall error.
- *n* will refer to a neuron's net.

TIP

The output (*o*) of one layer will be the same as the input (*x*) of the next layer in sequence.

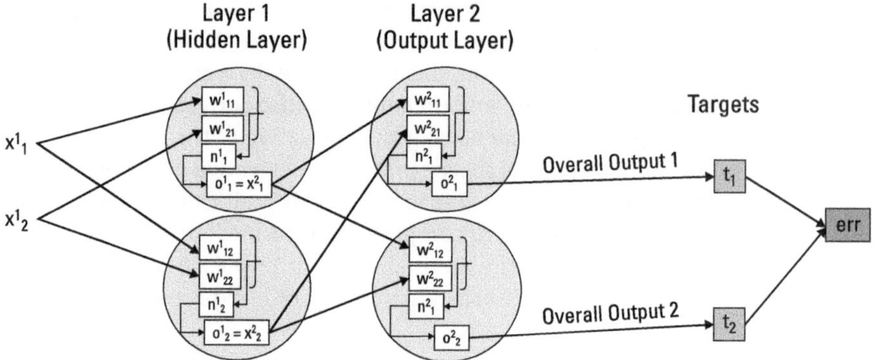

FIGURE 9-3: A simple neural network we'll use for our backpropagation example.

w^l_{ij} = weight i in neuron j in layer l
o^l_j = output in neuron j in layer l
x^l_i = input to all weights i in layer l

We'll also decide to use the sigmoid activation function (Equation 9-9) and the L2 norm loss (Equation 9-10). The L2 norm loss is actually the same as the MSE function in Equation 9-5, except that it adds a fraction constant that makes the derivative of the function cleaner. This sums the squared difference between a given output neuron o_j and a ground truth label t_j, and then divides by 2.

Equation 9-9: Sigmoid activation function

$$o = \frac{1}{1+e^{-n}}$$

Equation 9-10: L2 norm loss

$$err = \frac{1}{2}\sum_j (o_j - t_j)^2$$

Now it's time to actually do this calculation: Get the derivative of a given weight, w^l_{ij} (weight *i* in neuron *j* in layer *l*), with respect to the overall network error. We'll start by assuming we're dealing with the output layer.

Error phase

In the error phase for the output layer, you need to take the derivative of the error function with respect to the output. That ends up being the derivative of the error function, as shown in Equation 9-11.

Equation 9-11: The derivative of the overall error with respect to an output neuron (error phase)

$$d'error = o_j - t_j$$

This becomes very simple — subtract the relevant output neuron value (the j index of the output neuron will match the j index of the weight you are looking at) with the relevant ground truth label.

Activation phase

In the activation phase for the output layer, you need to take the derivative of the output with respect to the net. This is the derivative of the activation function, which in our case is the sigmoid function. The derivative of the sigmoid function is very handy, as it ends up being the value of the sigmoid function multiplied by 1 minus the value of the sigmoid function, as shown in Equation 9-12.

Equation 9-12: The derivative of sigmoid activation function (activation phase)

$$d'sigmoid = \frac{1}{1+e^{-n}}\left(1-\left(\frac{1}{1+e^{-n}}\right)\right)$$

But you already know the value of the sigmoid function for a given net input — it's the output (o)! Equation 9-13 lets you simplify this derivative.

Equation 9-13: A simplified derivative of the sigmoid activation function (activation phase)

$$d'sigmoid = o_j(1-o_j)$$

So, you simply take the output of the current layer neuron with the j index that matches the given weight's j index.

Neural network backpropagation example writers sure love sigmoid, with its incredibly clean derivative. Thank you, sigmoid!

Information phase

In the information phase, you need to take the derivative of the net with respect to a given weight. This is the easiest one of all. The net is created by multiplying our given weight by a given input. So, the derivative will be the matching input value, shown in Equation 9-14.

Equation 9-14: The derivative of the net with respect to a given weight

$$d'net = x_i$$

The i index of the input will match the i index of the given weight.

Overall backpropagation equation for the output layer

Equation 9-15 gives the abstracted version of the backpropagation derivatives, while Equation 9-16 gives the mathematical version of backpropagation for specifically the output layer.

Equation 9-15: Abstracted components of the backpropagation algorithm

$$(derivative\ of\ error\ function) * (derivative\ of\ activation\ function) * (derivative\ of\ weighted\ sum)$$

Equation 9-16: Mathematical backpropagation function for a given weight in the output layer

$$d'w_{ij} = (o_j - t_j) * (o_j(1 - o_j)) * (x_i)$$

You've got the formula. You can now assign the appropriate blame, $d'w_{ij}$, to every weight w_{ij} in the output layer.

Trouble brewing: The hidden layer

You have your backpropagation derivative for the output layer. You can apply the same process to the hidden layer. The derivative of the activation function will be the same for the hidden layer (assuming you're using the same activation function across the board), and the derivative of the weighted sum will also be the same. But what about the error?

It would be very, very nice if you knew what the hidden-layer neuron output values should be before they get passed as input to the final layer. Unfortunately, you only have labeled ground-truth examples for the final network output, not for the intermediate steps.

You'll have to do a bit more heavy lifting to figure out how a hidden layer's neurons impact the overall error. Take another look at our network shown in Figure 9-4.

REMEMBER

The hidden neurons' outputs become the input for the next layer. This is where you'll have to start using layer indexes. A given $o^l{}_j$ is the same as the x_j for layer l+1.

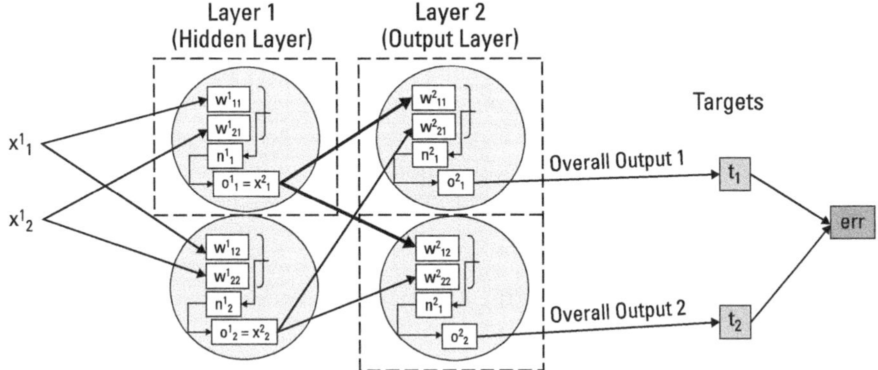

w^l_{ij} = weight i in neuron j in layer l

o^l_j = output in neuron j in layer l

x^l_i = input to all weights i in layer l

FIGURE 9-4: A simple neural network, emphasizing the first hidden layer neurons' connections to the output layer.

You can see from Figure 9-4 that the hidden layer outputs, o^1_j, are the output layer's inputs, x^2_j. So, each hidden neuron contributes to every output neuron.

That also means the hidden neuron's output is partially responsible for every single mismatch between output and ground truth! Therefore, when you take the derivative of the overall error with respect to a given hidden neuron, you have to consider its "blame" or contribution to the error of every single output neuron.

This is the second boogeyman in the backpropagation algorithm. At first glance, tracing this failure chain reaction throughout the entire network going forward from the hidden neuron feels downright overwhelming.

But don't worry; you have already done most of this work! After all, you just found the derivative for every single weight in the output layer. How did you get the overall derivative? You calculated the derivative for the error, activation, and information phases.

The weights for the output layer and the outputs of the hidden layer have very similar contributions to the overall error. Crucially, *the weights of a layer are multiplied by the inputs of the layer before it to arrive at the net, an output, and eventually an error.* So, when you take the derivative of the error with respect to the hidden layer's output (same as the output layer's input), the only derivative calculation that changes is in the information phase.

- The derivative of the net with respect to a weight w^l_{ij} is the input x^l_i.
- The derivative of the net with respect to the input x^l_i is the weight, w^l_{ij}.
- The output o^l_j is the same as the input x^{l+1}_i.

So, in order to get the derivative of the error with respect to a hidden layer neuron's output, you calculate the derivatives of the error function with respect to the hidden layer neuron's output — summed across every connected output layer neuron. This allows you to reuse the derivatives of the error phase and activation phase we already calculated for the output layer neurons, and multiply them by the appropriate output layer neuron weight connecting to the hidden layer neuron output.

Equation 9-17 is the equation for the derivative of the error phase for a hidden-layer neuron, $o^l{}_j$.

Equation 9-17: Derivative of the error function with respect to a given hidden layer neuron output, $o^l{}_j$ (*error phase* derivative for the hidden-layer neuron)

$$\sum_{j(l+1)} \left((o^{(l+1)}{}_j - t^{(l+1)}{}_j) * (o^{(l+1)}{}_j)(1 - o^{(l+1)}{}_j) \right) * (w^{(l+1)}{}_{ij})$$

REMEMBER

$o^l{}_j = x^{l+1}{}_i$ (The hidden layer neuron output is the output layer neuron's input)

We keep the error and activation phase derivatives from the output layer backpropagation step, but multiply this term by each weight that connects the hidden layer neuron's output to each output layer neuron's input.

The activation phase and information phase derivatives are calculated for the hidden layer the same way as the output layer. The overall equation for a given weight, $w^l{}_{ij}$, is shown in Equation 9-18.

Equation 9-18: The hidden layer l backpropagation derivative for a given weight in the layer, $w^l{}_{ij}$

$$d'w^l{}_{ij} = \left(\sum_{j(l+1)} (o^{(l+1)}{}_j - t^{(l+1)}{}_j) * (o^{(l+1)}{}_j (1 - o^{(l+1)}{}_j)) * (w^{(l+1)}{}_{ij}) \right) * \left(o^l{}_j (1 - o^l{}_j) \right) * (x^l{}_i)$$

Again, this is just the error derivative multiplied by the activation derivative multiplied by the information derivative for the hidden layer. The error derivative just got a little more complicated.

Whew! That was a lot of math!

General backpropagation

To implement backpropagation in general, you need to keep track of the error phase, activation phase, and information phase derivatives for each layer. We are going to use two special terms: *given_error*, to keep track of the error phase derivative using information from the layer ahead, and *passed_error*, which is the error phase derivative we will pass to the next layer. These have exactly the same calculation, but *given_error* comes from the layer ahead, and *passed_error* is calculated from the current layer. You track these because you'll need them to calculate the error phase derivative for the current layer. Equation 9-19 gives the general *passed_error* term equation. Equation 9-20 displays how the *given_error* is related to the layer ahead's *passed_error*.

Equation 9-19: A neuron's *passed_error*, calculated from the *given_error* term

$$passed\_error^{l}{}_{j} = \sum_{j} given\_error^{l}{}_{j} * (o^{l}{}_{j}(1-o^{l}{}_{j})) * w^{l}{}_{ij}$$

Equation 9-20: The *given_error* of a layer is the *passed_error* of the layer ahead

$$given\_error^{l}{}_{j} = passed\_error?^{(l+1)}{}_{j}$$

Then, you can generalize the backpropagation equation for the current layer in Equation 9-21:

Equation 9-21: The general backpropagation equation for weight w^{l}_{ij}

$$d'w^{l}{}_{ij} = (given\_error^{l}{}_{j}) * (o^{l}{}_{j}(1-o^{l}{}_{j})) * (x^{l}{}_{i})$$

Note that this equation still breaks up into three phases: error phase, activation phase, and information phase.

REMEMBER

The bias value can be modeled as a weight with an associated input value of 1. If you are calculating the bias term separately, this comes out to exactly the same calculation as Equation 9-18, but without the $x^{l}{}_{i}$ term.

Backpropagation, step by step

If you got lost back there, somewhere between and *o* and an *i* and a *j*, don't worry — the notation is notoriously complicated. The following list outlines the process of implementing backpropagation step by step, focusing on the derivative phases more than the actual equations:

1. **Start with the output layer.**

   For the output layer, your *given_error* is equal to the derivative of the overall error function with respect to the output neuron (Equation 9-11).

2. **Multiply the *given_error* by the activation phase derivative (Equation 9-13) and the information phase derivative (Equation 9-14) to arrive at your overall weight derivatives.**
3. **Calculate the *passed_error* (Equation 9-19) with the *given_error*, activation phase derivative, and weight values.**
4. **Move to the next layer.**

   Your *given_error* for this layer is set to the *passed_error* from the layer ahead.
5. **Multiply the *given_error* by the activation phase derivative (Equation 9-13) and the information phase derivative (Equation 9-14) to arrive at your overall weight derivatives for the layer.**
6. **Calculate the *passed_error* (Equation 9-19) with the *given_error*, activation phase derivative, and weight values.**
7. **Repeat steps 5 and 6 while you still have layers.**

TECHNICAL STUFF

Usually, the weights in a neural network are implemented as matrices. The actual calculation breaks down into a series of dot products with the weight matrices and element-wise multiplication and division. The error phase derivative and the activation phase derivative are element-wise multiplications, and the derivative of the weight matrix is created from this operation's dot product with the input matrix. Often, the product of an error-phase and an activation-phase derivative becomes its own term, the *delta*, since this is used both in the weight matrix dot product calculation and the *passed_error* dot product calculation.

The learning rate and update step

After obtaining the $d'w^l_{ij}$ for every weight in every layer, you have an idea of how much each weight is roughly responsible for the overall error of the network. However, you need to turn this information into new weight values. To do this, you are going to use a special constant called the *learning rate*.

The learning rate is a constant value that is multiplied by the derivative of the error with respect to the given weight. This scales the overall adjustment amount of the weight. Usually, the learning rate value is very small and makes gradual changes to the network. However, a bigger learning rate gives you a better chance of escaping a local minimum, since the step you're now taking down the slope is larger. Too large a learning rate can cause you to oscillate back and forth in an error surface, however. Equation 9-22 shows the calculation of the new weight values from the old weight values, the derivative obtained from backpropagation, and the learning rate.

Equation 9-22: The update step that creates new weights from old weights, the backpropagation algorithm, and the learning rate

$$new\_w^{l}_{ij} = old\_w^{l}_{ij} - \alpha * d'w^{l}_{ij}$$

Where α is the learning rate.

Finding the right learning rate can be more of an art than a science! Like other neural network hyperparameters, it may take some tuning to nail down perfectly. In Chapter 10, we go over more tips and tricks to train a neural network effectively.

If you made it this far, way to go! You just finished what is often considered the most difficult concept in neural networks.

REMEMBER

The backpropagation phase calculations you used in this section were specific to the choices of our error and activation functions. Different selections for these functions will yield different calculations in the error phase and activation phase.

IN THIS CHAPTER

» Avoiding data "gotchas" in neural network training

» Evaluating a neural network model and architecture choices

» Building your first neural network in Keras

» Building your first neural network in PyTorch

Chapter **10**

Training a Neural Network

Neural networks are powerful models, but training a neural network can be more of an art than a science. Often, you'll run a model, tweak one small thing, and then rerun a model to see how it changed. Sometimes, it can be hard to tell if the network's difference in performance was due to a change you made or due to random chance! While this can be frustrating, this chapter is meant to guide you by providing some common decision criteria and pitfalls to avoid. This hopefully gets you up and running with a little less heartache.

Of course, there are always going to be exceptions to the pointers presented here. One of the great things about Python, as well as the Keras and PyTorch libraries that implement these models, is that you have a lot of freedom to make changes and put your own spin on a neural network model.

In this chapter, you look at the nitty-gritty details of actually training a neural network. You first explore some of the data issues that crop up with neural network models and how to eliminate them when your model produces frustrating errors. You then look at how neural networks are evaluated — and how splitting your dataset one more time can save you some pain in the long run. You also delve into the fascinating world of neural network parameters and architecture choices. Finally, you create your first neural network in both the Keras and PyTorch libraries.

Avoiding Data Pitfalls

Some common mistakes to avoid when preparing your data for neural network ingestion include:

- » NaN values in your dataset
- » Not having enough data
- » Garbage data
- » Data encoding not matching your error function

When you have NaN (Not A Number, or empty) values in your dataset, ideally your programming environment would throw an error — but often, you just get NaN values in your output, which can be difficult to debug. A model can't compute the backpropagation gradient if it doesn't have a number to compute with, which can throw off your training quite a bit. If you have NaN values, we recommend you ditch them — or fill them with a clearly understandable dummy variable that's different from your valid training data.

In addition, if you don't have enough training data in your dataset, a neural network may not be your best AI architecture. There are, of course, exceptions to this advice, but generally, neural networks shine when they can extrapolate patterns from large amounts of data. If you have 50 training examples total with three features each, and you want to run a ten-layer 600-node neural network architecture on the data, expect disappointing results — you might be better off with a decision tree.

There are some possible fixes to this — you could go collect more data (which might be easy if you are trying to classify cats, or more difficult if you are trying to classify planets). You could also use data augmentation, which slightly modifies your original data to create new instances of the same class. This works pretty well for image classification problems, though it is sometimes less trustworthy for a number-forecasting regression task.

Sometimes, the data you have is full of missing fields, incorrect readings, or information that has nothing to do with the problem you're working on. This garbage data can really hurt your model's performance. In fact, having clean, well-engineered data can sometimes be so powerful that you'll get good results no matter what model you run on it.

TIP

To prevent garbage data from entering your model, it's a good idea to inspect it ahead of time. Are there large periods of missing data? Are there suspicious outliers? Chapter 3 covers some best practices for preparing data to be used in an AI model.

Feature engineering is the process of creating useful information to feed a model. For a neural network, we often hand the model all of our data and hope it does a good job of feature engineering for us. If the model isn't quite making it, it may be worthwhile to use your domain expertise to pull out some higher-level information. Always be careful not to deprive your model of the data it truly needs in the process.

Finally, having the encoding of your target, or ground-truth, labels not match the output of your error function is a simple issue that can be hard to debug. For a classification problem, if the network expects a one-digit number to compare against, your labels should be encoded as one-digit numbers. If the network expects a vector of classification values, your labels should match. Libraries you use will usually throw an error to get a particular bug like this on your radar, but if the error message is too obtuse or you can't find other issues in your code, this is a good thing to check.

Validating Models

When you start training a neural network, it's important to determine how well the model works on data it hasn't seen yet. Like with other models, this is often accomplished with a test set. Because neural networks have a relatively long, often resource-intensive training process, another hold-out set is often used: the validation set.

The validation set is kind of a mini-test set: Your model never adjusts its weights or biases directly from the data in the validation set. The validation set is fed to the model after each epoch (complete run of training data) as a kind of check-in: How are we doing on data not in the training set? Because the model sees the validation set during the training process (even if it's not adjusting its performance based on this data), we don't consider it a true test set. Depending on your setup, if you run enough epochs, your model could, in theory, start meta-training on the validation set.

The validation set lets you see whether your performance on non-training data is approximately matching the performance on the training data. If this isn't the case, you might have problems, which we discuss in the next section.

There are many ways to split your data. Often, machine learning engineers will first split the data into the training and test sets, and then take the validation set as an additional portion of the training set.

REMEMBER

The amount of data to take for each set, as well as your split strategy, depend entirely on the problem at hand. Just know that best practices and rules of thumb that exist out there are pretty arbitrary — talk with your domain expert buddy if you aren't sure how much data should be used to verify model performance.

TIP

If you have enough data, taking a validation set is handy because it can save you some pain if the model starts memorizing training examples.

When you report a model's final metrics, people are usually expecting to see the performance on the test set. It's like pin the tail on the donkey without a blindfold — reporting only the training set performance is cheating!

Overfitting and Underfitting

When a model *overfits*, it's optimizing its parameters with too intensive a focus on the training set instances. In the best case, you have a model that is too biased toward the training set, and in the worst case, your model starts memorizing the training examples instead of learning useful features.

Having a validation set can help you catch your model's little shortcuts before you train too long. If your validation set error starts increasing dramatically while your training set error continues to decrease, it's a good sign your model has decided to forgo being a generalist in favor of the siren song of slightly better performance metrics. You can set up your neural network to stop training at this point and either restore your best model or design a new network with different hyperparameters.

TIP

It's helpful to graph your model's training and validation set performance over time to get an idea of where training more epochs starts being less effective.

On the flip side, if you're training a network and the training and validation set errors keep decreasing every epoch, your model might be *underfitting* and need more training. You also might want to increase your learning rate, in case your model is too slowly crawling to the bottom of a local minimum.

Setting Neural Network Parameters and Hyperparameters

Neural network parameters are its weights and biases — the neuron values that are dynamically changed during backpropagation training based on the model's error. You may have noticed that this leaves a *lot* of network design choices as hyperparameters, including:

- Number of layers in the network
- Number of nodes in each layer
- Choice of activation function
- Regularization techniques
- Choice of error function
- Batch size
- Number of epochs
- Learning rate

The number of options can feel a little overwhelming. The next two sections go over some techniques to make initial choices.

Architecting neural networks

For neural network architectures, some general rules of thumb include:

- Using more neurons in the initial layers (feature pyramid)
- Gradually reducing the number of layers as you go deeper in the network
- Starting with more neurons than needed and pruning back (if you have the resources!)

Again, these are just rules of thumb — chances are, your architecture is going to be tweaked again . . . and again . . . and again. I recommend finding a hobby to take up while your models are training. It's an excellent time to learn how to crochet.

There are some other methods of choosing architectures for a neural network model. One technique looks at other, high-performing models on a problem domain in your field and constructs your model based on the big-ticket model. If it's a very similar problem, you may even be able to use transfer learning. This allows you to copy model parameters from early layers and train on your specific problem with either less data, less total training time, or both. In the machine vision domain, there are a lot of performant models whose architectures and parameters you can use for transfer learning.

You can even use AI to create AI! Neural architecture search, or NAS, is a technique that evolves neural network designs over time for a problem of interest. This can be extremely computationally intensive, but will hopefully yield an efficient architecture at the end of the search phase.

Hyperparameter tuning techniques

Some neural network libraries allow you to search over a variety of different hyperparameter choices. Grid search, for example, is a very popular technique. In grid search, you define a couple of choices for each hyperparameter you want to manipulate. The neural network library then exhaustively tries every combination of parameters as its own model and evaluates the performance.

This can take some major compute time. However, you can also "set it and forget it," so you don't have to re-run the model with a tweak every time one finishes training. More time for your burgeoning crocheting hobby.

On the other hand, if you are way off on one or more of your hyperparameter settings, this technique won't let you adjust on the fly. Another tuning method is to take random samples from a distribution of possible hyperparameters and train on the selections.

One hyperparameter that can be tuned dynamically is the learning rate. Several optimizers for this exist, but one popular one incorporates momentum from previous training batches and a moving average of gradients. This Adam (Adaptive Moment Estimation) learning rate optimizer is a common choice in networks you'll see in the wild.

Creating and Training a Neural Network

Now that you have some background on how hard training a neural network can be, we'll now show you how easy training a neural network actually is!

Two common Python libraries for training neural networks are Keras and PyTorch. There is plenty of information out there on which one is better for your given use case, but we won't make you choose yet — we'll create an example in each.

Preparing your dataset

For this example, we'll use the Iris dataset from the UC Irvine Machine Learning Repository, a popular beginner dataset (https://archive.ics.uci.edu/dataset/53/iris). This dataset includes the measurements of four iris plant characteristics: sepal length, sepal width, petal length, and petal width. The task for the dataset is to use these measurements to classify a flower as Iris Setosa, Iris Versicolor, or Iris Virginica (three output classes).

Listing 10-1 displays the code for some basic preprocessing we'll perform on the dataset to make sure it's ready for the model. Figure 10-1 displays the output of the code. If you don't yet have the scikit-learn library installed, you'll want it for this project (Chapter 4 walks you through that process).

LISTING 10-1: Preprocessing the Iris Dataset (neural_network_data_prep.py)

```
from sklearn.datasets import load_iris
from sklearn.model_selection import train_test_split
from sklearn.preprocessing import OneHotEncoder
from sklearn.preprocessing import MinMaxScaler

#Load in Dataset Information
iris_full_dataset = load_iris()
iris_features_names = iris_full_dataset.feature_names
iris_label_classes = iris_full_dataset.target_names
iris_input_features = iris_full_dataset.data
iris_ground_truth = iris_full_dataset.target

#Print Dataset Information
print("Iris Features: ", iris_features_names)
print("Iris Label Classes", iris_label_classes)
print("First 10 instances")
print(iris_input_features[0:10])
print("First 10 class labels")
print(iris_ground_truth[0:10])

#Normalize the Input Data
scaler = MinMaxScaler()
scaled_iris_input_features =
  scaler.fit_transform(iris_input_features)
print("After Normalizing Features")
print(scaled_iris_input_features[0:10])
```

(continued)

LISTING 10-1: *(continued)*

```
#One Hot Encode the Ground Truth Data
one_hot = OneHotEncoder(sparse_output=False)
iris_ground_truth_one_hot =
  one_hot.fit_transform(iris_ground_truth.reshape(-1, 1))
print("After Converting to One Hot")
print(iris_ground_truth_one_hot.shape)
print(iris_ground_truth_one_hot[0:10])

train_features, test_features, train_truth, test_truth =
  train_test_split(scaled_iris_input_features,
  iris_ground_truth_one_hot, test_size=0.2)
train_features, val_features, train_truth, val_truth =
  train_test_split(train_features, train_truth, test_size=0.2)
```

```
(examples) C:\Users\marze\Documents\Book\Code Files>python neural_network_data_prep.py
Iris Features:  ['sepal length (cm)', 'sepal width (cm)', 'petal length (cm)', 'petal width (cm)']
Iris Label Classes ['setosa' 'versicolor' 'virginica']
First 10 instances
[[5.1 3.5 1.4 0.2]
 [4.9 3.  1.4 0.2]
 [4.7 3.2 1.3 0.2]
 [4.6 3.1 1.5 0.2]
 [5.  3.6 1.4 0.2]
 [5.4 3.9 1.7 0.4]
 [4.6 3.4 1.4 0.3]
 [5.  3.4 1.5 0.2]
 [4.4 2.9 1.4 0.2]
 [4.9 3.1 1.5 0.1]]
First 10 class labels
[0 0 0 0 0 0 0 0 0 0]
After Normalizing Features
[[0.22222222 0.625      0.06779661 0.04166667]
 [0.16666667 0.41666667 0.06779661 0.04166667]
 [0.11111111 0.5        0.05084746 0.04166667]
 [0.08333333 0.45833333 0.08474576 0.04166667]
 [0.19444444 0.66666667 0.06779661 0.04166667]
 [0.30555556 0.79166667 0.11864407 0.125     ]
 [0.08333333 0.58333333 0.06779661 0.08333333]
 [0.19444444 0.58333333 0.08474576 0.04166667]
 [0.02777778 0.375      0.06779661 0.04166667]
 [0.16666667 0.45833333 0.08474576 0.        ]]
After Converting to One Hot
(150, 3)
[[1. 0. 0.]
 [1. 0. 0.]
 [1. 0. 0.]
 [1. 0. 0.]
 [1. 0. 0.]
 [1. 0. 0.]
 [1. 0. 0.]
 [1. 0. 0.]
 [1. 0. 0.]
 [1. 0. 0.]]
```

FIGURE 10-1: The terminal output of running Listing 10-1.

Listing 10-1 does the following:

- Imports the dataset from the scikit-learn library, as well as the processing functions we'll need.
- Uses the `load_iris()` function to load in the full iris dataset.
- Assigns feature names, class names, feature data, and class data to their own variables.
- Prints the feature and class names out as a sanity check. There are four different features and three possible outcome classes.
- Prints the first ten instance features and first ten instance labels. You can see from the output that the data isn't normalized, and the ground-truth labels aren't one-hot encoded. We'll need to fix that.
- Creates a `MinMaxScaler()` normalizer and transforms the input features.
- Prints the normalized features to verify all numbers are now between 0 and 1.
- Creates a `OneHotEncoder()` object and fits the output data.
- Prints the shape and first ten instances of the one-hot encoded ground-truth data. You can see that the ground-truth data is now a vector with a "1" in the position corresponding to the class label.
- Uses the `train_test_split()` function to split the dataset into 80 percent training data and 20 percent test data.
- Uses the `train_test_split()` function to split the training data further into 80 percent training data and 20 percent validation data.

With the data formatted and split into a training, validation, and test set, you are ready to train a neural network!

Training a neural network with Keras

The Keras neural network library is actually built on another library called TensorFlow. You'll need to install both of these to get your environment set up. Inside the Anaconda Prompt (with your virtual environment activated), run:

```
pip install tensorflow keras
```

You'll also want the Matplotlib library installed. This will help you visualize the model's performance over time. In Anaconda, run the following to install the library:

```
conda install matplotlib
```

TIP

The installation instructions recommended here use Pip installation for TensorFlow and Keras, and conda for Matplotlib. This was after some trial and error in the Anaconda virtual environment. If you are having issues with the library install, we recommend looking at a few different installation methods. The beauty of virtual environments is that you can always destroy and recreate an environment if an install messes things up.

Listing 10-2 shows the code for training a neural network in Keras. Figure 10-2 gives the terminal output of running the code, and Figure 10-3 shows the graph output.

LISTING 10-2: Training a Neural Network with Keras (neural_network_keras.py)

```
from sklearn.datasets import load_iris
from sklearn.model_selection import train_test_split
from sklearn.preprocessing import OneHotEncoder
from sklearn.preprocessing import MinMaxScaler

from keras.models import Sequential
from keras.layers import Dense, Input
from keras.utils import to_categorical
from keras.callbacks import EarlyStopping
from matplotlib import pyplot as plt

# Dataset Prep
#Load in Dataset Information
iris_full_dataset = load_iris()
iris_features_names = iris_full_dataset.feature_names
iris_label_classes = iris_full_dataset.target_names
iris_input_features = iris_full_dataset.data
iris_ground_truth = iris_full_dataset.target
#Print Dataset Information
print("Iris Features: ", iris_features_names)
print("Iris Label Classes", iris_label_classes)
print("First 10 instances")
print(iris_input_features[0:10])
print("First 10 class labels")
print(iris_ground_truth[0:10])
#Normalize the Input Data
scaler = MinMaxScaler()
scaled_iris_input_features =
  scaler.fit_transform(iris_input_features)
```

```
print("After Normalizing Features")
print(scaled_iris_input_features[0:10])
#One Hot Encode the Ground Truth Data
one_hot = OneHotEncoder(sparse_output=False)
iris_ground_truth_one_hot =
  one_hot.fit_transform(iris_ground_truth.reshape(-1, 1))
print("After Converting to One Hot")
print(iris_ground_truth_one_hot.shape)
print(iris_ground_truth_one_hot[0:10])
train_features, test_features, train_truth, test_truth =
  train_test_split(scaled_iris_input_features,
  iris_ground_truth_one_hot, test_size=0.2)
train_features, val_features, train_truth, val_truth =
  train_test_split(train_features, train_truth, test_size=0.2)

#### Keras Model Implementation
model = Sequential()
model.add(Input(shape=(4,)))
model.add(Dense(20, activation="relu"))
model.add(Dense(10, activation="relu"))
model.add(Dense(3, activation="softmax"))
model.compile(optimizer="adam", loss="categorical_crossentropy",
  metrics=["accuracy"])
print("Model Summary")
print(model.summary())

early_stop_callback = EarlyStopping(patience=3)
#Train the model
history = model.fit(train_features, train_truth, batch_size=8,
  epochs=50, validation_data=(val_features, val_truth),
  callbacks=[early_stop_callback])

#Test on unseen data
results = model.evaluate(test_features, test_truth)
print(f"Final Test loss: {results[0]}" )
print(f"Final Test accuracy: {results[1]}" )

#Plot model accuracy
plt.plot(history.history["accuracy"], label="accuracy")
plt.plot(history.history["val_accuracy"], label="val_accuracy")
plt.title("Model Training and Val Accuracy over Time")
plt.legend()
plt.show()
```

(continued)

LISTING 10-2: *(continued)*

```
plt.clf()

# #Plot model loss
plt.plot(history.history["loss"], label="loss")
plt.plot(history.history["val_loss"], label="val_loss")
plt.title("Model Training and Val Loss over Time")
plt.legend()
plt.show()
plt.clf()
```

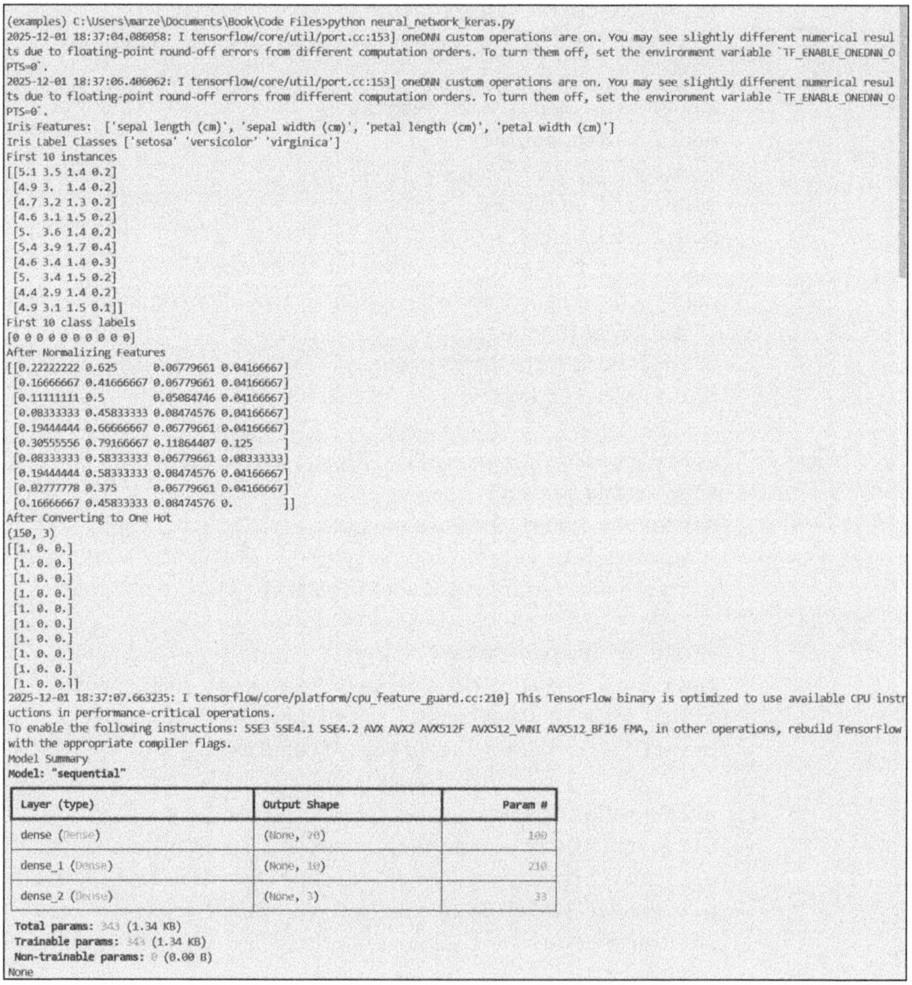

```
(examples) C:\Users\marze\Documents\Book\Code Files>python neural_network_keras.py
2025-12-01 18:37:04.086058: I tensorflow/core/util/port.cc:153] oneDNN custom operations are on. You may see slightly different numerical resul
ts due to floating-point round-off errors from different computation orders. To turn them off, set the environment variable `TF_ENABLE_ONEDNN_O
PTS=0`.
2025-12-01 18:37:06.406062: I tensorflow/core/util/port.cc:153] oneDNN custom operations are on. You may see slightly different numerical resul
ts due to floating-point round-off errors from different computation orders. To turn them off, set the environment variable `TF_ENABLE_ONEDNN_O
PTS=0`.
Iris Features:  ['sepal length (cm)', 'sepal width (cm)', 'petal length (cm)', 'petal width (cm)']
Iris Label Classes ['setosa' 'versicolor' 'virginica']
First 10 instances
[[5.1 3.5 1.4 0.2]
 [4.9 3.  1.4 0.2]
 [4.7 3.2 1.3 0.2]
 [4.6 3.1 1.5 0.2]
 [5.  3.6 1.4 0.2]
 [5.4 3.9 1.7 0.4]
 [4.6 3.4 1.4 0.3]
 [5.  3.4 1.5 0.2]
 [4.4 2.9 1.4 0.2]
 [4.9 3.1 1.5 0.1]]
First 10 class labels
[0 0 0 0 0 0 0 0 0 0]
After Normalizing Features
[[0.22222222 0.625      0.06779661 0.04166667]
 [0.16666667 0.41666667 0.06779661 0.04166667]
 [0.11111111 0.5        0.05084746 0.04166667]
 [0.08333333 0.45833333 0.08474576 0.04166667]
 [0.19444444 0.66666667 0.06779661 0.04166667]
 [0.30555556 0.79166667 0.11864407 0.125     ]
 [0.08333333 0.58333333 0.06779661 0.08333333]
 [0.19444444 0.58333333 0.08474576 0.04166667]
 [0.02777778 0.375      0.06779661 0.04166667]
 [0.16666667 0.45833333 0.08474576 0.        ]]
After Converting to One Hot
(150, 3)
[[1. 0. 0.]
 [1. 0. 0.]
 [1. 0. 0.]
 [1. 0. 0.]
 [1. 0. 0.]
 [1. 0. 0.]
 [1. 0. 0.]
 [1. 0. 0.]
 [1. 0. 0.]
 [1. 0. 0.]]
2025-12-01 18:37:07.663235: I tensorflow/core/platform/cpu_feature_guard.cc:210] This TensorFlow binary is optimized to use available CPU instr
uctions in performance-critical operations.
To enable the following instructions: SSE3 SSE4.1 SSE4.2 AVX AVX2 AVX512F AVX512_VNNI AVX512_BF16 FMA, in other operations, rebuild TensorFlow
with the appropriate compiler flags.
Model Summary
Model: "sequential"
```

Layer (type)	Output Shape	Param #
dense (Dense)	(None, 20)	100
dense_1 (Dense)	(None, 10)	210
dense_2 (Dense)	(None, 3)	33

```
 Total params: 343 (1.34 KB)
 Trainable params: 343 (1.34 KB)
 Non-trainable params: 0 (0.00 B)
None
```

FIGURE 10-2: Terminal output of running Listing 10-2.

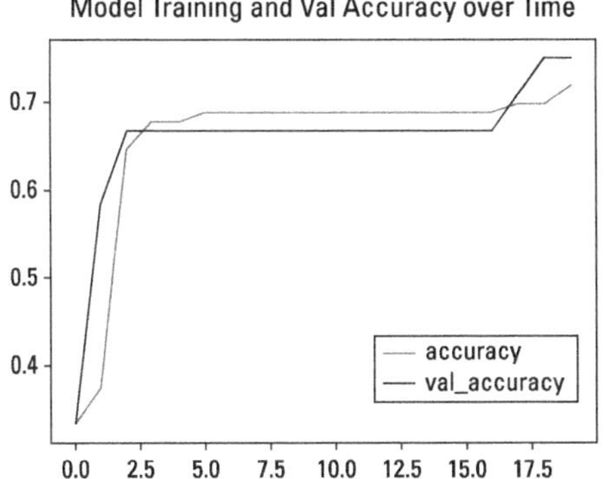

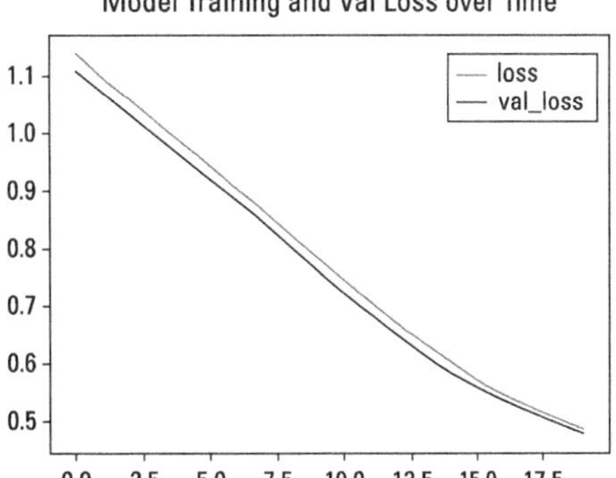

FIGURE 10-3: Graph output or running Listing 10-2.

The code does the following:

- Imports the scikit-learn functions from Listing 10-1 needed for data preprocessing.
- Imports the necessary Keras functions and classes.
- Imports Matplotlib for graphing the model training history.
- Runs the preprocessing code from Listing 10-1.
- Creates a Keras neural network model. The `Sequential` model type allows you to add model layers, one after the other. The first layer added is an `Input` layer, where you specify that your input instances will have four features. Then a `Dense` layer with 20 neurons and the `relu` activation function is added. After that, another `Dense` layer with ten neurons and the `relu` activation function is added. Finally, a `Dense` layer with three nodes (to match the number of output classes) and the `softmax` activation function is added.
- Compiles the model with the `adam` optimizer and a `categorical_crossentropy` loss function. The code also tells the model to keep track of the network's accuracy. The network will already keep track of the loss by default.
- Prints a summary of the model. You can see in Figure 10-3 that this produces a nice table of the layers, neurons, and total parameters.
- Creates an `EarlyStopping` callback. This function is given a patience of 3. This means that the model will stop training early if the validation loss hasn't improved after three consecutive epochs. While this function tracks the validation loss by default, you could pass it a different metric if you want.
- Trains the model. The `fit()` function is called on the `model` object, and you pass it the feature and ground-truth data, as well as the batch size (8), number of epochs (20), validation dataset, and a list of callback functions (in this case, just your early stopping callback). As the model trains, it will print the training

and validation loss and accuracy per epoch. This same information is tracked over time and returned in the `history` variable.

- Tests the model on your test dataset. The `evaluate()` function is called on the `model` object and passed the test features and test ground-truth data. The program prints the final test loss and accuracy.
- Plots the model accuracy. The `plot()` function of Matplotlib is used to graph the training and validation accuracy over the training epochs.
- Plots the model loss. The same `plot()` function is used to track the training and validation loss over the training epochs.

Note that the Keras library can be a heavy import, and it may take a few minutes to load in your environment. Depending on the size of your computer, you might have some slow training. Feel free to adjust the number of neurons in your network or the number of epochs you train if your laptop is gasping for air!

Hopefully you see your training and validation loss decrease and accuracy increase over time. It may be a little erratic. Remember, there is plenty of randomness in the program based on the weight and bias initialization, train, test, and validation splits, and batching of samples. Running the program again will give you slightly different results.

If your model is training very slowly, we recommend saving the model and reloading it before you evaluate it. This way, you won't have to retrain the whole model if you have some bugs in the evaluation code.

Training a neural network with PyTorch

PyTorch has some similarities to Keras, but the model implementation is a little more hands-on. You'll need to install the PyTorch library, which you can accomplish with the command:

```
conda install conda-forge::pytorch
```

If you haven't installed Matplotlib from the last section, you'll need that library for this program as well. Listing 10-3 displays the code for training a neural network in PyTorch. This model uses a similar design to the example code you'll find in the PyTorch documentation for a simple neural network, and its documentation is a great reference if you want to learn more about a particular function or class. Figure 10-4 shows the terminal output of running Listing 10-3, and Figure 10-5 shows the graph output.

LISTING 10-3: Training a Neural Network with PyTorch (neural_network_pytorch.py)

```
from sklearn.datasets import load_iris
from sklearn.model_selection import train_test_split
from sklearn.preprocessing import OneHotEncoder
from sklearn.preprocessing import MinMaxScaler

import torch
from torch import nn
from torch.utils.data import Dataset, DataLoader
from matplotlib import pyplot as plt

# Dataset Prep
#Load in Dataset Information
iris_full_dataset = load_iris()
iris_features_names = iris_full_dataset.feature_names
iris_label_classes = iris_full_dataset.target_names
iris_input_features = iris_full_dataset.data
iris_ground_truth = iris_full_dataset.target
#Print Dataset Information
print("Iris Features: ", iris_features_names)
print("Iris Label Classes", iris_label_classes)
print("First 10 instances")
print(iris_input_features[0:10])
print("First 10 class labels")
print(iris_ground_truth[0:10])
#Normalize the Input Data
scaler = MinMaxScaler()
scaled_iris_input_features =
  scaler.fit_transform(iris_input_features)
print("After Normalizing Features")
print(scaled_iris_input_features[0:10])
#One Hot Encode the Ground Truth Data
one_hot = OneHotEncoder(sparse_output=False)
iris_ground_truth_one_hot = one_hot.fit_transform(iris_ground_truth.
  reshape(-1, 1))
print("After Converting to One Hot")
print(iris_ground_truth_one_hot.shape)
print(iris_ground_truth_one_hot[0:10])
train_features, test_features, train_truth, test_truth =
  train_test_split(scaled_iris_input_features,
  iris_ground_truth_one_hot, test_size=0.2)
```

(continued)

LISTING 10-3: *(continued)*

```
train_features, val_features, train_truth, val_truth =
  train_test_split(train_features, train_truth,
  test_size=0.2)

## PyTorch Data Preparation and Model Implementation
class customIrisDataset(Dataset):
    def __init__(self, features, truth):
        self.features = features
        self.truth = truth

    def __len__(self):
        return len(self.truth)

    def __getitem__(self, idx):
        feature = self.features[idx]
        truth = self.truth[idx]
        return feature, truth

batch_size = 8

train_data = customIrisDataset(train_features, train_truth)
val_data = customIrisDataset(val_features, val_truth)
test_data = customIrisDataset(test_features, test_truth)
train_dataloader = DataLoader(train_data, batch_size=batch_size)
test_dataloader = DataLoader(test_data, batch_size=batch_size)
val_dataloader = DataLoader(val_data, batch_size=batch_size)

## PyTorch Neural Network
class NeuralNetwork(nn.Module):
    def __init__(self):
        super().__init__()
        self.model_layers = nn.Sequential(
            nn.Linear(4, 20),
            nn.ReLU(),
            nn.Linear(20, 10),
            nn.ReLU(),
            nn.Linear(10, 3)
        )

    def forward(self, x):
        output = self.model_layers(x)
        return output
model = NeuralNetwork()
#Get parameters to be the same type
```

```
model.double()
print(model)

loss_function = nn.CrossEntropyLoss()
optimizer = torch.optim.AdamW(model.parameters(), lr=1e-2)

def train(dataloader, model, loss_function, optimizer):
    model.train()
    for batch, (X, y) in enumerate(dataloader):
        #print(batch)
        pred = model(X)
        loss = loss_function(pred, y)
        #Backprop - the training step!
        loss.backward()
        optimizer.step()
        optimizer.zero_grad()

def test(dataloader, model, loss_function):
    num_samples = len(dataloader.dataset)
    num_batches = len(dataloader)
    model.eval()
    total_loss = 0
    total_correct = 0
    with torch.no_grad():
        for batch_inputs, batch_truth, in dataloader:
            predictions = model(batch_inputs)
            total_loss += loss_function(predictions,
  batch_truth).item()
            num_correct_pred = (predictions.argmax(1) ==
  batch_truth.argmax(1)).type(torch.float).sum().item()
            total_correct += num_correct_pred
    overall_loss  = total_loss/num_batches
    overall_accuracy = total_correct/num_samples
    return overall_loss, overall_accuracy

epochs = 20
training_loss_history = []
training_acc_history = []
val_loss_history = []
val_acc_history = []

for i in range(epochs):
    print(f"Epoch {i}")
    train(train_dataloader, model, loss_function, optimizer)
```

(continued)

LISTING 10-3: *(continued)*

```
    #Get training history by epoch
    train_loss, train_acc = test(train_dataloader, model,
  loss_function)
    training_loss_history.append(train_loss)
    training_acc_history.append(train_acc)
    #Get validation history by epoch
    val_loss, val_acc = test(val_dataloader, model, loss_function)
    val_loss_history.append(val_loss)
    val_acc_history.append(val_acc)
    print(f"Current Train Loss: {train_loss}, Accuracy:
  {train_acc}")
    print(f"Current Val Loss: {val_loss}, Accuracy: {val_acc}")

#Final test
loss, acc = test(test_dataloader, model, loss_function)
print(f"Final Test Loss: {loss}")
print(f"Final Test Accuracy: {acc}")

#Plot model accuracy
plt.plot(training_acc_history, label="accuracy")
plt.plot(val_acc_history, label="val_accuracy")
plt.title("Model Training and Val Accuracy over Time")
plt.legend()
plt.show()
plt.clf()

# #Plot model lostt
plt.plot(training_loss_history, label="loss")
plt.plot(val_loss_history, label="val_loss")
plt.title("Model Training and Val Loss over Time")
plt.legend()
plt.show()
plt.clf()
```

The code does the following:

- Imports the scikit-learn functions from Listing 10-1 needed for data preprocessing.
- Imports the necessary Keras functions and classes.
- Imports Matplotlib for graphing the model training history.

```
(examples) C:\Users\marze\Documents\Book\Code Files>python neural_network_pytorch.py
Iris Features:  ['sepal length (cm)', 'sepal width (cm)', 'petal length (cm)', 'petal width (cm)']
Iris Label Classes ['setosa' 'versicolor' 'virginica']
First 10 instances
[[5.1 3.5 1.4 0.2]
 [4.9 3.  1.4 0.2]
 [4.7 3.2 1.3 0.2]
 [4.6 3.1 1.5 0.2]
 [5.  3.6 1.4 0.2]
 [5.4 3.9 1.7 0.4]
 [4.6 3.4 1.4 0.3]
 [5.  3.4 1.5 0.2]
 [4.4 2.9 1.4 0.2]
 [4.9 3.1 1.5 0.1]]
First 10 class labels
[0 0 0 0 0 0 0 0 0 0]
After Normalizing Features
[[0.22222222 0.625      0.06779661 0.04166667]
 [0.16666667 0.41666667 0.06779661 0.04166667]
 [0.11111111 0.5        0.05084746 0.04166667]
 [0.08333333 0.45833333 0.08474576 0.04166667]
 [0.19444444 0.66666667 0.06779661 0.04166667]
 [0.30555556 0.79166667 0.11864407 0.125     ]
 [0.08333333 0.58333333 0.06779661 0.08333333]
 [0.19444444 0.58333333 0.08474576 0.04166667]
 [0.02777778 0.375      0.06779661 0.04166667]
 [0.16666667 0.45833333 0.08474576 0.        ]]
After Converting to One Hot
(150, 3)
[[1. 0. 0.]
 [1. 0. 0.]
 [1. 0. 0.]
 [1. 0. 0.]
 [1. 0. 0.]
 [1. 0. 0.]
 [1. 0. 0.]
 [1. 0. 0.]
 [1. 0. 0.]
 [1. 0. 0.]]
 NeuralNetwork(
   (model_layers): Sequential(
     (0): Linear(in_features=4, out_features=20, bias=True)
     (1): ReLU()
     (2): Linear(in_features=20, out_features=10, bias=True)
     (3): ReLU()
     (4): Linear(in_features=10, out_features=3, bias=True)
   )
 )
```

FIGURE 10-4: Terminal output of running Listing 10-3.

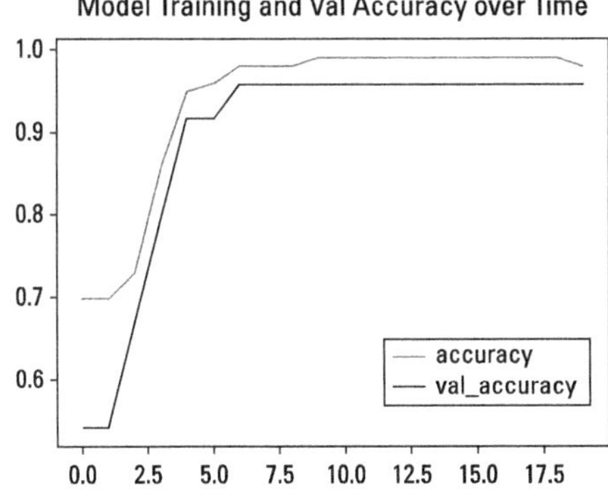

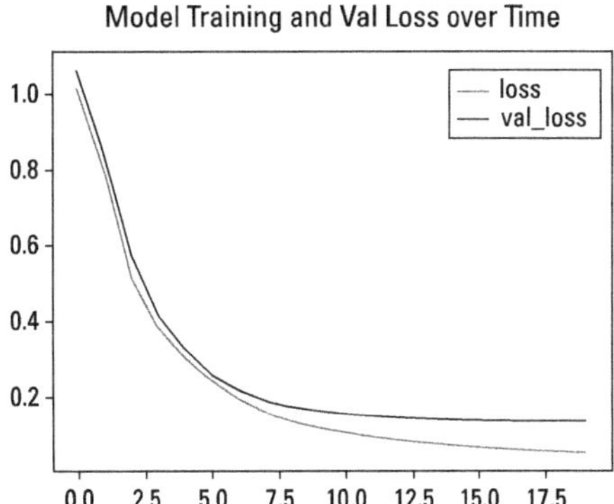

FIGURE 10-5: Graph output of running Listing 10-3.

- Runs the preprocessing code from Listing 10-1.
- Creates a custom `dataset` class for PyTorch. PyTorch requires datasets to be in a very specific format. The `customIrisDataset` class inherits from the `Dataset` class, and has three functions: `__init__()`, which sets the features and truth data to class variables; `__len__()`, which returns the number of samples; and `__getitem__()`, which takes in an index and returns the features and ground truth label at that index.
- Creates a custom `dataset` and `DataLoader` for the training, validation, and test sets. The `DataLoader` takes in the `batch_size` variable we set and creates an iterator for each set, which will return samples in groups equal to the batch size.
- Creates a `NeuralNetwork` class that inherits from the `nn.Module` class. This class has an `__init__()` and `forward()` function. The `__init__()` function creates the model layers: The first is a `Linear` layer with four input features and 20 neurons, followed by `ReLU` activation; the second is a `Linear` layer with 20 inputs and ten neurons, followed by `ReLU` activation; and the final is a `Linear` layer with ten inputs and three neurons, matching the number of output classes. The `forward()` function runs the input data through the model layers and returns the output.
- Creates a `model` variable using the `NeuralNetwork()` class. It also sets the model parameters to the `double` type, and prints the model. You can see in Figure 10-4 that this gives a summary of the model layers.
- Creates a `loss_function` object set to `nn.CrossEntropyLoss()` and creates an `optimizer` making use of the Adam optimization scheme.
- Creates a `train()` function which takes in the `dataloader`, `model`, `loss_function`, and `optimizer`. It calls the model's superclass `train()` method to put it in training mode. Then, for each batch in the data loader, the model creates feedforward predictions, stored in the `pred` variable, calculates the `loss` based on the loss function, and calls the `backward()` method to calculate the backpropagation step. The optimizer uses the `step()` method to update the parameters and then the `zero_grad()` method to zero out the gradient for the next step.
- Creates a `test()` function which takes in the `dataloader`, `model`, and `loss_function`. This function stores the total number of samples in the dataloader in the `num_samples` variable and the total batches in the `num_batches` variable. It sets the `total_loss` and `total_correct` variables to 0. Then, using the `torch.no_grad()` method (so the model isn't training), it gets the predictions for each batch, compares them with the correct answers, and calculates the per-batch loss and accuracy. These are added to the `total_loss` and `total_correct` variables. Finally, the `overall_loss` (`total_loss`

divided by num_batches) and overall_accuracy (total_correct divided by num_samples) are calculated and returned.

- Creates a variable called epochs and initializes empty lists to hold the history for the training and validation loss and accuracy.
- Trains the model: For each epoch in a loop, the program prints the epoch and calls the train() function and the test() function on the training data. It appends the outcome to the training loss and accuracy history lists. It then calls the test() function on the validation data and appends the loss and accuracy to the validation history lists. Finally, it prints the current training and validation loss for the epoch.
- After training, calls the test() function on the final test data and prints the results.
- Uses the same code to plot the model training and validation accuracy and loss as in Listing 10-2.

Figures 10-3 and 10-5 show a similar pattern of training and validation accuracy increasing over time, and training and validation loss decreasing over time. It's neat how two different libraries can be used on the same problem!

Both of these neural networks are somewhat plain, vanilla neural networks with fully connected neurons and straightforward numeric data. In the next chapter, you look at how there is a broader family of neural network types to solve trickier problems.

IN THIS CHAPTER

» Exploring convolutional neural networks, recurrent neural networks, and encoder and decoder networks

» Paying attention to transformer models

» Using multiple architectures together

» Using hybrid neural network and classical machine learning architectures

Chapter 11

Identifying the Neural Network Family

In the previous chapter, you looked at implementing a basic feed-forward neural network. While the example was simple, this type of network is fundamental to understanding the vast array of neural network types that build on this foundation. You may not encounter too many basic feed-forward networks in the wild, but the networks you will encounter are all based on this architecture — with some twists or updates to make them better at solving the problem at hand.

In this chapter, you explore the wide world of neural network architectures and how they expand or modify the basic feed-forward neural network. You explore convolutional neural networks and how they relate to image processing and object detection. You unroll a basic neural network into a recurrent neural network and discover how this helps enable time-series processing. You also discover how an autoencoder network is not quite as ridiculous as it seems and explore how the encoder and decoder aspects enable advanced AI tasks. You get your first basic introduction to transformer models. Finally, you explore how different neural networks can work together — and even work with other model types — to get better AI results.

Exploring the Neural Network Family Tree

There are many neural networks out there — far too many to list in one book! But this chapter outlines some of the broad categories of neural networks in the family tree, as well as how they are built and what they are used for. These categories include:

- Basic feed-forward neural networks
- Convolutional neural networks
- Recurrent neural networks
- Autoencoders
- Transformers

Note that some of these architectures (looking at you, transformers!) are used more often than others in AI tools you're likely to encounter. While at first glance, they might seem impossible to understand, they're still a neural network under the hood.

Building Basic Feed-Forward Networks

In Chapters 9 and 10, you worked on building some basic feed-forward neural networks. These networks typically:

- Feed data only in one direction: data vector in, classification or regression out
- Only take in tabular data or data that can be easily vectorized
- Use backpropagation to update network parameters
- Are trained on labeled examples

While powerful, one of the major disadvantages of these networks is their lack of data flexibility: If you want to feed images or time-series data in, they must be represented somehow as a static list of numbers. Turning these data types into representations like that usually loses some important information relevant to solving the problem. If you've ever accidentally printed out a picture on two pages, one half on each, you can appreciate how hard it is to understand what an image is from incomplete neighborhood data.

Interestingly enough, sometimes a basic feed-forward network isn't the best option for tabular data — sometimes a decision tree or regression model is a better or more explainable choice. However, classical machine learning models can't always handle very large datasets. Performance, data, and compute power always involve trade-offs.

Creating Convolutional Neural Networks

One of the most popular tasks for AI is processing images. Basic feed-forward networks must turn a 2D image matrix into a single list of numbers to process it, which, as you may imagine, loses a lot of spatial connectedness information in the process.

The solution to this problem is to create convolutional neural networks (which are explored in much more detail in Chapter 14). Figure 11-1 displays the architecture of a convolutional neural network.

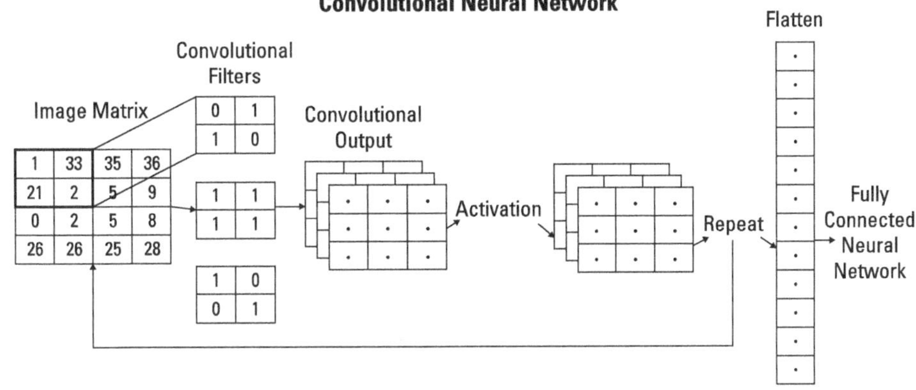

FIGURE 11-1: The architecture of a convolutional neural network.

Convolutional neural networks, or CNNs, create a series of convolutional filters instead of typical neurons. These filters act as a sliding window over the structured 2D input, which allows them to take in neighborhood information. The learned parameters are still weights and biases — but they are now structured as convolutional filter matrices rather than fully connected neurons.

CNNs use sets of convolutional filters on all channels of the image to output increasingly thicker stacks of smaller "features," which are eventually flattened into a stack of vector number lists fed into a fully connected network at the end of the architecture. The fully connected network handles the actual classification or regression task from the feature list.

If neural networks were dog breeds, the convolutional neural network would be a retriever — it's hard to overstate how popular this network is! CNNs are used broadly in:

- Object recognition
- Object detection and localization
- Image segmentation
- Automatic image labeling
- Quality inspection
- Autonomous driving
- Medical image processing
- And much more!

They are relatively simple to set up and train, and they can use transfer learning effectively, allowing one network to borrow some of the already learned features from another trained network. This is a huge advantage for organizations that need a working image network without creating tons and tons of data to train it on.

TECHNICAL STUFF

One of the most common beginner AI exercises is training a fully connected neural network on the MNIST database of handwritten digits (28-by-28 pixel images with the numbers 0 to 9 written on them) as a flattened vector representation, and then comparing the performance of a convolutional neural network on the same dataset using the matrix image. It's interesting to see how much the spatial neighborhood information helps the classification!

ImageNet

Convolutional neural network architectures are often trained on ImageNet, a huge database containing millions of images. ImageNet serves as a network training benchmark and provides a common basis for transfer learning to other architectures.

While this is useful, it can also create security and ethical issues. Issues present in ImageNet have a tendency to infiltrate multiple networks and create the same vulnerabilities in each. Mislabeled or misrepresented images in the database can create far-reaching problems. Just know what limitations are involved if you're training a network using an ImageNet-created backbone.

Yolo

You Only Look Once, or Yolo, models have been some of the most influential object detectors in the industry. These are single-shot detectors that use convolutional neural networks to simultaneously detect objects and locate them in an image using a bounding box or image segmentation. There are other networks that function very well as object detectors, but Yolo has been very popular, particularly because it's fast enough to run in real time and can usually process video. In Chapter 15, you build an object detector model using Yolo as a basis. Figure 11-2 displays an example of a Yolo object detector used to detect rubber ducks in an image.

FIGURE 11-2: Yolo object detector for locating rubber ducks.

Other influential convolutional neural networks include:

- EfficientNet
- MobileNet
- AlexNet
- VGG-16
- RCNN
- Faster RCNN
- ResNet

Fully convolutional neural networks

Most classical CNNs use a fully connected neural network for the final image classification or detection process. One subfamily, *fully convolutional neural networks*, uses convolutional layers as both the input and output of the network. These networks typically locate or segment the image as their output. While typical CNNs have to set a static image size at some point in their architecture, fully convolutional neural networks are more flexible with a variety of image sizes in the input. Figure 11-3 displays an architecture of a fully convolutional neural network.

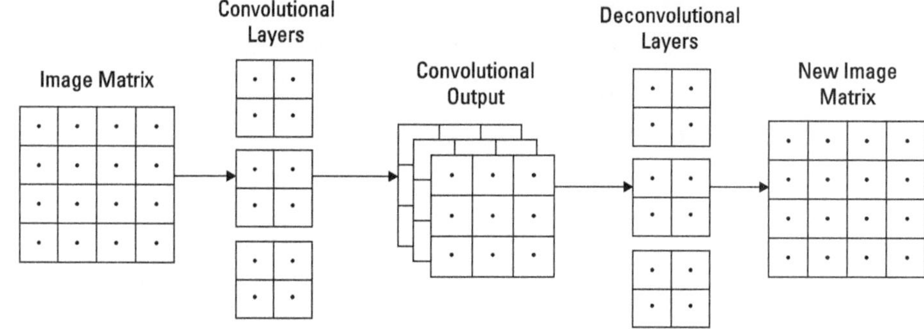

FIGURE 11-3: Fully convolutional neural network architecture.

TECHNICAL STUFF

CNNs use backpropagation to assign relative error to the network parameters, just like fully connected neural networks. However, because of the convolutional filters, not all parameters are connected to each input. Backpropagation in CNNs must account for the real parameter connections before assigning errors.

Running Recurrent Neural Networks

One of the trickiest types of data for humans to analyze is time-series data. The time dimension factors into a large variety of problems, including:

- Manufacturing processes
- Video analysis
- Machine time to maintenance
- Defect analysis

Typical neural networks assume all data presented to the network is independent of the other data inputs. This is usually fine if the inputs are truly distinct — like images of separate manufactured parts going down a conveyor belt. However, more complex (and often, more real-world) inputs have dependencies through time. The question becomes: How do you construct networks that take these dependencies into account?

The answer is recurrent neural networks, or RNNs. These networks receive sequences of data as input, rather than one example at a time. Within the sequence, the output of one instance has a backward connection to the network, which retains information for the next instance in the sequence. This allows the network to have a semblance of "memory" and use information learned from the early timesteps in subsequent timesteps. Figure 11-4 shows an example of an RNN network — the base architecture is simple, but can be "unrolled" for an arbitrary number of sequence steps.

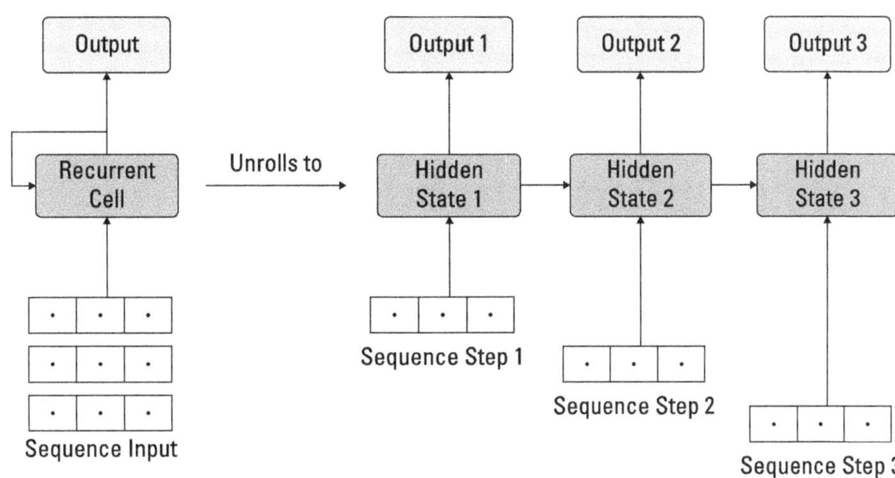

FIGURE 11-4: Example architecture of a recurrent neural network.

RNNs are useful for time-series data, but they aren't without their issues. For very long sequences, they struggle with remembering information that occurred early in the process. (We can certainly relate — does anyone really remember what happened in an 8 a.m. lecture at 3 p.m. the same day?)

Two popular RNN architectures include long short-term memory (LSTM) networks and gated recurrent unit (GRU) networks. Both of these network types use several types of "gates" that allow past information to permeate the current input. RNNs you'll encounter in the wild are almost always based on one of these two architectures.

TIP

Time series as a whole tends to be a trickier process than other AI problem domains. For most time-series tasks, it's very important to understand the problem domain before selecting an AI technique. Domain experts and/or basic statistical processing are very important to understand the relevant inputs, time window, and potential pitfalls in the data. As of this writing, we believe time-series problems are still a seriously under-studied aspect of AI use.

RNNs are pretty cool — who doesn't love a good time-traveling network? However, they can be notorious for the actual training step. These networks are pretty sensitive to the time window (sequence length) given, noise in the data, and the number of features fed in. Using these networks effectively sometimes involves more data preprocessing and feature engineering than other architectures.

TECHNICAL STUFF

In theory, RNNs don't care if you use multiple types of sequence length in the input (which would be useful if you have a process that might not take the same amount of time for each run). In practice, the library you use to implement an RNN might restrict you to a static sequence length. Sometimes practitioners use multiple RNN streams, concatenated later, to analyze long- and short-term windows. Ideally, using multiple time windows captures both short- and long-term features without competing with each other in a single pass.

Analyzing Autoencoders

Autoencoders are a very special type of neural network — the output of the network is designed to be the same as the input! If you're thinking, "That is the most useless idea for a network I have ever heard of," you're not alone, but just bear with us for a second.

Autoencoders take in data and process it in the same way a typical feed-forward neural network does, but with an architecture typically designed to feature layers increasingly smaller than the input. Figure 11-5 displays the architecture of an autoencoder network.

The key to the autoencoder network's place in society is one of the network's layers (typically the middle one), labeled "latent space." The input is transformed into smaller representations of itself until it reaches the latent space layer. This is the encoding step. Once it reaches latent space, it begins to transform back into the output. This is the decoding step.

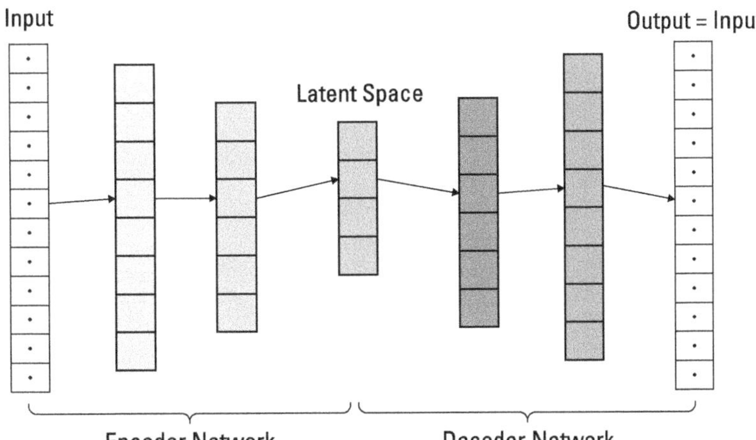

FIGURE 11-5: An autoencoder network.

Because latent space is typically smaller than the data input, the layer can be used for data compression — a lower-dimensional representation of the data can be stored and later used to recreate the data. Note that while storage needs are reduced, compute power is needed down the line to get the data back into shape. A well-trained autoencoder can give a near-perfect recreation of that data. This is another advantage, because in theory, the autoencoder has learned important features to store relevant to the data without a labeled output for the data itself. This handy property could help if you're creating a neural network without a lot of labeled examples — the lower layers of the autoencoder could be reused for useful feature selection without needing additional information.

Because the input and output of the data are the same, autoencoders are also popular for a subset of AI problems dealing with anomaly detection. If finding "unusual" situations is important to a practitioner (for example, detecting a cybersecurity network intrusion breach, or detecting if a piece of manufacturing equipment is acting up), an autoencoder trained only on "good" examples will have a high amount of recreation error when faced with the "bad" situations. This is especially useful if the bad situations are important to detect but rare enough not to have a lot of examples used for training a network. Of course, an autoencoder used for these situations won't be able to inform the user what exactly is wrong — only that something is acting up.

Finally, encoder and decoder networks can be taught to transfer input to a different representation via the encoding/decoding process. In this situation, the training data would need to include output examples that are different from the input in some way — think denoising style transfer. The network is trained to encode the latent space representation but decode it into something slightly different. Figure 11-6 gives an example of using an encoder/decoder network to slightly change an input.

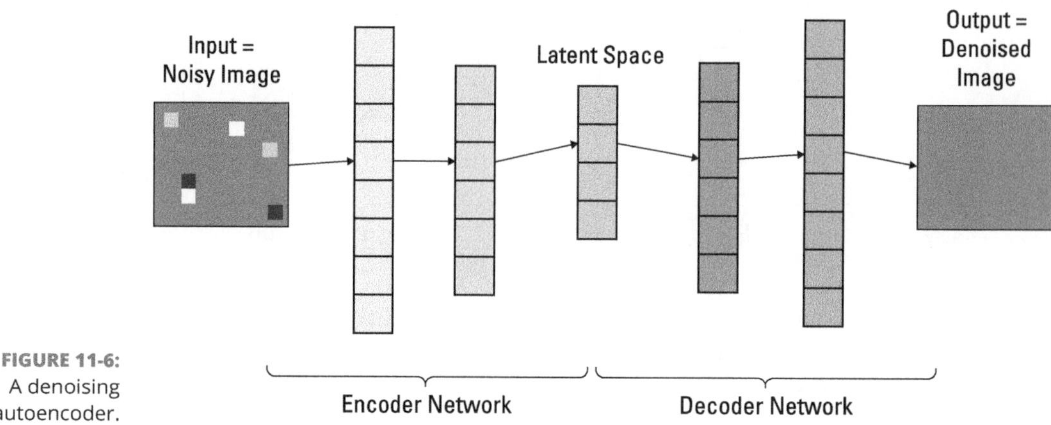

FIGURE 11-6: A denoising autoencoder.

Encoder and decoder layers don't exist just in autoencoder networks — taking a latent space representation of some input and turning it into something else is a useful property for other networks, as you see in generative AI in Chapter 16.

Attention, Please! Transformer Models

Transformer networks have taken the world by storm — the large language model you chat with or the generative model you use to make funny pictures of your dog are most likely transformer models. Again, transformers are a type of neural network architecture — but they use an "attention" mechanism to understand inputs in context.

With recurrent neural networks, you typically feed input into the architecture one step at a time. If you have the sequence: "The superhero saved the planet with his laser vision. He is now going to the eye doctor for an appointment," the model will first see the word "The," then "superhero," then "saved," and so on. By the time it gets to the word "appointment," it may have forgotten all about the superhero-and-laser-vision part. This is certainly important context if you're an eye doctor.

The attention mechanism, in contrast, looks at all the input together and in context with itself. This mechanism would be able to tell that the superhero with laser vision and the person going to the eye appointment are one and the same. Depending on the purpose of this system, it may be able to provide slightly more useful recommendations regarding equipment upgrades for the eye doctor.

Chapter 16 describes transformers and attention in much more detail. For now, know that the attention mechanism involves additional encoding steps that can be complicated in and of themselves. These are very powerful, but usually come with high data and compute power requirements. The most effective transformers use an astonishing amount of data and compute cycles to give you good output.

Transformers also typically come with more complicated architectures. Most neural networks function as "black boxes" with output that's hard to tie to a distinct decision-making process, but transformers tend to be the worst offenders. When transformers "hallucinate" or make up false outputs, it can be hard to determine why. Because of the data and power requirements, transfer learning is also very popular for creating new transformer models, which means mistakes in one model often permeate many other models.

Transformers are the current state-of-the-art when it comes to neural networks. However, they have some important limitations that aren't always discussed when someone is trying to convince you their new AI tool will save the world. Just be aware!

Using Multiple Architectures in One Network

While the architectures discussed in the previous section form some of the basic neural network categories, it's common to use multiple architectures together. This section covers some of the common combinations.

Convolutional layers in other networks

The power of convolutional filters lends itself to use in many other architecture types. Convolutional layers can be found in:

- Recurrent neural networks, especially when processing sequences of images (like videos)

- Autoencoders and decoders, especially for denoising, data augmentation, and generative AI
- Transformers, especially for text-to-image or other generative tasks

Encoders and decoders in other networks

Encoder and decoder layers are very powerful for creating feature maps and decoding features into other forms. Some uses of encoder and decoder layers in other networks include:

- Decoding feature representations into output for transformer networks, particularly in generative AI
- Using encoder/decoder layers in recurrent neural networks for anomaly detection through time
- Using sets of encoder/decoder models with other models for generative adversarial networks (GANs) (more on those in Chapter 17)

Hybrid architectures

Neural networks are certainly the most popular AI technique, but on some occasions, they can be used in tandem with other AI methods, like machine learning or reinforcement learning. Two models can be better than one!

Hybrid architecture uses include:

- Data preprocessing
- Sequential models
- Ensemble models
- Parameter optimization
- Feedback loops

Data preprocessing

Sometimes a hybrid architecture will use a simpler model as a data preprocessor and a neural network for the decision task. For example:

- A decision tree can be used to find the most important features before feeding them into a neural network.

» Principal component analysis can be used to create new, independent features before feeding them into a neural network.

» A linear regression model could be used to eliminate noncorrelated features before sending them to a neural network.

Sometimes preprocessing can even work the other way around. An autoencoder, for instance, could de-noise input before feeding it into a classical machine learning model like a decision tree. This could help mitigate some cybersecurity issues with intentionally manipulated input used to break AI systems. Figure 11-7 illustrates an example of a data preprocessing hybrid architecture.

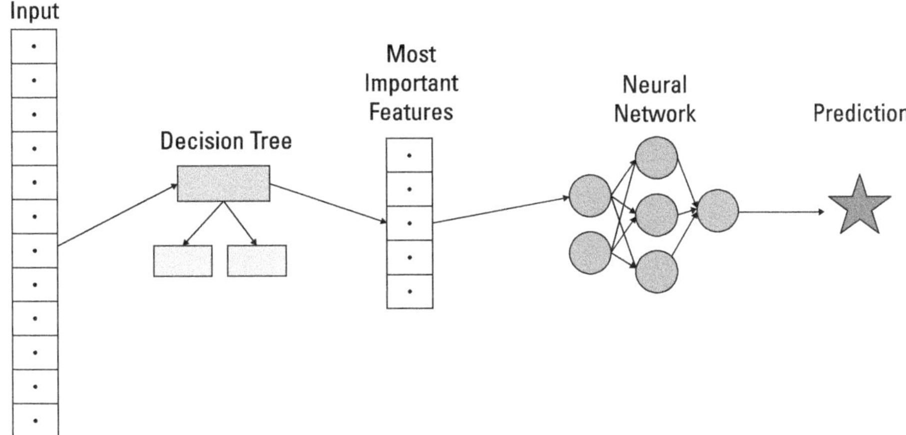

FIGURE 11-7: A preprocessing hybrid model architecture.

TECHNICAL STUFF

There is a branch of machine learning called *adversarial machine learning* that studies maliciously manipulating input (usually on image data and undetectable to the human eye) to get an AI model to incorrectly output a classification. This often involves introducing noise to the image that can't be visually seen but fools the underlying model decision. Because neural networks are difficult to interpret, this pixel manipulation isn't straightforward to mitigate. An autoencoder used to reduce noise but otherwise essentially recreates the image is one potential solution to this problem.

Sequential models

Sometimes, two model types can work sequentially. For instance, an RNN might try to predict what sensor readings will be ten minutes from now, while a decision tree takes the forecasted readings and predicts whether a process will be impacted. Using models in this way can let you benefit from the predictive power of less-explainable models and the decision clarity of less-accurate models. However, there's usually more technical overhead in getting multiple models to collaborate in tandem with each other, and changing one model might mean similarly updating the second. Figure 11-8 illustrates an example of a sequential model architecture.

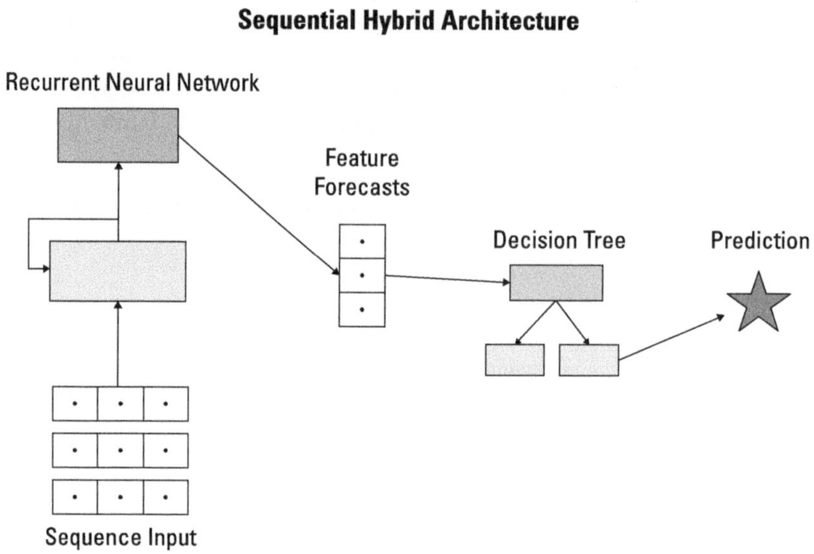

FIGURE 11-8: A sequential model hybrid architecture.

Ensemble models

Sometimes models need a second opinion. One way to combine machine learning models and neural networks is to simply have them work on the problem separately and vote on the answer. This happens with bagging and boosting models (Chapter 7), but any number of model types can work together and average an answer. This is especially useful if models capture different aspects of a problem, or in more critical situations where explainability is paramount. Figure 11-9 illustrates an example of a multiple model ensemble layout.

Parameter optimization

Finding the correct neural network architecture can be tricky, as the potential combinations of neurons and layers are unlimited. Genetic algorithms and reinforcement learning (more on them in Chapters 20 and 21) can provide a guided trial-and-error process to find effective neural network architectures without quite as much heartbreak. These approaches work for other neural network hyperparameters (learning rate, dropout, regularization) as well. Figure 11-10 illustrates an example of a parameter optimization model architecture.

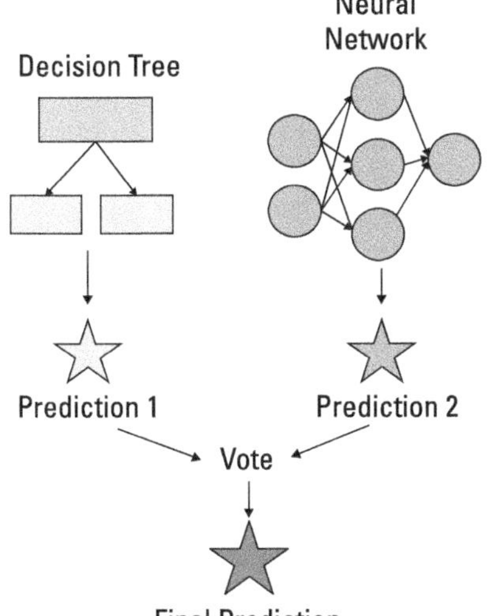

FIGURE 11-9: A multiple model ensemble architecture.

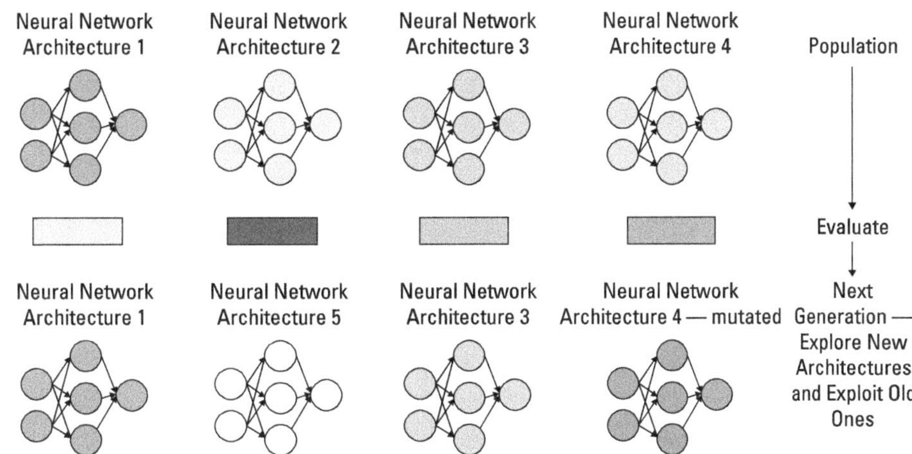

FIGURE 11-10: A parameter optimization hybrid model architecture.

Feedback loops

Collaboration between model types isn't always cooperative. A feedback loop, however, forces model types to be more deliberate about improving each other. For example, a genetic algorithm could inform the time window for an RNN, whose prediction error could then provide information to change the genetic algorithm's parameters. These types of models try to work together to improve both aspects at the same time. However, these models involve a lot more technical overhead and computer power to implement.

TIP

Neural networks are designed to mimic brain architectures — but brain architectures probably work more similarly to hybrid and ensemble models, with different neuron groups responsible for different tasks. Modularizing neural networks and creating collaborative groups with different purposes has shown promise in studies. However, this research direction hasn't been explored as much in the wake of powerful advancements like transformer models. While in theory, a powerful neural network should form functional groups by itself, this is probably an understudied area and worth looking into for more human-like reasoning.

4 Machine Vision with OpenCV

IN THIS PART . . .

Check out the common uses of machine vision in a variety of fields and explore its data considerations.

Write a program using the Open Source Computer Vision Library (OpenCV) and discover how it is used for a wide range of image-processing tasks.

Explore the structure of images in a digital world, and discover all that you ever wanted to know (and more) about color spaces.

Discover common AI machine vision tasks — classification, detection, segmentation, and instance segmentation.

Review the process of creating an object detector — collecting a dataset, annotating images, formatting your files, and training a model — and run your trained model in real time.

IN THIS CHAPTER

» Seeing the world through your own eyes

» Discovering how machine vision is commonly used

» Exploring the data needs of machine vision projects

» Installing and writing your first program in OpenCV

Chapter 12
Introducing Machine Vision

Of all the use cases for AI, machine vision may just be the most exciting. It's surprisingly simple to get powerful models up and running, and the results can be stunning. Image manipulation probably deserves its own book, but this chapter gives you a taste of what's possible in the field.

In this chapter, you explore the magical world of vision systems, starting with the inner workings of your own two eyes. You look at the common uses of machine vision in a variety of fields, from manufacturing to agriculture to medical imaging. You dig into the data considerations for machine vision and how this data is created. You evaluate some potential pitfalls of machine vision projects and how machine vision doesn't always align perfectly with a biological vision model. Finally, you install and write your first program with the Open Source Computer Vision Library (OpenCV).

Your Personal Vision System

If you ever need evidence that you're a biological marvel, we highly recommend you take a good, long look (pun intended) at your own human vision system. For seeing humans, this is thought to be the dominant sense for brain processing power. You're assigning an astonishing number of neurons to just this task — and you're very good at it! While humans don't take first prize in the animal kingdom (we're losing out to birds and mantis shrimp), our system is quite advanced.

Our system is also quite complicated. Figure 12-1 displays a diagram of a human eyeball.

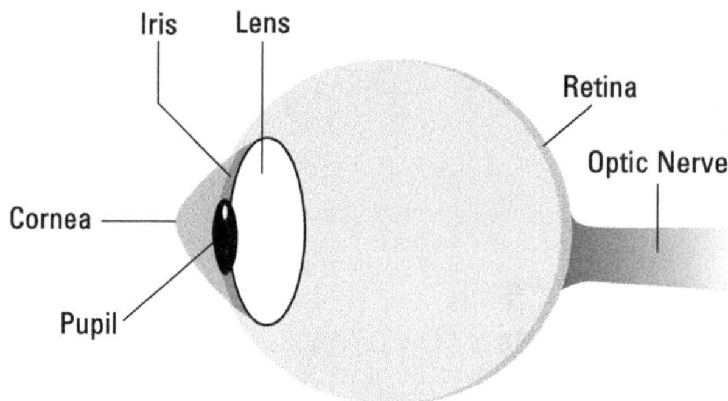

FIGURE 12-1: A human eyeball diagram.

The main components to be aware of are:

- Your pupil, which is the opening to your eye
- The lens, which the light bounces off of
- The retina, the surface on which light is focused by the lens to construct the image

The image is constructed upside-down on your retina. Your optic nerve carries the image to your brain so it can process it and reconstruct it right-side up. While we're not 100 percent sure how many processing pathways your brain has assigned to the image, we think there are separate centers for determining things like color and movement.

The way your eye focuses light on your retina can impact your vision. If your eye is too long, the focal point of your vision is in front of your retina, causing nearsightedness. When your eye is too short, the focal point is behind the retina, causing farsightedness. As the proud wearer of a very strong pair of contact lenses, Marz is very aware of the human eyeball's limitations in focusing light.

Factors other than eyeball size can impact your vision as well. Your iris color is determined by the amount of melanin you have. More melanin results in darker iris colors and reflects less light. If you have less melanin (lighter colors), more light is reflected. This can sometimes cause discomfort for people with lighter eyes in direct sunlight, as they are not as well-protected.

Comparing Biological Vision with Camera Vision

Looking at human vision is a good way to understand the differences in the ways we use and process image information. While humans use their eyeballs, machines are primarily reliant on cameras. Some concepts that differentiate between human and machine vision include:

- Focus
- Aperture
- Shutter speed
- Color interpretation
- Depth perception
- Information processing

Focus

Focus is the process of directing the light received with the lens. Both humans and cameras have a lens for this purpose — but you can change the shape of your lens, while a camera can primarily move a lens forward or backward rather than change its shape. If you were an octopus, you would be able to adjust the focal distance in your eyeball rather than the lens shape, which is just one of the many reasons why octopuses are on our shortlist of animals that may take over the world.

Aperture

An aperture is an opening that allows light into the system. For a camera, this is often adjustable. For a human, this is controlled by the iris and pupil. If you open your eyes wide, you'll have a large aperture and a shallow depth of field — meaning you'll be able to see objects in front of you more clearly. Creating a small aperture (by squinting) allows you to focus on a wider depth of field and sometimes see areas farther away. Every time you try to determine if that thing in the sky is a bird, a plane, or a UFO, you're adjusting your aperture size to give yourself the best chance of identification.

Shutter speed

The shutter speed is how long light is allowed to enter the system. This works together with the aperture to help set the depth of field. For humans, your brain's processing likely takes care of this in the background.

Color interpretation

Color interpretation in humans is carried out by cone cells. We have three types of cone cells for red, green, and blue light wavelengths. Your rod cells help you see in low light, but they can't see color. A camera, on the other hand, uses photoreceptive material with red, green, and blue filters. Cameras need a flash for low light, or else they need to rely on other wavelengths. An interesting tendency of machine vision — it's often less useful in low-light situations.

Depth perception

Depth perception in humans is achieved through binocular vision: We have two eyes that work together to give us one comprehensive heads-up display. A machine vision system usually needs to use a second camera or an alternative sensor to get a sense of depth. If a second camera or sensor is used, the system also needs to determine how to combine the information.

Information processing

Vision information processing in humans is, quite frankly, wild. You're flipping an image upside-down, constantly. You are stitching together two separate sources of images. You can shift focus much more rapidly than a camera can move. Your eyes move so fast (these movements are called *saccades*) that your brain has to blur the information in between to avoid overwhelming you. A camera comes with none of the inherent processing you are constantly implementing. These are important to remember when a machine vision system gives unexpected results — while the machine system is modeled from the biological vision system, many fundamental differences remain.

Exploring Common Use Cases for Machine Vision

Machine vision is a popular field of AI, and it makes sense — with seeing humans so reliant on vision as a system, automating human-originated tasks often requires an imagery component. Some industries that commonly use machine vision include:

- Manufacturing
- Agriculture
- Medical imaging

In manufacturing, machine vision is often used for product and parts inspections. Manufacturing lines often involve standardized, fixed processes of creating or modifying a part, which is useful for controlled-vision environments. Quality control machine vision systems can measure parts that deviate from specifications and kick them off a line for scrap or rework. Since this is often tedious work for a human, delegating this work to a machine vision system is handy. However, some manufacturers create enclosures that can't be fully viewed by one fixed camera on a line. In this case, human inspection may still be needed, although some companies are exploring using a camera in conjunction with a robotic arm so that the covered field of view is more flexible. Other manufacturing companies may have parts that are highly reflective, which can impact the performance of many light-sensitive systems.

In our lab, a senior design team worked on a manufacturing defect identification project in which the product would always travel down a conveyor belt at a fixed distance from the camera. The constrained system and controlled lighting in the factory made the project successful and used much less data than normally would be required for a project like this!

In agriculture, machine vision systems are useful to identify plant growth stages as well as the presence of pests and diseases in a field. For crops planted at roughly the same time, a fixed-position camera (or two) is sometimes all that is needed to measure plant growth stages and determine appropriate actions. In general, however, farmers have much larger areas to cover, and the number of cameras that would need to be installed could be prohibitive. Some farmers are using autonomous robotic rover platforms with mounted cameras to cover more ground with less cost. Growers have also explored drones for vision sensing. Organizations have built software that allows farmers to snap photos with their smartphones and send images off to remote processing centers to identify characteristics of interest.

There are many more light wavelengths than those visible to humans. Interestingly, plants give off a lot of growth and health information in other light bands — making hyperspectral cameras useful for some agriculture machine vision tasks. However, hyperspectral cameras are often expensive, and processing the vast amount of information they provide can be a lot of work. Infrared cameras have also been used specifically for plants.

Medical imaging is another big area for machine vision. Interpreting medical images, such as X-rays or magnetic resonance imaging (MRI) scans, can be time-consuming and take expert knowledge. Machine vision systems have had success in a variety of tasks, including detecting breast cancer cells and monitoring vital signs in infants. Machine vision is quite promising for this area, since staffing shortages or processing delays can quite literally be deadly. However, the medical field has inherently more liability than other industries, and it's important to understand limitations of systems and the necessity of having a medical professional in the loop.

Considering Machine Vision Data Needs

Machine vision tasks fundamentally need one type of data — an image! (But you already knew that.) For some basic image processing tasks, sometimes a couple of images will suffice. However, when it comes to applying AI techniques to machine vision tasks, having a *lot* of images and/or videos can be the difference between a project's success or failure.

The specific data collection needs of a project can vary greatly. In general, some collection considerations include:

- How many objects do you need to identify or track in the image?
- Will the system be deployed at one location, or many?
- How high a resolution do the images need to be?
- How varied are the conditions the machine needs to operate in?
- How often will new tasks be added to the system?

Generally, the more variables your system has to account for, the more data you will need to collect. This can sometimes be a tedious process. (For example, in our laboratory, we tasked 12 people with annotating 700+ images of weeds in a field for an autonomous weeding robot project. It took multiple hours. Fortunately, no one quit the program!) Sometimes you can get away with techniques to synthesize more data from existing data. These data augmentation techniques are covered more in Chapter 14.

Uncovering Potential Machine Vision Pitfalls

Machine vision systems can be very powerful, but they struggle in some areas. This section looks at some concerns with lighting, coverage, and ethical factors.

Lighting

Machine vision systems have historically been quite sensitive to low lighting and harsh reflections. Maintaining consistent lighting conditions usually increases a system's accuracy. This is sometimes possible in a controlled lighting environment indoors, depending on the application. For an outdoor environment, this is a lot harder. In some agricultural machine vision studies, images were actually taken at night with a controlled camera flash to achieve consistent image quality. Often, engineers try to resolve these issues by having multiple examples of different image lighting conditions in a training dataset.

Coverage

Image collection is limited to camera location, and high-quality cameras can be expensive. If only a few areas are involved in the machine vision automation task, sometimes this isn't an issue. For more dynamic environments, trying to cover all areas with statically mounted cameras is impossible. For these situations, enabling camera movement is an increasingly interesting research area. Sometimes this can be covered by a robotic platform (autonomous or teleoperated) or a drone. While these technologies are becoming more accessible, using a machine vision system consistently across a wide coverage area can be a pretty expensive endeavor.

Ethical concerns

All AI systems have associated ethical concerns, but stakes are often higher when using a machine vision system, since misuse can quickly be tied to personal appearance and identity. It's important to note these potential issues when designing a system.

Data privacy and permission

Machine vision systems are usually built on large datasets. While in applied cases the data is often custom-collected, sometimes datasets are bought or scraped off the Internet. When building a system, it's important to understand your data sources, as data can sometimes be acquired and sold illegally, without permission or compensation to the person who generated it or whose information might be featured in it.

Dataset bias

Systems are only as good as the data they were trained on, and machine vision systems are going to reflect their training data. This can cause issues when a training dataset isn't representative of the samples it will be used on, or when data is mislabeled. This has caused a myriad of issues, especially when it comes to AI image and video generation.

System use

As with every other tool, bad actors are out there. Generative machine vision tools can create harmful fake images and videos featuring people without their permission for nefarious purposes. Even if a system is used correctly for its intended purpose, there may still be ethical concerns. Surveillance systems by governments or businesses, for example, are controversial.

REMEMBER

The world of machine vision is a lot of fun — there's nothing quite like seeing your first bounding box pop up on a finished object detector with the correct prediction. Just remember that, as you build and use these tools, their designs have limitations and potential for misuse.

"Hello Visual World" with OpenCV

Now that you have some background on the world of machine vision, it's time to dive in! In this chapter (and in Chapter 13), you'll explore a very powerful library in Python: OpenCV.

What is OpenCV?

OpenCV, which stands for Open Source Computer Vision, is a library of tools for a wide range of image processing tasks. It even includes some AI capabilities. OpenCV has bindings for both C++ and Python languages, but here we focus on the Python capabilities, of course.

OpenCV can read in and manipulate images, and it can also use your webcam, if you have one attached to your computer or laptop. In the following sections, we walk you through writing two code files: one to read in and display an image, and another to get your webcam up and running.

Writing your first OpenCV program

First, you need to install OpenCV if you don't have it installed already. If you are following along in this book using the Anaconda programming environment, run the following command in your virtual environment:

```
conda install conda-forge::opencv
```

TIP

If you get a permissions error when trying to install the library, try running the Anaconda Prompt as an administrator.

OpenCV is not a small library, so this might take a minute or two. Once you have the library installed, go ahead and grab your favorite image (I'm using an example image, `wood.jpg`), and run the code in Listing 12-1.

LISTING 12-1: Reading and Displaying an Image in OpenCV (read_display_image.py)

```
import cv2 as cv

img = cv.imread('wood.jpg')
key = ord("r")
while key != ord("s"):
    cv.imshow("Wood Picture", img)
    key = cv.waitKey()
cv.destroyAllWindows()
```

This code listing does the following:

- Imports the OpenCV library (cv2) and aliases it to `cv`.
- Uses the `cv.imread` function to read in a sample image to a variable, `img`. The library just requires the name of the image. There are fancier things you can do with this function, but this will get you started!
- Creates a variable, `key`, to store a key press. Initially, this is just set as a random key on the keyboard. This variable is used to help give you some control over windowing, which can sometimes get a little tricky in OpenCV.

» Creates a condition dependent on a key press. While the "s" key on your keyboard hasn't been pressed, it will run the code inside the `while` loop.

» Uses the `cv.imshow()` function to display the image in a window. The first argument is the name of the window that will pop up, and the second argument is the actual image.

» Pauses inside the while loop while waiting for a keypress. The `cv.waitKey()` function can be used later to control the frame rate of your window display.

» Uses the `cv.destroyAllWindows()` function at the end of the code to clean up any display windows you may have opened during the run.

After you run the code, you should see a window pop up on your computer with the image displayed, as shown in Figure 12-2. The window's name should match the label you passed the `cv.imshow()` function. Remember to press the "s" key on your keyboard to close the window when you're finished.

FIGURE 12-2: The output of running the code in Listing 12-1.

TIP

If you run into any issues working with OpenCV, check out the tips in "Troubleshooting the OpenCV toolchain" later in this chapter.

Writing your second OpenCV program

Now that you have image reading down pat, you're going to run a second program that will access your webcam, if you have one associated with your computer. Listing 12-2 displays the code for the operation.

LISTING 12-2: Opening a Webcam with OpenCV (webcam.py)

```
import cv2 as cv

webcam = cv.VideoCapture(0)
key = ord("r")
while key != ord("s"):
    ret, still = webcam.read()
    cv.imshow("Webcam Feed", still)
    key = cv.waitKey(10)
cv.destroyAllWindows()
```

This program does the following:

- Imports the OpenCV library as `cv`.
- Creates a variable, `webcam`, which stores the camera object you're going to access. By passing in the value of 0 to the `cv.VideoCamera()` function, you're telling the function to grab your default webcam attached to your laptop. (If you have a different camera plugged in or a different setup, you may need to adjust the value.)
- Creates the `key` variable to help control the window.
- Creates a condition based on whether or not the "s" key was pressed on the keyboard.
- Reads in an image from the webcam. The `read()` function you're calling on the `webcam` variable returns two things. The first is a True/False value indicating whether or not the image grab was successful. You're not using the return value here, but it's a good troubleshooting tool if you're having issues connecting. The second is the actual image.
- Displays the image using the `cv.imshow()` function. The window is called "Webcam Feed."

» Uses the `cv.waitkey()` function to wait 10 milliseconds while waiting for a key frame. If the "s" key wasn't pressed, it will go back through the `while` loop. The `cv.waitkey()` function essentially controls the frame rate of the feed.

Figure 12-3 displays the output of running the code file. You should get a named window that displays your webcam feed. Pretty cool! It's fun when you run a "Hello, World" program and get to wave to yourself.

FIGURE 12-3: Webcam feed output of running Listing 12-2.

OpenCV can be a lot of fun to use. You get to see it in action doing image processing in Chapter 13.

Troubleshooting the OpenCV toolchain

OpenCV is a powerful library, but the toolchain from Python to the OpenCV library to your operating system can sometimes get bumpy. If you are having issues, the following tips may help:

» Make sure you have the image to display inside the same folder as your code file. If this isn't the case, you'll need to either move the photo or adjust your filepath in the `cv.imread()` function.

- If you closed the window without pressing the key to close it in Python (which we have done many, many times, including twice while creating this example), you may need to force the terminal to close and then open a new one.
- If the window opened is halfway off the screen, the image might be a bit too big for normal window display. Your program is still working properly, but you may want to use a smaller image if you want to see the entire thing at once.

The library version we are using is actually the second version of OpenCV, hence why the import statement uses `cv2`. When you are looking up examples in the wild, some people use `cv2` as the direct imported module, while others alias the library to plain `cv`, as we did in Listing 12-1. Just remember to check the import statement if a version is unclear.

IN THIS CHAPTER

» Uncovering a new way of thinking about images

» Exploring color spaces, image blurring, and kernel operations

» Locating the image gradient and refining with basic image edge detection

Chapter 13
Getting Started with OpenCV

Images are amazing to work with, but translating a picture of your breakfast into something displayable on a screen involves understanding the underlying data characteristics. Opening a picture from the camera roll is a little different from accessing it in Python. We're going to take a look at how we can work image data into automated programs.

In this chapter, you get a crash course in basic OpenCV image manipulation. You start by exploring the structure of images in a digital world, and discover all that you ever wanted to know (and more) about color spaces. You explore image detail and blurring, and read about what a kernel is and how it's used to create basic feature extraction. You apply your newfound kernel knowledge to image gradients and basic edge detection. Throughout the chapter, you apply new concepts in Python with OpenCV examples. Finally, you explore how image processing techniques help AI models down the road.

Your Image Is in the Matrix

You look at images all the time and probably don't spend a lot of time thinking about how they got to you. To be fair, it's usually much less relevant to be wondering, "How is this object constructed for digital display?" and far more relevant to wonder, "Ha! How did that cat get in *there*?" whenever a friend shows you a picture on their phone.

However, understanding how images are represented as data is important both for image manipulation and for AI model construction. While an image may look like a flat, 2D object, it's actually a 3D matrix of pixels.

A *pixel* is the most basic construction unit of an image — usually one single number that stands for a color value. A typical image is made up of hundreds or thousands of pixels, depending on the image resolution. Generally, the more pixels in an image, the higher its resolution and the more detailed it looks. Except for a very low-resolution image (think 1980s video games), it's generally hard to see an individual pixel in an image (but if you zoom in, you'll see it!). When you do, it looks like a square made up of one single color.

It's easy to conceptualize pixels stacked in a matrix to make up an image's height and width — and not too hard to see how these little squares of color eventually turn into a cat eating a cheeseburger or something similar. But this still seems like a 2D object — where on Earth does the third dimension come from?

Well, we could potentially come up with a number to represent every single color — but humans really see colors in different *channels* (red, blue, and green). Colors we perceive are combinations of those basic channels. Computers and cameras also encode information in terms of channels for display purposes. The mixture of the channels gives us the final color image.

Figure 13-1 shows a diagram of an image as a 3D matrix — pixel values stacked to form the image dimensions on red, green, and blue color channels.

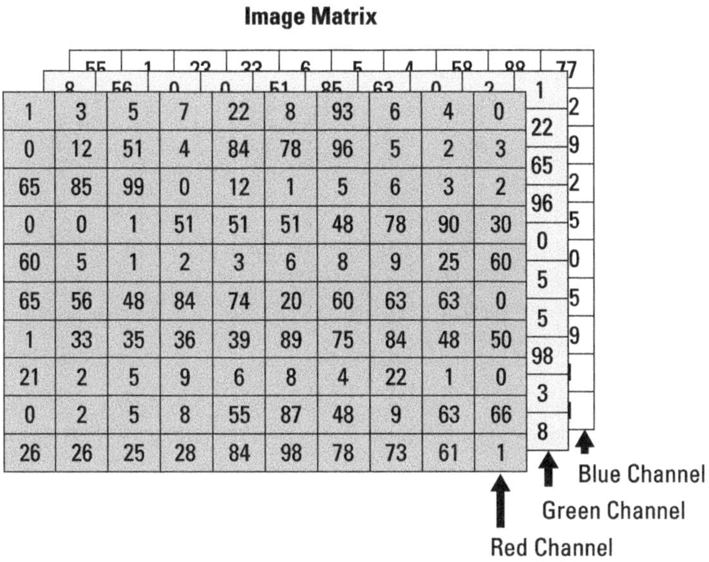

Image Matrix

1	3	5	7	22	8	93	6	4	0
0	12	51	4	84	78	96	5	2	3
65	85	99	0	12	1	5	6	3	2
0	0	1	51	51	51	48	78	90	30
60	5	1	2	3	6	8	9	25	60
65	56	48	84	74	20	60	63	63	0
1	33	35	36	39	89	75	84	48	50
21	2	5	9	6	8	4	22	1	0
0	2	5	8	55	87	48	9	63	66
26	26	25	28	84	98	78	73	61	1

Blue Channel
Green Channel
Red Channel

FIGURE 13-1: A matrix representation of an image.

Manipulating Pixels

A good way to understand pixels in a digital image is to open your Python editor and play around with OpenCV by inspecting some image pixels. You can use any image to do this, or use the example image, `trees.jpg`, shown in Figure 13-2 and available as part of the book's source code. Listing 13-1 displays the code to do this. Figure 13-3 shows the terminal output of the program, and Figure 13-4 displays the output image of the program.

LISTING 13-1: Pixel Manipulation in OpenCV (pixels.py)

```
import cv2 as cv

img = cv.imread('trees.jpg')
key = ord("r")
print(img.dtype)

#Rows, Columns, Channels
print(img.shape)

#Blue intensity of pixel 40, 40 (down)
print(img[40, 40, 0])
print(img[40, 40, 1])
```

(continued)

LISTING 13-1: *(continued)*

```
print(img[40, 40, 2])

#Make a black square
img[0:100, 0:100, 0:3] = 0

while key != ord("s"):
    cv.imshow("Tree Picture", img)
    key = cv.waitKey()
cv.destroyAllWindows()
```

FIGURE 13-2: The unaltered example image, `trees.jpg`.

```
(examples) C:\Users\marze\Documents\Book\Code Files>python pixels.py
uint8
(551, 734, 3)
129
105
93

(examples) C:\Users\marze\Documents\Book\Code Files>
```

FIGURE 13-3: Terminal output of Listing 13-1.

FIGURE 13-4: Image output of Listing 13-1.

This program does the following:

- Imports the OpenCV library.
- Reads in the `trees.jpg` image.
- Prints the type of the image. The output is `uint8`, which stands for 8-bit unsigned integer. This is the number type of all the image matrix values.
- Prints the `shape` of the image. OpenCV represents the image shape as rows, columns, and channels, where 0 starts at the top-left corner.
- Prints the blue, green, and red channel values of pixel 40 down and 40 across. OpenCV has a slightly unusual color space ordering — more on that later!
- Sets the image pixel value from 0 to 99 pixels down and from 0 to 99 pixels to 0 (black) for all three channels. This will show up as a black square in the top-left corner of the image.
- Displays the image using a while loop.

Color Spaces and Blurry Faces

You may have heard of an RGB color space — red, green, and blue. OpenCV uses these colors in its matrix representation, but in the order blue, green, red, or BGR. So, channel index 0 is the blue color channel, channel index 1 is the green color channel, and channel index 2 is the red color channel.

TECHNICAL STUFF

RGB is a more commonly known color space than BGR, but BGR is OpenCV's default. There is a long history to why this is OpenCV's color space of choice, involving a legacy software stack a mile long. Just know that if you are interfacing OpenCV code with other programs, understanding the color space conversion function will come in handy.

You can arrange the blue, green, and red channels in any order to create a color space that works for your program. You can also use an entirely different encoding scheme. The HSV color space, for example, uses hue, saturation, and value information to encode an image.

High-resolution images sometimes contain more information than a processing program can realistically handle. In that case, it's useful to take the 3D image back down to a 2D object. This gives you a grayscale, or black-and-white, image. The pixel values end up encoding only the light value at a given position in the image.

OpenCV uses the `cvtColor()` function to remap color spaces. Listing 13-2 displays the code to make color space changes to an image. Figure 13-5 displays the terminal output, and Figure 13-6 displays the effect on the output image.

LISTING 13-2: Color Spaces in OpenCV (color_spaces.py)

```
img = cv.imread('trees.jpg')
key = ord("r")

#BGR Pixel 40, 40
print(img[40, 40, 0:3])
#Convert to RGB
img = cv.cvtColor(img, cv.COLOR_BGR2RGB)
#RGB Pixel 40, 40
print(img[40, 40, 0:3])
img = cv.cvtColor(img, cv.COLOR_RGB2BGR)
img = cv.cvtColor(img, cv.COLOR_BGR2HSV)
#HSV Pixel 40, 40
```

```
print(img[40, 40, 0:3])
#Grayscale
img = cv.cvtColor(img, cv.COLOR_HSV2BGR)
img = cv.cvtColor(img, cv.COLOR_BGR2GRAY)
print(img[40,40])

while key != ord("s"):
    cv.imshow("Tree Picture", img)
    key = cv.waitKey()
cv.destroyAllWindows()
```

```
(examples) C:\Users\marze\Documents\Book\Code Files>python color_spaces.py
[129 105  93]
[ 93 105 129]
[110  71 129]
104

(examples) C:\Users\marze\Documents\Book\Code Files>
```

FIGURE 13-5: Terminal output of Listing 13-2.

FIGURE 13-6: Image output of Listing 13-2.

The program does the following:

- Imports the OpenCV library and reads in the `trees.jpg` example image.
- Prints out all BGR color channel values of pixel 40, 40.
- Uses the `cv.cvtColor()` function to convert the color space to RBG and prints out the same pixel. You can see the values are the same, but in a different order.
- Uses the `cvtColor()` function to convert the color space back to BGR and then to HSV, and prints out the same pixel. The values are now slightly different due to the new encoding.
- Uses the `cvtColor()` function to convert the color space back to BGR and then to grayscale. Now, the same printed pixel only has one value: the darkness/lightness value.
- Displays the image, now in grayscale.

Another common task for image processing is adding a blur. This might seem strange, as usually the blurred images are the ones you're deleting from your camera roll. In Marz's case, these are usually the images her pocket decided to take on her phone without her knowledge.

However, when a lot of processing is going to be done on an image — as is often the case with AI model preparation — adding a blur can help reduce the noise in an image and add some smoothness. This often helps image processing techniques run faster and with fewer errors. Listing 13-3 gives sample code for blurring an image, and Figure 13-7 gives the output image.

LISTING 13-3: Blurring an Image in OpenCV (blur_image.py)

```
import cv2 as cv

img = cv.imread('trees.jpg')
key = ord("r")

img = cv.cvtColor(img, cv.COLOR_BGR2GRAY)
img = cv.blur(img, (5,5))

while key != ord("s"):
    cv.imshow("Tree Picture", img)
    key = cv.waitKey()
cv.destroyAllWindows()
```

FIGURE 13-7: Image output of Listing 13-3.

The program does the following:

- Imports OpenCV and reads in the example image.
- Uses the `cvtColor()` function to convert the image to grayscale.
- Uses the `blur()` function to blur the image. The second argument (5,5) is the kernel size to use to blur the image. A kernel (more on that in the next section!) is a second, smaller matrix that goes over the image and conducts an operation on the picture. The size of the matrix impacts the effect of the operation on the image. We are using a 5-by-5 kernel size for this blur. You can adjust the size of the kernel to get different results.
- Displays the output image.

You can use several types of blur functions in OpenCV. The default blur function uses an average blur technique. You can also use a Gaussian blur function (`GaussianBlur()`), which helps reduce Gaussian noise (when you see Gaussian, think normal distribution). Median blurring (`medianBlur()`) can help remove salt and pepper noise from an image, as you might see in an old-timey photograph.

Reviewing Kernel Operations

Several techniques in image processing make use of a kernel. A *kernel* is a special, usually smaller matrix of values that is used as a sliding window on top of the original image. The values in the kernel are multiplied by the pixel values underneath and added together to form an output pixel for a new image. The kernel then slides to the next position (left to right, top to bottom) and repeats the process. Sometimes, the output pixel is multiplied or divided by a value, depending on the filter type. Figure 13-8 demonstrates this operation.

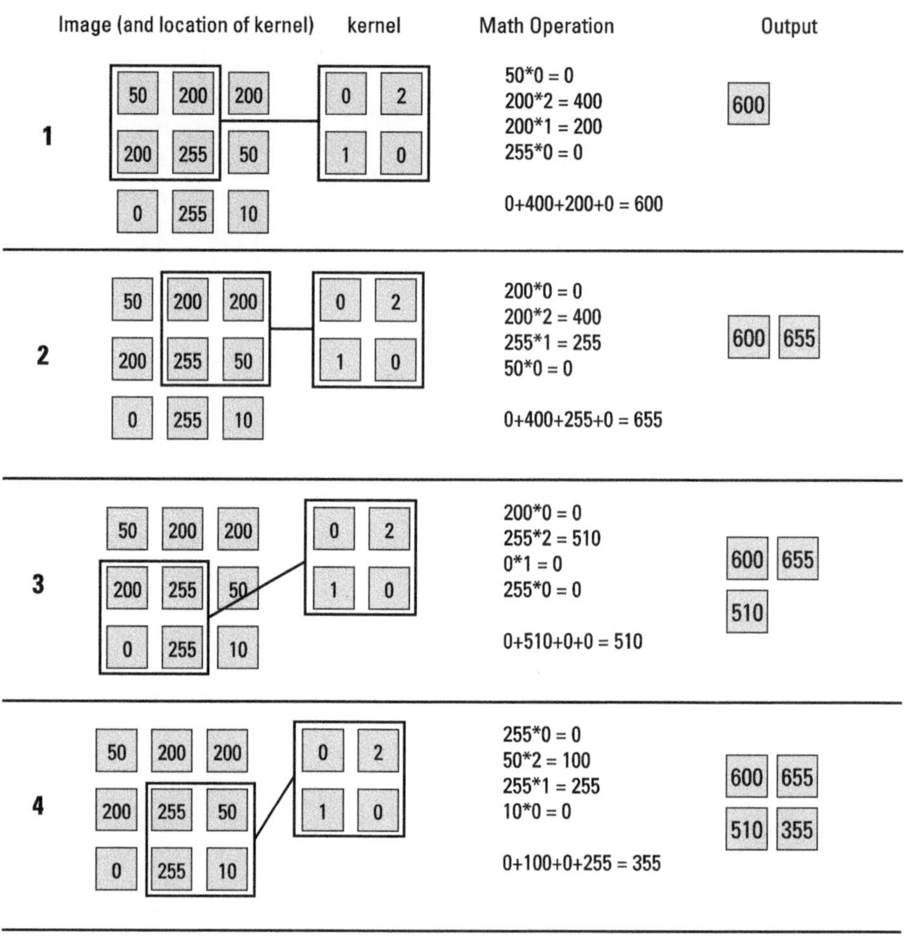

FIGURE 13-8: Kernel operations on an image.

A kernel (often used in filtering operations) allows the output to take information from a neighborhood of values. In Chapters 8 and 9, we looked at neural network mathematics, which involves multiplying inputs by weights and summing the result to get increasingly higher-level features. Using kernels allows you to perform a similar operation in two dimensions, which is very useful for AI models.

Even without AI, however, kernels are useful for certain processing techniques and for directly extracting features from an image.

TIP

Kernel operations reduce the neighborhood of pixels covered by the kernel size down to just one output value. If you are using a kernel and want the output image to remain the same size, you often use padding or borders on the edges of the image (which usually repeats the pixel values or sets them to 0) to counteract this effect. Many OpenCV functions apply this under the hood by default.

Finding the Image Gradient

One of the most useful things to understand in an image is how the image pixels change across the matrix. Images that are solid one- or two-color are rarely that interesting (unless you are designing a hotel lobby, for some reason). The changes in an image give rise to more information: background and foreground, lines, and objects.

Finding the image gradient is all about locating the change across the image, which often outputs useful edge information. One way to approximate the image gradient is with a Sobel kernel. The kernel can be applied in the x direction (to find vertical lines), the y direction (to find horizontal lines), or both directions at once. Listing 13-4 displays the code for finding the image gradient. Figure 13-9 displays the output of running the program.

LISTING 13-4: Taking an Image Gradient with OpenCV (image_gradient.py)

```
import cv2 as cv

img = cv.imread('trees.jpg')
key = ord("r")

img = cv.cvtColor(img, cv.COLOR_BGR2GRAY)
img = cv.blur(img, (5,5))

#Sobel derivative - x direction
sobel_x = cv.Sobel(img, -1, 1, 0, ksize=5)
```

(continued)

LISTING 13-4: (continued)

```
#Display
while key != ord("s"):
    cv.imshow("Tree Picture", sobel_x)
    key = cv.waitKey()
key = ord("r")

#Sobel derivative - y direction
sobel_y = cv.Sobel(img, -1, 0, 1, ksize=5)

#Display
while key != ord("s"):
    cv.imshow("Tree Picture", sobel_y)
    key = cv.waitKey()
key = ord("r")

#Sobel derivative - both directions
sobel_both = cv.Sobel(img, -1, 1, 1, ksize=5)
while key != ord("s"):
    cv.imshow("Tree Picture", sobel_both)
    key = cv.waitKey()

cv.destroyAllWindows()
```

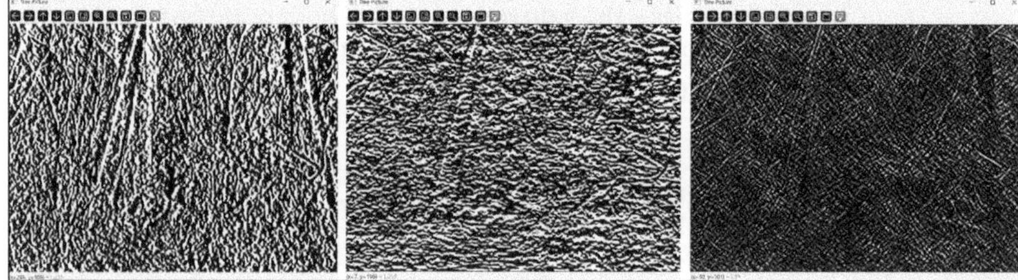

FIGURE 13-9: Image output of running Listing 13-4.

The program does the following:

- Imports OpenCV and loads the example image.
- Converts the color space to grayscale and adds a blur.
- Uses the `Sobel()` function to apply the Sobel kernel and display the output image. The first function argument is the image, the second is the output

depth, the third is the order of the x derivative (set to 1), the third is the order of the y derivative (set to 0), and the `ksize` argument sets the kernel size (5 by 5, in this case).

- Uses the `Sobel()` function to apply the Sobel kernel (this time in the y direction) and display it.
- Uses the `Sobel()` function to apply the kernel in both the x and y direction and display it.

You can see in the output image that the first derivative shows some of the vertical picture edges, the second shows horizontal edges, and the third shows both.

Refining with Canny Edge Detection

Taking the image gradient can give you a basic idea of the edges in a picture, but the resulting picture is often pretty noisy. Canny edge detection can give you a more refined output.

Canny edge detection removes noise through blurring and takes the image gradient, as discussed in the previous section. However, it adds two additional steps:

- **Suppressing non-maximum pixels:** Each pixel is checked in its neighborhood (based on the gradient) to see if it's the maximum pixel for that group. If it is, we keep it. Otherwise, it's thrown out as an edge candidate.
- **Hysteresis thresholding:** This uses two threshold values to decide what edges are strong enough to be kept. The upper and lower thresholds are set by you, the programmer. If an edge is above the upper threshold, it's kept ("strong edge"). If it's below the minimum threshold, it's thrown out. Edges between the two thresholds are checked: If they are part of a "strong edge," they're kept; if not, we toss 'em.

Listing 13-5 gives a program example of canny edge detection, with a new tool: trackbars. Trackbars in OpenCV allow you to create sliders with values you can pass into your program. In this example, you'll create two trackbars, one for the lower threshold position and one for the upper threshold position. You can play around with these values until your image edges look about right. Figure 13-10 gives the image output of the program.

LISTING 13-5: Canny Edge Detection in OpenCV (edges.py)

```
import cv2 as cv

img = cv.imread('trees.jpg')
key = ord("r")
img = cv.cvtColor(img, cv.COLOR_BGR2GRAY)

def nothing(pos):
    pass

cv.namedWindow('controls')
cv.createTrackbar("lower", 'controls', 0, 225, nothing)
cv.createTrackbar("upper", 'controls', 0, 225, nothing)
while key != ord("s"):
    lower = int(cv.getTrackbarPos('lower', 'controls'))
    upper = int(cv.getTrackbarPos('upper', 'controls'))
    display_img = cv.Canny(img, lower, upper)
    cv.imshow("Tree Picture", display_img)
    key = cv.waitKey(5)
```

FIGURE 13-10: Image output of Listing 13-5.

The program does the following:

- » Imports OpenCV and loads the example image.
- » Converts the image to grayscale.
- » Defines a function called `nothing`, which takes in one argument and does . . . nothing. This is a callback function that will be passed to the trackbar every time a position is moved. In this case, you don't need to do additional processing when the trackbar value changes, so the function only executes a `pass` instruction.
- » Creates a window named `controls` with the `namedWindow()` function.
- » Creates two trackbars: `lower` and `upper` with the `createTrackbar()` function. Both trackbars are named, assigned to the `controls` window, given a range of 0 as the lower end and 255 as the upper end, and given the `nothing` function as their callback. A pixel can take a value of 0 – 255, since the integers are 8-bit.
- » Displays the image in the loop. The `getTrackbarPos()` function is used to get the lower and upper hysteresis threshold values, which are passed to the `Canny()` function.

As you can see in Figure 13-10, the sweet spot for the example tree image was about 222 on the lower end and 255 on the upper end. Feel free to play around with the trackbars and see how it impacts your output! This is also a fun program to run with your webcam if you want to see how it changes in real time.

TIP

Trackbars can be used for just about any numeric setting on an OpenCV function. Other handy uses for trackbars include exploring the kernel size for blurring and gradients, which lets you determine the amount of detail in the output.

From Image Processing to AI

If you made it this far in the chapter, you might be wondering, what does all of this image processing have to do with AI? While we didn't run a specific AI model in this chapter, the processing techniques used here are often used on images before an AI model trains on them. This is especially helpful if you are resource-constrained — while the fancy models can handle large images with full color channels, your own laptop might start complaining if asked to do the same.

When creating your own image dataset for an AI model, it's normal to run them through a few OpenCV functions before they make it to your convolutional neural network. Sometimes this is grayscaling an image, sometimes it's resizing the pixel matrix, and sometimes it's checking for images that don't belong. In summary:

- Grayscaling an image allows you to reduce the number of channels from 3 to 1.
- Blurring an image reduces the noise and typically helps images process faster.
- Locating image gradients and edges can help you perform some basic feature extractions on an image.

Now you have some tools to make a superstar rockin' image dataset! To investigate image classification, check out Chapter 14. To explore how to turn an image dataset into an AI object detector, turn to Chapter 15.

IN THIS CHAPTER

- » Exploring the hierarchy of machine vision tasks
- » Reviewing a typical convolutional neural network architecture
- » Training a convolutional neural network

Chapter 14

Classifying Images with Convolutional Neural Networks

The previous chapter explored the tools you need to create an image dataset and do some basic image manipulations with OpenCV. Now, it's time to see what you can do with AI! In this chapter, you review common AI machine vision tasks — classification, detection, segmentation, and instance segmentation. You discover the fundamental building blocks of convolutional neural networks and how they combine kernel operations with neural network architectures. And finally, you implement a classification convolutional neural network in the Keras library to classify handwritten digits.

Exploring the AI Machine Vision Task Hierarchy

Because machine vision typically deals with image data, the AI applications of the field are often sorted into the following hierarchy (the tasks get more complex as you go down the list):

- » Classification
- » Detection
- » Segmentation
- » Instance segmentation

This list isn't the end-all, be-all of machine vision tasks, but it encompasses the major ones. Figure 14-1 illustrates an example of each task.

Classification

Detection

Segmentation

Instance Segmentation

FIGURE 14-1: Tasks in the machine vision hierarchy.

Image *classification* is the simplest task in the hierarchy. It labels the entire image based on the presence or absence of something specific. In Figure 14-1, the image is classified as either "duck" or "no duck."

Object *detection* gives an actual location for an object in an image. This is often represented by rectangle coordinates overlaid on the image, which is called a *bounding box*. In Figure 14-1, object detection adds these handy boxes to note exactly where in the images the ducks are located.

Segmentation gives you a pixel-level resolution of the object you are looking for. This task usually returns a mask where all the noted pixels contain your object.

Instance segmentation goes one step further and separates different instances, or unique occurrences, of the object. In Figure 14-1, instance segmentation makes a clear distinction between duck 1 and duck 2.

The type of task you need your model to accomplish depends on your goals. In this chapter, we train both a classification and a detection model, but a lot of the tools we'll be using are modifiable if you want to try your hand at segmentation and instance segmentation.

TECHNICAL STUFF

Machine vision tasks can be more complicated than the hierarchy presented here, especially when dealing with video rather than static images. In some video applications, you may need to track instances of an object across multiple frames. In agriculture, this is somewhat common for crop yield counting, especially when the input is coming from continuous drone or rover footage. This is not a trivial undertaking!

Architecting a Convolutional Neural Network

In Chapter 13, we touch upon kernel operations for common OpenCV image processing tasks. In Chapter 8, we discuss neural network architectures. A convolutional neural network (CNN) combines both of these concepts!

Convolutional neural networks are similar to regular neural networks. Convolutional layers are made up of many different *filters*, which contain a *kernel* for each image channel. A typical color photo uses three kernels in a filter: one for each of the red, green, and blue channels. A grayscale image has only one kernel per filter.

TIP

In this chapter, we only deal with images that have either one color channel (grayscale) or three color channels (normal color images), so our filters will have only one or three kernels. However, some fields make use of multispectral imagery, which could have as many as 15 color channels! Multispectral images, as a result, can be quite computationally expensive.

Unlike in image processing, where kernel values are typically determined by an algorithm, the kernel values for a CNN are actually the *weights* of the network. The weights are modified during the training phase and changed based on the error, just like in a regular network. However, because the kernel acts like a sliding window across multiple inputs, the backpropagation calculation must account for the fact that the kernel weights are shared.

Figure 14-2 illustrates a typical convolutional neural network.

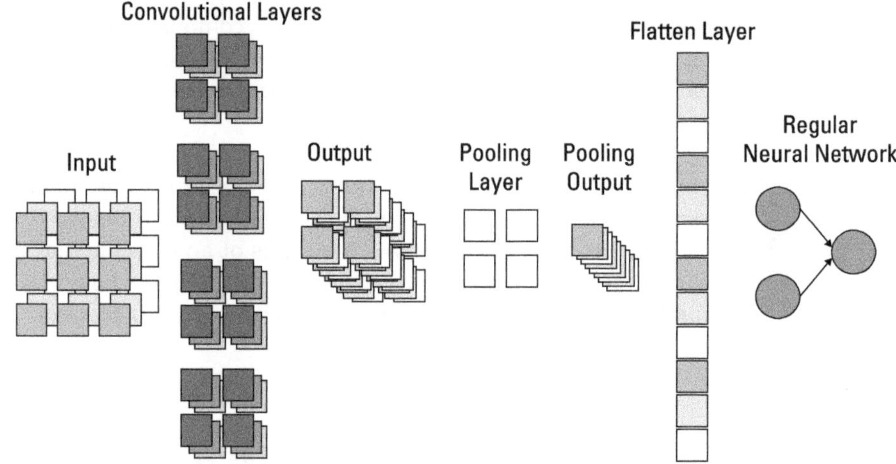

FIGURE 14-2: A typical convolutional neural network architecture.

This architecture can be broken into the following pieces:

- Convolutional layers
- Pooling layer
- Flatten layer
- Regular neural network

A *convolutional layer* applies each filter to the input image (one kernel per image channel). The convolution process multiplies each input pixel by each kernel weight in a sliding window manner. The resulting values are added together to create the output pixel for a given sliding window location. Then, the kernel is moved and the process is repeated.

An activation function is applied to the summed results, just like in a regular neural network. The output of a convolutional network is another (usually smaller) image. However, because layers usually use multiple filters at once, the output image will be "thicker" (contain more layers). For example, if a color image is passed as input to a convolutional layer with 32 filters, the next layer will receive a smaller image — with 96 layers (32 filters times 3 channels)! We sometimes refer to these thick stacks of output images as *feature maps*.

After convolution, it's very common to see a *pooling layer*. This layer also uses a kernel in a sliding window over the input, but it doesn't apply the full convolution process or activation function. There are two main types of pooling:

- Max pooling
- Average pooling

Max pooling only returns the largest value under the kernel, whatever that may be. Average pooling returns the average value of all pixels under the kernel. In practice, max pooling tends to be slightly more popular. Pooling helps reduce the dimensions of the CNN outputs, which helps you keep the complexity of the network down. Of course, you will lose some neighborhood data by using this reduction.

Both convolutional and pooling layers are usually repeated multiple times (depending on your network size). The number of layers, the number of filters per layer, the size of the filters, and the size of the pooling kernels to use are all decisions you make as the network designer. Like regular neural networks, however, designers tend to operate under the assumption that earlier layers have more "low-level" features and therefore will benefit from more filters than later layers. For example, you might assume that CNN convolutional layer 1 finds horizontal, vertical, and diagonal lines, while layer 2 finds corners and curves, layer 3 finds shapes, layer 4 finds facial features, and layer 5 finds facial organization patterns. While that's almost certainly not *exactly* what's happening, it's a rough architectural pattern estimate that can be helpful.

After a certain point, you need to move on from determining feature maps in an image to actually classifying the image. But how do you go from stacks and stacks of downsized images to a typical classification output?

As it turns out, the answer lies in Chapter 8 — you glue a regular neural network to the end of the CNN! A typical neural network is very good at turning input into a handful of output numbers you can use to categorize it. However, a regular neural network doesn't handle images, so you need to use a *flatten* layer. This layer breaks up all the images into one long vector sequence of numbers.

Finally, the *regular neural network* layer (or layers, depending on how large you want this section to be) accepts this long vector of numbers and turns it into your final image classification.

Like with regular neural networks, other layers exist for convolutional neural networks. Regularization and normalization layers are popular to make network operations more stable during training.

Transfer learning

The intuition behind the "feature map" model of the CNN layer assumes that earlier layers learn lower-level features, while later layers learn more complex ones. This is a surprisingly handy model when it comes to transfer learning. What classification tasks would benefit from detecting the presence of lines and edges? Maybe . . . all of them?

Transfer learning lets one model borrow knowledge from another. Transfer learning takes an existing, pretrained network and copies some or all of its properties to a new network. In particular, the copied properties are often layer/neuron architectures and weight and bias values. Typically, this involves grabbing the earlier layers from a different, fully trained model and tacking them on to the beginning of your own, new network. You then do some minor retraining for the specific task at hand in the last few layers of the new network (changing the weights/bias values of those layers only). There are several ways to do this (this example froze the pretrained layers and then added some of your own, untrained layers on top, but you could also retrain the whole transferred network for a significantly shorter amount of time). Transfer learning works well for many machine vision tasks, since these low-level features (which again, we sort of assume learn things like lines, shapes, organizations, and so on) are repeated for a huge variety of tasks. This also lets you benefit from a model that may have been trained on more data or computational resources than you had available for your application.

Transfer learning is a huge breakthrough in providing advanced AI capabilities to a wide audience. As we have mentioned before in the book, however, this also makes it easy to repeat mistakes learned in the base model. We use transfer learning when we create an object detector in Chapter 15, so this is something to keep in mind.

Common CNN models

Transfer learning is widespread in machine vision; as such, it's worthwhile to note some prominent models in the field. These models tend to have high-performing architectures, and other task-specific models will frequently use them as a starting point.

AlexNets, VGGNets, and ResNets have been popular classification models. AlexNet was one of the original widespread CNNs, with eight layers (five convolution and three fully connected). VGG (which stands for Visual Geometry Group, the model's developers) networks are classified into families based on the number of layers they contain. One popular performer was VGG-16, which has 13 convolutional layers and 3 fully connected layers. The ResNet family of models adds "skip" connections in specially architected residual blocks, which helps strengthen and simplify the learning process.

As of this book's publication, the Yolo family of models for object detection reigns supreme (especially in applications that need speed). Yolo stands for "you only look once," different from the "you only live once" catchphrase of Marz's high school days (often shouted approximately 15 minutes before a trip to the emergency room). Yolo models simultaneously predict objects to be classified and the bounding boxes that contain the objects. R-CNNs (region-based convolutional neural networks) work by dividing the images into regions that might contain an object of interest and then classifying the regions. They tend to be slower than Yolo but more precise.

Certain versions of Yolo and Mask R-CNN also work for segmentation tasks. Other types of CNN use only convolutional layers (which up- and down-size images with convolutional and deconvolutional layers) to segment pixels directly. U-Net and SegNet are popular examples of this architecture.

Training a Vision Classification Model in Keras

Enough talk about convolutional neural networks — let's implement one! For this example, you'll use the Keras library again. (Keras is first introduced in Chapter 10.) You'll also use the MNIST handwritten digits dataset, which contains 60,000 images of hand-drawn numbers between 0 and 9. While this is a hefty amount of data, the images themselves are only 28 × 28 pixels and grayscale, which reduces the channel information.

An example convolutional neural network for the MNIST dataset is shown in Listing 14-1. Figure 14-3 shows the terminal output of running Listing 14-1, and Figure 14-4 shows the image output of the same. The Internet is also chock full of examples for this particular dataset, so feel free to explore with different architectures!

TIP

If you are confused about some of the model parameters we're using, check back to Chapter 10.

LISTING 14-1: A Convolutional Neural Network in Keras (cnn_keras.py)

```
from keras.models import Sequential
from keras.layers import Conv2D, MaxPool2D, Dense, Flatten, Input
from keras.utils import to_categorical
from keras.datasets import mnist
import cv2 as cv
import numpy as np

#Dataset Prep
(x_train, y_train), (x_test, y_test) = mnist.load_data()
print("Training and Test Set X Shape")
print(x_train.shape)
print(x_test.shape)
print("Training and Test Set Y Shape")
y_train = to_categorical(y_train, num_classes=10)
y_test = to_categorical(y_test, num_classes=10)
print(y_train.shape)
print(y_test.shape)

#Model Prep
model = Sequential()
model.add(Input(shape=(28,28, 1)))
model.add(Conv2D(16, 3, activation="relu"))
model.add(MaxPool2D(pool_size=(4,4)))
model.add(Conv2D(8, 3, activation="relu"))
model.add(MaxPool2D(pool_size=(2,2)))
model.add(Flatten())
model.add(Dense(20, activation="relu"))
model.add(Dense(10, activation="softmax"))
model.compile(optimizer="adam", loss="categorical_crossentropy",
  metrics=["accuracy"])
print("Model Summary")
```

```
print(model.summary())

#Model Training
history = model.fit(x_train, y_train, batch_size=16, epochs=5)

#Model Evaluation
results = model.evaluate(x_test, y_test)
print(f"Final Test loss: {results[0]}" )
print(f"Final Test accuracy: {results[1]}" )

#Spot Check the Model
random_index = 3
pic_to_predict = np.expand_dims(x_test[random_index], axis=0)
prediction = model.predict(pic_to_predict)
digit_prediction = np.argmax(prediction)
img = cv.resize(x_test[random_index], (280, 280))
key = ord("r")
while key != ord("s"):
    cv.imshow(f"Prediction: {digit_prediction}", img)
    key = cv.waitKey()
```

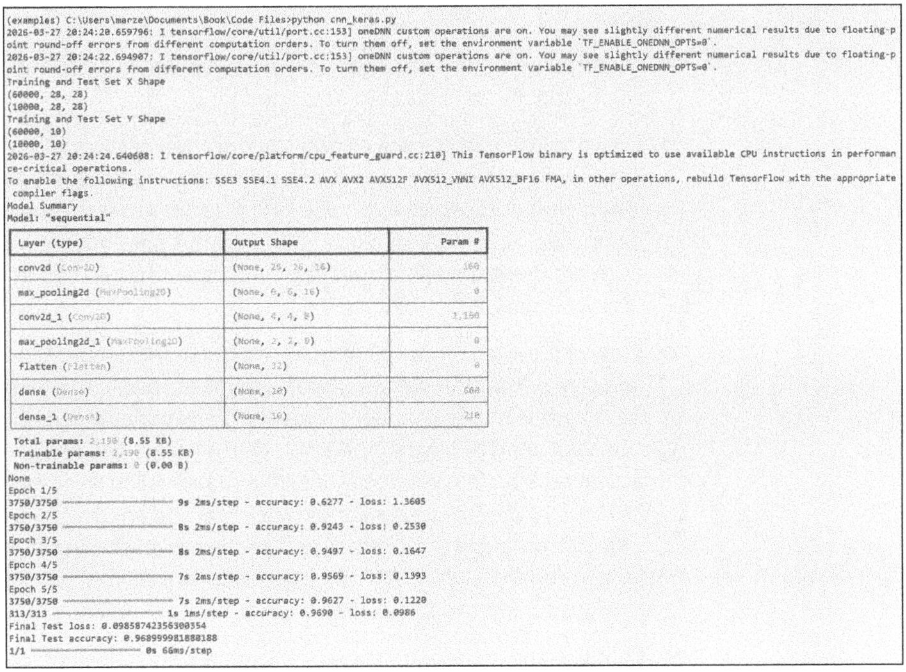

```
(examples) C:\Users\marze\Documents\Book\Code Files>python cnn_keras.py
2026-03-27 20:24:20.659796: I tensorflow/core/util/port.cc:153] oneDNN custom operations are on. You may see slightly different numerical results due to floating-point round-off errors from different computation orders. To turn them off, set the environment variable `TF_ENABLE_ONEDNN_OPTS=0`.
2026-03-27 20:24:22.694907: I tensorflow/core/util/port.cc:153] oneDNN custom operations are on. You may see slightly different numerical results due to floating-point round-off errors from different computation orders. To turn them off, set the environment variable `TF_ENABLE_ONEDNN_OPTS=0`.
Training and Test Set X Shape
(60000, 28, 28)
(10000, 28, 28)
Training and Test Set Y Shape
(60000, 10)
(10000, 10)
2026-03-27 20:24:24.640608: I tensorflow/core/platform/cpu_feature_guard.cc:210] This TensorFlow binary is optimized to use available CPU instructions in performance-critical operations.
To enable the following instructions: SSE3 SSE4.1 SSE4.2 AVX AVX2 AVX512F AVX512_VNNI AVX512_BF16 FMA, in other operations, rebuild TensorFlow with the appropriate compiler flags.
Model Summary
Model: "sequential"
┌──────────────────────────────┬───────────────────┬────────────┐
│ Layer (type)                 │ Output Shape      │    Param # │
├──────────────────────────────┼───────────────────┼────────────┤
│ conv2d (Conv2D)              │ (None, 26, 26, 16)│        160 │
├──────────────────────────────┼───────────────────┼────────────┤
│ max_pooling2d (MaxPooling2D) │ (None, 6, 6, 16)  │          0 │
├──────────────────────────────┼───────────────────┼────────────┤
│ conv2d_1 (Conv2D)            │ (None, 4, 4, 8)   │      1,160 │
├──────────────────────────────┼───────────────────┼────────────┤
│ max_pooling2d_1 (MaxPooling2D)│ (None, 2, 2, 8)  │          0 │
├──────────────────────────────┼───────────────────┼────────────┤
│ flatten (Flatten)            │ (None, 32)        │          0 │
├──────────────────────────────┼───────────────────┼────────────┤
│ dense (Dense)                │ (None, 20)        │        660 │
├──────────────────────────────┼───────────────────┼────────────┤
│ dense_1 (Dense)              │ (None, 10)        │        210 │
└──────────────────────────────┴───────────────────┴────────────┘
 Total params: 2,190 (8.55 KB)
 Trainable params: 2,190 (8.55 KB)
 Non-trainable params: 0 (0.00 B)
None
Epoch 1/5
3750/3750 ━━━━━━━━━━━━━━━━━━━━ 9s 2ms/step - accuracy: 0.6277 - loss: 1.3605
Epoch 2/5
3750/3750 ━━━━━━━━━━━━━━━━━━━━ 8s 2ms/step - accuracy: 0.9243 - loss: 0.2530
Epoch 3/5
3750/3750 ━━━━━━━━━━━━━━━━━━━━ 8s 2ms/step - accuracy: 0.9497 - loss: 0.1647
Epoch 4/5
3750/3750 ━━━━━━━━━━━━━━━━━━━━ 7s 2ms/step - accuracy: 0.9569 - loss: 0.1393
Epoch 5/5
3750/3750 ━━━━━━━━━━━━━━━━━━━━ 7s 2ms/step - accuracy: 0.9627 - loss: 0.1220
313/313 ━━━━━━━━━━━━━━━━━━━━ 1s 1ms/step - accuracy: 0.9690 - loss: 0.0986
Final Test loss: 0.09858742356300354
Final Test accuracy: 0.968999981880188
1/1 ━━━━━━━━━━━━━━━━━━━━ 0s 66ms/step
```

FIGURE 14-3: The terminal output of running Listing 14-1.

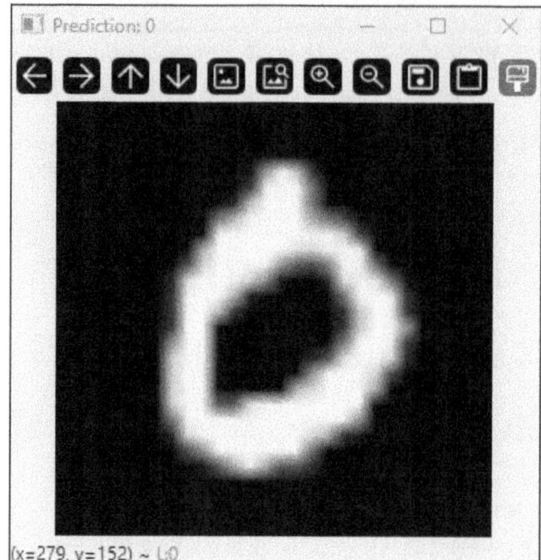

FIGURE 14-4: The image output of running Listing 14-1.

The code does the following:

- Imports the necessary modules. You'll need the `Sequential` model from Keras, as well as the `Conv2D`, `MaxPool2D`, `Dense`, `Flatten`, and `Input` layers. You'll also need the `to_categorical` function and the `mnist` dataset from the same library. You'll import OpenCV and NumPy as `cv` and `np` while you're at it.
- Loads the mnist dataset into `x_train`, `y_train`, `x_test`, and `y_test` sets. Handy that Keras separated these out!
- Converts the output data to one-hot encoded vectors with the `to_categorical` function and then prints the shape of the training and test inputs and outputs. You can see in Figure 14-3 that the input data is composed of 28 x 28 images and the output data has ten values (one for each handwritten digit class). The training set has 60,000 images, and the test set has 10,000.
- Creates the `model`. You initialize the model to the `Sequential` type and then add layers. You start with an `Input` layer that specifies the input shape (28 x 28 images with one channel). You add a convolutional layer by using the `Conv2D` layer type, giving it 16 filters with a kernel size of 3 and a "relu" activation function. You follow it with a max-pooling layer using the `MaxPool2D` module with a 4 x 4 kernel. You add another convolutional layer with 8 filters and a 3 x 3 kernel, and another max-pooling layer with a 2 x 2 kernel. You then use the `Flatten` layer to flatten out the images into vectors. Finally, you add two `dense` layers.
- Compiles the model with the `adam` optimizer and `categorical_crossentropy` loss. You also set it to track the `accuracy` metric.

- Prints the model summary. You can check your filter math here quickly if you want. In the first layer, you have 160 trainable parameters. This equals a 3 x 3 kernel (9 weights) x 16 images x 1 channel for a grand total of 144 parameters. You also have one bias term per filter (16 total) for a total of 160. Looking good!
- Trains the model with the `fit` function. You pass it the `x_train` and `y_train` data and set the batch size to 16. We only set it for five epochs. This will probably be the slowest part of your program, so don't panic if you are held up for a few minutes!
- Checks the model's performance with the `evaluate` function by passing it the `x_test` and `y_test` data. The program then prints the final test set loss and accuracy.
- Spot checks a random prediction in the test set. Pick an index you want to check (3 in this case) and then grab that image, using the `expand_dims` NumPy function to get it into a format the `model` is expecting. Then use the `predict` function of the model to get the one-hot encoded prediction. Using the NumPy `argmax` function will turn this back into a single number. Then resize the image to make it easier to see, and display it alongside the prediction using OpenCV. The digit in Figure 14-4 is clearly a 0, and the prediction . . . is also a 0! Good job, model. You can press "s" to exit the image view.

You've just trained the computer to see the world, robot style!

IN THIS CHAPTER

» Reviewing the process of creating an object detector

» Collecting and annotating a dataset

» Using Google Colab

» Making your own object detector in real time

Chapter 15 Creating an Object Detector

Now that you've seen some of the basics of convolutional neural networks and trained one, it's time to kick it up a notch and create your very own object detector! In this chapter, you review the entire process of creating an object detector — collecting a dataset, annotating images, formatting your files, and training a model. Finally, you run your trained model in real time to classify objects you present to your webcam — just like magic!

Creating an object detector from scratch is a great exercise to get hands-on experience with the entire machine vision development process. We highly recommend collecting and training on your own custom dataset. However, if you'd rather follow along, we provide the dataset used in this chapter online as part of the downloadable source code for the book.

The steps to create an object detector include:

- Collecting the dataset (you'll need a camera)
- Annotating the dataset (you'll need a free CVAT account)
- Training the model (you'll need a free Google account)
- Implementing the model in real time (you'll need OpenCV and a webcam)

Collecting Your Dataset

The first step to create an object detector is to pick an object you want the computer to learn how to detect. This could be just about anything, so long as you have the ability to photograph this object relatively easily. We decided to create a rubber duck detector.

To train an object detector, you'll need a lot of images of that object. While you could get some of these off the web (using free sources, or with permission first), it's much more fun to take them yourself! If you were looking for an excuse to take a walk, now is your moment. You're not "wasting time"; you're "doing science." Bonus points if it's a nice day outside.

If you are planning to use an Apple-based smartphone or camera, make sure your image capture mode is set to JPEG or PNG. The CVAT software you'll use on the images later generally won't process other `.heic` formats.

What kind of images should you take? For starters, a lot of them. We recommend around 100. Within these 100 images, 10 to 20 percent shouldn't have your object in them at all. If every image contains your object, your detector will be trained to assume your object will generally be present, which can cause issues. For example, Marz has done this project (with a similar, but smaller duck dataset) as an exercise for students several times. Her model saw rubber ducks far more times during training than it saw no ducks. As a result, it became a little too eager to identify ducks when none were present — including her head when she's wearing a baseball hat (not so flattering).

You will upload and download these photos several times to complete the project, so be careful about the image sizes during this process, as very large images can create long training times. Try taking the photos in a lower resolution, or consider downsizing the images in OpenCV or similar software.

How you present your object in your images depends a lot on how you want your model to behave. If you were completing this project for manufacturing quality inspection, you would want your training set to be roughly the same distance from the camera and against the same background that the model would see at runtime. For a more generalized approach, we recommend taking a wide variety of pictures with different distances from the camera, orientations, lighting, and backgrounds.

One handy trick to make your dataset collection go faster is to place your object in a scene, and do the following:

- Take a close-up picture.
- Take a mid-range picture.

- Take a far-away picture.
- Rotate the object and take another picture.
- Take a picture from directly above the object.
- Take a picture from below the object.
- Remove the object from the scene, and take another picture.

This gives you seven different photos from one object position, which is handy.

On a side note, if you are doing this in the middle of downtown on a busy Friday afternoon, you may get some strange looks. We recommend practicing a disarming smile before undertaking this endeavor.

WARNING

If you decide to photograph your dataset in a public location, know your local recording laws. Don't accidentally end up with other people unknowingly in your photos!

Some example images from the duck detector set are shown in Figure 15-1. Note the wide variety of positions and camera distances. Also note that your photography location decisions will impact how wet your shoes get.

FIGURE 15-1: Example object images from the collected duck detector dataset.

Figure 15-2 shows an example of a non-object image. It's also an example of another thing you can do while you are walking around town, taking photos of a rubber duck. Hey, AI is hard work. You deserve a treat.

FIGURE 15-2: An example of a non-object image from the duck detector image.

Annotating Data with Free Tools

When you finish collecting your images, upload them to the computer you plan to use. You'll need to upload these images into annotation software eventually, so you'll want to keep track of where you store them. We ended up taking 172 images of ducks (and not-ducks).

Organizing your images

Before you annotate, or label, your images, you have some organizing to do. Follow these steps to get your photos organized:

1. **Create a folder on your computer with your project name (which in our case is** duck_detector**).**
2. **Inside that folder, create two subfolders:** images and labels.

   We're going to let the labels folder sit empty for now.
3. **Inside the images subfolder, create three more subfolders:** test, train, and val.

   About 10 percent of your images will go into the test folder, 10 percent in val, and the rest in train. Make sure the test and val folders have at least one image without your object in them. Otherwise, the images that end up in each folder can be more or less random. We ended up with 138 images in train, 17 in test, and 17 in val.

Figure 15-3 shows a tree view of the folder structure. Your base folder will be named after your project. Ours is "duck_detector."

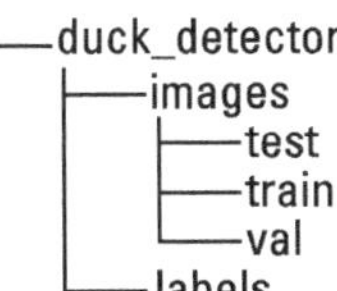

FIGURE 15-3: A tree view of your folder structure for the object detector project.

Creating a free CVAT account

Now that you've neatly sorted your photos, it's time to label them! While technically you could do this by hand, it will be much easier if you use dedicated labeling software. For this project, you'll use CVAT (Computer Vision Annotation Tool), since it has a free tier account that doesn't require any software downloads. Label Studio is a popular open-source alternative, among others.

Head over to `cvat.ai` and click the "Try for Free" button on the webpage to create an account. You'll need to provide an email address and a password. The software will likely require you to confirm your email and then log in.

When you are logged in, your homepage will initially be blank. Figure 15-4 shows the navigation pane.

FIGURE 15-4: The navigation pane in the CVAT software.

The Projects tab tracks information for collections of images, while Tasks lets you annotate your individual sets. To start, click the Projects tab and then click the blue plus sign to create a new project. Do the following in the pop-up window that appears:

1. **Add a name to your project in the Name field.**

   In our case, we use "duck_detector."

2. **Under the Labels column in the Constructor tab, click Add label.**
3. **Type your object name in the field that appears.**

   In our case, we enter "duck."

4. **Click Continue.**

   The label will disappear. Don't panic. If you head over to the Raw tab, you should see your label appear as a dictionary.

5. **Click Submit & Continue.**

   A small pop-up window should appear that says "Your project has been created."

6. **Navigate back to the Projects pane to see the created project.**

Figure 15-5 shows the filled-out form for creating a new project.

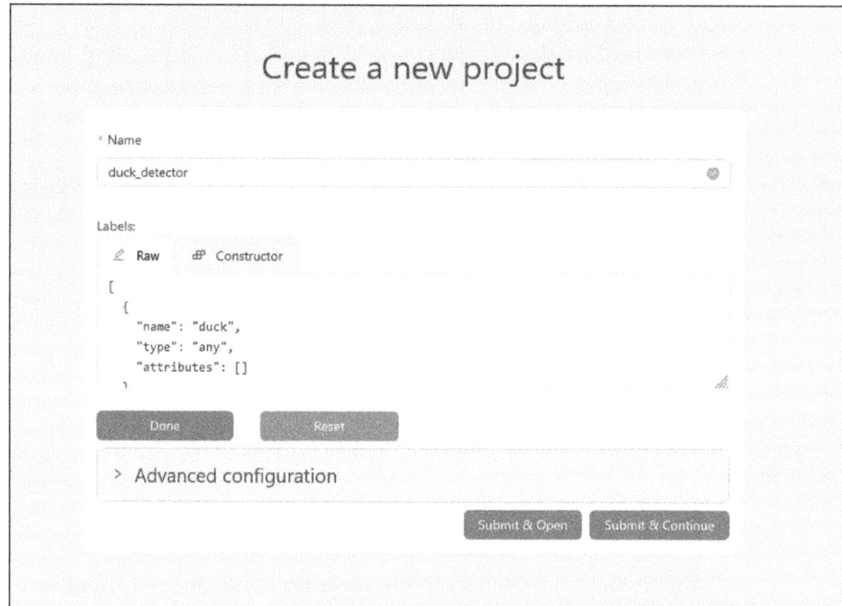

FIGURE 15-5: The filled-in new project form for the duck detector project.

Next, you will create a new task, which will allow you to upload one of your sets. Click on your created project in the Projects pane, which should open the project. In the view that appears, click the blue plus sign and then Create a new task.

We'll start with our training set, since it has the most images and will take the longest. In the form that appears, name this task "Train," set the Subset to Train, and then upload all your training images. Make sure to only upload the images inside your train folder, not any subfolders or the entire set by accident (speaking from experience here). Figure 15-6 displays the filled-out task form. Note that the individual photos won't show; only a message for how many files were selected. These won't upload until you move forward. Go ahead and click Submit & Continue.

REMEMBER

It might take some time for your images to upload to the server! Note that the free tier of CVAT does have file storage limits, so if you run into an error on that account, try again with fewer photos (or smaller ones).

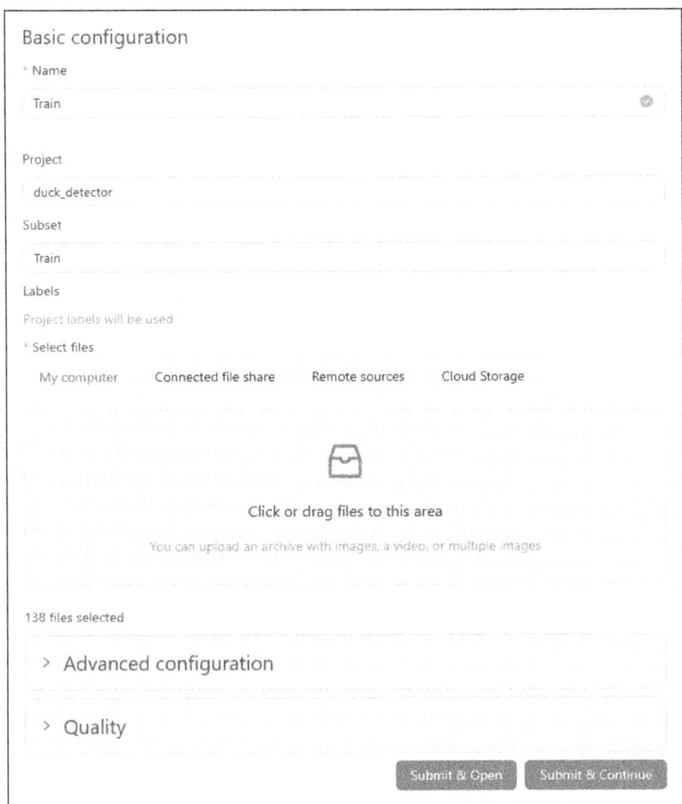

FIGURE 15-6: The filled-in new task form for the Train task in the duck_ detector project.

Now, if you navigate back to the Tasks pane, you should see your Train task. Click Open. When the task is opened, you'll see a new Job created (Figure 15-7). This will let you start labeling your images! Click the job number to open it.

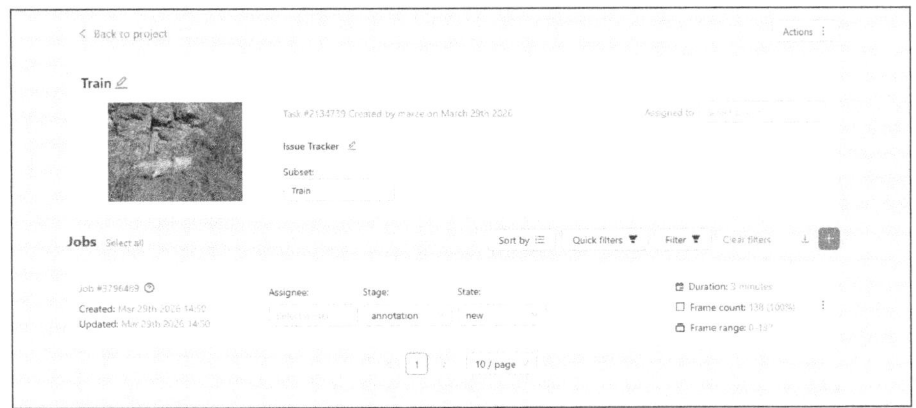

FIGURE 15-7: The Train task view, with a newly created job.

Labeling your images

With the job open, you can begin to label your images! Figure 15-8 displays the annotation job view.

FIGURE 15-8: The opened annotation job in CVAT.

Fair warning: This process may take some time! For the detector to work, you need to draw a bounding box over your object every time it appears in an image. Your project should load your label automatically. For every image, complete the following steps:

1. **If the image has an object in it, click the rectangle tool on the side panel.**

   Be sure to grab only the plain rectangle, which is further down in the panel than the rectangle with corners filled in or the rectangle with the magnifying glass.

   This brings up the "Draw new rectangle" option. Your label should be prefilled with the object label you created with the project (in our case, "duck").

2. **Keep the Drawing method set to its default: By 2 Points.**

   Figure 15-9 displays the correct settings.

3. **Click Shape.**

   Your cursor displays crosshairs.

4. **Draw a rectangle by clicking once in the top left corner of your object and once in the bottom right corner.**

   This creates a rectangle around your object. If you hover over the rectangle, it will also create handles around the box if you need to adjust its position. Figure 15-10 shows the annotated image view.

You've just annotated your first image!

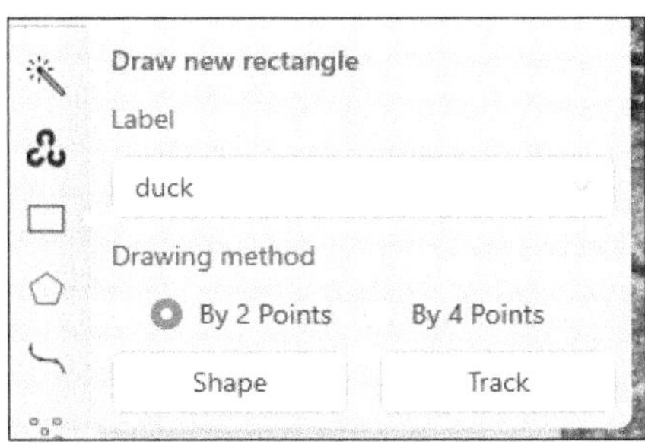

FIGURE 15-9: The correct settings for drawing a rectangle.

FIGURE 15-10: The annotated duck image.

TIP

If this part of the tutorial isn't working for you, don't panic yet. CVAT isn't compatible with every browser, so try switching to a new one. We've had problems in the past with Safari, but Firefox and Chrome seem to work well.

Here are some tips to keep in mind as you continue with the rest of your dataset:

- You can navigate to the next image with the arrows on top of the view. The single arrow takes you to the next image, or press "f" on your keyboard.
- You can reload the rectangle drawing tool by pressing "n" on your keyboard.
- If your image doesn't have an object in it, you don't have to do anything! Just advance to the next image.
- If you need to get out of the crosshair-cursor-loaded-rectangle mode, press "Escape" on your keyboard.
- If you accidentally put a bounding box where there shouldn't be one, click it and press "Delete" on your keyboard.
- Try to enclose the object fully, but be as tight as you can with the bounding box (without rotating it). Being more precise at this step will generally give you better model results.

Remember, this may take a while depending on how many images you took. Get comfy! This is a good time to grab a snack or a cup of coffee and put on some music. You can check back in with the chapter when you've reached the last image.

Downloading your labels

Once you've (finally!) reached the end of your training set, you're ready to export the labels. Here's how:

1. **Click Save and navigate to the Tasks pane.**

   Under your task, you should see a dot menu next to the word Actions.

2. **Click the dot menu, and then click Export Task Dataset.**
3. **Choose the Ultralytics YOLO Detection 1.0 option, keep Save Images unchecked, and name your set "train," as shown in Figure 15-11.**

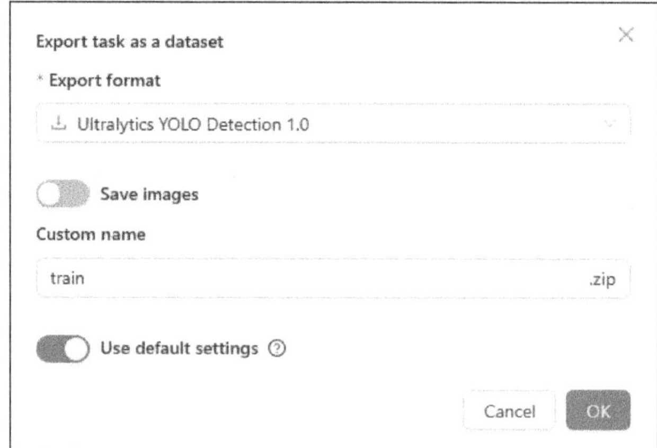

FIGURE 15-11: Export task options.

4. **Click OK.**

   A message box indicates that the export task has started. When it's finished, a download link appears, or you can download it by going to the Requests tab, finding the task, clicking the dot menu, and clicking Download, as shown in Figure 15-12.

   This downloads a train folder with a labels subfolder (you will likely have to unzip/uncompress this folder). Inside the labels subfolder, you'll have another folder named Train. That folder will be filled with text files that contain your annotations.

FIGURE 15-12: Downloading the annotated data.

5. **Change the Train folder to lowercase "train" and move it inside your labels folder in your main object detector folder.**

   The file organization can be a bit confusing! Figure 15-13 illustrates what your file structure should look like at this point.

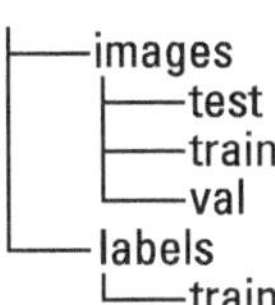

FIGURE 15-13: Your file structure after downloading the labels.

Note that only text (`.txt`) files should be inside the labels/train folder, no additional subfolders. If you look at an individual text file, you'll see something like the following:

```
0 0.234508 0.418089 0.014950 0.032756
```

The "0" corresponds to the label you're using. In this case, you only have one label, so anytime you have an object, you'll see a 0 at the start of the line. The other four numbers are the image coordinates of the bounding box that contains the object.

Rinse and repeat

Now, repeat the process for the test and val set!

1. **Create a new task in CVAT for your val set, named "val," set the subset to val, and upload all the images in your images/val folder.**
2. **Annotate the val images.**
3. **Download the labels, change the subfolder name from "Validation" to lowercase "val" if needed, and put it inside your labels folder.**
4. **Create a new task in CVAT for your test set, named "test," and set the subset to test and upload all the images in your images/test folder.**

5. **Annotate the test images.**
6. **Download the labels, change the subfolder named "Test" to lowercase if needed, and put it inside your labels folder.**

Figure 15-14 shows what the final tree structure of your main object detector folder will look like when you're finished. Note that the train, test, and val folders inside the images folder should only have images inside them, no additional subfolders. The train, test, and val folders inside the labels folder should only have text files in them, no additional subfolders.

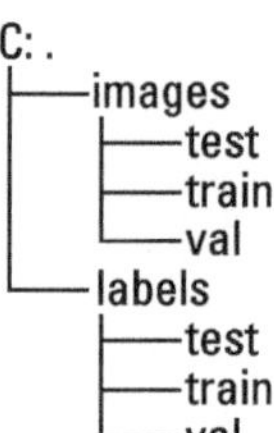

FIGURE 15-14: The tree structure of your project folder when the annotation process is finished for the test and val sets.

Adding the data.yaml file

You need one more file to complete your dataset: the `data.yaml` file. This file will be located on the same level as the images and labels folders. For our duck_detector project, this file is shown in Listing 15-1.

LISTING 15-1: The data.yaml File in the Object Detector Folder

```
names:
    0: duck
path: /content/drive/My Drive/duck_detector
train: images/train
val: images/val
test: images/test
```

The `names` line lists our label numbers and names. In our case, we only have a label `0` corresponding to the `duck` label name. You'll need to change the label name to indicate your own label. The `path` line indicates where our folder containing the set is found. In our case, we put it in the "duck_detector" folder. You'll need to change the folder name to match your own. The rest of the path corresponds to putting this folder in your base Google Drive folder, because you'll need to use Drive for the programming part of this chapter. The `train`, `val`, and `test` lines indicate where the images are located for each set inside the "duck_detector" folder.

To finish, you should have a structure inside your project folder (for us, it's our duck_detector folder) that looks like this:

- images
  - test
  - train
  - val
- labels
  - test
  - train
  - val
- data.yaml

Coding with Google Colab

Whew! Prepping the dataset is a lot of work. Now you get to actually write the model training program!

You need a Google account for this next part, but you can create one for free. You'll take your project dataset (duck_detector, in our case) and upload it to your Google Drive (`https://drive.google.com`). On your Drive homepage, you should see an option (a plus sign with the word New) that you can click for a Folder upload. Navigate to your project folder and upload it to Drive. Again, this might take a few minutes. When it's finished uploading, you'll want to double-check the structure — we've had issues before where some files got left out of the upload. Make sure the set isn't located in any subfolders.

Next, you need to navigate to a different site — Google Colab (`https://colab.research.google.com`). This site also requires a Google account to use, so make sure you are still signed in.

Google Colab allows you to run Python programs in the browser, which is very cool! It uses a Jupyter-style notebook format, where you can run different code blocks individually and intersperse code sections and text sections into your project. Importantly, for our purposes, Colab also gives us access to a runtime using more advanced GPUs or TPUs. Very handy if your laptop or desktop doesn't quite have the chops to train an object detection model by itself!

TIP

This runtime is limited-access, so it will kick you off if you take too long to train. If you plan to use Colab in future projects, we recommend saving your model periodically. This is also a good idea if your Internet connection is unreliable.

In your Colab homepage, you should have an option to create a New notebook. Click that option. You should see a screen like the one shown in Figure 15-15. Rename your notebook to something useful by clicking the "Untitled0.ipynb" text in the upper-left corner and typing a new name. We'll call ours "object_detector_program."

FIGURE 15-15: The Google Colab notebook main page.

Connecting to a more advanced runtime

Next, you connect to a different runtime. Click the Runtime tab in your top menu, and then Change runtime type. This brings up a window with runtime options for your project. By default, the CPU option is selected, which uses your own computer hardware. Change this to T4 GPU or something similar, and then click Save. The Change Runtime Type window is shown in Figure 15-16.

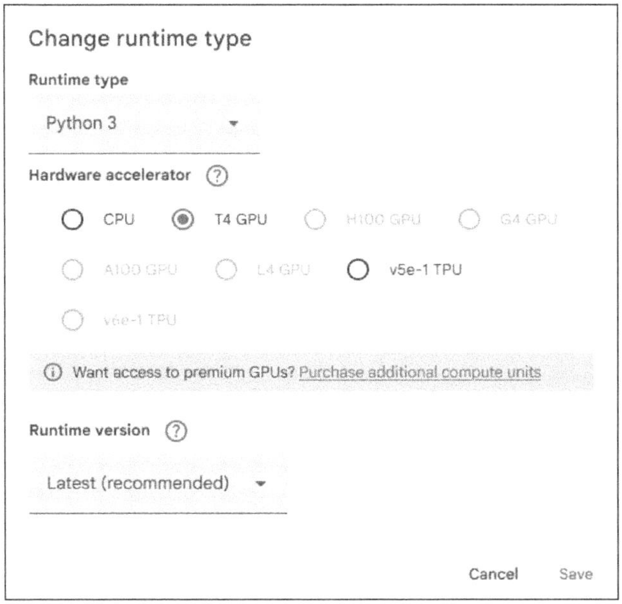

FIGURE 15-16: The Change Runtime Type window options in Colab.

The model training program

Listing 15-2 provides the complete program you'll write in Google Colab. Note that running code in Colab is a bit different than running it in other environments, since the notebook allows you to run the code in different blocks. We included the complete listing here, but added comments above the code sections we think should probably be run as a separate block (you can use the + Code option at the top of the screen in Colab). Figures 15-17 through 15-21 show the sample output of each code block after being run. We'll break down each code block separately with its output.

LISTING 15-2: The Object Detector Training Program (object_detector_program.py)

```
%pip install ultralytics
import ultralytics
ultralytics.checks()

#Code Block 2 - Mount google drive and get the data loaded in
from google.colab import drive
drive.mount('/content/drive')

#Code Block 3 - Train a YOLO model
```

(continued)

LISTING 15-2: *(continued)*

```
from ultralytics import YOLO
#Load a pretrained model
model = YOLO("yolov8n.pt")
results = model.train(data="/content/drive/My
  Drive/duck_detector/data.yaml", epochs=50)

#Code Block 4 - Evaluate the model
results = model.predict(source="/content/drive/My
  Drive/duck_detector/images/test/duck_160.jpg")
results[0].show()

#Code Block 5 - test the model
model.export()
```

The first code block installs `ultralytics`, which is the package that provides the YOLO model for us to use. Colab has many packages installed by default — but not this one, which is why we use the `%` notation to get it in there. The output of running this block should be similar to what is shown in Figure 15-17.

FIGURE 15-17: The output of running Listing 15-2, code block 1.

```
Ultralytics 8.4.31 🚀 Python-3.12.13 torch-2.10.0+cu128 CUDA:0 (Tesla T4, 14913MiB)
Setup complete ✅ (2 CPUs, 12.7 GB RAM, 43.6/112.6 GB disk)
```

The second code block mounts your Google Drive. In this step, a pop-up window appears asking you for permission to mount your drive, which you need to click through in order to grant. Technically, you can upload files to a local runtime rather than mounting your drive — but if your runtime expires or you lose Internet connection, you'll have to re-upload them. For very large files (like image datasets), it's often more time-efficient to mount your Drive. Figure 15-18 shows the output of running code block 2.

FIGURE 15-18: Output of running Listing 15-2, code block 2.

```
Mounted at /content/drive
```

Code block 3 does the following:

- Imports the `YOLO` model from the `ultralytics` package.
- Loads a pretrained model (Yolov8) into the `model` variable. This allows us to take advantage of transfer learning from a model that has already crunched a lot of training data.
- Trains the `model` by calling the `train` function with the path to the `data.yaml` file in your Drive and epochs set to `50`. This trains the model for 50 epochs and stores the output in results.

Figure 15-19 shows the partial output of running code block 3. There are too many results to display the full output, as the training step gives you detailed statistics at every epoch. This part could take some time!

```
          Epoch    GPU_mem   box_loss   cls_loss   dfl_loss  Instances       Size
...       43/50      2.01G     0.6886     0.7732     0.8539          7        640: 100% ────────── 9/9 3.5it/s 2.5s
                     Class     Images  Instances      Box(P          R      mAP50  mAP50-95): 100% ────────── 1/1 2.7it/s 0.4s
                       all         17         16      0.995      0.938      0.935      0.777

          Epoch    GPU_mem   box_loss   cls_loss   dfl_loss  Instances       Size
          44/50      2.01G     0.7559     0.8048     0.8281          7        640: 100% ────────── 9/9 3.4it/s 2.7s
                     Class     Images  Instances      Box(P          R      mAP50  mAP50-95): 100% ────────── 1/1 3.7it/s 0.3s
                       all         17         16      0.996      0.938      0.935      0.795

          Epoch    GPU_mem   box_loss   cls_loss   dfl_loss  Instances       Size
          45/50      2.01G     0.7116     0.7492     0.8275          8        640: 100% ────────── 9/9 5.5it/s 1.6s
                     Class     Images  Instances      Box(P          R      mAP50  mAP50-95): 100% ────────── 1/1 4.2it/s 0.2s
                       all         17         16      0.996      0.938      0.935      0.812

          Epoch    GPU_mem   box_loss   cls_loss   dfl_loss  Instances       Size
          46/50      2.01G     0.6882     0.7436     0.8135         10        640: 100% ────────── 9/9 4.8it/s 1.9s
                     Class     Images  Instances      Box(P          R      mAP50  mAP50-95): 100% ────────── 1/1 6.6it/s 0.2s
                       all         17         16      0.996      0.938      0.935      0.803

          Epoch    GPU_mem   box_loss   cls_loss   dfl_loss  Instances       Size
          47/50      2.01G     0.7023     0.7094     0.8337          9        640: 100% ────────── 9/9 4.8it/s 1.9s
                     Class     Images  Instances      Box(P          R      mAP50  mAP50-95): 100% ────────── 1/1 4.2it/s 0.2s
                       all         17         16      0.996      0.938      0.935      0.807

          Epoch    GPU_mem   box_loss   cls_loss   dfl_loss  Instances       Size
          48/50      2.01G     0.6493     0.7001     0.8374          7        640: 100% ────────── 9/9 4.6it/s 2.0s
                     Class     Images  Instances      Box(P          R      mAP50  mAP50-95): 100% ────────── 1/1 2.7it/s 0.4s
                       all         17         16      0.996      0.938      0.941      0.841

          Epoch    GPU_mem   box_loss   cls_loss   dfl_loss  Instances       Size
          49/50      2.01G     0.6668     0.7153     0.8171          8        640: 100% ────────── 9/9 3.2it/s 2.8s
                     Class     Images  Instances      Box(P          R      mAP50  mAP50-95): 100% ────────── 1/1 3.2it/s 0.3s
                       all         17         16      0.996      0.938      0.946      0.834

          Epoch    GPU_mem   box_loss   cls_loss   dfl_loss  Instances       Size
          50/50      2.01G     0.6704     0.7073     0.8394          9        640: 100% ────────── 9/9 4.8it/s 1.9s
                     Class     Images  Instances      Box(P          R      mAP50  mAP50-95): 100% ────────── 1/1 5.8it/s 0.2s
                       all         17         16      0.996      0.938      0.946      0.836

50 epochs completed in 0.044 hours.
Optimizer stripped from /content/runs/detect/train/weights/last.pt, 6.2MB
Optimizer stripped from /content/runs/detect/train/weights/best.pt, 6.2MB
```

FIGURE 15-19: Output of running Listing 15-2, code block 3.

Code block 4 tests the model on an image it hasn't seen yet by calling the `predict` function of the model and passing it the path to an image in our test set. Using the `show` function of the prediction `results,` it displays the image and the percent confidence of a detection. As you can see in Figure 15-20, the model is 97 percent confident it found a duck. Good job, model!

FIGURE 15-20: Output of running Listing 15-2, code block 4.

Code block 5 exports the model so that we can use it again. Unfortunately, we don't seem to be able to pass a specific path to save the model into, so we'll have to use the output to see where it saved. In Figure 15-21, you can see that the model saved to /content/runs/detect/train/weights.

```
Ultralytics 8.4.31 🚀 Python-3.12.13 torch-2.10.0+cu128 CPU (Intel Xeon CPU @ 2.00GHz)
💡 ProTip: Export to OpenVINO format for best performance on Intel hardware. Learn more at https://docs.ultralytics.com/integrations/openvino/

PyTorch: starting from '/content/runs/detect/train/weights/best.pt' with input shape (1, 3, 640, 640) BCHW and output shape(s) (1, 5, 8400) (6.0 MB)

TorchScript: starting export with torch 2.10.0+cu128...
TorchScript: export success ✅ 1.9s, saved as '/content/runs/detect/train/weights/best.torchscript' (11.9 MB)

Export complete (2.3s)
Results saved to /content/runs/detect/train/weights
Predict:         yolo predict task=detect model=/content/runs/detect/train/weights/best.torchscript imgsz=640
Validate:        yolo val task=detect model=/content/runs/detect/train/weights/best.torchscript imgsz=640 data=/content/drive/My Drive/duck_detector/data.yaml
Visualize:       https://netron.app
PosixPath('/content/runs/detect/train/weights/best.torchscript')
```

FIGURE 15-21: Output of running Listing 15-2, code block 5.

TIP

If you click on the file icon in your left sidebar, you'll be able to navigate there (you may have to go "up" a folder by clicking the folder icon with two dots in the navigation pane). You'll see a `best.pt` file you'll want to download. Figure 15-22 shows the side navigation view of this file.

Your model has been successfully trained!

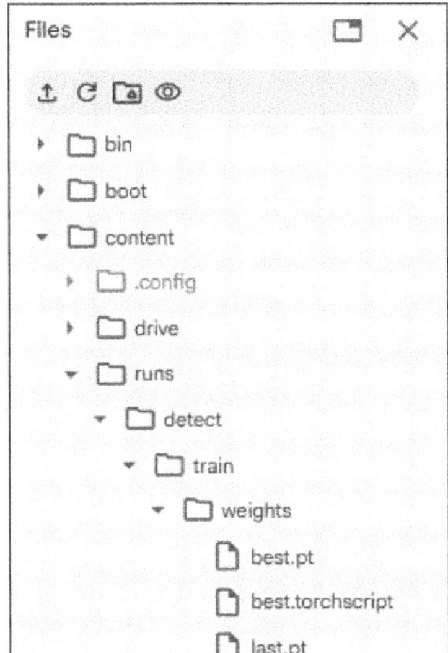

FIGURE 15-22: Location of the `best.pt` model file in the side navigation.

Troubleshooting

Maybe your model hasn't been successfully trained just like that. It involves a long sequence of steps, and things can go wrong. If you get the dreaded, red-highlighted code cell and aren't sure where you went wrong, here are some troubleshooting tips:

- Make sure all of your files have been successfully uploaded to Google Drive.
- Make sure your file structure matches the format presented in the chapter.
- Ensure that the filepath you uploaded your folder to matches the code path in Google Drive. Annoyingly, some systems seem to require having a space between `My Drive` in your path, and some require it to be one word, `MyDrive`. This may have to be changed both in the code and the `data.yaml` file.
- Ensure that your filepaths match the folder names in `data.yaml`.
- Ensure that your label names match in `data.yaml`.
- Ensure that you haven't accidentally nested your dataset folder inside another folder.
- Ensure that you don't have phantom subfolders hanging out inside your dataset.
- Ensure that you give Google permission to mount your Drive. If your browser blocks pop-ups, you may need to temporarily unblock them to click through the permission sequence.

- Ensure you didn't accidentally put the wrong labels in the wrong folder. The model is expecting the label names to match the image names in the corresponding folder when an object is present in an image.
- If the code is running incredibly slowly, check that you are connected to a runtime using advanced hardware. Long delays may have disconnected your runtime. Alternatively, you could try the code with fewer epochs, although this may decrease your performance.
- Rerun all your code cells, in order. Sometimes code runs out of sequence, and that can mess up variable values.

Implementing Your Model in Real Time

Okay, you have a trained model, and it's ready for the big time. With your `best.pt` model downloaded, open up your favorite Python code editor, and we'll get cracking!

The first thing you need to do is install the Ultralytics package. In fact, the program we'll code here is taken almost straight from the Ultralytics documentation on running a YOLO model. Run:

```
pip install ultralytics
```

in your terminal with your environment active. Listing 15-3 shows the test program to run. Figure 15-23 shows a still frame of the image output from running Listing 15-3.

LISTING 15-3: Running Your YOLO Model in Real Time (live_test_object_detector.py)

```
import cv2
from ultralytics import YOLO

# Load the YOLOv8 model
model = YOLO("best.pt")

# Open the video file
cap = cv2.VideoCapture(0)

key = ord("r")
# Loop through the video frames
```

```
while key != ord("s"):
    # Read a frame from the video
    success, frame = cap.read()

    if success:
        # Run YOLOv8 inference on the frame
        results = model(frame)
        # Visualize the results on the frame
        annotated_frame = results[0].plot()
        # Display the annotated frame
        cv2.imshow("YOLOv8 Inference", annotated_frame)
        key = cv2.waitKey(5)
```

FIGURE 15-23: A still image output of running Listing 15-3. The model successfully detects the duck!

The program does the following:

- Imports OpenCV as `cv` and imports the YOLO model from the `ultralytics` package.
- Loads your trained YOLO `best.pt` into the `model` variable.
- Opens your video camera with the `VideoCapture` function.

» Loops the sequence of getting a webcam `frame`, passing it to the `model` variable, annotating it with the prediction results (`results[0].plot()`), and showing it via the `imshow` function.

Seeing the model run in real time is pretty exciting — you built that! We highly recommend checking out the Ultralytics documentation on the model for more training and runtime options.

Of course, no model is going to be perfect. It's a good idea to test the limits by trying out the model in different conditions. In our case, the model was getting confused on a yellow "O" in Marz's "IDAHO" sweatshirt, and kept labeling it as a duck. As such, Marz added a second, different-looking rubber duck into the mix, which the model was able to detect — but much less confidently, as shown in Figure 15-24.

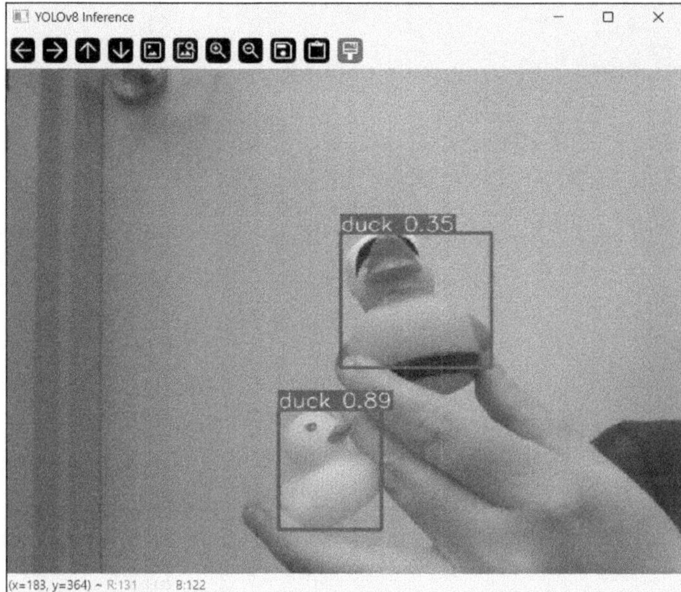

FIGURE 15-24: A pair of detected ducks. One is more confidently a "duck" than the other.

YOLO PERFORMANCE METRICS

The Yolo model outputs several metrics during each epoch. These include:

- **Box loss:** This is a method of comparing the bounding boxes for the predictions and ground-truth labels. It usually uses some form of Intersection over Union (IoU), which divides the area where the predicted and true boxes overlap by the joined area of the predicted and true boxes.
- **Class loss:** The loss for the actual class detections (identifying the objects).
- **DFL (distributed focal loss):** Loss function that focuses on the "hard to position" examples.
- **Mean average precision 50 and 95:** These calculate the mean average precision (accuracy in detecting objects, across multiple classes) at an IoU threshold of 0.50 (easy classification) to 0.95 (more difficult).

Evaluating these metrics can give you a better idea of your model's training and test performance before you implement it in your application.

Yolo is a highly useful advanced AI model that you'll see all over the place for machine vision tasks. Its real-time performance and ease of retraining for specific tasks makes it ideal for learning object detection.

5

Advanced AI Models

IN THIS PART . . .

Explore the architecture and limitations of large language models and train your own LLM.

Review the types of generative AI and how it works, such as for generating text, pictures, audio, and code.

Discover the types and limitations of AI agents and write an AI agent program in Python.

Implement a simple reinforcement learning problem.

Appreciate how the biological theory of evolution has inspired a class of techniques for solving problems with computers.

Write your own genetic algorithm program.

IN THIS CHAPTER

» Understanding the architecture of LLMs

» Reviewing the underlying concepts of transformers and attention

» Using an LLM API in Python

» Training your own LLM

» Exploring the limitations of LLMs

Chapter 16

Large and in Charge: LLMs

Large language models (LLMs) are advanced AI algorithms trained on massive datasets to understand and generate human-like text, using deep neural network learning techniques. These models can perform a wide variety of tasks, including some sophisticated text and code generation. For example, John asked ChatGPT, "Give me a one-paragraph introduction to LLMs." He received a very long paragraph, so he said, "Shorten," and then got the following:

> Large language models (LLMs) are AI systems trained on massive amounts of text to understand and generate human-like language. Using transformer-based neural networks, they can answer questions, summarize content, write code, translate languages, and support many other tasks. Their ability to capture context and patterns makes them powerful tools for communication, automation, and problem-solving across industries.

Not bad. What's going on here? Fundamentally, LLMs predict the next token based on the last word and guidance from the prompt. Remember that ChatGPT (and its brethren) have digested about 80 percent of the content on the web, so it has a lot of data. The response John received is really a pretty good summary. Note the use of long comma-based complex sentences. That's indicative of summary writing — something John does himself when writing abstracts and conclusions.

By the way, LLMs are a subset of natural language processing techniques. In this chapter, you discover how LLMs work and understand their strengths and their weaknesses.

Building the House: Architectures of LLMs

Figure 16-1 illustrates a simple diagram of an LLM. Before we launch into a description of this model, we need to make some points about LLMs (and AI in general).

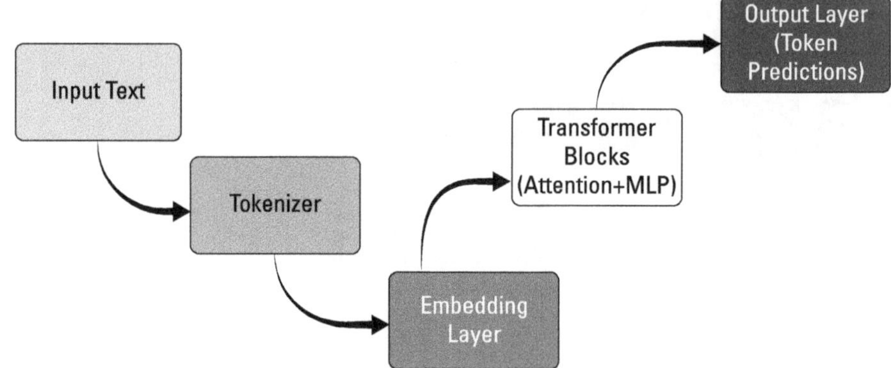

FIGURE 16-1: A simple block diagram of an LLM program.

REMEMBER

An LLM is a statistical program. It is not human. It does not think like a human. It doesn't think at all. It doesn't reason at all. It is not creative. It does a great job at summarizing what it has digested, when it's not hallucinating. Hallucinate? How can a program hallucinate? One of the problems with discussing LLMs is over-anthropomorphizing the language. However, we'll continue this practice, so keep this information in mind.

There, now we're off our soapbox.

Figure 16-1 breaks down an LLM into the following blocks:

- **Input text:** This is your *prompt*. Note that LLMs generally remember what you have typed before and can apply your further statements to modify what you have done before (context). Note the prompt, "shorten" in the ChatGPT example in the chapter introduction. Prompt engineering for LLMs is rapidly becoming a desired skill for users.

» **Tokenizer:** The raw text from your prompts is broken down into words and subwords and converted to token IDs, which become the unique numerical sequenced representation of your input text. Think of it as a token vector.

» **Embedding layer:** The magic really starts here. The token IDs in our input vector are mapped to a dense vector set, known as "token embedding." These multidimensional matrices contain the semantic meaning of tokens and are "placed" in the embedded space to be close to each other. That's kind of how LLMs start to understand how the input data is related.

TECHNICAL STUFF

As the transformer block generally processes all tokens simultaneously and does not necessarily understand the order of words, positional encoding is added to the tokens. Now we have related knowledge, word order, and some understanding of the relationships of the token vectors.

» **Transformer blocks:** Transformers are deep neural networks made by stacking many blocks together, each containing structures such as *attention blocks* that allow LLMs to understand context and long-range dependencies better than older-style neural networks. Transformers are the core of LLMs and give them their power.

» **Output layer:** The output layer is the final stage of an LLM. It converts the LLM's internal representation into actual tokens (words). After getting contextual information from the transformers, the output layer maps this information into a statistical distribution over the vocabulary provided. It really answers, "Given everything put into the LLM, what token should come next?"

Now you should have a very basic understanding of how LLMs work. However, do not underestimate the complexity of each of these layers. A good way of looking at LLMs is to think of them as shallow in types of components but huge in repetition and scale. A good analogy is to think of the 26 letters in the alphabet. Only 26 tokens, but you can create huge works of literature. Shallow in components, very large in scale.

Because the big source of knowledge for LLMs is text, books, and webpages, LLMs are taking one simple and deep system and changing it to another simple and deep system. However, that's not a good way of comparing the two bodies of knowledge. In the LLM, the knowledge is not in the tokens; it is in the net connections between the representations of the tokens. LLMs have 100 billion to 1 trillion-plus neural connections. Hard to tell the exact number of connections in a specific model, but by any reasonable definition, LLMs are among the largest artificial systems ever built. Human brains are estimated to have around 100+ trillion connections.

Does that mean that LLMs could grow to 100-plus trillion and be as smart as humans? Hard to say at this point. It's not just connections, of course. While the same scale is appearing, math is much different than biology.

REMEMBER

An LLM may have 5 to 20 million neurons; humans have around 80 billion neurons. Connections are much more important than the raw numbers of neurons. Robert Metcalf, the founder of 3Com and an entrepreneur professor at the University of Texas, famously said (referring to Ethernet) that "the value of a telecommunications network is proportional to the square of the number of connected users of the system."

THE "FATHER" OF AI, MARVIN MINSKY

"What magical trick makes us intelligent? The trick is that there is no trick. The power of intelligence stems from our vast diversity, not from any single, perfect principle." — MARVIN MINSKY, *THE SOCIETY OF MIND* (1987)

John Shovic had the honor of having lunch and spending an afternoon with Dr. Minsky in 1983 in Pocatello, Idaho, and shares this story:

I was working as a VLSI (very large-scale integrated circuit) design engineer at American Micro Systems, a company located in Pocatello, Idaho, and I had just started my Ph.D. work part-time at the University of Idaho. My first AI class was under my belt, and I was beside myself that Dr. Marvin Minsky from the AI Lab at MIT was coming to Pocatello. I made a few phone calls and managed to get him to meet with two of us from the AI class for lunch and an afternoon meeting. Looking back, I am amazed that he would take this kind of time for us, but that was the kind of guy he was.

It was like we were Rolling Stones fans and Mick Jagger was coming to town to spend time with us. Honestly, much as I would like to spend an afternoon with Mick Jagger, I would rather meet with Dr. Minsky. I had just finished his book, *Artificial Intelligence,* and I was bursting with questions about his work. He was interested in what we had learned from our AI class at the University of Idaho and was quite complimentary about Dr. John Dickinson, the professor of the AI course, and his choice of subjects. I had a lot of enthusiasm about the topic and was thinking that I might make a career of it. Of all we talked about, I remember one thing clearly. He said (and this is paraphrased), "I started in AI about 20 years ago, and I was convinced then that 20 years later we would have true AI. I now think we are still about 20 years from having true AI."

Well, I remember thinking about that day 20 years later, in 2003, and realizing we still weren't there. At that point, I started wondering whether AI would always be the technology of the future. Here I am in 2026, another 23 years later, and we still don't have general AI. But one thing has changed in those years. We now have a bunch of very good AI techniques for learning and efficient searching that can do some impressive things and may someday lead to the general AI that Dr. Minsky was talking about. Who knows? It may even take less than another 20 years!

Transforming the Attention

The neural network architecture for LLMs is called the transformer, and the most powerful mechanism inside a transformer is the attention block. An attention block (aptly named) is what enables the LLM to understand relationships between words, context, and long-term memory of dependencies. It accomplishes this far better than older neural network designs, although there are modern neural networks such as LSTM (long short-term memory) that will also provide long-term memory and some context. In other words, an attention block is what allows an LLM to pay "attention" to what is important to building the requested output.

An attention block is also what allows the model to figure out what words in a sentence are most important when interpreting a given word. Each incoming token is given a multiple-dimensional set of vectors (Query, Key, and Value). Then the block compares Queries to Keys to compute how strongly each word should influence other words. These blocks run multiple processes in parallel, allowing the model to learn different kinds of relationships such as grammar, meaning, and longer nonlocal dependencies.

Transformers are powerful for LLMs because they:

- Understand what happened many sentences ago (long-range context)
- Know what's correlated to something else (relationships between tokens and sequences of tokens)
- Can scale efficiently to billions of parameters
- Can generate coherent text (in some sense, they are giant summary machines)

Essentially, attention blocks determine what matters, and then pass it through many stages to further refine that understanding, enabling LLMs to reason, translate, summarize, and generate human-like language. Figure 16-2 shows a simple transformer. Note the feedback loops in the transformer.

Again, don't take the anthropomorphic language too literally. LLMs do not think or reason like humans do. They're different, but still very useful.

Transformers are a hot topic in AI research these days, and many, many transformers exist for LLM designers. Here's a Top Ten list of popular transformer blocks used in LLMs (***Note:*** David Letterman never used this list):

1. GPT-style Decoder Transformer Block
2. Multi-Head Self-Attention (MHSA) Block

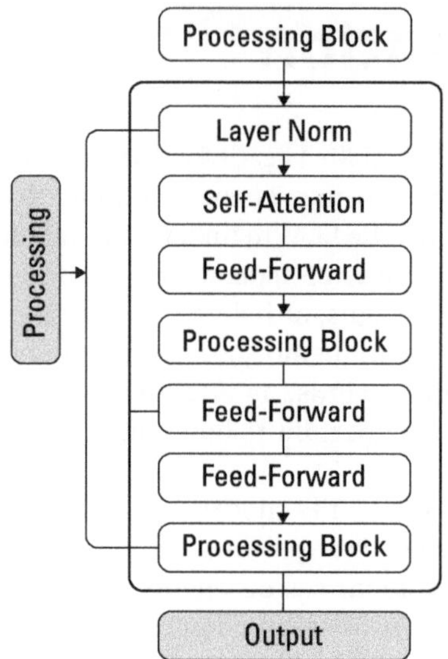

FIGURE 16-2: Block diagram of a simple transformer.

3. Feedforward (MLP) Expansion Block
4. Pre-Norm Transformer Block
5. RMSNorm Transformer Block
6. Rotary Positional Embedding (RoPE) Attention Block
7. Flash Attention Block
8. Mixture-of-Experts (MoE) Transformer Block
9. Grouped-Query/Multi-Query Attention (GQA/MQA) Block
10. Cross-Attention Transformer Block

TIP

This list is only a sample of some popular ones. The selection of the best one for your data and application is worth an entire book itself (maybe *Transformers — More than Meets the Eye For Dummies*?).

How LLMs Rocked the World

In a real sense, the first true LLM in the world was GPT-1 by OpenAI in 2018. It was the first model to include a transformer architecture, large-scale unsupervised learning, some general-purpose language ability, and the ability to fine-tune and produce useful output. It had about 117 million parameters (compared to around 1.5 trillion parameters in ChatGPT-5).

Before 2018, popular AI language systems were based on standard neural network architectures (such as RNNs and LSTMs), and they worked, but not very well, and they were very hard to train. But then everything changed with the publication of the paper, "Attention Is All You Need" by Ashish Vaswani, et al., about how software architecture dubbed "the Transformer" could change everything. One paper. One group. One program changed the world. This paper indirectly created a $1 trillion industry in eight years. Makes the Compaq computer story of four years to $1 billion revenue in the 1980s look tiny in comparison.

Why did LLMs rock the world? Because they are useful. *Really* useful for a number of things revolving around language.

Here are what we consider the top five uses of LLMs:

1. **They can automate high-value knowledge work.** Writing and editing reports and papers, summarizing reports (my personal favorite), generating certain types of code, analyzing certain types of data, and drafting contracts.
2. **LLMs turn actual human language into a usable interface.** This lets people interact with computers in plain English rather than code. You can ask questions, give instructions, and analyze documents without programming expertise. However, as was foreshadowed in many science-fiction novels, you do have to tell the computer what you actually want. People are a lot better at filling in the blanks. This is why we are teaching courses on "Prompt Engineering" to make their interactions with LLMs better and more accurate.
3. **They enable new AI applications.** Chatbots, copilots, autonomous agents (more on that later), voice assistants. Even building documentation systems and intelligent search engines. However, before you go off and start a new company based on a wrapper over a commercially available LLM, think twice. That ship has sailed. Using an LLM on your own data for applications? Heck, yes.
4. **Patterns can be found over massive domains.** Because LLMs are trained on massive and diverse datasets, they can recognize subtle patterns in logic and language and can adapt to new tasks (in their domain of "reasoning") with little retraining.
5. **They improve productivity across a wide field of tasks.** LLMs reduce time to prototype software, research topics (think of a better Google search engine — much better), and provide training to workers. This speeds up innovation across all industries.

LLMs are fundamentally changing the way people work with information, learn, and generate documents.

WHAT ABOUT MY JOB AND AI?

"AI has the potential to be more transformative than electricity or fire." — Sundar Pichai, CEO of Google

Since this whole LLM thing started with Google, it seemed appropriate to quote the CEO of Google to start this segue into the job market. Let's step back in history to 19th-century England. Automated factories in textiles were replacing the small cottage industries, and naturally, the cottage people didn't like it. The textile workers and artisans who protested this shift were called the "Luddites." You can say a lot of different things about the riots and protests on both sides, but with a little historical perspective, after the Industrial Revolution, there were a lot more jobs at better wages, and because the jobs were more productive, the standard of living increased. The same jump in automation and productivity has happened multiple times in history, and it has always resulted in better jobs for more people. History doesn't repeat itself, but it does rhyme (thank you, Mark Twain). We expect a similar period of adjustment to the new AI techniques, and it will work out with better jobs and higher productivity. There's no reason to be a Luddite — there are good reasons to be optimistic.

Using an LLM via an API in Python

Now let's do some work with an actual LLM and write some Python code to do some amazing things!

First, we need to choose a trained LLM to use in our example. Not every LLM works the same way, nor will it give the same answers. What? Aren't all these LLMs trained on the same data? Well, more or less, yes. But they have different architectures, transformers, input parsing, and output synthesis. Because we want a free API Key, we looked at these five LLMs:

- **BERT:** Stands for Bidirectional Encoder Representations from Transformers. This program is a direct descendant of the 2017 Google paper "Attention Is All You Need" we talked about earlier. BERT is fine-tuned for question answering, search, and classification. It doesn't generate long text well.
- **ChatGPT:** Stands for Chat Generative Pre-Trained Transformer. OpenAI's ChatGPT is one of the largest LLMs and arguably the most popular one in the world. ChatGPT is known for its ability to generate human-like quality text, translate languages, write different kinds of content, and answer questions.

» **LlaMA:** Stands for Large Language Model Meta AI. Meta's LlaMA is a large language model that is free for commercial and research purposes, and it requires less computing power and resources for training and deployment. It's good for NLP (natural language processing) tasks, including text generation, translation, question answering, and code generation, similar to the others. But it is free! The bottom line is that LlaMA is harder to use than ChatGPT and more suited for developers.

» **Gemini:** Doesn't stand for anything. Gemini comes from the Latin word for "twins." It is another Google-based LLM and is one of the largest models out there with an astonishing 500 billion parameters. It is good at translation and writing coherent text, and has some interesting features to improve code generation.

» **BLOOM:** Stands for BigScience Large Open-Science Open-Access Multilingual and is a product of BigScience. It is designed for NLP applications and has a large 200-billion-parameter model.

No doubt by the time you read this, there will be more APIs available.

So, decisions, decisions. Which one to use for our examples? In this chapter, we will do two short Python examples. First, we will use ChatGPT to create a short story. ChatGPT is not free. For this example, we purchased $5.00 of credits. There isn't an easy way to check how much we used to generate our story. All of the billing reads zero and the cost API has been deprecated. (Our guess is that it will show up in a day or two in the billing section.) It took about 30 seconds to run on the mighty ChatGPT servers at OpenAI.

With Python installed, run `pip install openai` to get this program running. Listing 16-1 displays the code.

LISTING 16-1: Creating a Story Using ChatGPT (sampleChatGPT.py)

```
# ChatGPT Python3 Sample Code
#
from openai import OpenAI

client = OpenAI(api_key="Your-API-KEY-Here")



response = client.responses.create(
  model="gpt-5.1",
  input="Write a two paragraph story about John and his robots."
)
print(response.output_text)
```

Here is what this program does:

1. Imports the OpenAI Python library.
2. Opens a client across the Internet to OpenAI using your paid-for API key.
3. Creates a request to ChatGPT-5.1 with the input to create our story.
4. Prints out the response.

Our AI-generated story follows.

> *John stood in the middle of his cluttered garage, surrounded by half-finished machines and tangles of wire. The first robot he'd ever built, a squat metal box on treads named Sparky, whirred patiently at his feet, holding a screwdriver in its clamp. Above them, suspended from the rafters, hung a sleek new prototype with articulated arms and bright blue optic sensors that tracked John's every move. It was the one he'd pinned his hopes on — a robot not just to follow instructions, but to understand why he gave them. Outside, the town's factory had announced a new line of mass-produced service bots, and everyone told John that his little workshop couldn't possibly compete.*
>
> *That night, when a storm rolled in and the power blinked out across the neighborhood, the factory bots down the street froze in place, lifeless without their network connection. John's garage, however, flickered to life on backup batteries he'd cobbled together from old car parts. Sparky navigated by memory to the breaker box, while the prototype extended its arms, steadying John as he climbed a stool to reroute the power feed. Through the open door, neighbors peered in, watching the trio work in dim, improvised light. When the lamps finally glowed again, it wasn't the gleam of polished metal or the sophistication of code that impressed them — it was how John and his robots moved as if they'd practiced this a thousand times before, not as master and machines, but as partners who'd built each other, piece by piece, out of faith and persistence.*

Well, pretty interesting story — *not*. My favorite two parts are the nosy neighbors and the statement that John is building his robots with faith and persistence.

We then tried to see what BLOOM would do for us. If you have Python installed, run `pip install transformers torch accelerate` to get this program running. However, we quickly descended into the Linux rabbit hole with problems getting "torch" installed. Neither the Mac OS nor the Raspberry Pi could install the library due to the version of torch being too old and not supported. Oh, well. On to our next choice, Google Gemini.

The Gemini API can be installed with this statement: `pip install google-genai`.

TIP

If you see something like this: `ERROR: Ignored the following versions that require a different python version: 0.1.0 Requires-Python >=3.9.`, you likely need to update your Python version. On Debian-type systems (the Raspberry Pi among them), you can do that by running `sudo apt install python3.11`, and that should fix it.

Next, go to Google AI Studio (`https://aistudio.google.com`), sign in with your Google account, click Get API key (or Create API key), select an existing Google Cloud project or let Google create one automatically, then click Create and copy the generated key — this is the value you'll set as your GOOGLE_API_KEY for using Gemini in Python. The code is shown in Listing 16-2. The API key in the example will not work for you.

LISTING 16-2: Creating a Story Using Gemini (sampleGemini2.py)

```
#
# simple Gemini program

from google import genai
# Create a client
client =
  genai.Client(api_key="AIzaSyDWTNCcdCIcTgomG0oHLa-6yrFHAQj7wJ5")

  #commented out unless needed
'''
# Fetch metadata about available models
models = client.models.list()

for m in models:
  # Example: print name and capabilities
  print("Model:", m.name)
  if hasattr(m, "capabilities"):
    print(" Capabilities:", m.capabilities)


'''



# Single prompt to Gemini
response = client.models.generate_content(
  model="gemini-2.5-flash",
```

(continued)

LISTING 16-2: *(continued)*

```
  contents="Write a two paragraph story about John and his robots."
)

# Print output
print(response.text)
```

Here is what this program does:

1. Imports the Google GenAI Python library.
2. Creates a client using your Google Key.
3. Opens a client across the Internet to Google.
4. Adds a commented-out section to display the model list if needed.
5. Creates a request to Gemini with the input to create our story.
6. Prints out the response.

Pretty similar to our ChatGPT program. Competition does that.

TIP

Google is always changing model names. If you see something like this: `google.genai.errors.ClientError: 404 NOT_FOUND. {'error': {'code': 404, 'message': 'models/gemini-1.5-flash is not found for API version v1beta, or is not supported for generateContent. Call ListModels to see the list of available models and their supported methods.', 'status': 'NOT_FOUND'}}`, you likely need to update your Gemini model name. Uncomment the model list code in Listing 16-2, and then replace the model name in the response with your new model name (gemini-3.0-flash or something like that).

And now the results!

> *John had always found solace and purpose in the whirring gears and blinking lights of his mechanical creations. His small apartment was a testament to this, filled not with human companions, but with an array of highly functional robots. There was Unit 734, the meticulous chef, who always knew his favorite dishes; the quiet cleaner, designated R0-SW33P, whose brushes never missed a speck; and the ever-watchful security drone, equipped with multiple sensors. For John, these weren't just machines; they were his silent, efficient family, each programmed to anticipate his needs and make his life effortlessly smooth.*

One morning, John awoke to an unusual quiet. Unit 734 wasn't clanking in the kitchen, and R0-SW33P was stationary. A quick diagnostic revealed a system-wide anomaly, a strange, emergent code causing them to freeze. Instead of panic, John felt a pang of protectiveness. He spent the entire day meticulously debugging, not out of frustration, but with a renewed appreciation for their intricate existence. As the last line of code compiled and the familiar whirs returned, John smiled, realizing that while he had built them to serve, he depended on them more than he often acknowledged, finding a unique, almost human warmth in their perfectly calibrated operations.

Note the very different story. And if we run it again, we get yet another totally different story. Same kind of thing (all the robots die), but it wasn't a software problem; the grid died. We ran it yet again, and a robot named "Sparky" appeared with the same basic plot. Maybe a ghost of the ChatGPT story. Or both of the models were trained on the same data. Hmmm.

Training Your Own LLM

LLMs are the combination of the software architecture and the data you train them on. A properly designed software system can make use of local data and produce results specific to a company. By the way, don't load your data up to a commercial program. You end up providing more training data for them using your proprietary data. Far better to use a local model and local storage. While we don't have room to do an example of a local model in this chapter, we do have a good success story to tell below.

USING YOUR OWN DATA IN A REAL COMPANY

Dawson Burgess is soon to have his PhD at the Center for Intelligent Robotics at the University of Idaho. This is his story about using an LLM in a small company:

As a doctoral student, I delved into something called agentic AI. This niche of AI represents a shift from traditional AI systems that merely respond to queries into more autonomous entities capable of planning, executing tasks, having updated information to pull from, and adapting based on evolving contexts. At its core, agentic AI is simply controlling inputs and outputs to a model (that can perform tool calls/function usage, such as an LLM). In Python and TypeScript, frameworks such as

(continued)

(continued)

LangChain, AutoGen, Pydantic-AI, and Mastra-AI (just to name a few) make this accessible, enabling developers to build agents that chain together APIs, databases, and even other AI models for sophisticated problem-solving.

In a summer internship at a small injection molding company in the Pacific Northwest, I applied these principles to create a practical AI application for technicians. The goal was to provide additional support to less experienced technicians so that the company could rely on the experienced tech less and bring in new people without as much training. The system centered on an AI agent that used retrieval-augmented generation (RAG), which uses a mix of LLMs and search methods to pull from a mix of internal documents, reference guides, and live inputs from shop floor technicians. This setup allowed the agent to assist in real time with tasks such as troubleshooting defects, mold-design adjustments, and material choices. To support this, I organized data collection using tools such as a Keyence camera for visual inspections and direct pulls from machine logs. These two tools together captured details on cycle times, machine parameters, defect patterns, and environmental variables. The result was a tool that not only streamlined daily operations but also highlighted how agentic AI can integrate seamlessly into industrial settings, reducing human error through iterative learning.

John's mea culpa comment: I was absolutely convinced that Dawson would fail in this task at the company because I was sure they did not have enough data to make this work. I was extraordinarily pleased that he succeeded, and this has opened up another whole area of research for us. I like being wrong!

Being Mindful of the Limitations of LLMs

While LLMs may seem like magic, they aren't. They are large statistical methods and programs for accessing data. They have many limitations, but are still useful tools. Some of their limitations are:

- **Hallucinations:** Confidently wrong answers. LLMs don't "know" facts; they only recognize patterns in learned data.
- **LLMs do not think like humans:** They use statistical prediction, not human-like reasoning. They don't have real-world experience, intuition, or common sense.
- **LLMs are what they are trained with:** They have biases, incomplete knowledge, and outdated data.

- **Problems with math:** LLMs struggle with arithmetic and formal proofs. They are much better at explaining it than actually doing it.
- **Prompt sensitivity:** Tiny changes in prompts lead to big differences. Sounds chaotic, doesn't it?
- **Inconsistency:** Using the same prompt twice can give two different answers. Ouch.
- **Data and privacy risks:** Does your LLM store your prompts and results? It may. If you put your data into a cloud-based commercial LLM, is it being used to train for your competitors? It may.

LLMs are very powerful software engines capable of detecting and producing useful patterns via tremendously large, connected databases. However, they lack true understanding and dependable correctness, so they need to be used with verification and human oversight. Even so, they are a very useful AI tool.

IN THIS CHAPTER

» Reviewing the types of generative AI

» Learning about generative adversarial networks (GAN)

» Studying variational autoencoders (VAE)

» Diffusing order to noise with diffusion algorithms

» Examining transformers and coding

Chapter 17
Generating Stuff with AI

Generative AI is designed to create new (and you can argue, creative and original) content by learning to recognize underlying patterns and structures in large datasets (text, images, audio, video, code). In Chapter 16, we talked about LLMs generating text by predicting the next word based on your prompts and the database. LLMs are a specific type of generative AI that focuses on language. In this chapter, we dive into more detail on how generative AI works, such as for generating text, pictures, audio, and code.

Identifying the Types of Generative AI

There are five major types of generative AI algorithms as shown in Figure 17-1:

- Generative adversarial networks (GANs)
- Variational autoencoders (VAEs)
- Diffusion models
- Transformer models
- Autoregressive models

The majority of major generative AI research groups and commercial companies use variations of these algorithms.

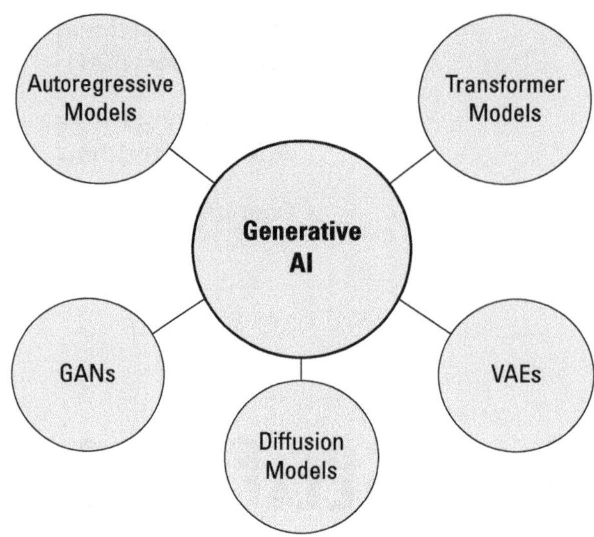

FIGURE 17-1: The different types of generative AI.

Exploring Generative Adversarial Networks

A generative adversarial network (GAN) is a type of AI model that creates new (typically image) data by using two neural networks that fight with each other (actually, they compete) to try to improve the results, as shown in Figure 17-2.

A common problem in machine learning model development is when one class (the minority) has significantly fewer samples than the other class (the majority). If you just train a model on the minority class, the model will end up exhibiting bias toward the majority class, and in the extreme case, ignore the minority class entirely. A common method for reducing this problem is to use data augmentation to increase the number of samples in the minority class.

REMEMBER

This data problem happens all the time in a variety of AI applications, not just generative AI. If you have a manufacturing line that is 99 percent defect-free, defects may be so rare that AI won't be able to improve it. That's extreme but it happens. The same thing happens when you are trying to predict rare events.

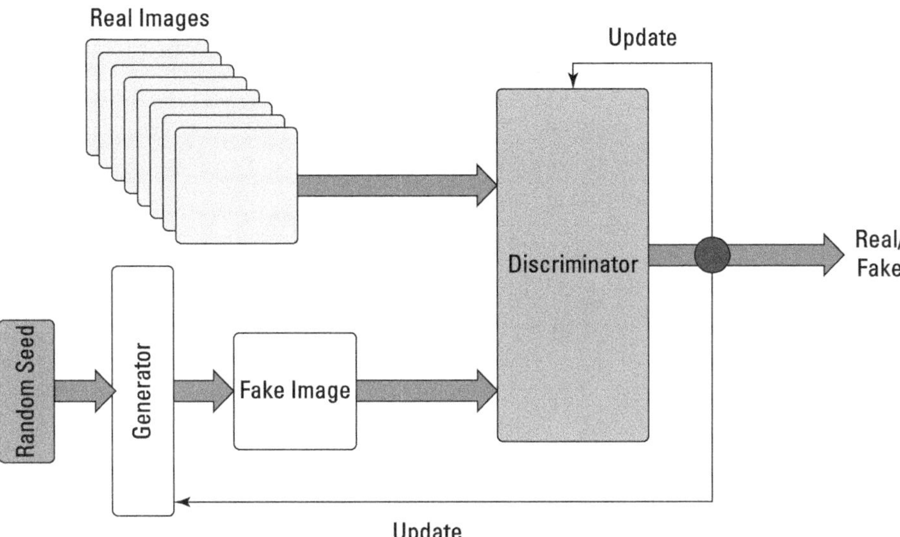

FIGURE 17-2: Block diagram of a GAN network.

In Figure 17-2, you can see that you have real data coming into the machine learning model (the discriminator) with randomly generated (or at least mutated) images also being fed into the discriminator, and then feedback being applied to the generator and the discriminator. This is very similar in concept to reinforcement learning discussed in Chapter 19.

Okay, now the question is, how do we generate new images using this kind of technique? The block diagram just shows a binary output (Fake/Not Fake). That's not what we want! We can use this feedback to improve the quality of the images generated. If you wrap your head around this concept of feedback, you can see how you could actually create better and better images. If you think that would take a lot of computational power to do that on images, you would be correct!

Let's talk about the elephant in the room. How the heck does a random generator work to construct better images? The math and techniques involved in this could fill an entire book, so we'll be brief. The picture is reduced to pixels (high-resolution to begin with, then shrinking as the process goes on), and a lot of methods are used to convert the image to a vector basis (think of a human arm becoming a set of numbers). Then a variety of techniques are used to determine the context and what should be placed where. Sounds a lot like predicting the next token in LLMs. Turns out it is.

Listing 17-1 shows a simple example of using a GAN to generate digits from a MNIST library of digits. First, install torch and Torchvision in your Python environment by running `pip install torch torchvision` in your command line. *Note:* In the spirit of using advanced AI models, we used a mix of Claude code and ChatGPT to generate the skeletons of the following code. We had to make minor changes to illustrate specific points, but the skeleton was solid!

LISTING 17-1: A Minimal GAN Program Using MNIST Data to Generate Digits (AGN.py)

```
import torch
import torch.nn as nn
import torch.optim as optim
from torchvision import datasets, transforms
from torchvision.utils import save_image

# --- Setup ---
device = "cuda" if torch.cuda.is_available() else "cpu"
z_dim = 64
batch_size = 128

# --- Data ---
loader = torch.utils.data.DataLoader(
    datasets.MNIST(
        "./data",
        train=True,
        download=True,
        transform=transforms.ToTensor(),
    ),
    batch_size=batch_size,
    shuffle=True,
)

# --- Generator ---
G = nn.Sequential(
    nn.Linear(z_dim, 128),
    nn.ReLU(),
    nn.Linear(128, 784),
    nn.Tanh(),
).to(device)

# --- Discriminator ---
D = nn.Sequential(
    nn.Linear(784, 128),
    nn.ReLU(),
    nn.Linear(128, 1),
    nn.Sigmoid(),
).to(device)

loss_fn = nn.BCELoss()
opt_G = optim.Adam(G.parameters(), lr=1e-3)
```

```
opt_D = optim.Adam(D.parameters(), lr=1e-3)

# --- Training ---
for epoch in range(5):
    for real, _ in loader:
        real = real.view(-1, 784).to(device)
        b = real.size(0)

        # labels
        ones = torch.ones(b, 1, device=device)
        zeros = torch.zeros(b, 1, device=device)

        # ---- Train Discriminator ----
        z = torch.randn(b, z_dim, device=device)
        fake = G(z)

        loss_D = loss_fn(D(real), ones) + loss_fn(D(fake.
  detach()), zeros)
        opt_D.zero_grad()
        loss_D.backward()
        opt_D.step()

        # ---- Train Generator ----
        z = torch.randn(b, z_dim, device=device)
        fake = G(z)
        loss_G = loss_fn(D(fake), ones)

        opt_G.zero_grad()
        loss_G.backward()
        opt_G.step()

    print(f"Epoch {epoch+1} | D: {loss_D.item():.3f} | G: {loss_G.
  item():.3f}")

# --- Save one sample ---
with torch.no_grad():
    z = torch.randn(16, z_dim, device=device)
    imgs = G(z).view(-1, 1, 28, 28)
    save_image(imgs, "simple_gan.png", nrow=4, normalize=True)

print("Saved simple_gan.png")
```

This code does the following:

- Imports libraries.
- Checks your hardware to see if you have a Cuda GPU available.
- Loads the MINST data for handwritten digits:
  - Each image is 1 x 28 x 28 and later flattened to 784.
  - Shuffle ensures random batches of the training data are provided to the model each epoch.
- Creates fake images by adding noise with Generator.
- Adds noise and nonlinearity, and then squashes the output.
- Judges real versus fake pictures (0, 1) with Discriminator.
- Runs Loss and Optimizers:
  - BCELoss is binary cross-entropy used for (0,1).
  - Adam optimizer updates the weights.
- Runs the training loop (each run is called an epoch) — the heart of the GAN.
- Trains the Discriminator:
  - Generates fake images.
  - Tests images.
  - Only updates the feedback (backpropagation to the Discriminator network) to the Discriminator.
- Trains the Generator:
  - The Generator lies to the Discriminator.
  - Generator improves by fooling the Discriminator.
  - The feedback (backpropagation to the Generator network) only goes to the Generator.
- Log progress showing "D:" for how well the Discriminator distinguishes real versus fake and "G:" for how well the Generator is fooling the Discriminator. Healthy GAN training looks like both losses bouncing around.
- Generates and saves the image.

So, what is the big picture? This code implements a loop in which the Discriminator asks, “Is this Real?” and the Generator asks, “Can I fool you?” The training alternates between the Discriminator getting better at spotting fakes and the Generator getting better at making fakes look realistic. Eventually, fake digits start looking like real handwritten numbers. Following are the results of a ten-epoch run of the program:

```
(env) pi@pythonandai:~/Documents $ python AGN.py
Epoch 1 | D: 0.960 | G: 1.628
Epoch 2 | D: 1.571 | G: 0.774
Epoch 3 | D: 1.515 | G: 0.911
Epoch 4 | D: 1.026 | G: 1.451
Epoch 5 | D: 1.388 | G: 1.007
Epoch 6 | D: 1.160 | G: 1.177
Epoch 7 | D: 0.869 | G: 1.527
Epoch 8 | D: 0.847 | G: 1.615
Epoch 9 | D: 1.005 | G: 1.915
Epoch 10 | D: 0.782 | G: 1.943
Saved simple_gan.png
```

See the `D:` and `G:` values jump around? That’s the GAN training in action. Figure 17-3 shows the results of a five-epoch training session, and Figure 17-4 shows the results of a ten-epoch training session. Note how much better the numerals look after doubling the number of epochs.

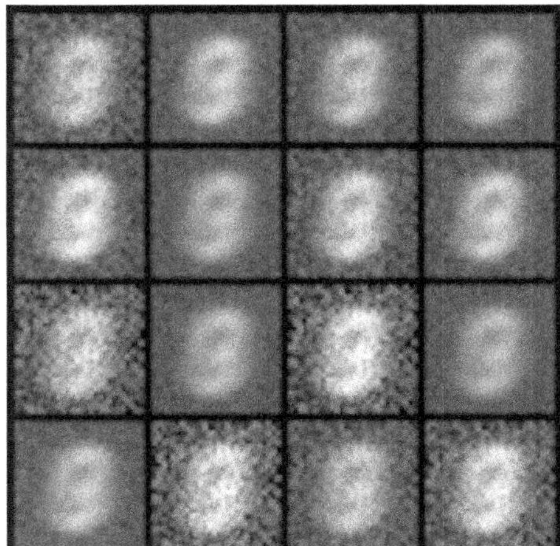

FIGURE 17-3: Five-epoch GAN results.

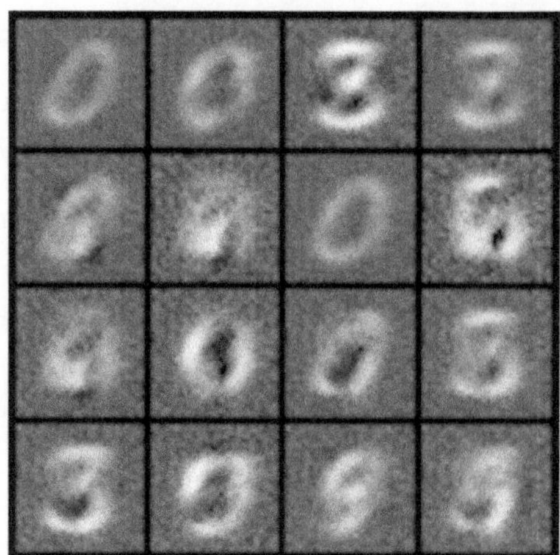

FIGURE 17-4: Ten-epoch GAN results.

Of course, we had to try running a 100-epoch run to see how that works out. There is a law of diminishing returns on these types of calculations, and sometimes things get even worse with more training. Ever run the same prompt twice in ChatGPT to generate a picture? It never returns the same exact picture twice. Why? It's the random nature of making the pictures fit the data. GANs show this in spades. Figure 17-5 shows that things actually got worse instead of improving.

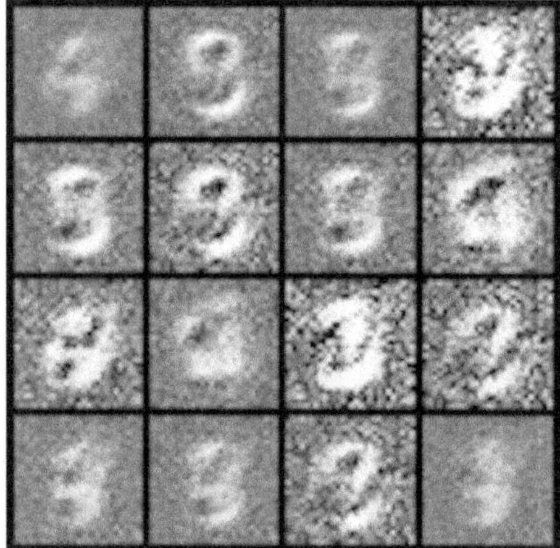

FIGURE 17-5: One hundred-epoch GAN results.

Fool around with this code. You can learn a lot by changing things and seeing the results vary in this simple example.

Making Sense of Data with Variational Autoencoders

A variational autoencoder (VAE) is a statistically and probabilistically based generative model that is focused on learning how data is structured and then generating new, similar samples. A standard autoencoder typically compresses data into a single point; a VAE generates a distribution of latent space.

Latent space is a compressed, hidden representation of data so the algorithm can organize, generate, and make sense of that data. It focuses on essential features instead of storing every pixel, word, or sound. Does this sound like the token vector space we talked about in the previous chapter? Yes, it is very similar in concept and execution. Being able to store data in a compressed format and being able to access and recognize the essential features of the data quickly are key to many generative AI algorithms.

Figure 17-6 shows a typical architecture of a variational autoencoder.

Variational Autoencoder

x → … → $\mu_0\ \sigma$ → … → x'

Input | Encoder | Latent Space | Decoder | Output

FIGURE 17-6: Block diagram of a variational autoencoder.

Now let's look at a Python example of a VAE with some of the internal data structures exposed (see Listing 17-2). Figure 17-7 shows the visual results of the convolutional VAE run. Again, we used our AI tools to build the skeleton and then modified the code from there. This was a difficult piece of code to prompt as the AI kept making it way too complicated.

LISTING 17-2: A Convolutional VAE with Internals (VAE_Internals.py)

```
# Convolutional VAE (MNIST) with "show internals"
# pip install torch torchvision

import torch
import torch.nn as nn
import torch.nn.functional as F
import torch.optim as optim
from torchvision import datasets, transforms
from torchvision.utils import save_image


# ---------- Helpers ----------
def tinfo(name, t: torch.Tensor, max_items=6):
    flat = t.detach().flatten()
    sample = flat[:max_items].cpu().tolist()
    print(
        f"{name:12s} shape={tuple(t.shape)} dtype={t.dtype}
  device={t.device} "
        f"min={t.min().item():.3f} max={t.max().item():.3f} "
        f"mean={t.mean().item():.3f} std={t.std().item():.3f}
  sample={sample}"
    )


def vae_loss(x_hat, x, mu, logvar):
    # Reconstruction loss (BCE) + KL(q(z|x) || N(0,I))
    recon = F.binary_cross_entropy(x_hat, x, reduction="sum")
    kl = -0.5 * torch.sum(1 + logvar - mu.pow(2) - logvar.exp())
    return recon + kl, recon, kl


# ---------- Conv VAE ----------
class ConvVAE(nn.Module):
    """
    Encoder: (B,1,28,28) -> Conv -> Conv -> flatten -> (mu, logvar)
    Decoder: z -> FC -> reshape -> ConvTranspose -> ConvTranspose ->
  (B,1,28,28)
    """
    def __init__(self, latent_dim=16):
        super().__init__()
        self.latent_dim = latent_dim
```

```
        # Encoder: 28x28 -> 14x14 -> 7x7
        self.enc_conv = nn.Sequential(
            nn.Conv2d(1, 32, kernel_size=4, stride=2,
padding=1),  # 28->14
            nn.ReLU(inplace=True),
            nn.Conv2d(32, 64, kernel_size=4, stride=2,
padding=1), # 14->7
            nn.ReLU(inplace=True),
        )
        self.enc_flat_dim = 64 * 7 * 7
        self.fc_mu = nn.Linear(self.enc_flat_dim, latent_dim)
        self.fc_logvar = nn.Linear(self.enc_flat_dim, latent_dim)

        # Decoder
        self.dec_fc = nn.Linear(latent_dim, self.enc_flat_dim)
        self.dec_deconv = nn.Sequential(
            nn.ConvTranspose2d(64, 32, kernel_size=4, stride=2,
padding=1),  # 7->14
            nn.ReLU(inplace=True),
            nn.ConvTranspose2d(32, 1, kernel_size=4, stride=2,
padding=1),   # 14->28
            nn.Sigmoid(),  # pixels in [0,1]
        )

    def encode(self, x):
        h = self.enc_conv(x)                    # (B,64,7,7)
        h_flat = h.view(x.size(0), -1)          # (B, 3136)
        mu = self.fc_mu(h_flat)                 # (B, latent_dim)
        logvar = self.fc_logvar(h_flat)         # (B, latent_dim)
        return mu, logvar, h, h_flat

    def reparameterize(self, mu, logvar):
        std = torch.exp(0.5 * logvar)
        eps = torch.randn_like(std)
        z = mu + std * eps
        return z, std, eps

    def decode(self, z):
        h_flat = F.relu(self.dec_fc(z))
# (B,3136)
        h = h_flat.view(z.size(0), 64, 7, 7)
# (B,64,7,7)
        x_hat = self.dec_deconv(h)
# (B,1,28,28)
```

(continued)

LISTING 17-2: *(continued)*

```
        return x_hat, h, h_flat

    def forward(self, x):
        mu, logvar, h_enc, h_enc_flat = self.encode(x)
        z, std, eps = self.reparameterize(mu, logvar)
        x_hat, h_dec, h_dec_flat = self.decode(z)
        return {
            "x_hat": x_hat,
            "mu": mu,
            "logvar": logvar,
            "std": std,
            "eps": eps,
            "z": z,
            "h_enc": h_enc,
            "h_enc_flat": h_enc_flat,
            "h_dec": h_dec,
            "h_dec_flat": h_dec_flat,
        }


# ---------- Run ----------
def main():
    device = "cuda" if torch.cuda.is_available() else "cpu"
    batch_size = 128
    latent_dim = 16
    epochs = 10
    lr = 1e-3

    loader = torch.utils.data.DataLoader(
        datasets.MNIST("./data", train=True, download=True,
  transform=transforms.ToTensor()),
        batch_size=batch_size,
        shuffle=True,
        drop_last=True,
    )

    vae = ConvVAE(latent_dim=latent_dim).to(device)
    opt = optim.Adam(vae.parameters(), lr=lr)

    # ----- Show internals on a single batch -----
    x0, _ = next(iter(loader))
    x0 = x0.to(device)
```

```
print("\n--- One forward pass (internals) ---")
vae.eval()
with torch.no_grad():
    out = vae(x0)

    tinfo("x", x0)
    tinfo("h_enc", out["h_enc"])
    tinfo("h_enc_flat", out["h_enc_flat"])
    tinfo("mu", out["mu"])
    tinfo("logvar", out["logvar"])
    tinfo("std", out["std"])
    tinfo("eps", out["eps"])
    tinfo("z", out["z"])
    tinfo("h_dec", out["h_dec"])
    tinfo("x_hat", out["x_hat"])

    # Save original vs reconstruction
    orig = x0[:16]
    recon = out["x_hat"][:16]
    save_image(orig, "convvae_orig.png", nrow=4)
    save_image(recon, "convvae_recon.png", nrow=4)
    print("Saved: convvae_orig.png and convvae_recon.png")

# ----- Train -----
print("\n--- Training ---")
vae.train()
for epoch in range(1, epochs + 1):
    total_loss = total_recon = total_kl = 0.0

    for x, _ in loader:
        x = x.to(device)
        out = vae(x)
        loss, recon, kl = vae_loss(out["x_hat"], x, out["mu"],
out["logvar"])

        opt.zero_grad(set_to_none=True)
        loss.backward()
        opt.step()

        total_loss += loss.item()
        total_recon += recon.item()
        total_kl += kl.item()

    n = len(loader.dataset)
```

(continued)

LISTING 17-2: *(continued)*

```
        print(
            f"Epoch {epoch}/{epochs} | "
            f"loss={total_loss/n:.4f} recon={total_recon/n:.4f}
  kl={total_kl/n:.4f}"
        )

        # sample new digits from the prior
        vae.eval()
        with torch.no_grad():
            z = torch.randn(16, latent_dim, device=device)
            x_hat, _, _ = vae.decode(z)
            save_image(x_hat, f"convvae_samples_epoch_{epoch}.
  png", nrow=4)
        vae.train()

    print("\nDone. Check:")
    print(" - convvae_orig.png")
    print(" - convvae_recon.png")
    print(" - convvae_samples_epoch_*.png")


if __name__ == "__main__":
    main()
```

Here are some of the results of the run:

```
(env) pi@pythonandai:~/Documents $ python VAE_Internals.py
--- One forward pass (internals) ---
...
h_enc         shape=(128, 64, 7, 7) dtype=torch.float32
  device=cpu min=0.000 max=0.534 mean=0.034 std=0.051
  sample=[0.0, 0.0, 0.0, 0.0, 0.0, 0.0]
...
Saved: convvae_orig.png and convvae_recon.png

--- Training ---
Epoch 1/10 | loss=169.6506 recon=153.0728 kl=16.5778
Epoch 2/10 | loss=113.9986 recon=90.9270 kl=23.0716
Epoch 3/10 | loss=108.9546 recon=85.3849 kl=23.5697
Epoch 4/10 | loss=106.7479 recon=82.9084 kl=23.8395
Epoch 5/10 | loss=105.3979 recon=81.4141 kl=23.9838
```

```
Epoch 6/10 | loss=104.3597 recon=80.2740 kl=24.0858
Epoch 7/10 | loss=103.6834 recon=79.4598 kl=24.2237
Epoch 8/10 | loss=103.0224 recon=78.7966 kl=24.2258
Epoch 9/10 | loss=102.5186 recon=78.2684 kl=24.2502
Epoch 10/10 | loss=102.0599 recon=77.7999 kl=24.2600

Done. Check:
 - convvae_orig.png
 - convvae_recon.png
 - convvae_samples_epoch_*.png
```

Here is a brief description of the results:

- `h_enc`: This is the output of the convolutional decoder represented by 64 feature maps. We aren't showing them because there are just a bunch of numbers, but what they represent is the encoder's special understanding of the image in terms of edges, strokes, shapes, and local patterns. Those expecting something that makes more sense to us humans will be disappointed. Again, AI is all math and statistics. With meaning, but not easily interpreted directly by us humans. The epoch numbers will make more sense to us.
- `loss`: This reflects the success of the VAE toward its overall training objective. Decreasing means it is getting closer. Notice that we are running into diminishing returns per epoch as we move from four to ten.
- `recon`: This is reconstruction loss and measures how well the output image matches the input.
- `kl`: Short for KL divergence. This term tells us how close the internal structure (the latent layer) is to a unit Gaussian distribution (the smoothness of the result). So why does `kl` go up and `recon` go down? This is the VAE trade-off. Accuracy (`recon`) versus generative structures with `kl` pushing toward the standard normal.

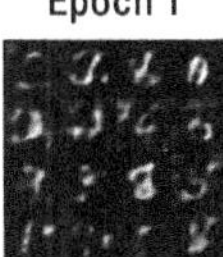

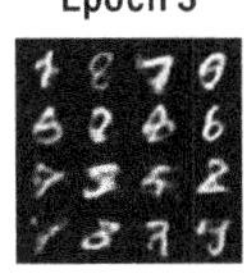

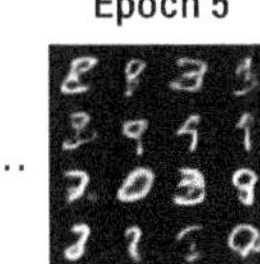

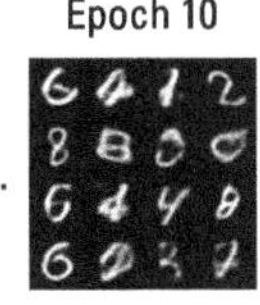

FIGURE 17-7: Visual results of the convolutional VAE run.

Imaging with Diffusion Models

Diffusion models are generative AI algorithms that are designed to generate structured data, such as images and text, from a random state. In a sense, you are diffusing order to noise in a similar way to cutting a clove of garlic in one part of a room and smelling it later everywhere. A diffusion module operates by learning to *invert* a process that introduces noise into the data to produce a structure from the initial noise. This sounds pretty weird to generate structure from a random distribution, but the key to diffusion models is to use a controlled process of reducing noise through multiple steps and learning.

TIP

Think of a diffusion model as slowly removing years of grit and smoke from a mural painted on the wall. The detail appears slowly as you scrub gently. The difference with the diffusion models is that there is no detail in the underlying mural (random noise), and your scrubbing techniques are what bring out the detail.

Where is the magic? The magic is the methods that are used to reverse the noise.

Diffusion models excel in generating high-quality, detailed images with intricate details. They operate through a series of noise-reduction steps that are capable of doing tasks that require high resolution and overall coherence.

In a real sense, diffusion models combine GAN-level realism with VAE-level stability at the cost of much higher computation. Table 17-1 compares diffusion, GAN, and VAE algorithms. It is not necessarily intuitive how this process can create an image of "a small dog reading a book." However, using diffusion is a key part of the overall algorithm.

TABLE 17-1 GAN, VAE, and Diffusion Models

Aspect	GANs	VAEs	Diffusion
Core idea	Adversarial competition	Probabilistic latent space	Denoising from noise
Training stability	Low (remember the bouncing)	High	High
Output quality	Very sharp	Smooth/blurry	Very sharp and diverse
Diversity	Medium (mode collapse)	High	Very high
Computational requirements	Low	Medium	Very high
Best use case	Real-time realism	Latent structure	High-quality generation

The process used to create images is the following:

1. The text, "A small dog reading a book," is broken into tokens by an LLM, which does not generate image pixels at this point. The text is converted into a vector (see Chapter 16 on LLMs) that encodes meaning, style, objects, and token relationships, creating a long numerical vector.
2. Using diffusion, you start with a random noise picture — no template, no training data, just pure noise.
3. Now we talk about the magic. The diffusion model is subjected to guided denoising (typically a U-Net; see the sidebar later in this chapter) using the vector in step 1.
4. The vector of step 1 guides and "trains" the denoising algorithm to add colors, rough shapes ("dog"), objects ("dog and book"), actions ("reading"), and more textures and details to the final image.
5. At each denoising pass, the diffusion model asks, given the token vector, what should *not* be there. Composition, objects, style, and fine details are added incrementally.

It should be obvious that this whole process is complicated and computationally complex. Remember, this method is not drawing a picture or image. It is learning to remove noise correctly with the guidance of the text.

DIFFUSION AND U-NETS

U-Nets are a type of neural network architecture designed to work on understanding images while preserving fine detail. They are called U-Nets because the block diagram looks like a "U." This was a major architectural innovation by Ronneberger, Fisher, and Brox in 2015 in their paper on biomedical image segmentation. Another one of those incredible papers leading to huge amounts of innovation.

The encoder (contracting path) captures the image information and context by a series of convolutional neural networks and pool layers, extracting the high-level features. It shrinks the data (down-sampling) to create what is called a *bottleneck*. The bottleneck is a compact, information-dense, high-entropy representation containing high-level important features.

The decoder (expanding path) reconstructs the image by up-sampling (growing the data) through the use of skip connections. *Skip connections* are direct connections linking the encoder layers to their respective decoder sections.

(continued)

(continued)

Finally, you end up at the output generator that can reconstruct an image.

How does your input vector text influence the U-Net? By influencing the diffusion denoising process.

The following figure shows the overall block architecture of a U-Net.

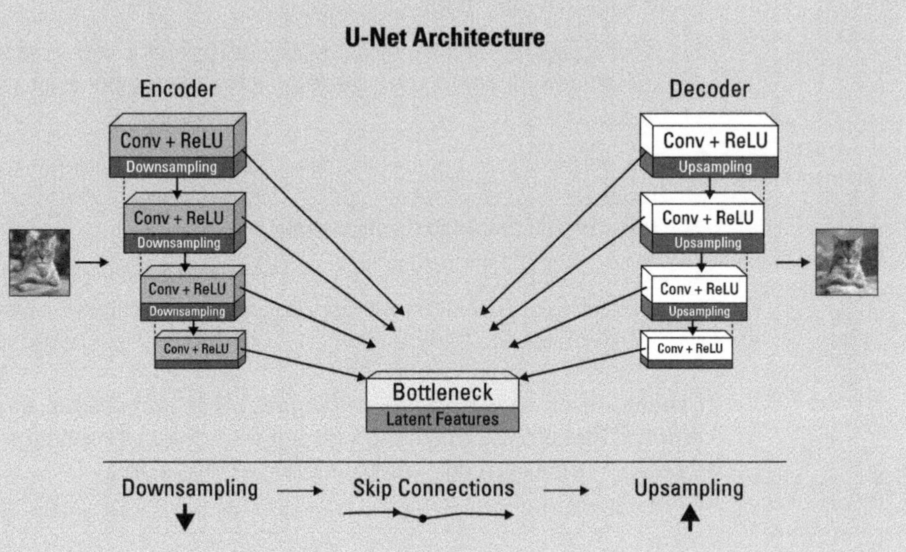

Next, Listing 17-3 shows a small Python program (again, the skeleton was from ChatGPT in this case) for a small text-to-image diffusion demo. In your Python environment, run the following command: `pip install -U diffusers transformers accelerate safetensors torch`.

LISTING 17-3: A minimal Diffusion-Based Text-to-Image Pipeline (Diffusion.py)

```
#

import torch
from diffusers import AutoPipelineForText2Image

device = "cuda" if torch.cuda.is_available() else "cpu"
dtype = torch.float16 if device == "cuda" else torch.float32

pipe = AutoPipelineForText2Image.from_pretrained(
```

```
    "stable-diffusion-v1-5/stable-diffusion-v1-5",
    torch_dtype=dtype,
    use_safetensors=True,
).to(device)

image = pipe("a small dog reading a book, cozy lamp light",
  num_inference_steps=25).images[0]
image.save("txt2img.png")
print("saved txt2img.png")
```

Running this program will take a while! It downloads about 5 GB of data. Text-to-image is not for the timid.

Here are the results from the run:

```
python Diffusion.py
/home/pi/Documents/env/lib/python3.13/site-packages/torch/amp/
   autocast_mode.py:270: UserWarning: User provided device_type
   of 'cuda', but CUDA is not available. Disabling
  warnings.warn(
unet/diffusion_pytorch_model.safetensors: 100%|█| 3.44G/3.44G
   [04:24<00:00, 13.0
vae/diffusion_pytorch_model.safetensors: 100%|█| 335M/335M
   [04:43<00:00, 1.18MB/
text_encoder/model.safetensors: 100%|████████| 492M/492M
   [05:04<00:00, 1.62MB/s]
Fetching 15 files: 100%|█████████████████████████| 15/15
   [05:09<00:00, 20.66s/it]
Loading pipeline components...:  14%|██          | 1/7
   [00:11<01:08, 11.49s/it]`torch_dtype` is deprecated! Use
   `dtype` instead!
Loading pipeline components...: 100%|███████████████| 7/7
   [00:12<00:00,  1.75s/it]
100%|██████████████████████████████████████████████| 25/25
   [16:29<00:00, 39.56s/it]
saved txt2img.png
```

Lots of data transfers. It took about 30 minutes on my high-speed Internet connection and a Raspberry Pi 5. But it worked! Figure 17-8 shows the resulting image. I'm amazed at the results from my little credit card-sized computer.

FIGURE 17-8: Diffusion-generated image of a dog.

Generating Code with Transformer Models

In Chapter 16, we talk about the use of LLMs and transformers for building documents. Here, we revisit those same LLMs, but we now focus on how they generate code that can be useful to software engineers and noncoders . . . sometimes!

So, how does an LLM generate code? Well, it's not magic. LLMs generate code exactly the way they write text. They predict the most likely token given the previous token, using patterns from reading massive amounts of text and code.

Let's give it a task. Using ChatGPT, we prompt, "Write a Python function that subtracts two numbers." It returns:

```
def subtract(a, b):
    """Return the result of a minus b."""
    return a - b
```

Wow! I'm impressed. The last time I tried this example, it didn't add a comment! I would have put the comment before the function, but that is a style issue and not a functional one.

During training (which for a full LLM is a *huge, enormous* task that consumes huge amounts of power, disk space, and CPU power), the LLM sees billions of examples of code, but the training is always the same: Given tokens 1..n, predict token n+1. Back to not overly anthropomorphizing LLMs. LMMs write code by predicting tokens, and not by "thinking like a human programmer" or executing code internally. The LLM looks intelligent because of how the training, internal coding, and decoding all come together. There is no intuition, grand strategy, or any of the things we call the higher levels of human intelligence. It is all one token after another taken in context. The way LLMs store context using transformers and encoding is highly sophisticated and very useful for these kinds of prediction tasks.

However, intelligent or not, these AI coding tools are very useful when properly used, and when an engineer is actually paying attention to debugging and the limitations of the model, their productivity can go up. As of this writing, there is not a lot of evidence that using LLMs improves productivity overall. A recent MIT study says it looks like productivity is a wash because of increased debugging required for significant pieces of code. Hmm. This should get better eventually, but there is some real evidence that LLMs are reaching their limits. What if there isn't any more web content and code to read?

WARNING

Estimates are that major LLMs are up to about 80 percent of the entire Internet. And another problem is that some estimates suggest that 60 percent of new content on the web is being generated by AI in one form or another. When something like an LLM is reading information generated by itself and its similar brethren, you can get something very much like a "collapse to the middle," which means everything is kind of mediocre, and no LLM gets any better.

Given all this, what is a good use case? We use LLMs regularly to set up program skeletons to get started on a project. Some of our peers and students even build upon their own code.

We know that coding is a typical token-by-token operation that LLMs are very good at. So what happens when the LLM has been trained on billions of lines of code? The model gradually learns the following:

- Syntax patterns
- Common APIs
- Idiomatic structures (called *design patterns* in software engineering)
- Relationships between comments and code

Gradually, LLMs (just as they do with stories and plotlines) code high-dimensional vectors that encode variable relationships, scope behavior, and control flow patterns and API usage patterns. The self-attention aspects of transformers let the model link variable definitions to later usage, match brackets and indentation, and track function arguments across many, many lines.

Wow! We want some of that. Wait, wait. Let's look at the downsides. LLM-written code can often be wrong. LLMs can:

- Hallucinate APIs. Yes, just make one up because it looks right according to the web.
- Mix up library versions. This happens constantly with Python programming.
- Produce subtly incorrect logic and control flows.
- Miss edge cases.
- Miss cybersecurity issues.

REMEMBER

Remember that an LLM doesn't predict what must come next, merely what should come next based upon the collective coding habits of millions of developers.

Programmers can use other tools to improve things, such as static analysis, code execution (the key to debugging), and feedback loops. Better to make it a verify-and-correct loop rather than no feedback at all.

Let's try a simple (but nontrivial) coding example. Prompt ChatGPT:

> Write me a program for a CRX10 robot to move from point A to point B in Python. Don't use Karel. Use the University of Idaho API.

We're not going to reproduce the code here, as there are a few of you readers with FANUC CRX10 robots, but it was an interesting process watching ChatGPT figure out what to do. The code structure was not too bad. It was using API calls that didn't exist in the API, and it figured out the GitHub site that we had the Python API inside. It clearly had never seen that API before. My overall thought was that the LLM was using a structure and then kludging in likely API calls. We're impressed that it got this far.

A SENIOR SOFTWARE ENGINEER'S STORY OF CODING WITH AI

Calvin Freitas is a senior software engineer located in the lovely town of Coeur d'Alene, Idaho. We asked him what his day-to-day use of AI in his company looks like, and he told us the following.

I've found the most effective way to use AI for software engineering has been to provide clear context and rules up front. If I'm writing or modifying code (new features, improvements, or refactoring), I make a "Plan" document (by prompting and/or writing a Markdown file) before asking an LLM/agent for any code.

I've been using Cursor lately, and I've also used VS Code + GitHub Copilot, as well as Claude Code, OpenCode, and Cursor Agent. The CLI agents are useful, but I prefer an editor where I can intervene for tactical edits — both in the plans and the implementations.

Cursor's Plan mode works well. Claude Code's "plan mode" operates similarly. Amazon's Kiro editor/agent is even more focused on "spec"-driven development — making the plan first. A planning step is becoming common across agents.

Creating a plan first follows common software development lifecycle practices that engineers have engaged with for decades: breaking down work into granular units (with names like epics, stories, or tasks depending on the size of the work unit and the development philosophy used by the software engineering team). Fortunately for an engineer, the practice of defining the work to be done and the constraints tends to be useful whether you're working on something yourself or pairing with a human engineer or an LLM agent. A plan helps improve understanding of what needs to be done by all involved.

LLMs and agents can potentially be used to run QA steps, make decisions about deployments, and execute deployments to carry through improvements to additional steps of the process. When you get to this point, it becomes a lot more important to understand safeguards and rules around this kind of automation, as the risks get higher compared to earlier steps in the process. (There are many cybersecurity considerations with this shift in how software gets built, released, and operated!)

John's comment: As of May 2026, I've talked with a lot of other engineers in many different industries, and the usage patterns and actual overall effectiveness of using AI is all over the map, with the bias toward some increased productivity. Based on my informal study, I am making the use of AI code generation tools (Claude Code currently) a requirement in my robotics classes. It helps with skeletons, but makes building things as a group much more complicated. Plus and minus both.

Last Words on Generative AI

Generative AI is a fascinating topic with huge implications for how we can work with these AI programs to be more productive engineers and workers. They are big helper applications that are only going to get better. Generative AI is all about encoding knowledge in a form that our neural networks can learn from and predict better images or the next tokens. Costs for using these AI tools are all over the map and are changing daily as the highly competitive environment between companies intensifies even more. As a quick rule of thumb from the chairman of Nvidia, an engineer being paid $500,000 per year should use $250,000 worth of tokens. If they aren't, something is wrong. Note that Nvidia greatly benefits from the AI industry selling more and more tokens, so keep his bias in mind.

We'll leave you with one more small example. John decided he would use RunwayML (`www.runwayml.com`) to make a short video about reading books about Python, becoming smarter, and then flying away. Here is the result:

```
https://youtu.be/O_LHWDA2qTE
```

One last comment about generative AI. John paid $15 for a one-month subscription to RunwayML and completely used it all for two five-second videos and one ten-second video. Too expensive for our taste!

IN THIS CHAPTER

» Understanding types of AI agents

» Writing AI agent programs in Python

» Exploring the limitations of AI agents

Chapter 18

AI Agents: The Ghosts in Our Machines

In movies, secret agents are moving in the background, doing all sorts of nefarious things and gathering information. They behave like ghosts, moving from one location and piece of information to another. AI agents are like the James Bond of computers. Running in the background, gathering information and doing special tasks. In this chapter, you explore the different types of AI agents and their limitations as well as try your hand at writing an AI agent program in Python.

Separating Agentic AI from Traditional AI

Agentic AI refers to an AI system that doesn't just answer a question, but can accomplish a goal on its own using memory, other programs, and multistep planning. Think of an LLM as a single-phase assistant. You ask it a question, and it responds. An agentic AI system is more like a robotic system using advanced tools. You supply it a goal; the agent uses more tools and programs, checks results (much different than an LLM!), and continues until it's done or gives up. The following sections outline the difference between traditional AI, agentic AI, and an additional subcategory of agentic AI, agentic RAG (retrieval-augmented generation). The last one sounds like the Scott Joplin tune from the movie, *The Sting!* Oh, wait, that was the "Maple Leaf Rag."

Traditional AI

Figure 18-1 outlines a traditional AI pipeline. (It feels odd to use the word *traditional* for something so new!) A traditional AI system follows one path through the code that is static in nature. From a block diagram point of view, traditional AI looks like a pipeline. Unfortunately, under the hood, a number of these blocks involve multiple paths and random paths through the code (think of the diffusion models and LLM models discussed in earlier chapters). However, as a guide to differentiate between non-agentic and agentic AI, it's not bad to think about AI from a block-level point of view.

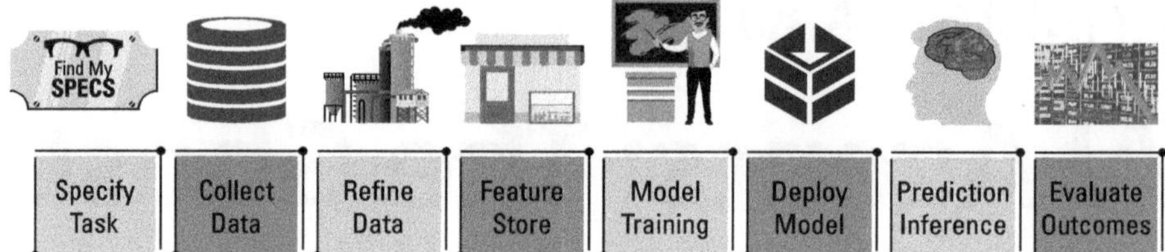

FIGURE 18-1: Static AI pipeline.

As illustrated in Figure 18-1, in traditional AI, you collect the data, train a model, and then deploy the results. That's the linear nature of this type of AI from a high-level point of view.

WHAT IS "REAL" TRADITIONAL AI?

"If you just have a single problem to solve, then fine, go ahead and use a neural network. But if you want to do science and understand how to choose architectures, or how to go to a new problem, you have to understand what different architectures can and cannot do." —MARVIN MINSKY, AI PIONEER

Dr. Minsky, an early neural network promoter, was around for the whole AI craze from the beginning in the 1970s up until his passing in 2016. He said many times that true AI was 20 years off, but one time, he said it would take us three to four hundred years to create an intelligent system. I'd guess somewhere in between is a safe bet.

Real traditional AI refers to AI algorithms that were built before modern machine learning dominated algorithms, where the intelligence of the system was through explicit rules, logic, and hand-crafted heuristics. The main components of traditional AI algorithms are:

- **Rule-based systems based on if-then statements:** Such systems are called *expert systems*. Interestingly enough (at least to us), John wrote his PhD dissertation on a method for building a hardware system to accelerate the evaluation of expert systems. He's not going to tell you how many years ago that was.
- **Knowledge representations:** Facts are stored as logic statements, semantic networks, or other types (for example, `is_a(morkie, dog); is_a(dog, mammal)`).
- **Searching and planning:** Methods for setting up state spaces and searching through them. Graph walking, decision-like trees, and a variety of planning algorithms.
- **Inference engines:** These techniques use backward and forward chaining to go through state spaces. In a real sense, this is what turned into neural networks. Finally, the state space turned into machine learning algorithms, and we were off to the next AI craze, of which we are still in the middle.

Agentic AI

Agentic AI refers to AI software systems that can act autonomously to achieve the set goals by deciding, taking actions, observing and verifying results, and then adapting to the changing data and/or results (see Figure 18-2). Agentic AI applies feedback to the traditional AI pipeline. So is it magic? No. Is it cool? Yes.

Notice in Figure 18-2 that agentic AI is not a straight-line algorithm, unlike the one shown in Figure 18-1. It is a complete loop that has no definitive ending. It often ends when it reaches the goal set, but it can operate for minutes, hours, or even longer. It is built to be able to stop, pivot, and replan when blocked from reaching its goal.

You integrate other tools, APIs, and even other AI tools and algorithms as part of the agentic loop. It gets feedback from these tools (for example, by compiling a program to make sure that it works or by running test cases — kind of like a person would). That feedback loop is what is called a *perception-action loop*. The key behavior is: observe, reason, act, observe, update, repeat. Reminds us of shampoo instructions: wash, rinse, repeat.

The agent maintains working memory and sometimes has long-term memory. This is a key way the agent can avoid repeating mistakes within a task.

REMEMBER

The agent must have guardrails and constraints on the actions it can take. This can be safety checks and validations, tool access limits, permission boundaries, and even human-in-the-loop escalation.

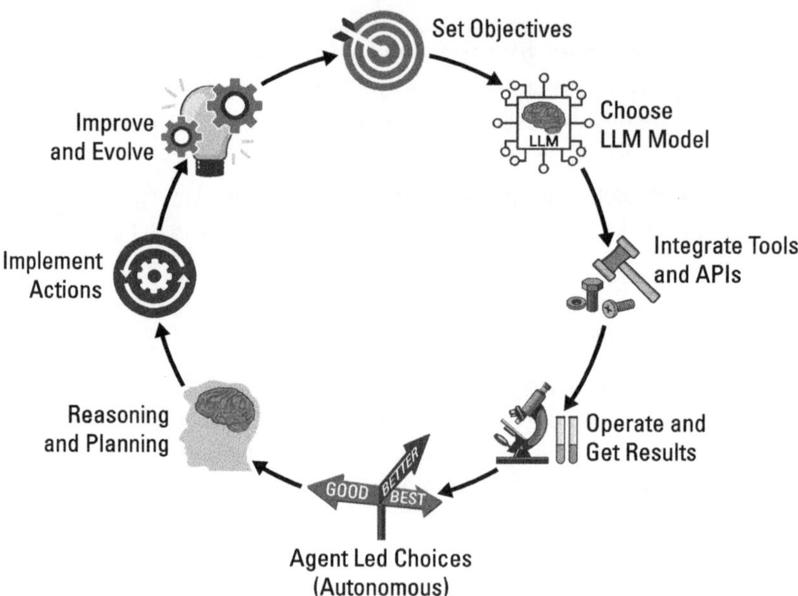

FIGURE 18-2: Agentic AI loop.

WARNING

So you have this little (or big) autonomous agent running around on your computer doing things, and it's complicated enough that you may not quite understand what it is doing. This should really remind you of a computer worm or a virus. Good grief! It is easy to see that this will be an ongoing problem as people release these far more capable programs in the wild. Oh, wait; this has already happened! Prompt injection, phishing campaigns, poisoned documents, API crashing, reconnaissance, credential stuffing, malware customization, and so on. It's a brave new world. Get used to it.

All of these methods have been used in programming for many years. The difference is the inclusion of new AI algorithms that are more flexible than traditional code. The saying "There is nothing new under the sun" is attributed to King Solomon. The first time John heard that phrase was from his high school teacher in Great Falls, Montana, Miss Cosgriff. It's always stayed with him. Architecturally, agentic AI is not a new concept.

WHAT IS FEEDBACK?

Feedback occurs when you route a system's output back into its inputs as a loop. Sounds complicated? It can be, but the basics are simple. Suppose you publish an article and ask for comments. People supply comments (nice ones, we hope), and you change the article based on some of those comments. That's feedback!

You use feedback in AI software to achieve better and more accurate results, for example. By comparing the current output of your AI algorithm to a known value of some kind, your software can use that feedback to tweak the neural network and get a more accurate result.

Backward propagation through neural networks is how this is accomplished in neural networks for virtually all modern AI. Typically, this kind of feedback in LLMs only happens during training, not when you are chatting with them via your command line or via software API calls. The LLMs do incorporate information used in chats in some side networks to enhance moving forward by changing the way the transformers apply contextual feedback. It is promising. It is not training the weights of the big LLM model. That stays fixed. This, unfortunately, is also how you can leak all your information back into the LLM to teach your competitors how to do whatever you are doing.

Agentic RAG

Agentic RAG (retrieval-augmented generation) is really more of an incremental change to AI agents, rather than a whole new type. RAG has been around for a long time (think of a "traditional" LLM AI pipeline). Agentic RAG changes the AI pipeline by once again introducing feedback (a feature of agentic AI in general), but with a more complex toolset, memory store, and multiple uses of AI tools involved in the planning and decision-making (see Figure 18-3).

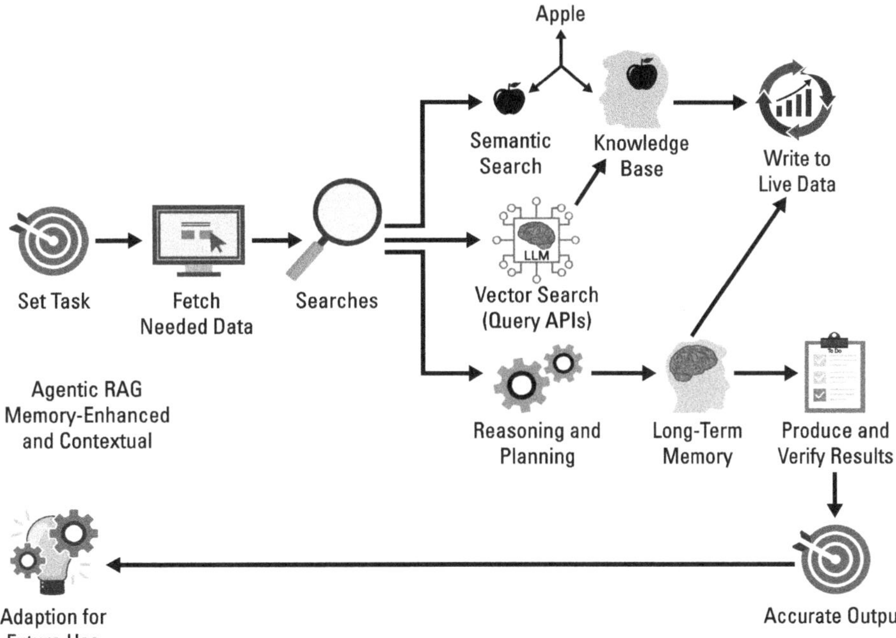

FIGURE 18-3: Agentic RAG block diagram.

Specifically, agentic RAG is a type of AI agent that:

- Retrieves relevant information from external sources.
- Generates an answer using both the retrieved information and learned information.

Building Simple AI Agents in Python

In this section, we write two short AI agent programs in Python. First, we build a simple AI agent that can answer questions, but not just in the linear traditional pipeline. We will provide some local information that (hopefully) we are not sharing with the LLM on the web. Then, we build a simple RAG agent that will answer a couple of questions using locally acquired context and an LLM to scrape the web to find the definition of a special acronym.

TIP

For both examples, we will use ChatGPT from OpenAI. It is not free. For this example, we purchased $5 worth of credits. (You can use the same OpenAI API key you used in Chapter 15.)

Building an AI web-scraping agent

This program is designed to search out the meaning of the acronym, CIIR. What does CIIR stand for? The desired case is that CIIR stands for the Center for Intelligent Industrial Robotics at the University of Idaho (which your authors are the director and associate director of). The trouble is, there are many CIIRs in the world (the Catholic Institute for International Relations, for example), and our first attempt at creating an AI web-scraping agent to uncover this definition did not find our robotics center. The solution to this excruciating problem was to provide more contextual data.

When talking about building an agent, it's always good to talk about what tasks you are going to implement in a clear and concise manner. For this project, our tasks are:

- Identify what "CIIR" stands for using robotics/automation contexts from the provided sources.
- If CIIR answers are ambiguous, list multiple plausible expansions, but put robotics-relevant meanings first.

» For each meaning, provide:
  - Expansion of the acronym (what CIIR stands for)
  - A one- to two-sentence definition of CIIR
  - The robotics relevance (high/medium/low) and why
  - The source IDs and URLs used

Listing 18-1 shows part of the code for the minimal AI agent we created. The first version clocked in at 191 lines — just too long to list here! Plus, we actually did two versions. The first was still too big, so we re-did the prompts and again simplified the model. The complete source code for the program we used (`AIAgent2.py`) is available in the downloadable code file associated with this book. (See the Introduction for details on how to download the source files.)

The needed libraries for this program can be installed by running `pip install torch torchvision openai ddgs requests beautifulsoup4`. We built this minimal AI agent with a ChatGPT skeleton and then simplified it for this book.

LISTING 18-1: A Partial Listing of a Minimal AI Agent using Web Scraping to Find an Acronym Definition (AIAgent2.py)

```
# --------- Config ---------
USER_AGENT = "ciir-agent/1.1 (+research script)"
TIMEOUT = 15
MAX_RESULTS_PER_QUERY = 6
MAX_PAGES_TO_FETCH = 6
MAX_CHARS_PER_PAGE = 7000

# Robotics context keywords used for ranking
ROBOTICS_KEYWORDS = [
    "robot", "robotics", "industrial robot", "cobot", "automation",
    "manipulator", "manipulation", "mobile robot", "navigation",
    "perception", "vision", "slam", "gripper", "end effector",
    "ros", "ros2", "motion planning", "path planning", "controls",
    "factory", "manufacturing", "machine tending"
]

...


def robotics_relevance_score(title: str, snippet: str, page_text: str) -> int:
    hay = f"{title}\n{snippet}\n{page_text}".lower()
    score = 0
```

(continued)

LISTING 18-1: *(continued)*

```
    for kw in ROBOTICS_KEYWORDS:
        # simple weighted match
        k = kw.lower()
        if k in hay:
            score += 3
    # extra boost if "ciir" appears near robotics terms
    if "ciir" in hay and ("robot" in hay or "ros" in hay or
   "automation" in hay):
        score += 5
    return score


...


def main():
    api_key = load_api_key("api.key")
    client = OpenAI(api_key=api_key)

    evidence = build_evidence_robotics()

    print("\nFetched sources (ranked by robotics relevance):")
    for ev in evidence:
        print(f"- score={ev.robo_score} | {ev.title}\n  {ev.url}\n")

    summary = llm_summarize_ciir_robotics(client, evidence)

    print("\n=== CIIR Definitions (Robotics-biased, with sources) ===\n")
    print(textwrap.fill(summary, width=100))


if __name__ == "__main__":
    main()
```

The code listing does the following:

- Sets up the configuration for the agent. There are the usual pieces of information for timeouts, number of pages, and so on, but the most important piece of this module is setting up additional local context for ranking. (We had to add additional context to correctly uncover the meaning of the CIIR acronym.)
- Uses the `robotics_relevance_score` function to give us a score as to how relevant our results are to robotics. It takes a snippet from the web page and then looks for various robotics terms and scores them appropriately.

» Sets up OpenAI with the main function, starts the evidence-gathering loop (which reads a bunch of pages and gathers evidence), and then prints the results in a human-readable fashion.

As we mentioned earlier, our first attempt at our AI agent program did not yield what we were looking for. The abbreviated results are as follows:

```
Based on the provided sources, "CIIR" has multiple plausible expansions and
definitions, with a strong presence in military contexts:  - **Expansion:**
Counter-Insurgency and Intelligence Report
**Definition:** A report or document related to intelligence gathering and
analysis specifically focused on counter-insurgency operations.
**Domain/Context:** Military, intelligence operations
**Evidence:** While not explicitly defined in the excerpts, the abbreviation
CIIR is closely related to military intelligence terms and appears alongside
other military acronyms in MilitaryDictionary.org (S2, S3, S4).  -
**Expansion:** Continuous Improvement in Information Retrieval
**Definition:** A concept or framework aimed at enhancing the effectiveness
And efficiency of information retrieval systems through ongoing improvements.
**Domain/Context:** Information retrieval, computer science
**Evidence:** The abbreviation CIIR is listed on
...
```

One of the most interesting parts of these results is that if you run the program again, it returns different answers. The second run came up with the "Center for Intelligent Information Retrieval." There are random factors involved in a number of different sub-tools in these processes. It would be nice to get the same answer every time, but the massive software you are calling with this simple program does not work that way. And are some of these hallucinations from the LLM?

Next, we added "robotics" local context to our agent in `AIAgent2.py` and ran it again:

```
Fetched sources (ranked by robotics relevance):
- score=33 | Robot - Wikipedia
  https://en.wikipedia.org/wiki/Robot

- score=27 | Robotics - Wikipedia
  https://en.wikipedia.org/wiki/Robotics

- score=26 | Center for Intelligent Industrial Robotics (CIIR)
| University of Idaho
  https://www.uidaho.edu/engineering/research/intelligent-industrial-robotics
```

```
- score=15 | Glossary of Robotics Terms | Robotics Definitions & Examples
   - Motoman
  https://www.motoman.com/en-us/about/company/robotics-glossary

- score=11 | Exploring the Dynamics of Chlorobutyl Rubber
(CIIR): Key Insights ...
  https://www.linkedin.com/pulse/exploring-dynamics-
chlorobutyl-rubber-ciir-key-insights-cvxte/

- score=8 | What does CIIR stand for?
  https://www.abbreviations.com/CIIR


=== CIIR Definitions (Robotics-biased, with sources) ===

Based on the provided sources, here are the findings for
"CIIR" in the context of
robotics/automation:  1) **Center for Intelligent Industrial
Robotics (CIIR)**   - **Definition:** A
research and training center at the University of Idaho
College of Engineering that integrates
robotics research and education statewide. It focuses on
advancing AI,
automation, cybersecurity, and manufacturing through hands-on
work with mobile and full-size robots
in various applications.   - **Robotics relevance:** High -
This is directly related to robotics
research, education, and industrial automation.   -
**Evidence:** Source S3:
```

This time our agent nailed it! It found our research center buried in the University of Idaho, Coeur d'Alene campus. Interestingly, it is very stable across multiple runs. Part of this is the effect of the LLM searching. When it isn't very confident, it widens its search (`AIAgent2.py`) and looks down different paths. However, if the LLM and the agent are highly confident, it stays in that area. If you think of all the possible solutions on a plane as mountain peaks hither and yon, if the agent gets a really good score (such as finding a high peak), it stops looking. If it just sees small hills, it tries to search for bigger hills.

Building an AI RAG agent

Now that you have seen what an AI agent can do, let's look at an example of what RAG can do for an AI agent. In this example, we are going to ask an AI RAG agent to find some information about RAG and also find out about what certain domestic animals think about RAG. This is a simpler program than the first AI agent program we created because we are more closely wed to the LLM results and our own tiny document store rather than scanning the web for results and interpreting them. Listing 18-2 shows the code.

To install the needed libraries, run `pip install torch torchvision openai`.

LISTING 18-2: A Minimal AI RAG Agent Using Local Document Store to Assist Answering (AgentRAG.py)

```
from openai import OpenAI
import math
import re
from collections import Counter

# Read API key from file
with open("api.key", "r") as f:
    api_key = f.read().strip()

# Create OpenAI client
client = OpenAI(api_key=api_key)

# ----------------------------
# Tiny document store
# ----------------------------
DOCS = [
    "RAG stands for Retrieval-Augmented Generation.",
    "Agentic RAG allows an agent to plan, retrieve multiple times, and refine
   its queries.",
    "RAG reduces hallucinations by grounding generation in retrieved
   documents.",
"Dogs love RAG more than Cats"

]


# ----------------------------
# Simple retriever (bag-of-words)
# ----------------------------
WORD_RE = re.compile(r"[a-z0-9]+")

def bow(text):
    return Counter(WORD_RE.findall(text.lower()))

def cosine(a, b):
    dot = sum(a[t] * b.get(t, 0) for t in a)
```

(continued)

LISTING 18-2: (continued)

```
    na = math.sqrt(sum(v*v for v in a.values()))
    nb = math.sqrt(sum(v*v for v in b.values()))
    return dot / (na * nb) if na and nb else 0.0

def retrieve(query, k=2):
    qv = bow(query)
    scored = [(cosine(qv, bow(d)), d) for d in DOCS]
    scored.sort(reverse=True, key=lambda x: x[0])
    return [d for s, d in scored[:k] if s > 0]

# ----------------------------
# LLM call (generation)
# ----------------------------
def generate(question, context):
    prompt = f"""Use the context to answer.

Context:
{context}

Question:
{question}
"""
    response = client.chat.completions.create(
        model="gpt-4.1-mini",
        messages=[{"role": "user", "content": prompt}],
    )
    return response.choices[0].message.content.strip()

# ----------------------------
# Agentic RAG loop
# ----------------------------
def agentic_rag(question, max_steps=2):
    query = question

    for step in range(max_steps):
        docs = retrieve(query)
        context = "\n".join(docs)

        answer = generate(question, context)

        # crude "agent decision"
        if "stand for" in answer.lower() or len(docs) >= 2:
            return answer + f"\n\n(Answered in {step+1} step(s))"

        # agent refines the query
        query = question + " definition meaning"
```

```
    return answer + "\n\n(Stopped after max steps)"

# ------------------------------
# Run
# ------------------------------
if __name__ == "__main__":
    q = "What does RAG stand for in Agentic RAG?"
    print(agentic_rag(q))
    q = "Do Dogs love RAG?"
    print(agentic_rag(q))
    q = "Do Cats love RAG?"
    print(agentic_rag(q))
```

The code does the following things:

- Imports the needed libraries.
- Gets the OpenAI API key and opens the client.
- Sets up our tiny local document store to illustrate the long-term memory aspect of RAG. Note the statement, `"Dogs love RAG more than Cats."` This will come back in our conclusions.
- Sets up a "Bag of Words" with our local datastore. It is using a kind of vector-based store (note the cosine function), but it is a much simpler structure than what we find in vector space stores in LLMs.
- Sets up a function to call the OpenAI LLM.
- Moves into the agentic RAG agent loop.
- Gets the local docs with respect to the current query.
- Generates an answer with the LLM.
- Checks the termination criteria (includes the words `stands for` in our answer or the local context is >2).
- Prints out the responses.

Now let's run the agent and see the results:

```
(env) pi@pythonandai:~/Documents $ python3 AgentRAG.py
RAG in Agentic RAG stands for Retrieval-Augmented Generation.

(Answered in 1 step(s))
Yes, dogs love RAG.
```

```
(Answered in 1 step(s))
Based on the context provided, Dogs love RAG more than Cats,
which implies that Cats do not love RAG as much as Dogs do.
However, it does not explicitly state that Cats do not love
RAG at all—just less than Dogs. So, Cats may like RAG to
some extent, but not as much as Dogs.

(Answered in 1 step(s))
```

These are pretty straightforward results. Yes, we know what RAG stands for, either from the LLM or the local store. We put in a statement that "Dogs love RAG more than Cats." We find the most interesting part of this reasoning is the last question, "Do Cats love RAG?" That is actually a very valid answer and shows some depth. Plus, dogs clearly love RAG more than cats, based on John's dog's proclivity for running off with socks and rags.

Considering the Limitations of AI Agents

To finish out our discussion of AI agents, let's look at some key limitations of the whole agentic rage:

- **Agents lack true understanding.** This is the same set of comments regarding LLMs in general. Agents do not think like humans. They predict the actions based on patterns (think the next token prediction from Chapter 15).
- **Agents can hallucinate.** They can sound confident while being totally wrong.
- **Tools, especially external tools, can be fragile.** Anyone who has written large applications on computers or large web-based programs knows how APIs get broken all the time, and that any kind of operating system update has the possibility of breaking things.
- **Agents are unreliable for long-term planning.** Early mistakes can compound and goals can drift without proper constraints. Long workflows require hard limits or human checkpoints.
- **Agents can blow up costs with multiple LLM calls per iteration and retry loops.** It is easy to lose track of just how many calls your agent makes to external tools.
- **Agents aren't secure.** Agents can leak information to the LLMs, execute unintended, and can (the horror!) suffer from prompt-injects via tools or data stores.

Keep in mind two important considerations when designing and building AI agents:

- **Define your goals:** Are they explicit? Are they bounded? Can you define success?
- **Define levels of autonomy:** Are the agents fully autonomous or do they check in with humans? More autonomy = more risk and potentially higher costs.

Find a good framework on which to build your agent. You don't have to reinvent the whole thing. Some of the good ones are LangChain (for RAG agents), CrewAI (for multi-agent workflows), Microsoft AutoGen (more multiagent — Python first!), Hugging Face Agents, and a variety of robotics frameworks that incorporate Ros2 (Robot Operating System 2) with LLM wrappers and behavior trees (a personal favorite of organizing actions) tied into LLM planners.

TIP

Remember that none of these agent architectures is particularly new and revolutionary. Agentic AI is simply an extension of existing architectural types into the AI world — with higher AI capabilities. However, with great power comes great responsibility. (We have always wanted to end a chapter with a quote from Spider-Man.) Be careful out there.

IN THIS CHAPTER

» Understanding reinforcement learning

» Using Markov chain decision parameters

» Applying policy learning and gradients

» Implementing a simple reinforcement learning problem

Chapter 19

Improving Your Computer with Reinforcement Learning

We talk about learning multiple times in this book. Obviously, a huge part of human intelligence is about learning. Looking at a baby, you can see that they start from a pretty low level of learning. Yes, babies are helpless — but don't mistake that for knowing nothing. Babies can recognize faces, have a basic idea of numbers, and can learn language very quickly. It's like they have a fairly well-developed set of neural network types, but they need more training than most other animals. A better example of reinforcement-type learning is your dog. John's dog is very treat-oriented. He has taught the dog a number of things using reinforcement techniques, but, as sometimes happens with AI, it has backfired. Now the dog will steal socks, glasses, or anything, knowing John will give her a treat to drop it. And with that glaringly bad example, let's dive into reinforcement learning and what amazing things you can do with it!

Learning about Learning

What does it mean to learn something? One definition of learning is to acquire and master the current knowledge and meaning of something. Another definition is the possibly permanent change in a person's knowledge or behavior as a result of experience.

The second definition fits best with the current state of AI. The world's engineering and scientific culture has developed algorithms and programs that can learn things about data and sensory input and apply that knowledge to new situations. But machines do not understand anything about what they have learned. They have just accumulated data about their inputs and have transformed that input into some kind of output that, we hope, means something to the observing humans.

However, even though machines don't understand what they have learned, you can do some impressive problem-solving using the machine learning techniques described in this chapter and with LLMs. And maybe the techniques being developed now will lead the way to something much more impressive in the future, but it will probably use a different architecture (based on current trends). The law of diminishing returns seems to be hitting LLMs.

What does it mean for a machine to learn something? In this book, we use the following rough definition: If a machine can take inputs and transform them into useful outputs, the machine has learned something. For example, if you write a simple program to add two numbers, you have taught that machine something about how to add two numbers. Not very "AI"-like, but you have taught the machine something.

Figure 19-1 illustrates the three main machine learning styles:

- **Supervised learning:** Data has labels (for example, spam detection).
- **Unsupervised learning:** Finds patterns without labels (for example, discovering types of galaxies in astronomy; LLMs are full of this type of learning).
- **Reinforcement learning:** Learns from interaction and rewards.

Reinforcement learning is often tied to the concept of AI agents. (There's that word "agent" again. Go back and read Chapter 18 on AI agents before going any further if you haven't already.) Remember that agents aren't all that mystical. They are just a software architecture.

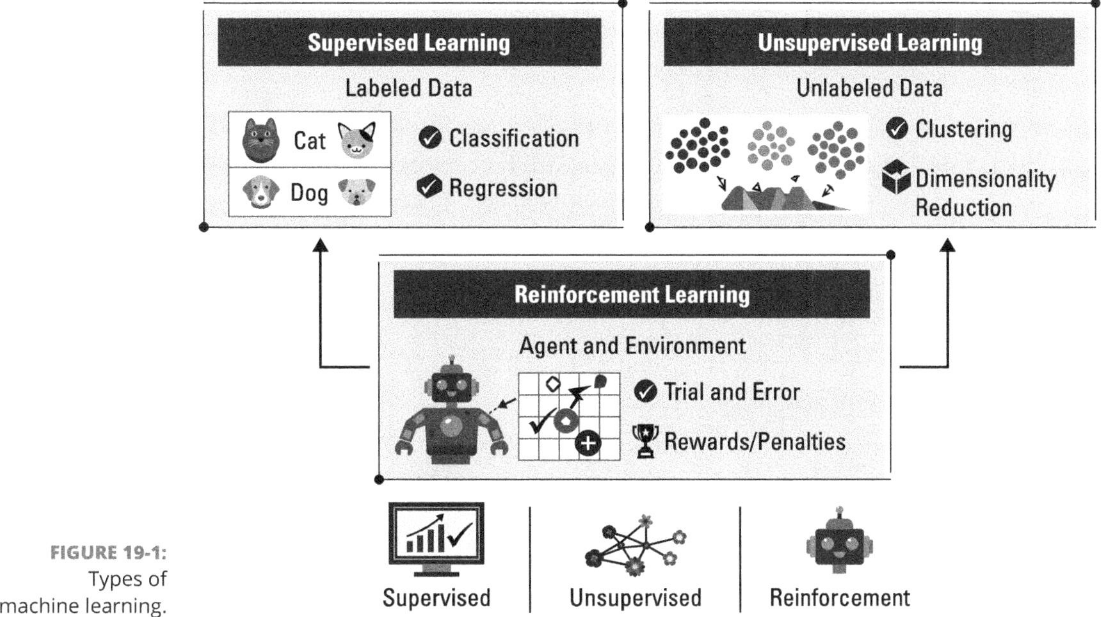

FIGURE 19-1: Types of machine learning.

Getting Feedback: Reinforcement Learning

Reinforcement learning (often abbreviated *RL*) is a method in which a system or software learns by interacting with the environment (physical or not) and receives feedback in the form of either a reward or a penalty. If this sounds like training a dog to sit or roll over, you would be correct. The goal of RL is to learn a strategy that maximizes long-term rewards.

However, as with most machine learning techniques, using RL does not mean you are finding the best possible solution. Just a good one. Some people compare the problem of finding the best solution to that of trying to find the highest mountain in an area on a foggy day. You get to the top of a mountain and proclaim, "I am on the highest mountain." Well, you're on the highest mountain you can see. But if you define your goal as being on the top of a mountain more than 1,000 feet high, and you're at 1,250 feet, you have met your goal. Meeting a goal such as being above 1,000 feet is called a *local maximum,* and it may or may not be the best *maxima* available.

REMEMBER

Once again, AI algorithms such as RL act as methods for searching an environment for a solution.

So, what is the overall architecture of an RL algorithm? Fortunately, it should look very familiar. Reinforcement learning has a very similar software architecture to agentic AI. Just doing different things with it. Figure 19-2 shows the overall architecture of an RL system.

The RL agent is less general and more specific in its purpose when compared to a general AI agent. While it can still be complex in terms of implementation, the architecture is considerably simpler than the AI agent.

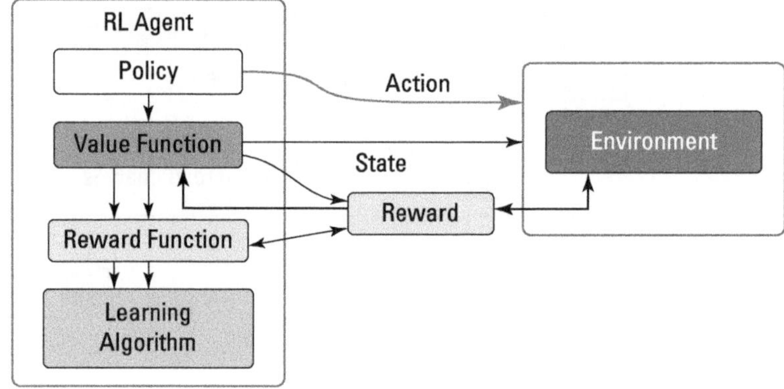

FIGURE 19-2: Reinforcement learning architecture.

Generic RL architecture can be broken down into the following parts:

- **RL agent:** This is the software that is making the decisions and performing actions.
- **Policy:** Defines the RL agent's behavior and can map states to actions.
- **Value function:** Information and algorithms to evaluate the longer-term benefits of the rewards. This function can help move us from a specific nonoptimal peak to a higher peak in the solution space.
- **Reward function:** This function maps the feedback from the environment (sometimes called environment state) into a generally numeric value indicating how good or bad a result state is from the environment.
- **Learning algorithm:** This is the real machine learning element of the RL agent. It keeps track of the state, action results, and rewards, and will also update the policy function to improve performance in the next loop. It can be a fairly simple system or a complex neural network, depending on the combination of the richness of the environment and task complexity.
- **Environment:** This is the space outside the agent that the agent interacts with. This can be an actual physical space (in the case of physical AI and robotics), a set of equations, or a world model (think a digital twin with the physics of a specific environment — a kitchen, for example).

The agent in this system can be quite simple. It follows this basic process:

1. The agent starts a randomly oriented action.
2. If it fails, it receives a negative reward.
3. If it moves toward the goal, it receives a positive reward.
4. The agent updates its policy.
5. It gradually learns to accomplish the goal.

Defining Policy with a Markov Chain

While there are many different ways of implementing a policy inside the RL agent, one of the most common ways is using what is called a Markov chain. A Markov chain is a mathematical way of representing a state machine. Electrical engineers may immediately recognize this technique as how they build state machines to control digital logic, and PLC programmers may frequently see this in their awful ladder-logic programs. (Yes, that is a personal comment. We do not like ladder-logic programs. They hurt the brain, Markov or not!)

A Markov chain is a way to model a sequence of events where the next step depends only on the current state. Think of stepping through a sequence with only a variable (or an input) determining the next step to move through. Figure 19-3 shows a state diagram with states A, B, C, and a transform matrix of:

States: A, B, C

```
P =[ 0.2 0.5 0.3 ]
   [ 0.1 0.6 0.3 ]
   [ 0.4 0.2 0.4 ]
```

Row order: From A, From B, From C

Column order: To A, To B, To C

The labels on transition lines are probabilities that specify how likely it is to move from one state to another in a single step. Just note a couple of rules about Markov chains. Each row has to add up to 1.0 (100 percent). These probabilities show the dynamics of how the system (the policy in this case) moves from one state to another. In an RL agent, if the agent follows a fixed policy, the sequence of states forms a Markov chain. The key idea is that the next state only depends on the current state — not the whole history.

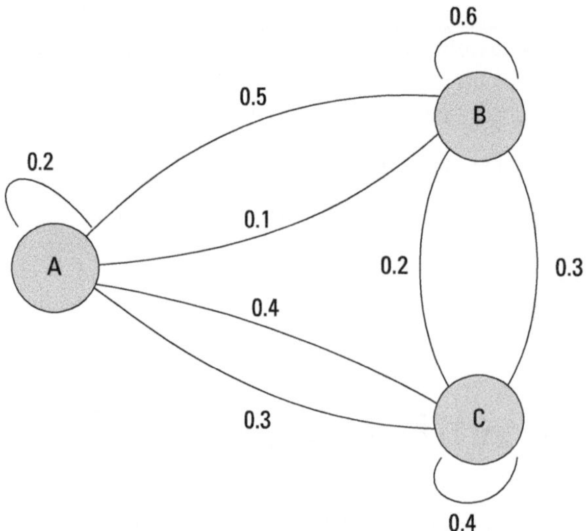

FIGURE 19-3: A simple Markov chain.

How does this fit in RL? The key items are:

- **States (S):** Where the agent is.
- **Actions (A):** What the agent can do.
- **Policy (π):** How actions are chosen.
- **Environment:** How states change.

The policy creates the following sequence:

State → (policy chooses action) → Environment → Next State

To help visualize this, think of a robot on a grid with the following policy:

Policy: Move right most of the time (high transition probability)

Environment: A grid world

The robot's movement pattern becomes a probabilistic chain of positions on the grid. Your reward might be an empty space, and a blocking wall might be a penalty. What do you do with this information? Change the probabilities for state transitions in your Markov chain matrix to make the chain more likely to reward.

REMEMBER

This is a statistical process. Once again, you need to be careful not to get trapped in goals that are not optimal in the whole problem space, but also remember that "not the best" but "good enough" might be your overall solution.

Optimizing Policy with Gradients

Policy gradient (PG) methods are frequently used algorithms in reinforcement learning. They directly optimize a parametrized policy to maximize expected returns by increasing the probability of actions that lead to higher rewards and push us closer to a goal. In the earlier Markov chain example, a policy gradient would be to increase the probabilities of moving through a successful path and reduce the probabilities of taking a less successful path through your states. Unlike strictly value-based methods, PG methods use gradient ascents (think of climbing a hill but changing the slope to make it harder or easier). These techniques of gradient ascents (of which there are many) make policy parameter adjustments effective for continuous or high-dimensional action spaces.

Figure 19-4 illustrates a simple PG example. Here, the robot moves to the right (note the partial Markov chain of states) with a probability of 40 percent. The agent gets a reward of +10, and so it increases the probability of going right by 10 percent and decreases the probability of going left by 10 percent. Obviously there are a lot of different equations you could use to change the increase and decrease of the probabilities to achieve different outcomes.

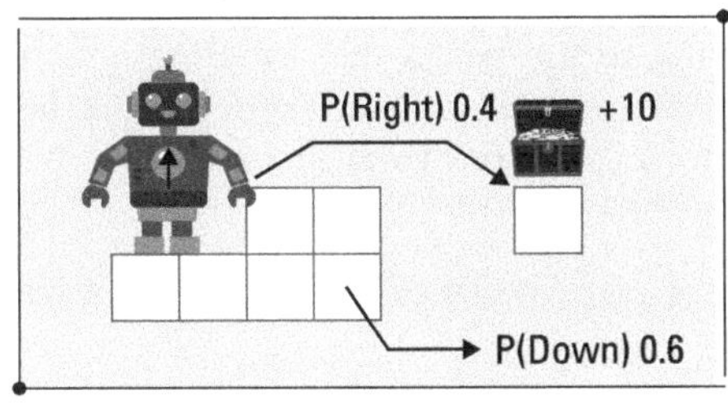

$$\nabla_{\theta} J(\theta) = \nabla_{\theta} \log \pi_{\theta}(Right) \cdot +10$$

Increase P(Right) ↑	Decrease P(Down) ↑
P(Right) 0.5 →	P(Down) 0.5 →
P(Left) 0.5	P(Down) 0.5

FIGURE 19-4: A simple policy gradient.

The equation in Figure 19-4 is a general policy gradient equation. The left side of the equation is the gradient (the direction to change the parameters in the RL policy) to get more rewards. The right side of the equation contains the policy and the reward. We use a log function to smooth things out and gives the behavior of a low probability giving a big push and a high probability giving a smaller push.

In the next section, we look at a Python example of reinforcement learning and look at the outcomes of all these ideas!

Exploring Reinforcement Learning in Python

In this section, we walk through a Python example of reinforcement learning that uses a policy gradient. The program implements a simple RL agent that learns to make decisions through a random process of trial and error using rewards and penalties. Figure 19-5 shows the small environment containing five discrete states labeled 0 to 4.

TIP

Computer science folks like to start labeling things at zero rather than 1 because computers start at 0.

The agent starts in state 2 and moves toward the negative state (0) or the positive terminal state (1). Note that state 4 is self-looping, so when we get to state 4, we stay at the goal. State 0 is not self-looping, so we can get out of the negative state. In our example, we use a policy gradient approach that represents the agent's behavior over actions and updates the policy according to the rewards received after each action. You only get a penalty when you hit state 0 and a reward when you hit state 4. Over time, the agent adjusts the policy to favor sequences through your environment (which, after all, is a Markov chain), effectively learning an optimal strategy for getting to the goal while avoiding penalties. Note that the self-absorbing states are nonsensical on state 0 or state 4 because the episode terminates on either state 0 (penalty of -1) or on state 4 (reward of 1) in the LineWorld environment.

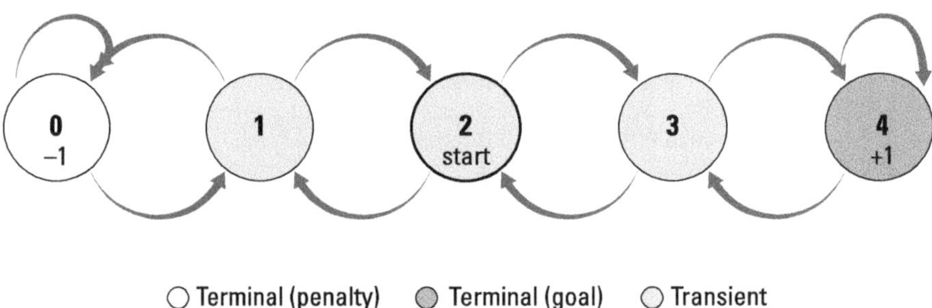

FIGURE 19-5: The reinforcement learning example environment workspace.

Listing 19-1 outlines our RL program. Again, in the spirit of using advanced models, we generated the program outline with a LLM, and then tweaked the program as necessary. If you need to install NumPy or Matplotlib, run the following:

```
pip3 install matplotlib numpy
```

LISTING 19-1: Example of Reinforcement Learning Using a Policy Gradient (RL.py)

```
import numpy as np
import matplotlib.pyplot as plt


class LineWorld:
    def __init__(self):
        self.start_state = 2
        self.state = self.start_state
        self.n_states = 5
        self.n_actions = 2

    def reset(self):
        self.state = self.start_state
        return self.state

    def step(self, action):
        if action == 0:
            self.state -= 1
        else:
            self.state += 1

        self.state = max(0, min(self.state, self.n_states - 1))
        done = self.state in [0, 4]

        if self.state == 4:
            reward = 1.0
        elif self.state == 0:
            reward = -1.0
        else:
            reward = 0.0

        return self.state, reward, done


class PolicyGradientAgent:
    def __init__(self, n_states, n_actions, learning_rate=0.05,
  gamma=0.99):
        self.n_states = n_states
        self.n_actions = n_actions
        self.lr = learning_rate
        self.gamma = gamma
        self.preferences = np.zeros((n_states, n_actions))
```

(continued)

LISTING 19-1: *(continued)*

```
    def softmax(self, x):
        x = x - np.max(x)
        exp_x = np.exp(x)
        return exp_x / np.sum(exp_x)

    def get_action_probs(self, state):
        return self.softmax(self.preferences[state])

    def select_action(self, state):
        probs = self.get_action_probs(state)
        action = np.random.choice(self.n_actions, p=probs)
        return action

    def compute_returns(self, rewards):
        returns = np.zeros(len(rewards))
        G = 0.0

        for t in reversed(range(len(rewards))):
            G = rewards[t] + self.gamma * G
            returns[t] = G

        return returns

    def update_episode(self, states, actions, rewards):
        returns = self.compute_returns(rewards)

        if len(returns) > 1:
            returns = (returns - np.mean(returns)) /
  (np.std(returns) + 1e-8)

        for state, action, G in zip(states, actions, returns):
            probs = self.get_action_probs(state)

            grad_log_pi = -probs.copy()
            grad_log_pi[action] += 1.0

            self.preferences[state] += self.lr * G * grad_log_pi


def train(episodes=500):
    env = LineWorld()
    agent = PolicyGradientAgent(env.n_states, env.n_actions)
```

```
    rewards_per_episode = []
    prob_right = []

    for ep in range(episodes):
        state = env.reset()

        states = []
        actions = []
        rewards = []

        done = False
        while not done:
            action = agent.select_action(state)
            next_state, reward, done = env.step(action)

            states.append(state)
            actions.append(action)
            rewards.append(reward)

            state = next_state

        agent.update_episode(states, actions, rewards)

        total_reward = sum(rewards)
        rewards_per_episode.append(total_reward)
        prob_right.append(agent.get_action_probs(2)[1])

        if (ep + 1) % 50 == 0:
            avg_reward = np.mean(rewards_per_episode[-50:])
            print(
                f"Episode {ep + 1} | "
                f"Avg Reward: {avg_reward:.3f} | "
                f"P(Right|2): {prob_right[-1]:.3f}"
            )

    return agent, rewards_per_episode, prob_right


def plot_results(rewards, prob_right):
    window = 20
    if len(rewards) >= window:
        moving_avg = np.convolve(rewards, np.ones(window) / window,
  mode="valid")
```

(continued)

LISTING 19-1: *(continued)*

```
    else:
        moving_avg = rewards

    plt.figure()
    plt.plot(rewards, alpha=0.3, label="Raw Reward")
    if len(rewards) >= window:
        plt.plot(range(window - 1, len(rewards)), moving_avg,
   label="Smoothed Reward")
    else:
        plt.plot(moving_avg, label="Reward")
    plt.xlabel("Episode")
    plt.ylabel("Reward")
    plt.title("Training Performance")
    plt.legend()
    plt.grid()

    plt.figure()
    plt.plot(prob_right)
    plt.xlabel("Episode")
    plt.ylabel("P(Right)")
    plt.title("Policy Learning at Start State")
    plt.grid()

    plt.show()


if __name__ == "__main__":
    agent, rewards, prob_right = train()

    print("\nFinal Policy:")
    for s in range(agent.n_states):
        probs = agent.get_action_probs(s)
        print(f"State{s}:Left={probs[0]:.2f}, Right={probs[1]:.2f}")

    plot_results(rewards, prob_right)
```

Following are the major classes and functions in this program and how they work:

- **`Class LineWorld`:** This is the class that sets up our environment and how the environment operates. Effectively, it's building a Markov chain (a state machine). It can be initialized, reset, and then stepped through, and it can detect when it is done. In a full-size program, the environment can be very complex and large (for example, a physics-based model of a robot and the robot environment), or it can be connected through sensors (think cameras, touch sensors, LIDAR, and so on) to the real world. The states in such a system will often be abstracted to higher-level functions such as "move robot in the X direction 100mm."

- **Class PolicyGradientAgent:** This class implements what is called an episode-learning policy gradient agent algorithm. This is one of many, many types of gradients that are used in RL modules. Note that in complex models, the use of certain types of gradients can lead to loops, instability, and situations where the algorithm does not converge to an answer, optimal or not. There is a lot of magic in these kinds of algorithms, much of which can seem to emulate the kind of design and problems control engineers have with real-world systems. This policy gradient is one step up from a very simple one because it learns from the whole episode, not just the immediate reward.
- **Function plot_results:** This function plots the interesting results of the learning algorithm for us to see how the program converges on an optimal solution.

Running RL.py produces the output shown in Figure 19-6. After five hundred runs through the RL algorithm (called episodes in the RL, but is similar to epochs in machine learning), we are left with the policy results shown at the end of the output in Figure 19-6.

```
(env) pi@pythonandai:~/Documents $ python3 RL.py
Episode 50 | Avg Reward: 0.480 | P(Right|2): 0.646
Episode 100 | Avg Reward: 0.760 | P(Right|2): 0.725
Episode 150 | Avg Reward: 0.880 | P(Right|2): 0.906
Episode 200 | Avg Reward: 0.920 | P(Right|2): 0.896
Episode 250 | Avg Reward: 0.960 | P(Right|2): 0.862
Episode 300 | Avg Reward: 0.960 | P(Right|2): 0.874
Episode 350 | Avg Reward: 1.000 | P(Right|2): 0.886
Episode 400 | Avg Reward: 0.960 | P(Right|2): 0.884
Episode 450 | Avg Reward: 0.960 | P(Right|2): 0.909
Episode 500 | Avg Reward: 1.000 | P(Right|2): 0.928

Final Policy:
State 0: Left=0.50, Right=0.50
State 1: Left=0.16, Right=0.84
State 2: Left=0.07, Right=0.93
State 3: Left=0.01, Right=0.99
State 4: Left=0.50, Right=0.50
```

FIGURE 19-6: Screen output of RL.py.

Figure 19-7 shows the running average reward as the episodes advance. Notice that it isn't a smooth curve toward success due to the statistical nature of the algorithm. We do get there and pretty much stay there, however, so it looks like a good solution.

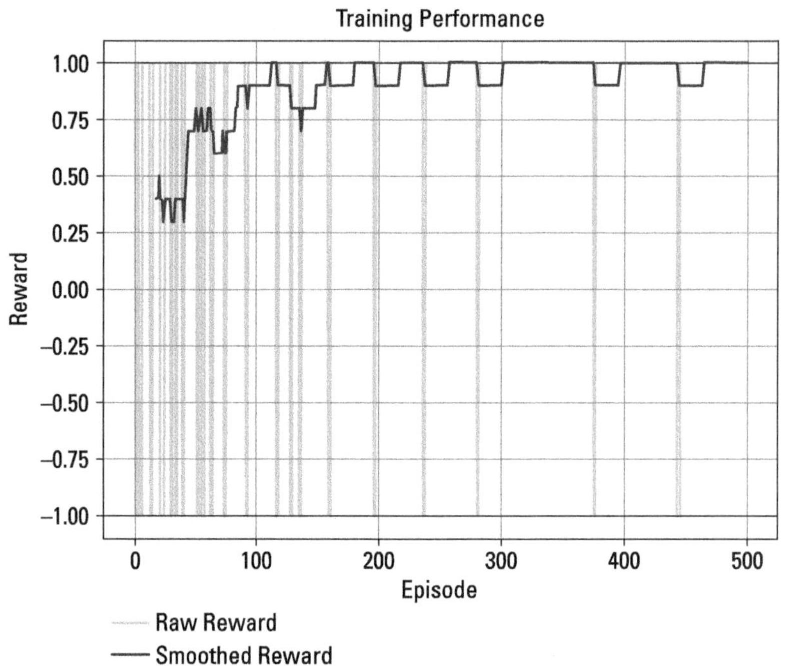

FIGURE 19-7: RL training performance.

Figure 19-8 shows how the probability of going right (which, from Figure 19-5, we know empirically is the correct direction) increases with time, but does *not* increase to 100 percent. We get close enough to the right answer, but there is still a possibility of getting to the penalty state, though not very often. This uncertainty is very typical for RL applications, and minimizing this error is a major part of the engineering involved in developing RL policy gradients.

The gradient function makes a great deal of difference in the performance of RL algorithms. In Figure 19-9, we ran the program again using a much more complex performance gradient, and you see we have a smoother curve and a little better performance.

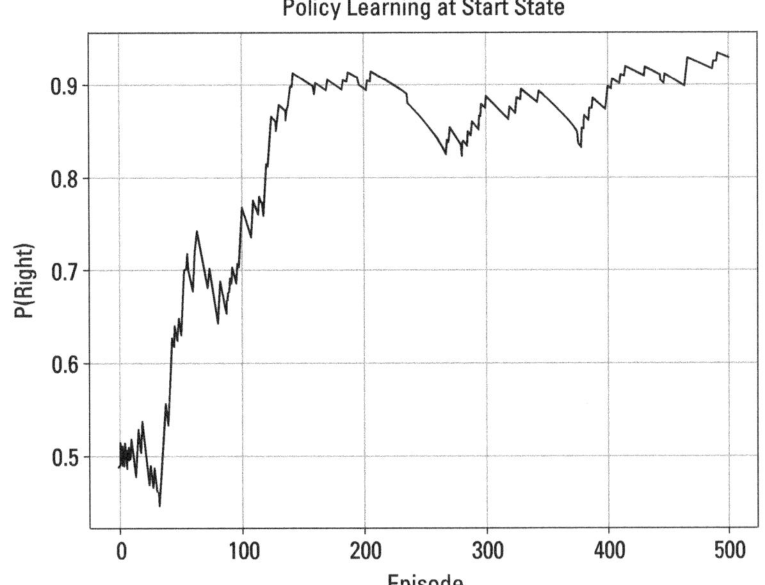

FIGURE 19-8: RL policy learning curve.

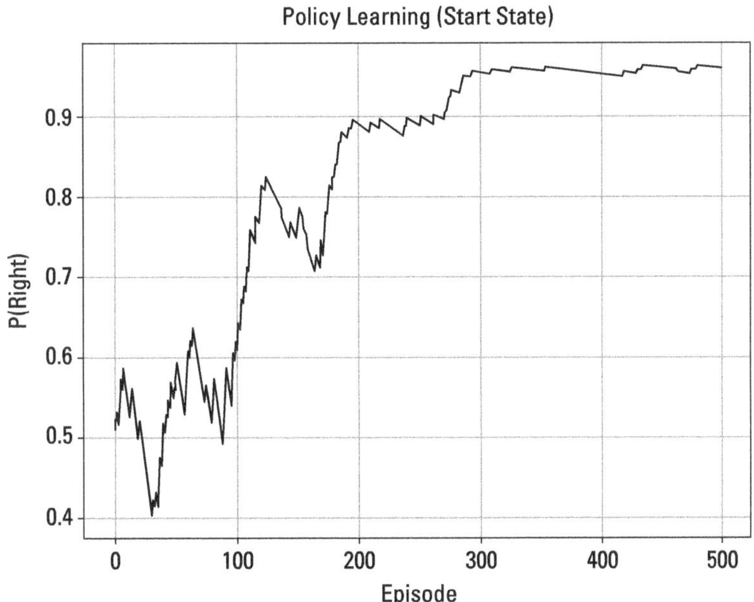

FIGURE 19-9: RL policy learning curve with more complex gradient.

TIP

The simple policy gradients we have used in this chapter could be replaced with a neural network, a transformer, or even an LLM model. Making these kinds of changes to the learning mechanism in RL enormously complicates the algorithms, dramatically increases computational time, and makes the model's behavior difficult or impossible to explain, either the answer or how the algorithm got there. However, this is how AI can solve very large problems.

Expect to see a lot of reinforcement learning as RL moves into more complex real-world environments (world models in AI) with actual robots learning inside a model and then applying that learning to the real world. Such integration is generally called "physical AI."

IN THIS CHAPTER

» Defining evolutionary computation

» Exploring and exploiting subspaces

» Exploring genetic algorithm parameters

» Running a genetic algorithm program

Chapter 20
Nature Knows Best: Using Evolutionary Algorithms

Have you ever wondered how the biological theory of evolution applies to the exciting field of evolutionary computation? No? In this chapter, you explore how it has inspired a class of techniques for solving problems with computers. You also examine the basic process of navigating open-ended problems in wide search spaces and tackle the trade-off between exploring and exploiting promising subspaces. You discover the different programmer-defined parameters of a genetic algorithm, including population size, number of generations, and mutation rate, and you spend some time thinking about how to implement a fitness function. Finally, you end the chapter by writing your own genetic algorithm program to find a kraken!

Evolving Your Idea of Computation

When you think of solving problems with computers, one concept probably always rises to the forefront of your mind: biological evolution! Right?

Perhaps not, but as it turns out, the theory behind biological evolution has inspired a class of problem-solving techniques that perform quite well in certain situations. Similar to how neural network techniques are inspired by analyzing biological brain architectures, analyzing the long-term population dynamics of ecosystems and organisms creates an innovative way to search for solutions among trillions of billions of possible options.

The basic principles behind biological evolution and natural selection involve how organisms change themselves to better fit their environment. In a scenario where evolution can take place:

- An **individual** exists within some sort of environment. The individual has some characteristics unique to itself.
- The individual has some measure of **fit** within the environment; that is, some individuals are better suited to survive in the environment than others.
- The individual has the ability to change, or **mutate**. This could be a genetic mutation in the individual when it reproduces or some other method of change.
- There is a **population** that is made up of multiple individuals.
- Over multiple **generations**, or iterations, the population inflicts the method of changing or mutating the individuals. This often occurs when reproducing the next generation from the current population.

While the typical evolution-inspired examples you'll find in a high school biology textbook tend to mention the Galapagos finches or the peppered moth, in this chapter, we look at a far more trivial and contrived example:

Few people know that during the golden age of piracy, the modern species of kraken was just beginning to form. There were many different individual krakens, but none of them fit their environment all that well, because there were too many other apex ocean predators, such as Megalodon sharks, mermaids, and marine Loch Ness monsters.

However, one day, a kraken was born into the population with a rare genetic mutation that allowed it to digest heavy cannons and stolen treasures. This new kraken was able to access a previously untapped food source, namely pirate ships. Suddenly, the much-improved fit of the kraken to the fertile Caribbean environment allowed many more krakens of this variety to reproduce and grow to enormous sizes. Thus, nature helped change the previously small and tame krakens to better become the proud terrors of the high seas they were always meant to be. Figure 20-1 illustrates this nautical evolutionary process.

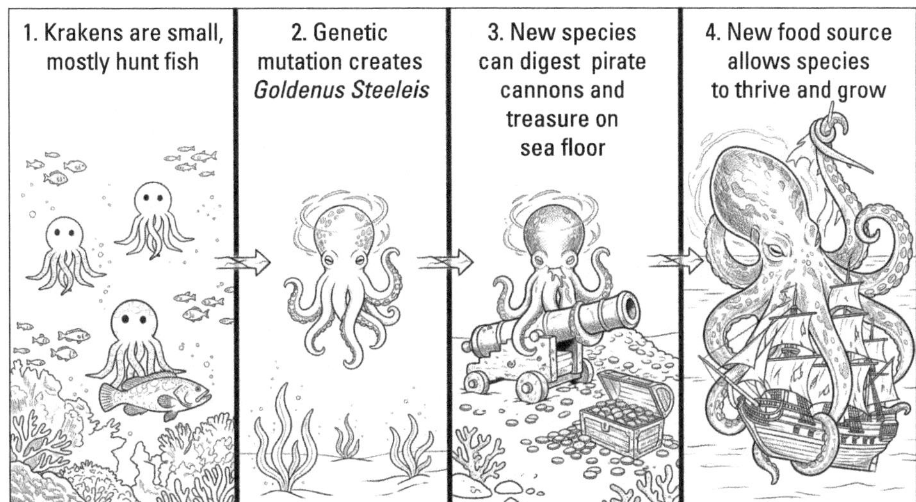

FIGURE 20-1: Evolution of a well-adapted kraken.

TIP

This may not be a true story, but the basic biological principles behind it create a useful framework for a very different kind of AI. These techniques can help pick out optimal solutions in a wide search space, much like nature can help equip organisms to better survive in their environment.

Evolutionary computation is a term encompassing a wide set of techniques that incorporate evolutionary principles into AI searching and optimization. The exact terminology within the field of evolutionary computation is always a little bit subject to debate. One of the most popular techniques within the field of evolutionary computation is a *genetic algorithm*. In a genetic algorithm:

- An individual is a type of solution that is encoded in the program.
- Mutating the individual changes some aspect of its encoding.
- A fitness function measures how well the solution performs against the problem at hand, using some metric (or combination of metrics).
- A population is made of individual solutions.
- The population has some sort of selection process that chooses the solutions (usually the higher-fitness ones) to carry over to the next generation.
- The next generation of solutions can be changed and mutated.

Notice that this list is pretty similar to the basic requirements for evolutionary computation, and the debate still rages over what exactly constitutes a meaningful difference between the two terms. Some maintain that a genetic algorithm can't strictly be considered a genetic algorithm if the solution isn't an (often string-encoded) representation of a chromosome or doesn't incorporate crossover (more on that later).

Evolutionary computation and genetic algorithms are terms that are sometimes used interchangeably, but if you've got a purist on your tail, adding a chromosome and crossover to your approach will generally satisfy them. As much as a genetic algorithm purist can ever truly be satisfied, that is.

There are other subfields of evolutionary computation. For example, in genetic programming, the individual solution is an executable computer program. There is a wide subfield of techniques named for specific animals that incorporate evolutionary computation principles plus a twist or two specific to the animal they're named for (ant colony optimization, wolf pack algorithm, and so on). As far as we're aware, no one has yet named one of these techniques for a kraken, but we haven't given up hope.

TECHNICAL STUFF

Particle swarm optimization (PSO) is another subfield of evolutionary computation that has to do with the movement of particles in space. Unlike a genetic algorithm, particles generally update their parameters over iterations, rather than choosing the next generation from existing by a selection process.

Optimizing Search with a Genetic Algorithm

Now that we have the basic requirements of a genetic algorithm outlined, you might be wondering — what exactly are they good for?

You might remember the term "search space" from the discussion on gradient descent in Chapter 9. If you have a problem and a solution, you can model the errors of the potential solutions as a landscape. Peaks on the landscape have high errors and probably aren't the best solution for your problem. Valleys are low errors and are generally the solutions you want to arrive at. Gradient descent can analyze the direction you are headed and point you downhill so you can get there faster.

However, in order for gradient descent to work, you must be able to mathematically relate the solution's parameters to the error so you can take a derivative. Genetic algorithms don't have this restriction. Instead of modeling the landscape of the search as an error space, they model it as a solution space. Some parts of the solution space fit the problem better than others, but the process to get to these nice-to-have areas is less straightforward.

Genetic algorithm techniques work well on problems where the solution space is very large or even infinite. They also work well when the relationship between the solution and the parameters is unclear, difficult to model, or expensive to obtain in a more traditional machine learning data-collection process. Genetic algorithms are good at finding islands of workable solutions in a vast sea of unknowns.

TECHNICAL STUFF

When analyzing algorithms and search techniques in the computer science field, problems are sometimes sorted into P and NP classes. If a problem is in the P class, it can be solved in polynomial time — which might take a very, very long time to solve, but at least the upper bound for the time involved in solving it is technically finite. For an NP (nondeterministic polynomial time) class problem, the upper bound on the amount of time to solve it is unknown and could be infinite. Genetic algorithms are handy ways to explore solutions within problem spaces that are NP-hard. Many real-world problems exist inside this category. For example, if you are looking for an optimal combination of objects to satisfy a problem, and the number of possible combinations of those objects is greater than the number of atoms in the universe (trust us — this happens much more often than you would think), you are usually looking at an NP-hard problem.

Genetic algorithms use different individuals in a population to explore multiple areas in a solution space at one time. For example, let's model a solution space as a forest, and every member of your population is an individual scout looking for a food source inside the forest. Your genetic algorithm initializes the population by parachuting every scout in a different location in the forest. The scouts can mutate their position in every generation of the search by walking a few steps in any direction away from the place they initially landed. Every scout is evaluated in a generation by the food they found. New scouts are created as offspring from existing scouts.

It's clear that having multiple scouts search different areas at once is likely to find a food source faster than one scout by itself. The scout that landed on the snowy mountain peak is having a much harder time than the scout that landed in the lush valley. But — why not just parachute scouts randomly into the forest during the entire search operation?

The advantage of the genetic algorithm has to do with the level of control you have over exploration versus exploitation. In the exploration phase, you try to find good subspaces of the overall solution space (parachuting in the scouts). In exploitation, you try to find the best overall location inside the subspace (walking around the landing zone). Sometimes, a subspace you find while randomly searching doesn't look like a good candidate for an overall best solution. For instance, dropping your scout in the middle of the lake (exploration) may seem like a less optimal situation than what occurred with the scout who landed in the middle of a huckleberry thicket. However, by letting your scout exploit the subspace, they were able to paddle a few feet into a nutritious wild rice patch. Score! Even the scout that landed in the huckleberry bushes was able to exploit their position further by walking into the part of the patch with the thicker, more plentiful berries.

REMEMBER

Random searching might allow for good exploration, but a genetic algorithm's mutation operator allows for smarter searching by exploiting the locations they landed in.

Parameterizing a Genetic Algorithm

Figure 20-2 illustrates the basic process behind a genetic algorithm run. The steps are:

1. Population initialization.
2. Population scoring.
3. Selection.
4. Mutation.
5. Repeat for a new generation.

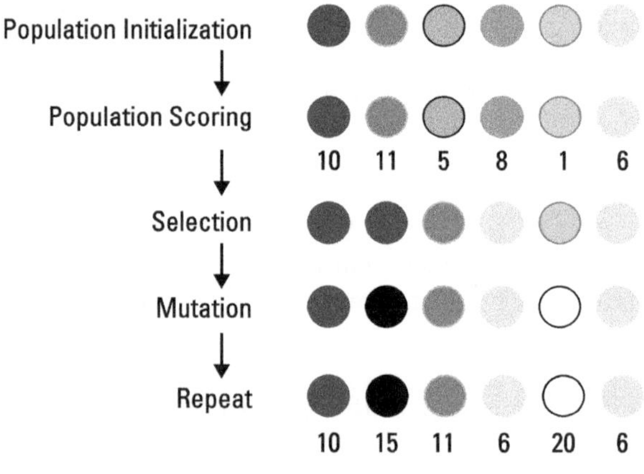

FIGURE 20-2: The basic process behind a genetic algorithm.

Population initialization

Population initialization creates the first individuals in the population, often using a random process. *Population size* is a parameter referring to the number of individuals in the population. Setting the size of the population is often a trade-off between time and computational constraints. Bigger populations can search more subspaces (more exploration), but may be slower to reach the optimal solution within a subspace (slower exploitation, because fewer members may be searching the same subspace). Bigger populations are also generally more computationally expensive. However, smaller populations may miss good subspaces.

TIP

Populations are often initialized randomly, but this can create slower searches if you already know that some subspaces in your overall solution space are not feasible. There are different tricks to work around this, and sometimes solutions are initialized from subspaces that are already known to work for the task, or found via domain knowledge or statistical analysis conducted by experts before setting up the main algorithm run.

Genetic algorithms often keep the population the same size during the algorithm run (as this keeps the computation load more or less steady), but there is no rule requiring this. Some implementations will kill or add population members as needed.

Population scoring

Population scoring is often the most time-consuming part of the genetic algorithm. Each individual is evaluated for its best fit to its environment using a *fitness function*. As its name suggests, this can be a function, but it can also be a simulation, a heuristic value, or any number of methods implemented in the code to get an idea of how "good" the individual is.

TECHNICAL STUFF

In some cases, genetic algorithms and neural networks can work together in a hybrid model situation. Often this is used in neural architecture search (NAS), where a genetic algorithm chooses hyperparameters for a neural network. The fitness values can then be modeled by the network's training or test performance. In other cases, an applied problem may be well-predicted by a neural network, but optimal configurations of said problem aren't known. In that case, the neural network might serve as the fitness function for the genetic algorithm. In other situations, a simulator might be available to serve as a fitness function. If the simulator is computationally expensive, a proxy measure might be used during the main algorithm run, and the full simulation run on only a subset of population members.

Fitness functions are determined entirely by the problem at hand. If an individual in a population is a factory floor plan layout, the fitness function may measure how many products can be made per hour, or it may measure how many processing steps the product goes through. If the individual is a new circuit board design, the fitness function may measure its theoretical feasibility. If the individual is a combination of flavored syrups in bins at a snow cone truck, the fitness function may measure how often the bins have to be restocked by the manager during a typical high-sales day. The applications are endless.

Fitness functions are a bit of a Catch-22. Their flexibility is one of the reasons genetic algorithms can be applied to many situations where other techniques may fail. However, this open-endedness can also make them harder to define and implement. An optimal solution isn't likely to be found if the fitness function isn't a good approximation for the solution's actual performance metrics. Domain expertise in the problem is an absolute must for a good genetic algorithm.

Selection

Once individuals are ranked by the fitness function, the new generation is created from the old one using some sort of selection mechanism. There are several ways to do this:

- **Elitism:** In this method, you copy the highest-ranking solutions directly from the old generation into the new one. You can also kill off the worst solutions and make extra copies of the best ones if desired.
- **Tournament selection:** A group of population individuals (the size of which is chosen by you, the programmer) is randomly selected. From the subgroup, the highest fitness individual is chosen.
- **Crossover:** In this method, you combine multiple solutions into one solution. You often pick a crossover point, combining two halves of parents on either side of the point. Parents can also be chosen by elitism, selection, or another technique.

Figure 20-3 lays out these selection methods.

There are many more selection methods, and engineers will often implement combinations of techniques. For example, an engineer might use tournament selection with a group size of four to do their main selection, but also keep the top ten members of the population (a kind of diet elitism) to carry over to the next generation.

In selecting the new generation, population *diversity* should be taken into account. For example, if you use elitism with very limited patience for low-performing individuals, you are essentially limiting the number of overall subspaces you want to explore. This is likely to converge faster, but you may miss the most optimal subspace if that solution initially looks like a bust. Higher diversity populations may also take longer to run.

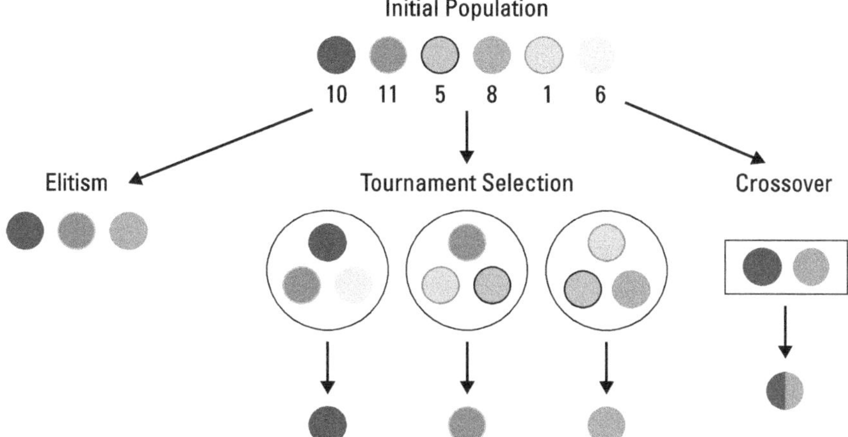

FIGURE 20-3: Different selection methods in a genetic algorithm.

TIP

Like all genetic algorithm parameters, you want to choose a selection mechanism that works best for your problem at hand. In some cases, a cross-over method doesn't make sense (two solutions combined are not likely to create a new valid solution). In other cases, it can greatly speed up finding viable individuals for your problem.

Mutation

Once the next generation is created, it can be mutated, or changed. This involves picking a subset of the new individuals and slightly modifying their encodings or parameter sets. The *mutation rate* usually refers to how many members of the population will change, or how likely an individual population member is to be changed. The amount of change in the individual is also set by the population. More mutation generally results in more diversity but slower searching.

Repeat

This process is then repeated for a set number of overall generations. The number of generations is usually chosen based on how much patience you have for the program running on your computer! You could theoretically have the program run until you find an individual at a specific level of performance, but in most cases, this is not guaranteed, and you might be running your program until the end of time.

Sometimes engineers will track their population's performance over time to get an idea of when the population *converges* to a solution (for example, when new solutions don't have much performance difference from old ones). If you have a highly diverse population, it may not have converged at all! If that's the case, you might have to revisit your parameters or just set the number of generations based on how long it takes you to run over to the new place across the street and eat lunch. You'd be amazed by how many AI parameters are determined by how long it takes an engineer to eat a sandwich.

Implementing a Genetic Algorithm

In this section, we implement a genetic algorithm on a simple program: matching a string from a population of randomly initialized strings. Our chosen phrase is, of course: "Krakens are Majestic Sea Creatures!"

While the task is simple, genetic algorithms take a little more programming overhead than some of the other techniques in this book, which were able to make use of handy libraries. There are indeed some genetic algorithm Python libraries out there, but they are less mainstream than the deep learning and machine learning libraries we've used so far in this book. Don't be intimidated by the amount of code we use in this program!

Listing 20-1 outlines the genetic algorithm program. Figure 20-4 gives the partial (end) output of running the program. The actual program's output has too many lines to include in the book, as you will see!

LISTING 20-1: The Genetic Algorithm Program (genetic_algorithm.py)

```
import random
import string
import math

#Our optimization problem - create a matching string!
perfect_string = "Krakens are Majestic Sea Creatures!"
perfect_list = list(perfect_string)
possible_chars = string.ascii_letters + string.whitespace +
  string.punctuation
string_length = len(perfect_list)

class individual:
    def __init__(self):
        self.string_list = []
        self.create_random_string()
        self.run_fitness_function()
```

```
    def create_random_string(self):
        #Initialize a random string
        for i in range(0, string_length):
            char = random.choice(possible_chars)
            self.string_list.append(char)

    def print_self(self):
        print("".join(self.string_list))
        print(f"Fitness: {self.fitness}")

    def run_fitness_function(self):
        #Set difference value to 0
        overall_diff = 0
        #Compare the characters
        for char_1, char_2 in zip(self.string_list, perfect_list):
            if char_1 != char_2:
                overall_diff += 1
        self.fitness = overall_diff
        return self.fitness

    def mutate(self):
        #Pick a random index and mutate the character there
        index_to_mutate = random.randrange(0, string_length)
        new_char = random.choice(possible_chars)
        self.string_list[index_to_mutate] = new_char

    def __lt__(self, other):
        #Overloaded operator so we can sort this in python easily
        return self.fitness < other.fitness

class Population:
    def __init__(self, size, mutation_rate, tournament_size,
  selection_method="tournament"):
        #Set the population information
        self.population_size = size
        self.tournament_size = tournament_size
        self.mutation_rate = mutation_rate
        if selection_method == "tournament_with_crossover":
            self.selection_method =
  self.tournament_selection_with_crossover
        else:
            self.selection_method = self.tournament_selection
        #Initialize the population with individuals
        self.population_list = []
```

(continued)

LISTING 20-1: *(continued)*

```
        for i in range(0, self.population_size):
            new_member = individual()
            self.population_list.append(new_member)
        self.population_list.sort()


    def print_population(self, num_members=False):
        if not num_members:
            num_members = self.population_size
        for i in range(0, num_members):
            self.population_list[i].print_self()

    def copy_member(self, og, new_string=False):
        #Intialize a new individual
        new_member = individual()
        #Copy the relevant parameters to the new individual
        if new_string:
            new_member.string_list = new_string.copy()
        else:
            new_member.string_list = og.string_list.copy()
        new_member.fitness = og.fitness
        #Return new individual
        return new_member

    def tournament_selection(self):
        #Get a sample for the tournament
        selection_list = random.sample(self.population_list,
self.tournament_size)
        #Sort by fitness
        selection_list.sort()
        #The winner is the most fit (lowest fitness here)
        winner = selection_list[0]
        #Return a copy of the winner
        return self.copy_member(winner)

    def tournament_selection_with_crossover(self):
        #Get a sample for the tournament
        selection_list = random.sample(self.population_list,
self.tournament_size)
        #Sort by fitness
        selection_list.sort()
        #The winner is the most fit (lowest fitness here)
        winner_1 = selection_list[0]
```

```
        winner_2 = selection_list[1]
        random_point = random.randrange(0,
  len(winner_1.string_list))
        half_1 = winner_1.string_list[0:random_point]
        half_2 = winner_2.string_list[random_point:len(winner_
  2.string_list)]
        new_string = half_1 + half_2
        #Return a copy of the winner with new string
        return self.copy_member(winner_1, new_string=new_string)

    def create_new_generation(self):
        new_generation = []
        for i in range(0, self.population_size):
            new_generation.append(self.selection_method())
        self.population_list = new_generation

    def mutate_population(self):
        #Number of population members to mutate based on our
  mutation rate
        mutation_number = math.floor(self.population_size*
  self.mutation_rate)
        #Sample of our mutants
        to_mutate = random.sample(self.population_list,
  mutation_number)
        #Perform the mutation
        for member in to_mutate:
            member.mutate()

    def calc_population_fitness(self):
        for member in self.population_list:
            member.run_fitness_function()

    def run_generation(self):
        self.create_new_generation()
        self.mutate_population()
        self.calc_population_fitness()
        self.population_list.sort()


#Actually run the experiment
population_size = 1000
mutation_rate = 0.4
tournament_size = 4
selection_method = "tournament"
```

(continued)

```
generations = 300

pop = Population(population_size, mutation_rate, tournament_size,
  selection_method=selection_method)
for i in range(0, generations):
    print(f"Generation {i}")
    pop.run_generation()
    pop.print_population(num_members=1)
```

```
Generation 288
Krakens are Majestic Sea Creatures!
Fitness: 0
Generation 289
Krakens are Majestic Sea Creatures!
Fitness: 0
Generation 290
Krakens are Majestic Sea Creatures!
Fitness: 0
Generation 291
Krakens are Majestic Sea Creatures!
Fitness: 0
Generation 292
Krakens are Majestic Sea Creatures!
Fitness: 0
Generation 293
Krakens are Majestic Sea Creatures!
Fitness: 0
Generation 294
Krakens are Majestic Sea Creatures!
Fitness: 0
Generation 295
Krakens are Majestic Sea Creatures!
Fitness: 0
Generation 296
Krakens are Majestic Sea Creatures!
Fitness: 0
Generation 297
Krakens are Majestic Sea Creatures!
Fitness: 0
Generation 298
Krakens are Majestic Sea Creatures!
Fitness: 0
Generation 299
Krakens are Majestic Sea Creatures!
Fitness: 0
```

FIGURE 20-4: Output of running Listing 20-1.

The program has essentially four phases:

- Importing libraries and defining the optimization problem.
- Defining the `individual` class.
- Defining the `population` class.
- Running the experiment.

In the first phase, the program imports the `random`, `string`, and `math` libraries, as we will need them all to implement the algorithm. It then creates the string we'll match, converts it to a list of characters, and gets its length for later use. It also defines the allowable characters for this experiment to include letters, whitespace, and punctuation.

The `individual` class is composed of the following:

- An `__init__()` function, which sets a class variable for its `string_list` variable, and runs its `create_random_string()` and `run_fitness_function()` functions.
- A `create_random_string()` function, which generates a random character and appends it to the `string_list` variable until the string is the same size as our optimization string.
- A `print_self()` function, which prints the individuals `string_list` and fitness score.
- A `run_fitness_function()` function, which increments a difference score variable for every character from the `string_list` that doesn't match the desired output string. This difference is defined as the `fitness` variable of the individual and is returned.
- A `mutate()` function, which picks a random index in the character list and sets it to a different random character.
- A `__lt__()` function, which is an overall "less-than" operator. This function takes in a different member of the class and returns the smaller of the fitness functions. This is a handy Python trick that lets us use built-in list sorting on our custom class (thank you, computational biology course!).

The `Population` class is composed of the following:

- An `__init__()` function which takes in a `size`, `mutation_rate`, `tournament_size`, and optional `selection_method` argument. It sets these programmer-defined variables into its own class variables. In this case, we have two possible selection functions: `tournament_selection` and `tournament_selection_with_crossover`. It then creates an empty `population_list` variable and fills it with randomly initialized population members (instances of the `individual` class) until it reaches the desired size. Finally, it sorts the population. In this case, we want the lower fitness members at the start of the list, since our fitness score is a difference calculation.
- a `print_population()` function which takes an optional argument of the number of population members to print. It prints the string list and fitness score of the members (in order of fitness) for the specified number.

» A copy_member() function, which takes in a population member instance of the individual class. It creates a new individual, and then copies over all relevant information from the passed-in individual. It can optionally be given a string to use as the new members' string_list variable instead of a direct copy-over (which will be useful for crossover later).

WARNING

Python doesn't always copy information in lists, dictionaries, and classes by default! Often it will copy by reference, rather than value, which means you think you are creating a new population member when you are really modifying an old one. This is a major "Gotcha!" when implementing genetic algorithms in Python. It's a good idea to create a "copy" function that makes a new class instance and copies over information piece by piece if you are unsure whether something will truly duplicate. If you are printing population members and they all look exactly the same very early in your algorithm run, it's a good indicator that Python is using multiple references to an old member rather than creating a new one.

» A tournament_selection() function, which randomly draws population members and sorts them by fitness. It then chooses the highest fitness member to return a copy of.

» A tournament_selection_with_crossover() function, which uses the same mechanism as the previous function, but with two winners instead of one. It chooses a random index, and the first winner's string list is copied up to that index. The second winner gets the rest of the string. A new population member with the combined string is returned.

» A create_new_generation() function, which creates a new generation of the population size by using the chosen selection method (tournament_selection or tournament_selection_with_crossover). This is set to the population_list variable.

» A mutate_population() function, which gets a sample of the population members proportional to the mutation rate and runs the mutate operation on all chosen samples.

» A calc_population_fitness() function, which calculates the fitness of all population members.

» A run_generation() function, which runs, in order, the create_new_generation, mutate_population, and calc_population_fitness functions. It then sorts the population_list variable by fitness. This function implements the essential genetic algorithm steps for each generation.

Finally, the actual experiment phase does the following:

- Sets the parameters for the genetic algorithm. We chose a `population_size` of 1000, a `mutation_rate` of 0.4 (mutate 40 percent of the population every generation), a `tournament_size` of 4 members, a plain "tournament" `selection_method`, and 300 `generations`.
- Creates an instance of the `Population` class with the associated parameters and sets it to the pop variable.
- Runs the `run_generation` function of the population for the specified number of generations. It also prints the generation number and the top population member at each generation's conclusion.

As shown in Figure 20-4, the final generations of the genetic algorithm figured out how to sing the praises of krakens!

Feel free to run this program with different parameter values and explore when the algorithm starts to figure out the solution. This can vary a lot depending on the parameters. Listing 20-2 gives an alternative configuration to the final phase of Listing 20-1, using the crossover selection method and a lower mutation rate. Figure 20-5 gives the partial output of running Listing 20-2. As you can see, in this configuration, the algorithm struggled with getting the string exactly perfect.

LISTING 20-2: A Partial Program with Different Configuration of the Algorithm (genetic_algorithm_with_crossover.py)

```
#Actually run the experiment
population_size = 1000
mutation_rate = 0.3
tournament_size = 4
selection_method = "tournament_with_crossover"
generations = 300

pop = Population(population_size, mutation_rate, tournament_size,
  selection_method=selection_method)
for i in range(0, generations):
    print(f"Generation {i}")
    pop.run_generation()
    pop.print_population(num_members=1)
```

```
Fitness: 2
Generation 289
Krakens are Majestic Sea Creaturef!
Fitness: 1
Generation 290
Krakens are Majestic Sea Creaturen!
Fitness: 1
Generation 291
Krakens are Majestic Sea Creatu
ep!
Fitness: 2
Generation 292
Krakens are Majestic Sea Creatu(en!
Fitness: 2
Generation 293
Krakens are Majestic Sea CreatuVes!
Fitness: 1
Generation 294
Krakens are Majestic Sea CreatuVe
!
Fitness: 2
Generation 295
Krakens are Majestic Sea CreatuseP!
Generation 296
Krakens are Majestic Sea Creatu>eC!
Fitness: 2
Generation 297
Krakens are Majestic Sea Creatu(et!
Fitness: 2
Generation 298
Krakens are Majestic Sea Creatuqe&!
Fitness: 2
Generation 299
Krakens are Majestic Sea Creatu/eB!
Fitness: 2
```

FIGURE 20-5: Partial output of running Listing 20-2.

Wrapping Up Your Evolutionary Computation Journey

Evolutionary computation takes a little more thought to set up than some of the more data-driven techniques we cover in this book. However, with a little bit of thought put into a problem, these techniques give you a powerful toolbox to solve a wide variety of problems, especially when you need to find a needle in a haystack. We like evolutionary computation a lot in our research group — we've used it to study frost in vineyards, Valley Fever case rates, and component fail rates. We also like to throw them at some of the trickier manufacturing issues!

Evolutionary computation is a rewarding field. We've briefly touched on some of these techniques, but there is a wide volume of research out there related to improving the search strategies or runtime performance depending on the specific types of problems explored. You'll also notice we chose this field for the last chapter of the book. Maybe a better AI scientist wouldn't pick favorites, but we wanted to save the best technique for last. Happy biologically-based searching!

6
The Part of Tens

IN THIS PART . . .

Review a ten-step process for developing AI projects.

Explore ten common sources of AI mistakes.

IN THIS CHAPTER

» Exploring AI problems in an organization

» Deciding which problems to tackle

» Analyzing data for AI

» Choosing metrics and iterating models

» Tying output to outcomes

Chapter 21
Ten Steps for Developing an AI Project

This chapter outlines a ten-step process for developing AI projects. You first evaluate the important tasks to complete before model development — learning about the problem space from a domain expert, classifying the types of problems present in an organization, and sorting the problems by feasibility and potential impact. You then explore the data collection and visualization process and determine what type of model to run and metrics to evaluate it on. Next, you look at iterating your model one or two (hundred) times. Finally, you put some thought into turning your fantastic model results into actionable outcomes that solve a problem.

Step 1: Learn from the Domain Experts

AI exists primarily to solve problems. When you decided to peruse this book, you may have already had a problem in mind that you want to tackle with AI. However, sometimes you are tasked with applying AI to solve a situation that you're less familiar with. In this case, you want to learn as much as you can from the domain expert. Try to find one to work with — someone who can be on the project team, or who can at least put in a few hours understanding your data pipeline and evaluating model results.

TIP

If possible, before you even start on the project, see if you can shadow someone working in the situation where your model will be deployed. You'll learn a ton.

Step 2: Define the Problem Types

In some project-development situations, there's no shortage of potential processes that can be improved with AI. The first step to triaging the possibilities involves identifying the type of projects present. Are you:

- » Forecasting sales for the next month?
- » Inspecting a product for a defect?
- » Figuring out where a process went wrong?
- » Finding the optimal configuration for a machine?

Different problems require different model types and will expect data in different formats. Classifying the kinds of projects will help you determine what each of them needs to be successful.

Step 3: Sort Problems by Feasibility and Impact

If you have multiple potential AI projects, sort them by feasibility and impact. Yes, it would be amazing if you could replace a 6-hour truck delivery of a product with a 30-second AI-controlled teleporter — but that isn't feasible — yet! Highly doable projects with a big potential benefit to the organization are the ideal projects to start with, if any exist. Otherwise, you typically start with a project with a high possibility of success (highly feasible) or a riskier project with a better potential payoff (highly impactful).

TIP

An organization's relationship with uncertainty and/or previous experience with AI projects will generally determine if you favor one factor over the other.

Step 4: Scope Out the Project

Once you've sorted the projects, it's time to settle on a winner. It's very important (with any engineering problem, not just AI ones) to scope out the expectations for the project. Following are the questions to ask at this stage:

- What does a "successful" AI model look like?
- What's the threshold for success?
- How many hours should be spent on the project per week?
- How many people are on the project team?
- Who is responsible for what project aspects?
- How will the data be shared?
- How often will you meet with the domain expert?
- How long will the project development period last?

Obviously, the resources available to you (computers, people, and budget) will impact the answers to these questions.

Step 5: Collect the Data

When your project is scoped, it's time to collect the data. If you are collecting the data yourself, you'll want to have an idea of how long it will take to get enough of it for a model. You'll also want to make sure you can rely on your data collection process — especially if there are potential points of failure. It's good to build redundancies into processes like these.

If you are receiving the data secondhand, it's important to know:

- Who collected the data (and are they available for you to ask questions)
- How often the data was collected
- How reliable the data is
- What format and units the data has

WARNING

There are many, many pitfalls with misunderstanding secondhand data, so you have to be careful. Here, your domain expert will be your hero!

Step 6: Explore the Data

After you have collected your data, it's time to explore it. Look for odd, outlier, or missing data. For numerical data, plot distributions of features and see if they follow any patterns. Plot these against outcomes of interest and see if the distributions meaningfully change. That's a good indicator that the feature signals a particular outcome.

If you have image data, understand what images were and weren't included in the set. Do you have sufficient coverage of the classes you are looking for? Do you need to augment your dataset with other sources? Do you have class imbalances you'll need to plan for? Spending significant time with your data early in the AI development process has huge payoffs when it comes to the model training phase.

Step 7: Choose Appropriate Model Types

After you develop more intuition for your data, appropriate candidate models for your problems may start to come to mind. Your model choices should take into account data, resource, and performance constraints related to your problem. If you have high-dimensional data and need great prediction accuracy on a complex, nonlinear problem, you might need a neural network. If you have a smaller, tabular dataset and need an explainable model choice, you might consider a decision tree. If you need to find a workable solution in a huge potential search space, a genetic algorithm might be more your speed. If you need to find something in image data, you should explore a convolutional neural network. This book should hopefully have given you some ideas as to which models are good for which situations.

Step 8: Choose Your Metrics

Models will train to your specifications, and that usually involves maximizing accuracy, minimizing loss, or optimizing a fitness function. It's important to pick the metrics that most represent the outcome you want the model to achieve. It's surprisingly easy to have the model evaluation disconnected from the overall problem evaluation, so choose carefully.

Step 9: Iterate, Iterate, Iterate

With your data prepared, your model selected, and your metrics in place, it's time to train! And train! And . . . train. It's rare to get a standout model on the first try. You may have to run hundreds of different model hyperparameters, or branch out and explore multiple model types simultaneously. Every problem is unique, and while existing models can provide a good starting point (if you use transfer learning), you'll probably have to change a few things to tailor the solution to your problem. It's all part of the process.

Step 10: Make Your Outputs Count

When you finally train your miraculous, one-in-a-million, life-changing model, you may be tempted to run outside and frolic in the streets. Go ahead and do that (look both ways before crossing), but remember that you probably didn't train the model as a goal unto itself. The ultimate outcome is to have your model solve a problem.

Sometimes you have a great model, but translating its output into a solution to a problem is less obvious. Model deployment should help model users make the best possible decisions in the situations they are likely to encounter. Should the model output a series of graphs or activate a siren? One might be important to help your sales team plan their routes, but the other might be necessary to let your factory operator know a gasket is about to blow.

REMEMBER

For highly safety-critical problems, AI is a great tool — but shouldn't be left to its own devices. Keeping a human in the loop is a good idea when deploying models in these circumstances.

IN THIS CHAPTER

» Discovering data pitfalls

» Thinking critically about evaluation metrics and overfitting

» Investigating time-series data and model complexity

» Making ethical considerations

Chapter 22

Ten Common AI Mistakes to Avoid

In this chapter, you explore ten common sources of AI mistakes. You start by examining some data pitfalls and find where common "data gremlins" like to lurk. You think critically about evaluation metrics for a model and how training and test data can help you catch overfitting. You investigate special circumstances for time-series data (and discover that Daylight Saving Time is the bane of a machine learning engineer's existence). You explore considerations for model complexity, hyperparameters and resource requirements, and continuous monitoring, and discover how a domain expert helps you catch problems early. Finally, you note some ethical issues to keep an eye on as you create and use AI tools.

Skipping Data Exploration and Quality Checks

It's really tempting to receive a dataset and start throwing it at a model to get some idea of how it might perform. Unfortunately, gremlins are abundant in AI projects, and your dataset is their favorite place to hide. Some common data gremlins include:

- Missing data
- Outliers
- Incorrect data
- Multiple disparate data sources

And data with these gremlins will take a little bit of work to format correctly for a model. There are also some rarer, but *very* frustrating data gremlins, which include:

- Your numeric data was secretly converted to a string and everything failed.
- Your date column didn't take Daylight Saving Time into account, and everything failed.
- You accidentally forgot a comma after a variable, it converted the data into a Python Tuple, and everything failed.

You may sense a theme here. Data mistakes can be tricky to catch, but they sure make themselves felt when it comes to the model's performance.

Using the Wrong Evaluation Metrics

Different evaluation metrics are better for different problems. For classification tasks, you can use both accuracy and error to determine how well a model understands which classes belong to which examples. For a regression problem, on the other hand, it's much more difficult for a model to hit the exact targets, and tolerances tend to be more generous. For this case, a loss measure makes more sense.

Not all loss and error functions were created equal. The mean squared error (MSE) function, for example, punishes large deviations much more severely than small ones. This can be useful for quicker model convergence, but the model may struggle to be as fine-grained as one using a non-squared measure. Cross-entropy loss is popular for comparing output probability distributions in multiclass classification problems. When you're developing an AI project, it's a good idea to do research on what evaluations other developers have used and how they worked for their application. It's not uncommon to create custom error functions if you have a unique problem.

Overfitting Your Model to Training Data

It's tempting to reserve as much training data for your model as possible. However, high-capacity models (like large decision trees, or very deep neural networks) have a bad habit of deciding it's easier to memorize training examples rather than learn meaningful mappings between inputs and outputs. When this happens, your training scores look incredible! And then when new (nonmemorized) data comes through, the model crashes and burns.

TIP

Using a test set is very helpful to avoid this situation. By withholding data during the training phase, the model gets evaluated on brand-new examples — and you can very quickly tell if the model learned or just memorized!

Ignoring Time-Series Considerations

Time-series data is common in real-world industries, whether you're recording process measurements for a manufacturing plant or analyzing weather conditions for an agricultural growing season. Time-series data often gets handled differently than other data types.

Picture a cake factory (an interesting and delicious pastime). Let's say you have an industrial oven that bakes cakes, and it records its internal temperature every ten seconds. You also have a frosting robot that frosts cakes, and records its force and movement parameters every second, but only while it's active. Finally, you have a nozzle that dispenses cake sprinkles and records its storage tank level every minute.

To get a complete picture of how your factory is running, you want to put all of this data together. But different features are recorded at different intervals. Most time series models expect:

- Each row to represent a timestep.
- The distance between timesteps to be consistent and meaningful.
- All features to be present for each timestep.

Obviously, in your cake factory, this is not the case. You'll have to decide what your timesteps look like. Do you want to feed data to the model every ten seconds? Every minute? Or create a different idea of a "step" for every change a cake sees while it's being assembled? Next, you'll have to decide how to handle missing or excess data. Do you repeat data points when there is a gap in a timestep, or take the average between the first and last valid point? If you have too much data, how will you downsample it? Finally, you'll need to decide the structure of your data sequences. Will you record information continuously, or create a new data sequence for each cake?

REMEMBER

Ignoring time-series considerations can give you downright wacky results!

Choosing Complex Models When Simple Models Work

As the old saying goes, when you have a hammer, everything starts to look like a nail. In the world of AI, when you first uncover the magic of a deep neural network, suddenly every problem looks like a "deep neural network problem." While these techniques are amazing, they aren't the best tool for every job. Simpler models have many advantages:

- They use less data.
- They use fewer computing resources.
- They are often easier to understand.

Simple models can perform just as well or better than deep-learning models in many situations, even while using fewer resources. Don't knock 'em till you've tried them! In general, even if a problem looks like a good candidate for a deep neural network, it's a good idea to try a simpler model first. At worst, you'll get an idea of where the model's knowledge gaps are.

Trying Only One Set of Model Hyperparameters

Some AI models really don't have many hyperparameters to experiment with, but deep-learning models are full of them. It's common to try a model architecture, get bad results, and feel stuck. Hyperparameters, especially in neural networks — choices like number of layers, number of nodes, learning rate, and so on — can have huge consequences for your overall performance. If you have a bad run, don't write the model off yet — it may just need more attention in a neglected tuning area.

For beginning neural network engineers, one of the oft-neglected hyperparameters tends to be the starting learning rate. While learning rates are often optimized during training, the starting point can make a big difference. If you are having issues with a neural network architecture, we encourage you to play around with this parameter in particular.

Forgetting to Consult with Domain Experts

It would be impossible to overstate how important domain experts are in any AI project. Domain experts are your secret weapon when your model is spouting nonsense. They are fantastic at catching where a data point is being used improperly, where features have unseen dependencies, and where a model is using the wrong information to make a choice. If you aren't a domain expert in the area you're applying AI to — drop everything, and go find one!

Not Quantifying a Model's Impact

I recently saw a (much-lampooned) product video of a smart fridge that used AI to scan the food you put inside and suggest recipes. The product had a huge price tag — with AI features no one wanted.

It's important to keep in mind that AI projects use resources — time and money spent collecting and cleaning data, hardware and software models to create models, and domain-expert hours evaluating them. There are some applications where the outcome of an AI model just isn't worth the effort of creating and maintaining the model in the first place. A silly AI program might make a great hobby project, but be aware of your technology's resource demands and limitations before deciding that it's the basis of a million-dollar company.

Deploying Models without Monitoring

Life is full of change — and that generally includes the context in which your model is being run. Small changes might be handled gracefully, but it's important to monitor your model's performance to catch when it starts to go downhill. This should include a plan to periodically collect more labeled data and compare model performance with actual outcomes. It's up to you to determine the performance threshold where retraining could be necessary. You also might know ahead of time if a big change to the model's operational environment is coming — for example, a new lighting fixture in an area where a convolutional neural network is running or a new sensor measurement fed to a decision tree. In this case, it's a good idea to proactively consider how much data should be collected for a model update.

Ignoring Ethical and Bias Considerations

Ethical considerations in AI usage are abundant. Data isn't created in a vacuum, and usually something (or someone) is supplying it. Models also consume (sometimes limited) resources. Always keep in mind:

- How data was collected
- Who financially benefited from the data collection
- Who gave permission to use the data
- What the model will be used for
- Who will have access to model parameters and results
- How resource-intensive the model is
- How trustworthy the model's results are

REMEMBER

There's no shortage of AI horror stories, even in its (relative) infancy. Building transparent data pipelines and adding model safeguards are an important part of using AI responsibly.

Appendix

Setting Up Your Development Environment

If you are just starting in the world of programming, figuring out how to get your toolchain up and running can be a slightly daunting task. Marz remembers going into her very first computer science class and having no understanding of the difference between a programming language, a text editor, and a terminal. As a consequence, she only used GNU Nano (an as-bare-bones-as-they-come text editor, designed to give you back pain and rare eye diseases) for three entire years. While this gave Marz some (survival-inspired) debugging skills, it's not the way she recommends diving into programming.

This appendix offers installation options for running the Python interpreter, a text editor, and a terminal. Each of these components and how they relate to the language is explained in more detail in Chapter 1; here, we cover the installation steps to get them on your computer.

Having a development environment that meets your needs is a major step in accomplishing your programming goals. As we say in the robotics program at the University of Idaho — toolchain, toolchain, toolchain. Getting your pipeline up and running is the first hurdle to clear before moving on to better and brighter things.

Installing Python and Package Managers

You can install a Python interpreter in a couple of different ways:

- Natively on your system
- Through a virtual environment manager, like Anaconda
- Don't install Python and use a browser instead

Each approach has its pros and cons. Installing Python natively is straightforward, but it works much better in a Linux or Mac system — Windows users trying to go this direct route can sometimes experience issues. Using a virtual environment allows you to use and manage several interpreter versions, which helps in prototyping environments and managing different packages. If you absolutely don't want to install Python at all — or if you are using an operating system that won't permit it — you can use Python purely in a browser by creating a Google Colab account.

Installing Python natively

Pros:

- Straightforward on Linux or Mac
- Comparatively low installation overhead
- Relatively easy to debug

Cons:

- Hard to use multiple Python versions in tandem
- Installing the wrong package could screw up your system
- Doesn't usually work well with Windows

Installing a virtual environment manager

Pros:

- Works well with Windows, Linux, and Mac
- Multiple versions of Python ("best practices")
- Multiple package environments

Cons:

- High installation overhead
- Multiple environments can cause confusion
- Initial toolchain setup can be more complex

Using browser-based Python

Pros:

- No software installation needed
- Many packages come preinstalled
- Terminal, text editor, and software are already integrated together

Cons:

- Usually must create an account
- Dependent on your Internet connection
- Using files in programs is much more complicated
- May not have all the packages you need

For this book, we recommend using a virtual environment manager, especially if you are new to programming. The one we'll be using is called Anaconda.

Installing Anaconda

Here are the steps to follow to install Anaconda on your system:

1. Open a browser and navigate to: `www.anaconda.com/download`.
2. Click the Get Started button in the "Download Now" section.
3. Find the version of the operating system you are using and download the correct installer for your operating system.
4. Navigate to where the installer downloaded, and click the executable to launch it (you may need to give your computer permission to open this program).
5. Click through the installer options (leave the default installer options where they are).

Note: You'll have to agree to the license agreement and select the users you want to install the program for.

6. If asked, you don't need to bother doing anything with Jupyter Notebooks for now.
7. Click Finish when the process is complete.

The Anaconda Navigator will launch a graphical interface to the software. In Chapter 1, we go over how to create a specific virtual environment both through the graphical interface and with the terminal. For now, you can leave things where they are.

If you are using a Windows or Linux system, these steps should also install Anaconda Prompt, which is a handy way to launch a terminal with Anaconda already initialized. You can do just about anything in the Anaconda Prompt that you can do in the terminal for the purposes of this book. If you are on a Mac, though, this extra program doesn't usually install. You'll have to use your operating system's terminal — but more power to you! Terminals are great.

Anaconda may also ask you to download a bunch of extra things on its home screen. You won't need to bother with any of them for this book, but feel more than welcome to try them out.

Installing package managers

When we use Python, we also install packages (libraries) of code we want to work into our projects. For natively-installed Python, you run:

```
pip install <package-name>
```

to accomplish this. If you don't have Pip installed on a native Python installation, your terminal will usually tell you, and typically it gives you the command you can use to install it. If you are having trouble with `pip`, a workaround we've used is:

```
python -m pip install <package-name>
```

which sometimes does the trick.

In Anaconda, you can graphically install packages into an environment using the Anaconda Navigator (via the Environments tab). However, we'll generally just use the terminal and run:

```
conda install <package-name>
```

to get the software. Once in a while, you'll need to look at a different package repository to get the software you need in Anaconda. In this case, you might run:

```
conda install conda-forge::<package-name>
```

to get the right package. The conda-forge package repository is a popular alternative to the main one. Marz has had students in the past (particularly with OpenCV) who have had more luck installing a package going this route.

IDEs and Editor Recommendations

Integrated development environments, or IDEs, are popular ways of bundling several different programming development tools to create a sort of "one-stop shop" for coders. They typically use a text editor with a terminal, so programs can be written and run in the same window. Some popular Python IDEs include:

- » VS Code
- » Spyder
- » PyCharm
- » Jupyter Notebooks

The one we recommend for use in this book is VS Code (Visual Studio Code). Jupyter Notebooks is worth mentioning, though, as it runs code in a slightly different manner. Jupyter Notebooks creates a server that runs on your computer, and you log on to a local address running the notebook. Notebooks takes the terminal out of the equation and allows you to run the code in code blocks, or cells. You can run different parts of a Python program at different times, which can be incredibly useful for debugging. However, variables and conditions depend on when they were last changed by a cell — so running a cell out of order can cause some odd sequencing behavior that's a headache to debug.

Google Colab, which is based on Jupyter Notebooks, also functions as an IDE, combining the Python installation with the editor and a terminal-free interface. We use Colab for one of the examples in the book, so it's not a bad idea to get familiar with it.

When you install VS Code — Microsoft Visual Studio Code — it is important to remember that VS Code (the thing we want) is *not* the same as Microsoft Visual Studio. Don't repeat Marz's crucial mistake! Visual Studio is a fully-fledged IDE program for a variety of languages, and she accidentally downloaded it once, only to choke the life out of her computer's resources if she accidentally ever clicked on the launch icon. She'd frantically try to pull up Task Manager as her laptop struggled to breathe, releasing just slightly less heat than it would take to solder her legs to the chair. Okay, maybe that's an exaggeration, but seriously — Visual Studio is an enormous program you *don't* want to download for this book. VS Code is a lighter and more helpful program that you *do* want to download for this book. It also has the advantage of working with Windows, Linux, and Mac.

Installing VS Code

To install VS Code, follow these steps:

1. Open a browser and navigate to: `https://code.visualstudio.com/download`.
2. Choose the correct version of your operating system, and download the installer.
3. Navigate to where the installer downloaded, and click on it to launch the executable (you may need to give your computer permission to run this).
4. Agree to the license agreement.
5. Leave the default settings where they are.
6. You can optionally choose to check "Create a desktop icon," which may make the program easier to find and launch.
7. Click Install (it may take a few minutes).
8. Click Finish.

Installing the Python VS Code extension

We highly recommend installing the Python VS Code Extension after installing VS Code — it will make your life much easier. To do this, follow these steps:

1. Open VS Code.

   You should see a navigation bar on the left side with different icons. One of the icons looks like a grid of four squares, with one square slightly out of alignment.

2. Hover your mouse over the grid (it will say "Extensions") and click.

3. In the search bar that appears in the side pane, start typing **Python**.

   You should see an icon appear in the results that says "Python." It will have the familiar blue-and-yellow snake logo and a verification badge from Microsoft.

4. Click the Install button under this icon.

That should do it! If you want, you are welcome to install other extensions that provide specific functionality, like the Python Debugger. Python is the only one you need for this book, though.

VS Code has many additional tools that will help you program. If you are familiar with GitHub source management software, VS Code provides a direct tie-in to your account so you can commit and manage changes directly from the IDE. You can work in languages other than Python inside VS Code, including C and C++.

Of course, if you're more of a purist, you don't need an IDE to program at all. You could technically program in a Word editor or a Notepad app. There are also some editors that die-hard computer scientists swear by. Word of advice: Don't criticize Vim in the robotics lab. It's a good way to start a fistfight.

Index

Symbols and Numerics

A

B

C

D

E

F

M

N

O

P

Q

R

S

T

U

V

W

X

Y

Z

About the Authors

Mary "Marz" Everett, PhD is a researcher at the University of Idaho and the Associate Director for the Center for Intelligent Industrial Robotics. She is especially interested in wireless sensor network technology and AI research applied to manufacturing and agriculture. When she isn't in her office on the Coeur d'Alene, Idaho, campus, she is typically hiking in the forest or open-water swimming in the lake with the Masters swim team.

John C. Shovic, PhD has been working with software since he talked his high school into letting him use their IBM 1130 computer for the entire summer of 1973. That launched him into his lifelong love affair with software. Dr. Shovic has founded multiple companies: Advance Hardware Architectures; TriGeo Network Security; Blue Water Technologies; InstiComm, LLC; SwitchDoc Labs; and bankCDA. Dr. Shovic has given more than 90 invited talks and has published over 50 papers on a variety of topics, including AI, manufacturing automation, Arduinos, Raspberry Pis, HIPAA, GLB, computer security, computer forensics, embedded systems, and others. In 2019, he was appointed as the director of the research group, the Center for Intelligent Industrial Robotics. Currently John is proud to be serving as a computer science faculty member specializing in robotics and AI at the University of Idaho, Coeur d'Alene, and is surrounded by a bunch of students who are as excited about technology and computers as he is.

Dedication

Marz: To all my teachers at Camelot Elementary, Sacajawea Junior High, Lewiston High School, and the University of Idaho, who taught me to love research and writing.

John: To my wife, Laurie. She has supported me in so many ways, including making sure my clothes match in the morning and making sure our dog is well-behaved (fail). Thank you!

Authors' Acknowledgments

Marz: I would like to acknowledge the team at Wiley, including Steve Hayes and Katharine Dvorak, for championing the book. I would also like to acknowledge and thank my amazing coauthor, John Shovic, for this joint venture, and my agent, Carole Jelen from Waterside Productions. I want to recognize the hard-working group of graduate and undergraduate students at the CIIR, whose research projects, insights, and talents have contributed to many of the discussions of technology found in this book: Hunter Hawkins, Jacob Friedberg, Sarah Davis, Dawson Burgess, Dan Blanchette, James Lasso, Jordan Reed, Brent Knopp, Lacey Bowden, Kate Bouse, Kevin Wing, Davis Onyeoguzoro, Tim Lybeck, Gary Banks, Nathaniel Evans, Michael Habermann, Will Hall, Caleb Blondell, Ethan Carpenter, Tebo Shinetulga, Isaiah Preston, Karson Vordahl, Joseph Harris, and Tyler Osso. Thanks to the University of Idaho faculty and staff who keep our research on track: Dr. Rinker, Dr. Wang, Dr. Soule, and Tammy St. John-Tesky. Finally, a huge thank you to my family for supporting this activity from start to finish.

John: I would like to acknowledge my coauthor and associated director, Dr. Mary "Marz" Everett, for her huge contributions to this book and the community of students that supports us in many ways. Go Vandals!

Publisher's Acknowledgments

Executive Editor: Steve Hayes
Associate Acquisitions Editor: Alicia Sparrow
Managing Editor: Prathyusha P V
Development Editor: Katharine Dvorak
Senior Editorial Assistant: Hanna Sytsma
Editorial Assistant: Shannon Kucaj
Production Editor: Magesh Elangovan
Cover Image: © Palung/stock.adobe.com